VÁCLAV HAVEL

VÁCLAV HAVEL

A POLITICAL TRAGEDY IN SIX ACTS

JOHN KEANE

BLOOMSBURY

First published 1999

Copyright © 1999 by John Keane

The moral right of the author
has been asserted

Bloomsbury Publishing Plc,
38 Soho Square, London W1V 5DF

A CIP catalogue record for this
book is available from the British Library

ISBN 0 7475 4458 1

10 9 8 7 6 5 4 3 2 1

Typeset by Palimpsest Book Production Limited,
Polmont, Stirlingshire
Printed in Great Britain by
Clays Limited, St Ives plc

CONTENTS

For Kathy O'Neil

PROLOGUE

Time can be a cruel despot. Acting on a whim, it sometimes pounces on particular lives, pushing them into custody, dragging them to a destination of suffering and unhappy endings. Such has been the fate of Václav Havel. Resembling a classical political tragedy, his life has been clamped by moments of sensation and moral gravity, episodes of joy ruined by sadness, courage mixed with vacillation, honesty tainted by knavery, triumph spoiled by defeat – and deathly climaxes linked to the struggle for power.

Havel is of course currently much better known world-wide for his dazzling achievements as a talented playwright, courageous dissident, and as a moral leader of the democratic world. This reputation is justified, but incomplete. Many pertinent episodes of his life remain unknown, including the one that currently grips the early winter of his life. Abroad, in countries like the United States, Japan, Germany and Britain, the name of Václav Havel is a synonym for integrity, probity, freedom. At home, within the tiny landlocked European country he governs, impressions are different. The final act of a splendid political tragedy is now unfolding. Public grumbling and grave personal illness, like a crowd of blanketed beggars, are huddling at the gates of his hilltop Castle in Prague. It is true that its young soldiers, dressed in red, white and blue, still dutifully stand guard, beneath the fluttering national flag. And each day, tourists with clicking cameras arrive in their thousands to walk its courtyards, marvel at the Spanish Hall, and listen to the chiming bells of St Vitus's Cathedral. But the harsh fact is that most of the citizens of President Havel's republic think less of him than they did a year ago. Some say that he is hindering the process of consolidating good government, or that he is too ill to be a statesman. More than a few have been calling for his resignation.

Havel's political star at home is evidently waning. It may do so abroad as well. Perhaps nobody should be surprised, for final-term, 'lame duck' presidencies are commonplace in other democracies around the world. The reason was once explained to me by a wise old politician. Political careers, he told me, usually end in failure. Especially during second or third or fourth terms of office – as Havel has had – politicians often suffer from the hardening of their political arteries, he explained. Their charisma fades. They fall into a pit of narcissism, or become cloth-eared and haughty, or lose their guard. Meanwhile, their critics and enemies have time to

group and regroup, which is why the terminal phases of a political
career are often scarred by scandals, public grumbling, and sounds
of sharpening knives.

Havel is currently in the grip of such trends, and it is therefore unsurprising that in recent times he has swung between
dejection and anger, and that he has considered resignation. His
opponents smile coldly as they clutch at their weapons, but before
they make their next moves, or draw their conclusions, they should
read this book. Within its pages, they may be surprised to discover
many things hitherto unknown about Havel. They will taste the
moments of joy, irony, farce and misfortune through which he
has lived. They will see that his life displays great generosity and
courage in the face of misery and defeat. They will understand
better why he, the 'post-modern president', has admirers in the
four corners of the earth. Above all, they will discover something
that both his critics and supporters must never forget: that Václav
Havel suffered the misfortune of being born into the twentieth
century, that his fate was politics, that by any standards of reckoning
he rose to become a flamboyant political animal who achieved
fame by teaching the world more about the powerful and the
powerless, power-grabbing and power-sharing, than virtually any
other of his twentieth-century rivals.

My grandiloquent suggestion that Havel will be judged by
posterity as among the most distinguished political figures of
our century is bound to raise eyebrows. He naturally has many
competitors. All kinds of famous twentieth-century heads of state
– Masaryk, Hitler, Brezhnev, Reagan, Gorbachev, Mandela, Kohl,
Clinton, to mention a few – have passed through the magnificent
gates of his splendid Castle. Not only that, but to predict that
he will be remembered as a great political figure of the century
presumes some things about the course of the past hundred
years. Our century has had many unique features, including the
way in which it stimulated awareness of the difference between
historical time and clock time and, for the first time, nurtured
the widespread perception that the twentieth century was indeed
a century, and that as a century it has meant various things to
many different people. So the century was ripe with technical inventions – the radio, the telephone, the automobile, the
refrigerator, the washing machine, the television, the computer –
whose diffusion has radically altered the sense of time and spatial

movements of millions of people. It was the century in which economic life finally went global, for instance in the fields of telecommunications and travel, thanks to which time and space barriers for some people were wiped out and the Grand Tour began to be democratized by becoming financially accessible to millions called tourists. The twentieth century saw the rise of modernist art – and 'post-modern' challenges to its penchant for self-edifying abstraction. And as Havel knows from bitter personal experience, the twentieth century will for ever be recorded as the century that perfected the arts of violently misusing power over others. Aerial bombardment became commonplace. There were planned attempts to exterminate whole peoples. Corpses were burned and recycled into gunpowder to make more skeletons from future enemies. There were bombs whose flash proved brighter than the sun. The domination of the world by European colonial empires, dating back to the eighteenth century, came to a bloody end. And just as comrade V. I. Lenin predicted, more people were pushed and bullied and killed in wars and revolutions than in all previous centuries combined.

Comrade Lenin was not completely right, however. His fascination with bossy power, revolution, war and state-building blinded him to the fact, clearer now than in his times, that the twentieth century saw a growth spurt in what can be called the modern democratic revolution. This quiet revolution began long ago, with such events as the Dutch resistance against the government of Philip II in the Low Countries, the bashed-up English revolution of the 1640s, the surprise defeat of the British Empire by the American colonists, and the disturbances that swept through Europe in 1848 – the year that marked the birth of the Czechs' long struggle for civil freedoms. The twentieth-century quest for democracy started out badly, but it subsequently yielded surprising results. Totalitarian regimes were defeated, not only by military action but also by the peaceful revolution of citizens. In the four corners of the earth, the power-constraining pinch of international humanitarian law, covering such matters as torture, rape and genocide, began to be felt for the first time. Heavily armed, nasty dictatorships were effectively resisted, or simply collapsed, on a breathtaking scale. Within the actually existing democracies, meanwhile, the century saw various experiments in rejuvenating the principle of non-violent power-sharing – think of the suffragettes dressed in purple and green, or the black and white protesters at Little Rock. And the century witnessed as well organized efforts to transport that slippery ideal into concrete institutions – from the workplace to the bedroom – that were previously untouched by the idea of publicly monitored and shared power, the principle for which democracies are justly famous.

Havel has always been sensitive to these trends – not only because from an early age his political instincts were opposed to power-grabbing, but also because his greatest political achievement is that he personally helped to make the growth spurt of democracy happen. As a sandy-haired young boy, he had a healthy disdain for troops in uniform, armoured cars, and the terror of air raids. During Stalin's times, as a young teenager, he daringly organized a remarkable literary circle called the Thirty-Sixers – so named because he and its other members were all born in the fateful year 1936. Havel soon mounted comical assaults on the socialist theatre establishment. His earliest – still unappreciated – plays like *You've Got Your Whole Life Ahead of You* and *Hitchhiking* matured into award-winning, side-splitting plays like *The Memorandum*, which granted him the gift of global fame for defending the view that theatre should raise more questions than it answers, that it should make people laugh at unaccountable power, and that theatre should democratically unnerve, not soothe or patronize its audiences.

Havel offered other gifts to the modern democratic revolution. His first important confrontations with the Communist authorities took place in the early 1960s, when he fancied himself as a blue-jeaned poet and essay-writer, and served on the editorial board of a revamped monthly journal called *The Face* (*Tvář*). That period blessed him with the reputation of 'clean hands' and it helped launch him into prominence as a playwright, radio announcer and street activist during the 1968 Prague Spring – the time when he first met Dubček and began to play something of a public-political role. Havel was soon forced to endure the miseries of the Cold War and Brezhnev-style 'real socialism'. Struggling to keep his sanity amidst terrible personal suffering, he staged a dramatic undercover version of John Gay's *The Beggar's Opera* and played a key role in convening the human-rights initiative called Charter 77. Praise for his efforts came from the lips of statesmen like Henry Kissinger and Zbigniew Brzezinski – alongside bitter Communist attacks on him as the spoiled son of '*nouveau riche* millionaires', or (as an American congressman once said) as a dropout wearing 'ten dollars' worth of clothes and badly needing a haircut'. Then came the revolutionary upheavals during the magical autumn of 1989 – the 'velvet' events which transformed him into a leather-jacketed hero, then into a besuited politician politicking on all fronts as his state and its citizens tread the dangerous path of consolidating a new configuration of institutions that are conventionally called democratic: precious institutions like the rule of law, free elections, parliamentary government, a civil society, and independent media and public life.

Havel's life has been so blown about by the winds of twentieth-century history that it is impossible to understand him without understanding the events that shaped and reshaped, racked and ruined not only the Czechs but the whole of Europe. In this book, I try to retell his life against the backdrop of the collapse of the Habsburg monarchy, the rise of Hitler, the Stalin trials, and the horror of the concentration camps. I show how his life and writings were later shadowed by the Berlin Wall and encouraged by the events of May 1968. I emphasize as well the 1989 revolutions against Communism, the collapse of the Soviet empire – the last modern empire in Europe – and all the key events that have since followed: the painful transitions to parliamentary democracy in central Europe, war in the Balkans, the global resurgence of free-market economics, and the accelerated growth of the world's most advanced experiment in regional integration, the European Union.

My treatment of Havel's life naturally tries to be sensitive to the Czech context into which he was born. There is admittedly little here about the collage of Romanesque, Gothic, Renaissance, baroque, art-nouveau and post-modern architecture that in comparison to Prague makes most other modern cities look like urban eyesores. The spas of Karlovy Vary, known for their beneficial effects on arthritis and constipation, hardly rate a mention. Tripe soup, dumplings, sauerkraut and roast pork are absent fare. So too are the fiery brandies tasting of cloves and plums. There are no stories of Bohemian bears and wolves – or Czech tennis and hockey players. The allure of the Škoda, the 'foreign' car that advertisers tell us is less likely than most other cars to be stolen in towns like Edinburgh, Hamburg, and Denver, goes unmentioned.

Some readers, unfamiliar with Prague – and having never visited his splendid Castle – nevertheless will happily encounter the influences of Franz Kafka, Karel Čapek and Milan Kundera. They will read as well about Havel's predilection for Moravian white wine, free-and-easy bohemian nights, good dinners and endless cigarettes. And they will learn about the Czech women in his life, his taste for Anglo-American politics and post-Heideggerian philosophy, and his love of the music of the contemporary Prague scene, from the scores of Smetana and Dvořák to punk bands like Plastic People of the Universe, and elderly pop musicians who are still loved in Prague, like Tina Turner, Lou Reed and the Rolling Stones.

There is more in this book than the minutiae of a remarkable life lived in a hapless country during an extraordinary century. In keeping with the style of Havel's plays, poems, essays, and speeches, my biography pays attention to its own form. Gone are the days when it could be presumed that biography was about recording the facts, and literature was about experimental fiction. My account of Havel's life is unavoidably 'factional'. By that I mean two things. Although I try hard to 'fill gaps' and to pay meticulous attention to all of the important details, the story that I tell is based on principles of selection and interpretation that unavoidably highlight certain aspects of his life, rather than others. Where there are 'facts' there are 'theories', and where there are 'theories' there are value-laden 'interpretations'.

The way a biography is written counts as one of these shaping conditions, which is to say that every 'factual' biography is a work of fiction. If that is so, then questioning and overturning the pseudo factual form of old-fashioned biographies becomes important. This I have tried to do, and it is the second sense in which my account of Havel's life is 'factional'. I have set out to tell an unusual story about his life by means of *tableaux vivants* that not merely pay homage to his love of theatre, but also resonate with the fragmentation of his life by historical events beyond his control. More than that, these *tableaux vivants* are designed to heighten readers' sense that his actions in the world are understandable as a tragedy; and to have the 'cubist' effect of producing deliberately broken narratives that warn readers from the outset that the stories told here are 'fabricated' by certain – but challengeable – points of view.

Havel's closest aides at the Castle – bearded, bow-tied Vladimír Hanzel, for instance – urged me to capture his many faces. The advice reminded me of Nietzsche's remark that 'one's own self is well hidden from one's own self; of all mines of treasure one's own is the last to be dug up'. Whether or not Mr Hanzel intended this, his advice in effect urged me not to mythologize Havel, to see that he is not always himself, that his own self-assessments should be believed and disbelieved. Hanzel was implying, probably against his will, that Havel is not fully comprehensible, that he will continually be out of reach, and, thus, that readers should accept that neither he nor anybody else is entitled to exercise ultimate power over defining exactly who Havel is. That being so, it follows that Havel himself – presuming that he has the time and energy to read the book – will not necessarily accept all or most of the viewpoints that I use to structure my account of his tragic life.

My probe into his life and writings also presents a philosophical reflection upon a subject that is of perennial importance, because it is inextricably bound up with the human condition: the subject of power. Philosophers and political thinkers tell us that power (originally from the Latin *posse*, to be able) is the ability of actors – individuals, groups, organizations, whole states or international bodies – to make a difference upon the people and things within their environment. It is said that the term power refers to humans' ability to make their marks on the world; that power is the production of desired or valuable effects; and that power is the capacity to achieve whatever effects are desired by drawing upon certain resources, such as money, guns, or images, even in the face of stiff controversy and opposition. It follows from such definitions that to study power in any context is to consider who gets what, when and how, and whether they ought to have done so.

Havel's life, deeply ensnared as it is with the political crossroads of Prague and the Bohemian lands, provides rich material indeed for taking a new look at the old subject of power. Havel has of course written many essays and plays on the subject. His speeches as head of state sometimes dwell on the same theme. He has also been unluckily privileged to live through virtually all of the major changes of power in twentieth-century Europe. Five-sixths of Havel's life has been lived under anti-democratic regimes of one kind or another. The hands of a breathtaking variety of power regimes – I count eight altogether – have in fact touched him.

He was born into a republican bourgeois family shaped by the Habsburg empire, whose collapse was hastened by the First World War and the birth of the Czechoslovak parliamentary republic led by the philosopher-president Masaryk, who was personally known to Havel's family. That First Republic was Havel's Athens: understandably so, since it was the most successful parliamentary republic in middle Europe, until British and French politicians knifed it in the back with the Munich agreement. Havel went on to live his early years under Nazi occupation and the threat of total war. He tasted a brief period of multi-party social democracy that was forcibly terminated by the cunning and violence of the 1948 *coup de Prague*. As a teenager and then as young man, he and his family suffered under Stalinism, but he contributed actively to Czech efforts, culminating in the 1968 Prague Spring, to liberalize that Soviet model of totalitarian power. For the next two decades, Havel was tormented by various forms of persecution at the hands of what I call 'late-socialism' – a post-totalitarian regime that felt like one big grey prison ruled by a single party. Then came the magical 'velvet revolution' of the autumn of 1989 – a dramatic upheaval that radically altered the patterns of who got what, when and how and catapulted Havel into the office of President of the Czechoslovak Republic. The wildest of his wild dreams came true. And now, for the past ten years of your life, he has headed a state that has trodden the unknown path of post-Communism.

Since this is a study of these different – mainly despotic – régimes of power that have criss-crossed, moulded and complicated Havel's life, readers should not be surprised to find that I have chosen to write the book as a political tragedy. As with all tragedies, there are some memorable moments of triumph and *jouissance*, certainly. Like the assassination of Heydrich. Or Havel's first public address during the Hungarian Revolution. Or his release after four years in prison. Or the day of his election as unchallenged charismatic ruler of a landlocked country called Czechoslovakia. But these are exceptions, for within the stories that I tell Havel appears more often as a tragedian – as an actor in a prose drama riddled with calamities, injustices, and unhappy endings. Many readers outside the Czech Republic will be surprised to find that the past decade, when supposedly the world has been his oyster, has been no exception to this set pattern. If anything – some will recoil from this claim, even though Havel himself knows that it's true

– this period has been the most crisis-ridden of his life. It is now taking its toll. Death and public grumbling are camped outside his Castle gates. It is as if he is being punished for living most of his life in unfreedom. One of his oldest friends told me recently that Havel still might be rescuable from this sad fate, but that that would require the political kidnapping of the century, followed by strenuous efforts to rehabilitate his best qualities. That friend's joke was revealing. It suggested that Havel's greatest misfortune in life is to have found that his final big dream – to become a president – came true. It seems that the words of his favourite relative, Uncle Miloš Havel, written after being bullied into exile in Germany by Czechoslovak Communists, applies well to Havel himself: 'In the free world, I continue to suffer from lack of freedom.'

Aristotle recommended (in his *Poetics*) that a tragedy should be structured in such a way that those who encounter it 'thrill with horror and melt to pity at what takes place'. The sad stories told about Havel here may well leave readers with feelings of sorrow aroused by his suffering. They are not likely to be left with the impression that his life deserves heroization. Typically for someone of my generation, I have never believed in heroes, and I certainly never became interested in Havel and his work because I thought of him as a hero – a substitute for Mahatma Gandhi, or Martin Luther King, or Jack Kennedy, or Che Guevara, or Chairman Mao, or God. I remember well the first time we met. It was 1984. We were supposed to discuss the English version of his *The Power of the Powerless*, which I was then editing. Havel had just come from a long spell in prison, and his circumstances were difficult, to say the least. But he didn't look like much of a hero to me. If anything, I felt sorry and upset for him. He seemed like a hapless victim of the absurdity of so-called reality. He was exhausted, overweight, depressed, his restless fingers shook. He grated the gears and several times got lost when he drove me and a friend around Prague in his old Mercedes. He seemed baffled by the streets of his birthplace. Whisky and cigarettes and words seemed to be his anchor in life.

When, some years ago, we corresponded about my decision to embark on this book, I stressed to Havel that I did not believe in the genre of 'authorized biography'. I explained that I did not need his permission to tell his life as I thought fit. Nothing subsequently changed. Since Havel too believes in 'living in the truth', since this is a new approach to the understanding of power, and since my vocation is that of a political thinker and writer intent on stretching the concept of power into the most private domains – to uncover the naked bodies in the bedroom, or to peek through the keyhole into the top-secret meeting taking place behind closed doors – my book publicly scrutinizes his life in great detail, without apologies, without illusions. I have tried my best to research things meticulously, to write accurately, to draw conclusions and to make judgements without malice – in the same spirit of honesty and openness that Havel himself has championed at various points in his life. There may be comments recorded and tales told in this book that he finds unsettling. Some incidents may cause him discomfort, either because he does not remember them, or because he disagrees with the interpretations proffered, or even because he considers them potentially ruinous of his political reputation. I cannot apologize for these possible reactions. For it is the duty of political writing to call things by their proper name, to refuse nonsense and to scale down the pompous – to say things that shake the world and stop it from falling asleep.

My ultimate aim in writing this study of power in biographical form is to invite comparison with the 'classic' attempts to treat questions about who gets what, when and how, and whether they ought to. In early modern times, say from the early sixteenth century onwards, two different but related genres of the study of power began to crystallize, and then to dominate the field. One type is the so-called 'realist' account of power. An early version is on display in Niccolò Machiavelli's research into the contemporary politics of the emergent states around Firenze, which led him to write tracts like *Il principe* (1513), which aimed to serve as a guide or handbook for rulers like the Medici, to enable them better to rule their subjects. This approach to power concentrates on the political manoeuvring for the levers and resources of government. It emphasizes, for instance, the necessity of foresight and flexible planning for the future; the importance of winning friends and allies; the vital political role of trickery, which depends upon deception, secrecy and surprise; and the need to avoid halfway measures. The aim of political struggle, it is said, is state power over its subjects, the people, just as the military commander's aim is power over the defeated enemy.

Then there is the inverse approach, let us call it the obedience view of power, an early example of which can be seen in the writings of the seventeenth-century political analyst, Thomas Hobbes. His reflections on the revolutionary upheavals in England during the 1640s resulted in works like *De Cive* (1642) and *Leviathan* (1651), which are less manuals of statecraft than grammars for obedient subjects. This second approach shares with the first a belief in the need for institutions of top-down government, and in the unavoidability of cunning and knavery in human affairs. But in contrast to the first view, it concentrates less on the power dynamics in the alpine regions of state institutions and more on the importance of laying down the ground rules of obedience for subjects living in the valleys and on the plains below. Observing that men and women are proud and passionate and prone to disorder and violent conflict, this approach specifies the morally binding laws that must be observed by everybody in order for a stable political community to survive through time. 'I put for a general inclination of all mankind,' wrote Hobbes, 'a perpetual and restless desire of power after power, that ceaseth only in death.' That being so, individual subjects are required to enter into a peace contract. It specifies that everybody must obey the civil laws laid down by the individual or council whom they recognize as their sovereign ruler. In return for their obedience, all individuals receive the assurance that each will honour their agreement. They have the assurance, backed by the sovereign's threat of force, that each will abide by the rule: Do not do unto others what you would not have them do unto you. If anybody steps out of line – if at the outset they refuse to enter the contract of obedience, or if they subsequently express infidelity to the contract by breaking the law – then woe betide them. Following the Book of Job, Hobbes with good reason compared the necessary sovereign ruler to Leviathan, whom God called 'King of the Proud'. The job of the Leviathan is to rule by making subjects permanently afraid – that if they break the laws then they will be punished severely, certainly with death.

Burdened by these two different but complementary approaches, the study of power in modern times has been skewed in favour of the powerful. The capacity for action and entitlements of the governed – the dark side of the moon of modern accounts of power – have been badly neglected. A third approach, one that explores power from the standpoint of the governed, is required. This is what I have attempted here. The new probe into power stands firmly within the modern democratic revolution. It certainly recognizes that state institutions are important for the maintenance of the lives and livelihoods of people, wherever they live; and it recognizes as well that subjects' consensual obedience to state institutions is critical for the survival of good government. I do not suppose that power contests, hubris and fear can be made to disappear from human affairs. But that is exactly why the inbuilt prejudice of the two orthodoxies against the entitlements of the governed needs to be counterbalanced with a radically different perspective.

So this study of Havel's life and times might be described as a manual for democrats. It supposes that the lust for power is polymorphously perverse, that power, wherever it is exercised, is therefore always in need of public monitoring and control. It further supposes that such monitoring is best done within a democratic order marked by non-violent power-sharing arrangements, including limits on the scope and potential arrogance of governmental institutions. A democracy, ideally conceived, is a fractured and self-monitoring system of power in which there are daily reminders to governors and governed alike that those who exercise power over others – whether in the bedroom or on the battlefield – cannot do just anything they want, and that (as the Dutch Jewish political philosopher Spinoza put it) even sovereigns are forced in practice to recognize their own limitations, to admit that they cannot make a table eat grass.

The spirit of democracy in this sense is evident throughout this book, for instance in its accounts of the causes and – sometimes grotesque – effects of various power-thirsty anti-democratic regimes that straitjacketed Havel's life for fifty years. The concern for democracy can be seen as well in the *tableaux vivants* structure, which aims to discourage readers from 'understanding' the text as indisputably True, and instead to encourage them to 'overstand' the text, that is, to read the accounts with frowns on their faces in order better to make up their own minds about the subject of power – and about Havel himself. And this is a manual for democrats in a third sense: in its attempt to explore dimensions of power that for too long have been neglected. The *tableaux vivants* sketched here try to inject life into conventionally stale, power-related topics such as parliaments, freedom of expression, and civil society. But I have tried to do more than resuscitate dead subjects. Topics such as courage, fear, and temptation are also shown to be integral to the subject of power. So too are matters like theatre and literature, prison and sex, folly and cunning, friends and enemies, birth and death.

Such themes conspire to produce a political tragedy, albeit with a difference. Tragedy is of course a form of writing, not of living. The stories I tell display many of the ingredients of classical tragedy, defined as it was by figures like Aristotle and Seneca, Shakespeare and Lessing. In this book, the private anguish of a single individual – an innocent and courageous mortal with marked imperfections – is re-enacted on a public stage that is cluttered with great evil and suffering caused by violent struggles for power over others. Like the classical tragic form as well, my book offers insights into how the tough-skinned victim is exposed and broken by forces that are, in the circumstances, neither fully understandable nor controllable by prudent calculation. This political tragedy, like those written before it, also aims to arouse concern and pity, and so to uplift its reading audience. Tragedy most certainly does not aim to make us love our misery. It is potentially a source of *catharsis* and *pleasure* and *political wisdom*. By confronting readers with some terrible episodes of human history, tragedy can arouse and discharge compassion for the undeserved misfortune of the victims, partly because readers can recognize *themselves* in the misfortune. Tragedy thereby demonstrates (as Shakespeare observed) that great griefs are powerful medicine, that excessive human suffering can incite human claims to dignity and freedom.

To these familiar ingredients of classical tragedy I add certain 'modern' elements, like the absence of Absolutes. Traditional forms of tragedy supposed the omnipresence of the gods, or of a God who although not on stage is always there as a spectator, watching and judging the action, capable even of maddening or destroying the central characters. In this book, the suffering of the main character is not traced to irresistible forces that are divinely destined, cosmic forces that hunger for retribution against those who have bared their behinds to the divine order of things. The cautionary tales about power told here see Havel's suffering as contingent rather than necessary, as an effect of certain historically specific regimes of power, especially those in which some men –

like the Titans who set off to scale Mount Olympus – acted as if they were God. My democratic form of tragedy turns its back on talk of unchanging 'human nature'. It also rejects the bias of classical tragedy towards fixed hierarchies of worldly power, whose victims were the playthings of aristocracies, armies and monarchs. The political tragedy that follows is simply the sad but inspiring story of an individual whose astonishing life was pushed and pulled, twisted and torn by all of the tumultuous political forces of a century – thankfully – which is now past.

London and Prague
May 1999

THE YOUNG PRINCE

(1936–1945)

BEGINNINGS

Those who gathered around tiny 'Venoušek' from his first day in the world – Monday, 5 October 1936 – had no doubt that he was special. His family luckily believed in the power of recorded images so that, unusually for this period, his first few months are well preserved as black-and-white home movies. Although inexpertly shot by his father, the granular frames leave behind a striking impression of a child swaddled in high expectations – a child whose early months were not only coddled but *crowned*. At two weeks of age, freshly home from his birthplace at Dr Záhorský's private hospital on Prague's Londýnská Street, he appears as a wispy cherub robed in white, crying, showered in words by his proudly smiling, brown-haired mother. A few months later, sitting but not yet able to walk, he appears in various poses: enveloped by admiring, kissing, stroking relatives eager to attract his attention at a summer garden party; propped up on a sofa, cornered by a toy dog that he regards with deep suspicion; seated in a stroller entertained by a moustached man, dressed up in the suave style of Adolf Hitler, clasping young Venoušek's rattle; and, most strikingly, watched by the Mayor of Prague, sitting in a wooden high chair, enthroned ceremoniously by his father with a crown made of summer flowers, confidently looking straight at the camera, backgrounded by an ivy-clad wall and a bronze plaque of his famous grandfather, himself a friend of T. G. Masaryk, founding President of the fledgling Czechoslovak Republic.

Like all past relics that defy the ruthlessness of time, these photographic images can be interpreted in a dizzying variety of conflicting ways. Havel himself emphasized their absurdity. 'In those films,' he once mused, 'I am a small baby who is constantly the subject of everyone's attention, a pampered bourgeois child attended by governesses, relatives, friends, even the Mayor of Prague himself.' Pestering admirers, he continued, made him feel a deep sense of loneliness amidst love. 'This love is so overpowering and burdensome that the child seems constantly to be petrified and astonished. This I think developed in me at an early age a strengthened sense of the absurdity of the world, a certain distance from it, even a kind of fear of the world.'[1]

---

[1] Cited in *Václav Havel: A Czech Drama*, a BBC documentary programme in the Bookmark series (London, 1987).

Probably Havel here inflated his earliest powers of perception, as well as understated the ways in which he, like all newcomers on earth, yearned for comforting breasts and chests, exactly because the world is an unintelligible, potentially frightening place. Havel nevertheless correctly put his finger on the unusual cluttering of his early months with admirers. Not many new arrivals on earth were so showered with privileged well-wishers, with adult faces exuding the magic of birth, the excitement and joy evoked by beginners in the world. Many of the curled and scratched photographs in the Havel family albums are additional testimony to this power of beginning – to the human ability to create a being which did not exist before, and so to ensure that the world does not remain at a standstill.

Some beginnings, such as revolutionary upheavals, are of course unplanned spectacular events that take humans completely by surprise. Birth, by contrast, is both a regular and ineradicable – but no less special – feature of the human condition. The human species is naturally bound and gagged in its absolute dependence upon birth for its survival and reproduction. Yet birth is not just a natural event – as if birth is merely a shield against death, or merely the prelude to death. Birth is more interesting than that, and it is little wonder that it is marked with rites of passage – gifts, visits, celebrations, the giving of names – and proverbial turns of phrase about its importance. The beginning is half the whole, some say. Others add: things are always best in their beginning; from small beginnings grow mighty things; and all glory comes from daring to begin. The first yelps and whimpers of blue-eyed Venoušek confirmed all this. They proved yet again that birth is a vital moment of beginning. Here was a single individual – like all other individuals – endowed with unique and unpredictable qualities making his appearance in the world. He weighed only 3.27 kilograms and stretched a mere 50 centimetres, but the world was never again to be the same. His birth, like the birth of all other human beings, was a beginning pregnant with unforeseeable consequences. Venoušek's arrival might even be said to have been beginning's revenge upon those who wanted to resist novelty and to keep the world predictably on course. Like all newborns – his first admirers wrote – he had within him the potential power of the newcomer to begin something anew, that is, to act not only within but upon the world. 'Your Honour, Esteemed Sir', began

the very first correspondence he received. It was a postcard signed
by the tenants and servants at the family's country house called
Havlov. 'We dare to send you our greetings full of respect,' they
continued. The tone resembled that of royal petitioners humbly
waiting upon their new king. The conclusion squeezed into the
corner of the card was equally deferential. 'We trust that you are
in the best condition of health,' they wrote, 'and we hope when
we see you that you will show favour on us.'[1]

[1]The postcard, dated 11 October 1936 and signed by Alice Moraweková and others,
is reproduced in *Václav Havel 97* (Prague, 1998), p. 7.

FOLLY

The learned ability of the newborn to flourish in the world's fields of power is always fragile and risky. There are times when the cries of innocents are extinguished by stupidity, squalor, hunger, violence. Even when they survive the perils of birth, the newborn find their lives complicated by the power dynamics of families, communities, business firms, whole economies, parties, governments, and states. Such organizations are menacing. They tower over them like colossi. Organizations make the innocent look and feel small. The newborn are turned into the playthings of power relations – of which they know little, let alone can understand, or tame or control.

Young Venoušek's early years were exactly like this. It has often been said – by card-carrying Communists, sceptical conservatives, guilted liberals – that he enjoyed a comfortable 'bourgeois' upbringing. The sad truth is that his life as 'a well-fed piglet'[1] began badly within a family whose ideals were smashed up by folly, military occupation, surveillance, air raids, war, and totalitarianism. Venoušek took his first steps in the early autumn of 1937 – at precisely the moment that Czechoslovakia was pushed to its knees by the power-posturing of neighbouring states and alliances. Not everybody saw what was happening. Or they foolishly turned a blind eye, as did the most popular contemporary guide for foreign travellers to Prague.[2] First published in the month of Venoušek's birth, the guide conjured his home town into an exotic haven. The guide marvelled over Prague's green spaces and wooded surroundings; the breathtaking views of the city from the heights of Petřín, Hradčany, and Letná; and the wealth of architectural beauty – Romanesque, Gothic, Renaissance, rococo, and especially baroque buildings resonating its varied history from the time of the seventh century. Praise was heaped upon the Prague diet of freshwater trout and carp; goose, duck and venison; pilsner, dark beer from Smíchov, fiery plum brandy and agreeable Moravian wine; only a small frown was reserved for the 'unexpected' local sandwiches, consisting of *topless* slices of buttered bread covered in salami, egg, pickled cucumber, fish or ham. The guide noted that

[1] Václav Havel, *Letters to Olga*. June 1979–September 1982 (New York, 1988), p. 180.
[2] The guide, written by an Honorary Foreign Member of the Masaryk Academy of Work, Gerald Druce, is entitled *In the Heart of Europe. Life in Czechoslovakia* (London, 1936).

central heating of residences was common; that road traffic moved on the left; and that a system of red letter-boxes for the quick delivery of letters franked with 90-heller stamps functioned well. Although sugar was rationed, commodities like soap and matches were plentiful, while the commercial hub in St Wenceslas Square was often thronged with shoppers, said the guide.

The guide admired Prague's modernist feel. It pointed to the example of 'a new suburb' called Barrandov, built on a rock cliff overlooking the River Vltava and offering magnificent views of the city. The text left unmentioned that it was owned by the Havel family; it simply noted that Barrandov had 'a magnificent restaurant which has become a popular afternoon and evening rendezvous for those wishing to escape from the city for an hour or two. It has a well-equipped bathing pool and numerous tennis courts.'[1] The guide went on to report the popularity of bookable cinema performances, theatres, music halls, cabarets, low-price symphonies, the opera performances of Smetana's *Libuše*, Dvořák's *Rusalka* and Janáček's *Jenůfa*, and the amusing comedies of Voskovec and Werich. The guide noted the enthusiasm in Prague for public performances by Sokol gymnasts, at which thousands of young women in loose Romanesque dresses and young men dressed in red shirts and feathered caps together performed exercises in lines and patterns designed to highlight the values of self-control, cool courage, and the synchronism of body and mind. The guide reported that in matters of recreation young people were keen on tennis, volleyball, *házená* (a handball game played by women), football, ice-hockey, skating, skiing, athletics, and (thanks to the local Barrandov studios) the new medium of cinema. The professional classes, the guide reported, seemed unusually knowledgeable about world and current affairs, no doubt because for two or three hours per week on average they frequented cafés well stocked with a wide range of domestic and foreign newspapers and periodicals, both illustrated and literary. The guide reserved a short epilogue for politics and international affairs. It noted that the citizens of Prague had every right to be proud of their country's achievements. There had been a steady consolidation of its various territorial units. The Czechs and Slovaks were setting an example to other nations by practising tolerance and respect towards the claims of the

[1] *In the Heart of Europe*, op. cit., p. 166.

minority populations of Germans, Hungarians, Poles and others. Czechoslovakia enjoyed warm relations with its neighbours. The country was an ardent supporter of the League of Nations. The recent resignation (on 14 December 1935) for health reasons of the great statesman, eighty-five-year-old President T. G. Masaryk, had changed nothing. 'At the election held in the Vladislav Hall of the Prague Castle,' the guide concluded, 'Dr Edward Beneš was elected to succeed him. Thus, after having been its Foreign Secretary ever since the republic was founded, Dr Beneš became Czechoslovakia's second President and a continuity of the country's internal and external policies, with Dr Milan Hodža as Prime Minister, was assured.'[1]

The words harboured foolish thinking, proving yet again that fools enjoy serenity in the company of knaves. The unpleasant fact was that Havel's country of birth was about to be strangled alive by a Nazi Germany on the loose in central Europe. Ever since late 1933, when Hitler had pulled Germany out of the League of Nations, the tiny middle-European state of Czechoslovakia had begun to look and feel ever smaller. During the summer of 1934, in clear defiance of the Versailles settlement, the Nazis had managed a coup in Austria by murdering its Chancellor, Dr Engelbert Dolfuss, who favoured a one-party dictatorship but anti-Nazi state. In 1935, by means of a plebiscite envisaged in the Versailles Treaty, the Saarland had been incorporated within the Reich. Hitler promptly compounded the victory by reconstituting the Luftwaffe, reintroducing conscription, and renouncing any commitment to disarmament. In the spring of 1936, in open defiance of the Treaty, the Nazis marched into the demilitarized zone in the Rhineland, and during the course of the next year they signed the Anti-Comintern Pact with Mussolini's Italy and withdrew from the British-backed Non-Intervention Committee that was aiming to shield Spain from foreign armies. Then in March 1938 – Havel was eighteen months old, still in nappies but mincing his first words – the Nazis tasted their greatest triumph yet: the engineered *Anschluss* or 'annexation' of Austria, the proclamation of a Greater German Reich, and the welcoming of Hitler's splendid cavalcade in Vienna by flag-waving, cheering crowds kept orderly by Austrian police proudly wearing Nazi insignia.

[1] *In the Heart of Europe*, op. cit., pp. 222–223.

The Western powers reacted to expansionism with foolish fumblings. Especially given that Hitler had no prepared timetable for his forays, and that his so-called policy of 'peaceful aggression' relied at this stage mainly on huffing and puffing, big-mouthed bluffing and local cuffing – he judged that he could get his way mainly by localized conflict that fell short of war – the reactions of states like Britain appear in retrospect to be nothing short of political lunacy. It seemed obvious to the British in particular that the best antidote to Hitler was on the one hand to recruit France and the Soviet Union as counterweights to Nazism, thereby re-creating the security triangle of the Great War, meanwhile hoping that Germany could be lured into playing the role of anchor state in a new European security zone. This episode of balance-of-power politics produced perverse results.

For many contemporary observers, the specifically modern principle of the balance of power among territorial states – a power-sharing arrangement that ensures that 'a tiny republic is no less a sovereign state than the most powerful kingdom'[1] – was the dominant principle, the fundamental law of interstate relations in the European region. It had indeed been so since the emergence, during the Renaissance, of a system of armed territorial states. British foreign policy supposed that the principle was still operative, but the commitment produced evil contradictions. Quite apart from the problem of complicity with the most horrendous programme of organized murder that Europe had ever seen – Stalin was in the middle of liquidating more Communists than any despot of the twentieth century – the British vision required giving the Nazis precisely what they wanted: more room in middle Europe to secure and expand the *Volksmasse*, the racial community of Germans not yet united under one state.[2] For various reasons, the requirement came easily to the British. Influential conservatives in that country considered that Germany had suffered unjustly at the hands of the victors at Versailles while British policy-makers, too ignorant about German politics to grasp the novelty of totalitarianism, took Hitler at his word in presuming that Nazi ambitions were strictly limited to areas inhabited by Germans. Prime Minister Neville Chamberlain

[1] M. de Vattel, *Le droit des gens, ou principes de la loi naturelle* (Leiden, 1758), p. 6.
[2] See 'The Hossbach Memorandum', in *Documents on German Foreign Policy 1918–45* (London, 1949), series D, i, pp. 29–30.

even hoped that Hitler would turn out to be another Bismarck. If Germany were satisfied by concessions, he supposed, it would prove to be a safeguard of European security – thereby overcoming the instability caused by France's little ally Czechoslovakia, and all the other weakling states of central-eastern Europe created by the controversial Versailles settlement.

It followed from this view of Germany as a steadying force that Prague would need to be pressed into concessions to Berlin. Czechoslovakia, the most resilient parliamentary republic of central Europe, was to be turned into a devil's playground. It did not follow automatically that Czechoslovakia had to be sacrificed without any tangible security guarantees from the Nazis, but that was to be the tragic outcome. During the second half of September 1938, Chamberlain met thrice with Hitler. 'In spite of the hardness and ruthlessness of his face,' the Prime Minister mused of the ex-Austrian ex-corporal, 'I got the impression that here was a man who could be relied upon.'[1] At their meeting at Berchtesgaden on 15 September, Hitler insisted on the right of 'Sudetenland' to secede from Czechoslovakia. He added positively that this was 'the Führer's last demand'.

Like a dog returning to its vomit, the fool Chamberlain returned to his folly. The fools listened. Chamberlain agreed to give Hitler's demand careful consideration, but he did not expect Hitler to move so swiftly, as he did on 23 September at Godesberg by demanding the evacuation and annexation of the Sudetenland within five days. While the British cabinet initially rejected the ultimatum, France and Germany began to mobilize their armies, and at Munich on 29–30 September, in the presence of the Führer, Mussolini and the socialist Edouard Daladier, the spineless and clueless Chamberlain willingly caved in.[2] The British in effect did the work of the Nazis. Chamberlain, who said he was *pleasantly* tired after nine long hours with Hitler, was certain that there would now be no war. He immediately issued an ultimatum to the Czechoslovak delegation, huddled in an adjoining room, that they should accept the amputation of their state or else suffer more dramatic consequences, like the death of their body politic. Between yawns, Chamberlain spoke

[1] Keith Feiling, *A Life of Neville Chamberlain* (London, 1946), p. 367.
[2] See Igor Lukes, *Czechoslovakia between Stalin and Hitler. The Diplomacy of Edvard Beneš in the 1930s* (New York and Oxford, 1996), especially chapters 5–7; and Boris Celovsky, *Das Münchener Abkommen 1938* (Stuttgart, 1958).

fine words about how the big powers would protect the rump
Czechoslovak state. The Czechoslovak delegates were told that
their response was not required, and that they should leave. In the
same spirit as the Nazi-saluting English football team playing against
Germany earlier that year in Berlin, Chamberlain then proceeded
to put his hopes in a draft declaration on Anglo–German friendship,
some version of which was waved in the air as he stepped from his
plane in London, announcing with a triumphant smile the outbreak
of 'Peace in our time'.

These foolish words of a man who thought himself wise but
made his folly sovereign turned out to be the elixir of Hitlerite
power. In this fools' paradise called Europe, foul-tempered Hitler
– nicknamed the *Teppichfresser* (carpet-eater) by some diplomats
– drank delight. Folly nourished his worst qualities. He shouted,
threatened violence, grudgingly promised to keep the dogs of war
leashed for a while, then shouted and threatened violence again.
'*Es hat keinen Sinn weiter zu verhandeln* [There's no sense at all
in negotiating further],' he bellowed to Chamberlain's emissary.
'Germans are being treated like niggers,' he screamed. 'No one
would dare to treat even the Turks like that.' Like a rapist, he then
lowered his voice, and growled, 'On 1 October [1938] I shall have
Czechoslovakia where I want her. If France and England decide to
strike, let them strike.'[1]

This kind of behaviour, succoured by Chamberlain's foolishness,
disgraced the art of negotiation, undermined Western support for
further talks with Hitler, and convinced him, and probably Stalin
and Mussolini as well, that further 'peaceful aggression' elsewhere
in Europe would reap easy dividends. The policy of appeasement
spelled immediate disaster for the rump Czechoslovak polity,
which under the initial leadership of President Beneš was forced
to suffer textbook lessons in the art of destroying a state by
stages.[2] Verbal threats followed by confusion; the confiscation
of land; the spreading fever of fear; growing military pressures
from without: all this served within the republic to create power

---

[1] Nevile Henderson, *Failure of a Mission, Berlin 1937–1939* (New York, 1940), p.
163.
[2] Compare the classic account of the earlier breakdown of the Weimar Republic –
the ways in which it passed sequentially through the phases of loss of power, power
vacuum, and the takeover of power – presented by Karl Dietrich Bracher, 'Auflösung
einer Demokratie: Das Ende der Weimar Republik als Forschungsproblem', in
Faktoren der Machtbildung, ed., Arkadij Gurland (Berlin, 1952), pp. 39–98.

vacuums within which politicians and other actors seemed to float helplessly.

The immediate effect of the Munich appeasement was to intensify the powerlessness of the state authorities. In matters of foreign policy, Czechoslovakia slipped to the status of a mere satellite state. At home, its parliamentary republican institutions suffered paralysis. Indistinct leadership, directionless policy-making, the open flouting of laws began to pave the way for a peaceful transition from democracy to dictatorship. As if hypnotized by their Nazi neighbours, the Czechoslovak political class tried desperately to forestall German interference in their affairs and to promote political recovery by emulating certain key features, but not the excesses, of Nazi rule. Within a few months of the Munich fiasco – young Venoušek was now just over two years old – pre-publication press censorship was introduced. Political exiles from Germany were extradited into the hands of the Gestapo without any vocal opposition. The National Assembly authorized the executive to legislate by decree in cases of emergency. The Communist Party was abolished and trade unions were merged into a single organization dominated by the right-wing social-democratic National Labour Party. Jews were encouraged to emigrate and many of them encountered growing discrimination by the authorities in both the private professions and state-sector employment. The election, on 30 November 1938 by the National Assembly, of Emil Hácha as third President of the country (which was soon to be renamed 'The Protectorate of Bohemia and Moravia') symbolized all these developments. So did his foolish cabinet address shortly after his election. Formulated in the rear-view mirror of time, it perfectly reflected the new-fangled policy of appeasement. 'Czechoslovak statesmen should take the national saint, Prince Wenceslas, as their model,' he told his ministers. 'Prince Wenceslas fought for German–Czech understanding, although initially he did not find understanding with his own people.'[1]

---

[1] Cited in Vojtech Mastny, *The Czechs Under Nazi Rule. The Failure of National Resistance, 1939–1942* (New York, 1971), p. 23 (translation altered). See also F. Lukeš, 'K volbě Emila Háchy presidentem tzv. druhé republiky', *Časopis Národního musea*, Social Science series, CXXXI (1962), pp. 114–120; and Hácha to Beneš, 10 December 1938, in Edvard Beneš, *Memoirs of Edvard Beneš: From Munich to New Year and New Victory* (London, 1954), p. 97.

REPUBLICANS

VÁCLAV HAVEL

Hácha's advice was insulting to young Venoušek's family. The historical analogy he drew was not merely unfortunate – Prince Wenceslas was murdered in A.D. 935 by his younger brother Boleslav, whose sibling jealousy was combined with strong disapproval of Wenceslas's political concessions to the German Empire. Pressured by Great Britain, abandoned by France and the Soviet Union, the Czechoslovak government's capitulation to the Munich agreement and to the growing military power of Nazism was understandable. But it flung the whole Havel family into turmoil. Václav M. Havel, Venoušek's father, was a strong-minded entrepreneur-citizen with definite anti-fascist views. 'We reject the prophets who want to solve the Depression by a return to lower levels of culture and economy,' he wrote shortly after Hitler had come to power. Wavy-haired, grey-blue-eyed, tiny Mr Havel was known to be a kind and generous man of calm moderation. He held firm political views. 'We do not want to go backwards in civilization', he wrote. He found repugnant 'nationalism', 'irredentism' and 'racialist messianism'. These evils needed to be wiped out – principally by embracing the power-sharing, social-liberal principles of 'openness and truthfulness, purity of political ends and political means, intelligent and honest politics'.

Venoušek's father thought that these high principles required a new system of welfare-state-regulated capitalism and parliamentary democracy guided by a 'cultural elite'. A modern-mannered republic was his ideal. 'To avoid any misunderstanding,' he once said in a speech, 'by "elite" we do not mean a closed caste, but rather an unorganized, unorganizable partnership of creative spirits, who thanks to their strong cultural values form a cultural authority in society, a spiritual government which – free of all means of power – is a durable and continuous guardian of successful social improvement.' The task of the cultural elite, of which he clearly considered himself a member, was to work for a polity defined by the non-violent sharing of power. Mr Havel was not a man of the Left. He usually voted for the National Democrats – a party founded by Karel Kramář, who in 1919 became Prime Minister of the new Czechoslovak state. Mr Havel stood for open government, full employment, socially responsible investment, the cultivation of individual conscience and creative responsibility through education, and nurturing 'mutual assistance and co-operation' through civilized corporatist bargaining among unions, businesses and professions. 'Democratically onwards!' he liked to say to his friends. He usually added, in the next breath, that the world of international politics now needed to cultivate genuine patriotism among citizens, support for peace through the League of Nations, and the protection of sovereign autonomy of nation states. His conclusion was utterly old-fashioned. 'The unity and independence of the Czechoslovak state,' he said, 'are not subjects open for discussion.'[1]

These patriotic social-liberal views were redolent of an old and respectable family whose known roots stretched back into the late eighteenth century. Young Venoušek was soon to hear tales, told by his father and mother, of the family's fair share of misfits and tragic figures: a great-great-grandmother who died in childbirth; a distant cousin who was taken by tuberculosis; a great uncle Rajmund who probably drank himself to death; another uncle, a butcher by trade, who died young of blood-poisoning. The family otherwise consisted of stolidly bourgeois stock. A rare photograph of Venoušek, a smiling four year old, dressed in a heavy coat and beret and clutching an umbrella, shows him standing in Prague's Košíře cemetery, beside the soon-to-be-destroyed family tomb that contained family members dating back 200 years. His great-great-grandfather, Václav Julius Havel was the first-born son of a well-known Prague miller and citizen; his wife, Terezie (1816–1882), who died suddenly from an attack of pneumonia, came from a family of moderately prosperous farmers. Venoušek's great-grandparents were prominent merchants and restaurateurs, while his grandfather, a successful Prague building contractor who married a much sought-after wealthy beauty, lived and worked, surrounded by servants, within a 'bourgeois milieu'.[2]

Venoušek's grandparents were also members of the 'cultural elite' that favoured independence from the Austro-Hungarian empire. They grew up as Czech patriots within a territory whose ruling group remained instinctively 'Austrian'.[3] Unlike Lieutenant Lukáš – a character in Jaroslav Hašek's The Good Soldier Švejk – the Havels were not Czechs who equated being a Czech with

---

[1]See 'Před nástupem mladých' (a speech in March 1933) and 'Barrandovská skupina' (minutes of a discussion group convened at Havlov, 24–28 May 1933) in V. M. Havel, Mé vzpomínky (Prague, 1995), pp. 229–247 and 247–260.
[2]Mé vzpomínky, op. cit., p. 16.
[3]Ibid.

membership of some kind of secret organization, who spoke German in society, wrote German, and who read Czech books and said to others in confidence: 'Let's be Czechs, but no one need know about it.' The Havels refused to educate their children in German-speaking schools. Young Venoušek's industrious grand-father, Vácslav Havel, 'employed only Czechs wherever he could'. He built the first indoor ice rink in Prague; sited on Primátorský Island, it was called Harmonia, and quickly proved to be a popular meeting point for Prague's cultural elite. His greatest project was the design and construction, from 1905 onwards, of Lucerna, the first and largest modern entertainment complex in Prague. It was inspired by his travels to such cities as Paris, Copenhagen, Milan and Berlin and by his patriotic faith that one day Prague would become a European metropolis.

In political terms, Venoušek's grandfather openly described himself as a 'Young Czech'. That meant that he had a poor opinion of the Habsburg dynasty that ruled over the Bohemian lands for 300 years. It was bad rule, he thought. The dynasty had destroyed religious freedom and suppressed the Czech language. It had driven the elite of the nation's nobility and church into exile, distributed estates and offices to alien caretakers, and turned the Czechs into an impotent minority within an ill-administered province. Venoušek's grandfather was proud of the 1918 declaration of Czechoslovak independence. He considered it a brave revolution, in which not a drop of blood was spilled, no windows were broken, and in which the first law passed by the revolutionary committee declared: 'All existing laws remain in force.'

These opinions counted. Venoušek's grandfather was well connected within the worlds of Prague business, medicine, arts, education, and politics. He was good friends, for example, with Karel Kramář, a well-known founder of the Czechoslovak state and political rival of Tomáš G. Masaryk. He kept company with the Deputy Mayor of Prague, Dr Štech, and was well acquainted with Professor Jan Jesenský, the father of Milena Jesenská, and Alois Rašín, who later became Minister of Finance in the First Republic of Czechoslovakia. Venoušek's grandfather was also active in theatre circles. He was treasurer of the National Theatre Association (among whose members his nickname was 'The Finance Minister'). He and his wife, who was a renowned cook, were regular hosts of lavish dinner parties, whose invited guests included many well-known artistic personalities, among them the lyric poet and dramatist Jaroslav Kvapil, and the most famous Prague poet of the day, Jaroslav Vrchlický, revered for his weaning of Czech literature away from German domination and (as his blurred images in the Havel family archives reveal) notorious for refusing to sit or stand still before the magnesium lamp camera, to which he had a principled aversion.

Venoušek's father – according to the rather dry account he gave of his own early years – thought of himself as a faithful carrier of this family tradition of republican Czech bourgeois respectability.[1] By European standards, the family was 'apparently wealthy'.[2] Although considerable debts were incurred from building the Lucerna complex, its assets enabled the family to lead a life of cosmopolitan luxury. As a young boy, before the First World War, Venoušek's father was taken on family trips to Italy, France, Belgium, and to Holland, where in Oostende (according to family folklore) he heard a performance of the great Italian opera singer, Caruso. The family often took holidays abroad. During the First Republic, they travelled on summer holidays to seaside resorts in Germany and Italy, and to the breathtaking lakeside setting at Bled, located in today's Slovenia; in wintertime, they liked to stay closer to home, at favourite ski slopes in Mnichovice and in the Giant Mountains (Krkonoše). After Venoušek was born, the Havel family liked to stay in their spacious summer residence at Havlov, a few hours by car from Prague. Accompanied by servants, the family also loved to venture out of Prague on fine-weather Sunday outings, especially by car, and then steamboat down the Vltava River to Braník, where they were ferried across the river to picnic and climb the cliffs of Barrandov in search of trilobites. Venoušek's father and mother also hosted visits to Havlov from Prague notables. Painters, lawyers, politicians, writers – what they called 'educated Prague society' – were regular guests at the family table. Among them was the most influential Czech writer of the First Republic, the witty and wise Karel Čapek, whose novel *War with the Newts* (published in the year of Venoušek's birth) satirized fascism, colonialism and greedy capitalism, all in the spirit of what Czechs like to call *lidskost*: down-to-earth sympathy and kindness for others.

[1] *Mé vzpomínky*, op. cit. especially parts 1, 3.
[2] From an interview with Václav Havel in the television programme, 'Pracovat a nezatrpknout', directed by Dita Fuchsová, Česká televize (21 February 1999).

True to the family's Young Czech instincts, Venoušek's father was sent to his father's old school, the Czech reálke, located in Ječná Street, near Charles Square, in central Prague. He later went on to study construction engineering at the Czech Polytechnic in Prague, where amidst the fears and hopes, disruption and destruction generated by the Great War, he became active in student politics. Shortly after the end of hostilities, at the moment of the birth of Czechoslovakia in 1918, he was elected as the first Chairman of the Union of Czechoslovak Students. The political experience made him 'a life-long democrat, an admirer of Masaryk'.[1] He was attracted to Masaryk's ideal of a 'perpetually self-reforming democracy' and he became convinced, for the rest of his life, that politics was important and that thinking and acting as an informed citizen was a duty, not a luxury. 'Political activity or inactivity is a question of conscience,' he later wrote. 'We are the state – and each of us is therefore responsible for its condition and future. If we tolerate a defective system, it is because we have not yet created anything better; bad people will make decisions only until such time as better people have acquired the courage, strength and ability to replace them. A new political programme requires creativity, activity and radicalism, both intellectual and moral.'[2]

The spirit of republicanism pervaded his visionary advice to an audience of young people, given in the month of Hitler's accession to power, to work for a 'quality democracy' in the new Czechoslovakia. Contemporary democracies like Czechoslovakia, he argued, suffered from a variety of ailments, most of them traceable to the tyranny of 'the mechanical spirit'. Venoušek's father here drew upon the authority of a family friend, the Brno philosopher J. L. Fischer, to condemn the hegemony of mechanical reason. Mr Havel disliked the bad habit of supposing that both nature and society can and should be observed, numbered, recorded, planned, and ordered about at will. The mechanical spirit, he told his young audience, had colonized the dominant ideologies of the times. Liberal individualism, which presumes like an accountant that each and every individual is 'an absolutely free unit' guided by the criteria of 'size and number, minimum expense and maximum benefit', was a case in point. Bossy forms of collectivism pushed

[1] Václav Havel in 'Pracovat a nezatrpknout', op. cit.
[2] All quotations in the following passages are taken from Václav M. Havel, 'Barrandovská skupina', in *Mé vzpomínky*, op. cit., pp. 247–260.

in the same direction. Fascism perversely worships the Nation and state-building, while Communism, guided by the doctrine of the dictatorship of the proletariat, ends up doing the same by greedily monopolizing power over its subjects in the name of class struggle.

Despite the rise of German fascism, Mr Havel predicted that these ideologies of impersonal mechanization would eventually lose their grip upon the world. His stated belief in human progress was often put so fulsomely that the faces of its nineteenth-century exponents would have flushed. 'Every thought and every organism goes through a certain development,' he wrote. 'The times call for new relations and contexts. Progress then assumes that the positive values and achievements bequeathed to us by the past and still unsurpassed will be preserved. Those, however, which have lost their significance cannot be permitted to be an obstacle to new development. That is the principle of evolution.' Venoušek's father used this principle to predict the end of liberal democracy. 'The idea of the responsibility of the individual for the whole, and of the whole for each individual' was gaining ground. So too was the related insight that the individual, far from being an atom whose motion is calculable, is rather 'a person and personality variously capable of various tasks and continually changing'. All this was plainly evident in contemporary architectural designs that favoured simplicity, horizontality and function, rather than mere form. The trend was evident as well in industrial experiments, like the Baťa employee autonomy-and-performance schemes in the field of shoe-manufacturing. And it could be seen in the magnificent Sokol rallies, held to the sound of loudspeaker music. 'Everyone who has watched the undulating masses during physical training notes with interest the individuals, the beauty of the function of man in relation to the tremendous whole. More striking, however, is the way that every individual is trained in his unit to develop his own unique characteristics and attitude, despite the tremendous and uniform appearance of the whole.' Such experiments, observed Mr Havel, signalled the demechanization of life and the birth of a *quality* democracy that values power-sharing, choice, personal responsibility, equality of opportunity, patriotism, functionalism [*účelnost*], voluntary discipline, beauty, openness, public account-ability, and personal belief in a God. 'I am convinced that there is a more effective form of democratic government than today's,' he concluded. 'It is the task of all who acknowledge the high moral value of democratic ideals to strive, without delay and with every ounce of energy, for the reconstruction of our democracy in the spirit of the times.'

DEVIL'S PLAYGROUND

The times were unripe for such dreaming. The fledgling parliamentary republic of Czechoslovakia was on the verge of becoming the unlucky testing ground for something new in the ways and means of power. A bizarre symbol of things to come was the kowtowing of one head of state to another. The old Chinese custom of touching the ground with one's forehead as a sign of worship or absolute submission to power (*k'o-t'ou*, from *k'o*, knock, *t'ou*, head) – the Czechs call it crawling up someone's arse – was repeated on the evening of 14 March 1939, when the top-hatted, stooping President of the Czechoslovak Republic, Emil Hácha, hurried by train from Prague to Berlin to keep an appointment with Hitler. It is unclear just how well Hácha along the way had digested the ominous news that that same evening, at 17.30 hours, the crack SS Bodyguard 'Adolf Hitler' had begun to occupy the Ostrava region, in the north of the country. It is known that Hácha's appointment began badly. The moody film buff Führer – the man who seemed to regard total war as a big-budget film – made his counterpart wait two hours so that he could finish watching a movie. It was an escapist romance, recommended to him as usual by Goebbels, appropriately enough entitled *A Hopeless Case* (*Ein Hoffnungsloser Fall*).[1]

Business got under way at a quarter-past one in the morning, by which time the old and frail Hácha had been mesmerized into playing the role of the mouse before the lion. Hácha was the first to open his mouth. He repeated what he had said publicly before leaving Prague: that the Czechoslovak state indeed belonged both geographically and historically to the sphere of German power.[2] Apparently so surprised by Hácha's submissiveness, Hitler, sipping his favourite mineral water, quickly roared that within six hours the German armed forces would invade Czechoslovakia from three sides, crushing ruthlessly any resistance along the way. It was a lie. German airfields were at that moment enshrouded in fog. But the lie had instant effect. The faint-headed Hácha collapsed into the arms of the Führer's personal physician, Dr Morell, who injected him at once with dextrose and vitamins. The kowtowed Hácha with eyes barely open was then told by Göring that the Luftwaffe would smash any Czech resistance by reducing Prague to a pile of

[1]Wilhelm Keitel, *The Memoirs of Field-Marshall Keitel* (New York, 1966), p. 79.
[2]Karl Megerle, 'Deutschland und das Ende der Tschecho-Slowakei', *Monatshefte für auswärtige Politik*, VI (1939), p. 770.

rubble. The bluffing worked. Hácha telephoned Prague to order that there be no resistance to the invading troops. He then reassured Hitler and his entourage of clever thugs that Czechoslovakia would do anything to avoid bloodshed. Sitting beside Hitler just before dawn, Hácha concluded the meeting by signing a statement prepared by the Nazis. 'The Czechoslovak President declared that . . . he confidently placed the fate of the Czech people and country in the hands of the Führer of the German Reich,' the statement ran. It was a masterpiece of political deception. 'The Führer accepted this declaration and expressed his intention of taking the Czech people under the protection of the German Reich and of guaranteeing them an autonomous development of their ethnic life as suited their character.'[1]

The words were to be written like foul-mouthed graffiti over the young Václav Havel's life during the next six years. Hácha's faint-headed behaviour before Hitler fitted perfectly the stereotype of Czechs as self-pitying, childlike subjects skilled at stepping away from responsibility – subjects who are then forced by others to pay heavily for their cowardice and to wallow in a 'martyr complex'.[2] It was later said in Hácha's defence that he tried his best under difficult circumstances to protect his fellow citizens. And Hácha himself claimed that he had sacrificed the state to save the nation. But the bitter truth was that the Czechs were forced to pay heavily for their leader's kowtowing. The Czechoslovak state was rapidly dismembered. Ruthenia was forcibly annexed by Hungary. Slovakia was reorganized into an independent state with limited sovereign powers. And Bohemia and Moravia, once the heartlands of the republic, were pushed and shoved through several stages of Nazification.[3]

'*Es kommt der Tag* [The day will come],' Czech friends of the Nazis used to whisper, and here it was. Hours after Hácha's fateful meeting with Hitler, in blizzard conditions, German troops

[1] *Documents on German Foreign Policy, 1918–45*, Series D, volume 4 (Washington, 1949–1958), p. 270.

[2] Vít Vlnas, *Jan Nepomucký, česká legenda* (Prague, 1993), p. 69; and the fine study by Robert Pynsent, *Questions of Identity. Czech and Slovak Ideas of Nationality and Personality* (Budapest, London and New York, 1994), pp. 190–196.

[3] The following draws upon Vojtech Mastny, *The Czechs under Nazi Rule*, op. cit., Detlef Brandes, *Die Tschechen unter deutschem Protektorat*, volume 1: 1939–1942 (Munich, 1969); Sheila Grant Duff, *A German Protectorate: the Czechs under Nazi Rule* (London, 1942); Callum MacDonald and Jan Kaplan, *Prague in the Shadow of the Swastika: A History of the German Occupation 1939–1945* (Prague, 1995).

poured into Prague, red-faced by sleet and frost, and perhaps even a touch of shame. Hitler followed, checking in to Prague Castle at Hradčany on the evening of 15 March. Initially, the Nazis treated their prey with caution. Militant pragmatism dictated that the Czechs were to be exploited for the Nazi war effort with a minimum outlay of German resources. Talk of Czech–German co-operation abounded. The important independent powers of the provinces of Bohemia and Moravia – customs and monetary affairs, military authority and defence, foreign affairs, and postal and telecommunications facilities – were all wiped out by decree. All governmental institutions were placed under the immediate authority of the 'Reichsprotektor', an office filled by the former German foreign minister, Baron von Neurath, who from here on countermanded 'in the interest of the Reich' any measures of the government of the Protectorate. The Czechoslovak army was disbanded. Parliament was dissolved. All political parties were suspended. Privileges were extended to the ethnic German-speaking minority, such as the right of Reich citizenship, immunity from Czech courts of justice, and promotion within the administration of such cities as Prague, Brno, Olomouc, and České Budějovice. Meanwhile, 'sensible' measures against Jews were taken, which meant that a climate of fear and suspicion was nurtured, for instance by sacking Jewish civil servants and banning the Jewish population from purchasing or disposing of their property.

Following the declaration of war on Germany by Britain and France on 3 September 1939, but especially after the posting to Prague two years later of Reinhard Heydrich, former boss of the Reich Security Office (*Reichssicherheitshauptamt*), the Nazis toughened their methods of governing. Stimulated by military victories against the Soviet Union, and confident in their own ability to deal with reported Czech resistance, and keen to win what Goebbels liked to call the 'chess match for power,' the Heydrich administration swiftly moved in for the kill. Martial law was declared. The Gestapo undertook large-scale arrests, turning first mainly to German political *émigrés*. Rounds of summary court judgements and executions followed. Material concessions to peasants and workers were combined with policies aimed at terrorizing and weeding out intellectuals. The Czechs were entitled to live a private existence so long as they didn't think or act publicly. Colleges and universities were closed and their buildings assigned either to the German University in Prague or used for different functions, as happened to the building of Prague's college of law, which was turned into a *Schutzstaffel* (SS) barracks. Student dormitories were ransacked. Thousands of students and staff were arrested. The 'ring-leaders' among them were summarily shot. Many others were carted off as hostages to the Oranienburg concentration camp, from which they were set free by handfuls and permitted to return home, frightened by their brush with death.

Nazi government in this form bore the stamp of Heydrich, under whose leadership the Protectorate was changed by fits and starts into a well-functioning system of total power, the likes of which Czechs had never before experienced. This was no dictatorship or despotism. It was an entirely new configuration of power, whose contours defied all traditional categories of political thought. It was soon to be called 'totalitarian'. The word has subsequently lost much of its sting through familiarity and misuse, but for descriptive purposes it remains chillingly apt. Under conditions of totalitarianism, nobody – not even its commanders – was safe from persecution, or death. Totalitarian rule was specifically geared to organizing, breaking up and destroying everything that was living, dead, inert. Land, shared historical memories, men, women, and children: these were the objects of totalitarian rule, which more savagely rampaged through the world only *after* its adversaries were defeated and destroyed.

The totalitarian power that the Nazis brought to Prague was unhinged power. Balzac (in *Cousine Bette*) noted that 'arbitrary rule is power gone mad', but the madness of totalitarian power was beyond the bounds of his wildest imaginings. Transforming the world into a hell-hole, totalitarianism was uninhibited power enjoying a monopoly of the means of available violence. Totalitarian power was the unrestricted capacity to organize and push people and things down the path of complete annihilation. Totalitarian power produced total powerlessness. It even regarded suicide as an insult, and it did all it could to prevent it by emaciating and grinding down the bodies of its victims – in the last instance by means of torture, or by a bullet through the head of the one trying to reach the electrified fence. Totalitarian power naturally created an inferno of fear and uncertainty for everybody and everything. Nobody was safe from annihilation. Totalitarian power certainly relied upon formal organizations: specialized administrative staff;

hierarchies of command; the scheduling of services; codes of conduct and discipline for personnel; systematic record-keeping. In this way, totalitarian power could function well by ensuring smooth administration, even if its staff were second-rate, or prone to rivalry, protection and corruption. Totalitarian rule also certainly put to good use individuals who were careerists, or who had a strong sense of duty and a knack for organizing things and getting jobs done. Yet totalitarian power was most definitely not a species of bureaucratic rule. For one thing, it cultivated and required its victims' willingness to take the initiative in performing the dirty business – for instance by informing on others, or supervising prison work-squads. For another thing, totalitarianism recognized no hindering rules or restrictions; it was self-propelling power that thrived on crashing through the world, demolishing all barriers along the way. Totalitarian power tended to undermine bureaucratic rule. It ignored considerations of economic utility or *Realpolitik*. And it did away with talk of moral or ethical restrictions. It treated such talk as rubbish left over from a corrupted past.

The totalitarianism of the Reichsprotektorat dispensed with ideological convictions. Although it operated under the canopy of a totalizing ideology – the ideology stressed the animal-like struggle of the new Reich against its enemies, and the imperative of building a new Europe modelled on the emerging *Volksgemeinschaft* of the Third Reich – totalitarian power effectively broke free from all such ideological self-justifications. The old maxim that power is only effective when it is legitimate in the eyes of the ruled was disproven by totalitarian power, which was not at all a type of rule guided by principled aims and calculations of how to achieve certain ends. Or, rather, totalitarian power was guided by only one end: the annihilation of its designated enemies. Totalitarian power was impulsive, arbitrary, terroristic, murderous. Not even its unlimited power of culling and sewing a label on whole categories of the population – Jews, homosexuals, Romanies, Poles, Jehovah's Witnesses, the unfit – was free of arbitrariness, uncertainty and disorder. Everything became provisional. The essence of totalitarian power was terror – soul- and body-destroying fear driven by the expectation that death and destruction at the hands of the secret police, army or 'unidentified thugs' were just around the corner.

Thanks to the Reichsprotektorat, everybody, including the

administrators and accomplices of the regime, was potentially superfluous. 'Force should be right,' said the totalitarian voice, 'or rather, right and wrong should lose their names, and so should justice.'[1] The living were flung into a merciless struggle of each against all. The boundaries between life and death dissolved. Past and present and future collapsed into each other. Each minute was potentially the last minute. A second could feel like a lifetime. Or like nothing at all. Everyone was 'raw material'. Each individual was on terror's hit list. Anyone – in the Auschwitz jargon – could be turned into a walking dead *Muselmann* ('Muslim') whose body and soul disintegrate before the eyes of others. Anyone could be disposed of without trace. Murder naturally succoured this form of power. It demonstrated its omnipotence. Cruel excess was constantly required. Talented and ingenious barbarism functioned as a form of self-assertion – as sadistic proof that there were no external barriers to power, that those who were acting on the world were capable of anything, that the unthinkable was real.[2] It was therefore not surprising that bizarre forms of dastardly evil resulted. Totalitarianism was a killing field, which is why the mass grave and the concentration camp, in which subjects were stripped of the right to have rights and then exterminated, were its perfect manifestations – and not somehow embarrassing exceptions. Extermination of individuals and whole groups – one might even say all of humanity – was the logical and practical end point of totalitarian power.

[1] William Shakespeare, *Troilus and Cressida*, Act 1, Scene 3.

[2] Jean Améry, *Jenseits von Schuld und Sühne* (Stuttgart, 1977), p. 67. Compare also the insightful work by Wolfgang Sofsky, *Die Ordnung des Terrors. Das Konzentrationslager* (Frankfurt am Main, 1993), especially part 1.

ZOOLOGY

The frightening novelty of the regime convinced the Havel family to remove young Václav and his little brother Ivan from the hell-hole of Prague to the relative tranquillity of their country house, near Tišnov in Moravia. Havlov served for a time as something like a rural retreat. The half-wooden, white-plastered villa with green window-frames and a swimming pool was tucked away within a forest, above a little stream called Bobrůvka, within hiking distance of old Pernštejn Castle. The house was also within walking distance of a school in the nearby village of Žďárec, which Havel began attending during the first week of September 1942. The decision to move the children and send them to a country school was his mother's. Božena Havlová, like many other thinking Czechs, tried to act as if life were normal, all the while knowing that the world was now being divided, violently and irreversibly, between those who valued human omnipotence and those for whom utter powerlessness was a simple fact of life.

Reinhard Heydrich, who prior to his rule of Czechoslovakia had been among Himmler's closest collaborators, was emblematic of the trend.[1] Here was a new type of ruler, unfamiliar to most Czechs, a man convinced of his own omnipotence and skilled in the art of repeatedly insulting his opponents to demonstrate to everybody that they were not merely flesh-and-blood opponents but 'objective enemies'. Those who knew him personally – the Havel family did not – confirmed his habit of regarding friends as potential foes, and rivals as enemies, 'not as individuals, but as carriers of tendencies endangering the State and therefore beyond the pale of the National Community'.[2] His obsession with 'objective enemies' evidently led down the path of reducing them to nothing, or killing them in 'self-defence'. This meant the extermination of whole categories of flesh-and-blood mortals. Heydrich was of course temporarily interested in Jews and in Romanies – thousands of whom reportedly died from 'typhus', which meant beating, starvation, transportation to Auschwitz as slave labourers, gassing in nearby Birkenau, or

[1] See Günther Deschner, *Heydrich: the pursuit of total power* (London, 1981); and S. Aronson, *Reinhard Heydrich und die Frühgeschichte von Gestapo und SD* (Stuttgart, 1971).
[2] The description is provided by the Nazi jurist and SS member, R. Höhn, in an obituary printed in the *Deutsche Allgemeine Zeitung* (13 June 1942) and quoted in Ernst Kohn-Bramstedt, *Dictatorship and Political Police. The technique of control by fear* (London, 1945), p. 160.

being burned, tossed into latrines, or buried in mass graves in forests. But the list of future potential victims was infinitely expandable. It was well known to the Havel family, and to others in informed Prague circles, that as early as 1941 proposals had been circulating among the Nazis to treat the entire Polish population as Jews: making them the objects of compulsory changes of name if they were of German origin; forcing them to wear the P-sign, which would function like the yellow star worn by Jews; and making sexual intercourse between Germans and Poles punishable by death. Many Czechs, the Havel family included, naturally began to fear that they might be next in line.

Their fears were laced with rumours, deliberately planted by the German authorities, that they would deport or eliminate hundreds of thousands of Czechs. Driven by expectations of total victory in Western Europe, plans for the deportation of the Czechs – what later would be called 'ethnic cleansing' – were indeed drawn up. The Havel family knew that tens of thousands of Czech workers were being compulsorily drafted into work teams and sent to the Reich. They knew that Jews were receiving orders to hand over their typewriters and musical instruments, furs and microscopes, that they were now forbidden to enter certain streets and parks, that they were now prevented from disposing of their property, or making gifts. The family also knew that the once-small fortress town of Terezín (Theresienstadt) was being transformed into a 'self-administered' ghetto for Jews, even those who considered themselves Czechs and Christians. The Havels knew as well that Jews were cruelly saddled with the jobs of selecting candidates for 'resettlement lists', which meant transport to death camps elsewhere, and of apportioning the starvation rations of a few grams of bread and potatoes and teaspoonfuls of soup to inmates too old or exhausted to work.

The implication was clear: the punishment of non-Germans and 'unfit' Germans was a precondition of the triumphant will to total power over others. World conquest required breaking down the division between the conquering regime and the conquered territories. Even the distinction between 'at home' and 'abroad' had to be dissolved. A totalitarian conqueror like Heydrich had to act as if the territory he had conquered were his very own home – by eliminating strangers who did not belong. And so the Nazis' ultimate aim – as Heydrich clearly stated in his first speech after assuming office – was to undo the work of young Czechs like Havel's father, to 'Germanize' Bohemia and Moravia by incorporating them fully into the Reich. Hitler's 'table conversations' about the Czechs made it clear that while the Nazis aimed within their borders to build a suave totalitarianism, this involved no sympathy or respect for the Czechs. 'Germanizing' them meant expelling or exterminating elements of the population 'unsuited' for Germanization. It also meant acting like locusts within the country's rich fields of political culture and inherited republican parliamentary institutions. The final aim was to be linguicide. 'By firmly leading the Protectorate,' said Hitler during the third year of occupation – young Venoušek was now five and a half years old – 'it ought to be possible in about twenty years to push the Czech language back to the importance of a dialect.'[1] All this required that the Nazis had to be cruel. But, in order not to trigger explosions, or simply to avoid strikes and sabotage, or even guerrilla warfare behind the lines of the German army, the Nazis had to be kind. They had merely to be cruel by stealth. The aim was to kill the Czechs with kindness. So although the Führer stressed just how useful threats of expulsion of the Czechs from their homeland were as a means of government, he also instructed his Prague henchmen that Czechs should not be involved directly in the war effort. If that happened, they would likely raise their demands. Better then to seduce the Czechs into obedience and hard work by 'good treatment' and 'double rations'.[2]

The dilemma hiding within the Nazis' conquering power over the Czechs mirrored a dilemma lurking within the ranks of the conquered, young Václav included. From the side of all Czechs of (potential) anti-Nazi sentiment, threats of arrest, deportation, murder, imprisonment and extermination were self-evident from the moment of occupation. Like the man who worked in the crematorium in Prague at the time of the Nazi occupation – the

[1] Gerhard Ritter ed., *Hitlers Tischgespräche im Führerhauptquartier, 1941/1942* (Bonn, 1951), p. 91; second edition (Stuttgart, 1963), p. 363.
[2] Ibid., pp. 85, 91, 176–177, 288; second edition, pp. 349, 359, 363, 434–435. Heydrich's hardline speech of 2 October 1941 is reproduced in Václav Král, *Die Vergangenheit warnt. Dokumente über die Germanisierungs und Austilgungspolitik der Naziokkupanten in der Tschechoslowakei* (Prague, 1960), pp. 121–132.

'hero' of Ladislav Fuks's novel, *The Cremator*[1] – virtually every household was touched by the thought that individuals, groups, indeed the whole population would suffer interrogation, or arrest, or extinction. Various reactions were thinkable, including stashing weapons in sofas, cupboards and coffins, and martyrdom in the form of open resistance. Yet the nasty experience of the Poles when resisting Nazi occupation, combined with the fact that the Czechs themselves had already been the victims of appeasement at Munich, made many Czechs think twice about this option. It encouraged them to conform, to tiptoe across puddles of blood, to take the road of self-abasement in order to guard themselves against the dreaded outcome.

At Havlov, Havel's parents heard through radio reports of the huge rally of 200,000 Czechs packed into Wenceslas Square in the mid-summer of 1942, singing the national anthem whilst pledging allegiance to the Third Reich and giving the Hitler salute. It depressed them. The rally demonstrated to them, and to every thinking person, that collaboration in the exact sense of the word was widespread among Czechs. Sometimes the co-operation assumed crude forms, symbolized by the case of Colonel Emanuel Moravec, a former prominent nationalist member of the Czechoslovak Legion, who accepted from the Nazis the job of heading the Ministry of Education and the new Office for Public Enlightenment.[2] Such arse-crawling by Czech stooges and quislings was abnormal. Quite a number of Czech governmental and political-party figures, for instance, saw instead that their interest lay in keeping calm, maintaining order, keeping the population politically alert, and, wherever possible, subtly 'throwing sand into the cogwheels'. The response of many civil servants ran in a parallel, but different direction. They certainly knew that if they caused trouble they would lose their jobs and suffer police action. So they stayed at their desks not out of simple opportunism but rather because they were titillated by the vague hope that the country would survive in the eye of the storm of totalitarianism if they zipped their lips and kept their heads down.

Then there was the disquieting response of those whose reaction to total power is best described as zoological: better to live well

[1] Ladislav Fuks, *The Cremator* (London, 1984).
[2] Emanuel Moravec published several booklets, including *Tatsachen und Irrtümer. Der Weg ins neue Europa* (Prague, 1942). He committed suicide on 5 May 1945.

fed and quietly than not to live at all. As a type of collaboration, zoologism was a complex matter hedged in by dimly expressed motives. Zoologism supposed a tacit agreement between rulers and ruled that peace and quiet served the interests of both. Bearers of the 'contract' understood that it was renewable daily by possible annihilation and the impossibility of calm calculation; that fear ate the brain and soul; and that when the fear-stricken ruled thought about it at all, martyrdom in the face of total power seemed pointless, simply because their own superfluousness had been decided in advance. For these 'reasons' alone, plenty of Czechs adjusted their lives to the simple obligatory maxims of zoologism: Powerless of the Great German Reich! Quietly comply! Conform and be dull! Tell yourselves as you look in the mirror each day that it is better not to die. Forget about a most basic freedom, the freedom to tell others what they don't want to hear. Get on with existing. Do whatever you feel like doing! Shave, wash, work, shop, cook, eat, drink, chat, bathe, make love, fall asleep. Keep your chins up. Keep your noses clean. Clink glasses. Grumble quietly. Tell jokes, if you can. And no matter what happens, avoid thinking, let alone uttering the word collaboration. If you do, regard it as a meaningless slip. Then quickly change the subject. Define away questions about whether co-operation with the powerful is ever shameful, or treasonable. Above all, regard collaboration as a non-existent word.

RESISTANCE

C zech pusillanimity later became the butt of Czech humour. Among the favourites that circulated in the Havel household was the one about the Yugoslav and Czech tourists who meet on a pebbled summer's beach in Dalmatia. 'Whenever we came across Germans in uniform, we used to shoot them or, to save bullets, slit their throats,' said the reminiscing Yugoslav, matter-of-fact. Replied the Czech: 'Well, you know, we would have liked to do the same thing, but at the time in our country it was against the law.'

It was later easy to laugh. But in the dark times of the Reichs-protektorat the rampant conformism of many Czechs validated the fear, shared by the republican-minded Havel family, that the world was dividing into omnipotence and powerlessness. In the lugubrious circumstances, it seemed out of the question that Reinhard Heydrich, the superman of total power, could himself be harmed by powerless conformists. But it happened. On the morning of 27 May 1942, a great drama – one that young Venoušek Havel was old enough to remember for the rest of his life – was performed in the streets of Prague. Two of seven parachute agents sent by the Czechoslovak government-in-exile in London successfully launched a bomb attack on Heydrich's car as it rounded a sharp bend into the street V Holešovičkách in the grey factory district of Prague-Libeň. A lorry from a nearby factory jammed the road, forcing Heydrich's driver to brake suddenly. Tommy-gun shots rang out. Heydrich fired twice from his service revolver, but both shots missed their target. Two bombs then exploded in quick time, ripping out the car's undercarriage. Heydrich was rushed to the nearby Bulovka hospital, where he died nine days later from infected wounds.

Heydrich was the only leading Nazi to be assassinated during World War II. The whole Czech population was made to pay for the daring act. On the evening after Heydrich's death, the body was carried through the ghostly curfewed streets lined with SS men wielding flaming torches. The cortège passed through the hilltop Castle gates at exactly the moment the city clocks below chimed midnight. The precise timing was a wicked omen. Terror straightaway stalked the streets of Prague. Each morning and evening, firing squads in the Prague-Kobylisy execution grounds could be heard ruining lives. It was announced that anybody suspected of concealing knowledge of the assassins would be shot, along with their entire families. Suspicion was soon directed (mistakenly) at the village of Lidice, near Prague, whose men, women and children were ritualistically murdered, deported to Ravensbrück concentration camp, or (the fate of small children) physically separated and adopted out in preparation for 'Germanization'. Rumours were deliberately planted that every tenth Czech would meet the same fate unless the parachute assassins were apprehended. Then Himmler ordered the SS to arrest and murder 30,000 politically active Czechs – a final solution that proved unnecessary after Heydrich's assassins were finally cornered, two weeks after his death, in the Church of St Cyril and St Methodius on Resslova Street, several blocks from the Havels' house in central Prague. Following a shoot-out with the *Waffen-SS*, the men took their own lives in dignity, rather than surrender in humiliation to the Nazis.

The Nazis' revenge against the Czechs undoubtedly complicated lives, including the Havels'. It felt as if the whole nation now lived in a house suffering a great misfortune. Silent lips quivered. Daily life trudged heavily uphill. Resistance to totalitarianism in any form became more difficult, not to say dangerous, but the miracle was that it did not disappear entirely. Quiet methods were mostly employed, ranging from private belly-aching and jokes – various forms of underhanded, petty, anti-authoritarian guile that the Czechs call *švejkovina* – to random acts of sabotage, and a special kind of resistance, one that harnessed the power of beginning. Women's efforts *not* to conceive by practising contraception are most often a form of resistance to power that governs them. But in the Reichsprotektorat the willingness to risk conception, although it bordered on nonchalance and added to the daily pressures on women, had a politically important effect: a substantial increase in the birth-rate from 15 per thousand in 1938 to 16.7 in 1940 and to 20.7 in 1943. Despite everything – during the five-year Reichsprotektorat up to 135,000 Czechs died from political persecution and in concentration camps, including the murder of about two-thirds of the Jewish population – births markedly outstripped deaths and the overall population of Havel's homeland increased by some 236,000.[1]

This was not the route Havel's mother took – her last child and

[1]See Albin Eissner, 'Die tschechoslowakische Bevölkerung im Zweiten Weltkrieg', *Aussenpolitik*, 13 (1962), pp. 328–334; Waller Wynne, Jr., *The Population of Czechoslovakia* (Washington, 1953), p. 44, table 3; and Helena Krejčová and Jana Svobodová (eds.), *Postavení a osudy židouského obyvatelstva čechách a na Moravé v letech 1939–1945* (Prague, 1998), p. 7.

second son, Ivan, was born on 11 October 1938 – which raises the pertinent question of which other methods, if any, she and her family used consciously to resist the Nazis. The surviving past fragments are few, and indistinct. During the course of 1944, for instance, Havel's father, who had Jewish friends and a history of acquaintances stretching back to his own father's business dealings with a Prague Jew named Kohn, was visited by the Gestapo and threatened with reprisals for allegedly sheltering a Jewish family in the Lucerna building. Fearing for their collective lives, the Jewish family had in fact already fled to Canada, perhaps with the secret assistance of the Havels, and no further action was taken, luckily so since it was a capital offence to shelter unregistered persons.[1]

More definite – and most instructive – are the surviving details of the fraught involvements with the Nazi-dominated Czech film industry of young Venoušek's Uncle Miloš. Good-looking, intelligent, youthful, always stylishly dressed, Miloš (1899–1968) was from an early age his nephew's favourite relative. Miloš was the sort of character who was bound to clash with the local Reichsprotektorat quislings. Since his teenage years, Miloš had had a keen eye for social justice and lived by the motto of 'the self-determination of the individual'[2]. His friends, most of them in the smart set of Prague, found him 'charming, generous, elegant, gifted . . . a man of great style who was capable of brilliant ideas'.[3] Miloš was a 'generous, gregarious'[4] figure who liked to drink wine and (as he put it) inhale 'the odd cigarette' in the company of theatre and film directors, actors and actresses, musicians, dancers and painters. He was a lifelong close friend of the famous writer-performer, Jan Werich, and his professional and personal contacts ran deep and wide. Women found him attractive. 'Many a proud mother would have found him a suitable husband for her daughter,' remarked his stolid brother, young Václav's father, but mothers and daughters alike were consistently disappointed. For convenience's sake, Miloš was briefly married in 1934 to an old friend, the daughter

[1] These points are based respectively on *Mé vzpomínky*, op. cit., and an interview with Jiřina Šiklová in Prague, 19 September 1996.
[2] From a letter to his parents written during the Christmas period 1917, cited in *Mé vzpomínky*, op. cit., p. 54.
[3] Interview with František Novák, one of his oldest surviving friends, London (7 February 1997).
[4] *Mé vzpomínky*, op. cit., p. 53.

of a wealthy Prague architect, Maria ('Mánička') Weyrová. At the beginning of the Reichsprotektorat, their platonic relationship was dissolved by mutual consent. Thereafter – the anachronism is descriptively appropriate – Miloš led a life that was openly gay.

That fact alone made Miloš a potential victim of Nazi terror. So too did his interest in the film business. He had been trained at the commercial academy in Prague, and had genuine entrepreneurial flair. 'Miloš was a natural-born boss,' noted his brother. 'He didn't shout or use insults or vulgar language, but he knew how to get his wishes and orders across; rarely was he opposed.'[1] The born boss had a soft heart – numerous times he intervened to prevent the sacking of his own staff accused of wrongdoing by their supervisors. He was most definitely not a bourgeois philistine: not a businessman who was an *épicier* (the word used by Gustave Flaubert to condemn the uncultured bourgeoisie), a colourless materialistic creature from head to toe, an unadventurous figure bereft of all sense of the extraordinary and the exotic. Miloš was averse to the seductions of the easy and as a member of the cultivated upper middle class he tried to combine business with strongly modernist sympathies for the unconventional. He liked motor cars and car-racing – he was among the first to drive a Mercedes in Prague – and he was excited by the new medium of radio. At a very young age, he founded Radio Lucerna, a company which successfully imported from England all the latest radios, including cheap crystal sets, which sold like hot cakes in Prague. During World War I, he became interested as well in film, and set up a cinema company called Lucernafilm and a cinema called Bio Lucerna. It released silent films (like American Westerns) never before seen in Prague; and in 1929, using Western Electric equipment, it was the first moviehouse in the country to introduce talkies like *Ship of Fools* and *Six Wives of Henry VIII*, starring Charles Laughton, both of which caused a sensation among audiences who found themselves returning again and again to see the same film.

Well before the Nazi invasion of Czechoslovakia, Miloš naturally explored the possibility of commercially producing Czech films.

---

[1] *Mé vzpomínky*, op. cit., p. 64.

He did so by setting up the Barrandov Studios – the Czech Hollywood – and a film-production company called AB, both of which instantly became the targets of fascist intrigue. The Nazis had an interest in retaining the services of Miloš, and in preserving and expanding the film industry as a whole. For the majority of the Czech population, cinema was the preferred entertainment amidst misery and, from the Nazis' point of view, it was an important added consideration that the Prague Barrandov studios were technically advanced and initially beyond the range of allied bombers. Soon after invading the country, the Nazis seized a 51 per cent stake in Barrandov and set up a new German front company, Prag-Film. It managed all aspects of film production, linked it to its German counterpart, and worked hard to improve the already excellent technical facilities by expanding the studio complex and building the largest sound stage in Europe. So long as the Czechs avoided 'stupid nationalism', explained Joseph Goebbels, they could play a key role in the cinema of the New Europe. European cinema, he predicted, would eventually eclipse Hollywood in its power of seducing audiences.

The reaction of employees at Barrandov varied. Some had to get out, like the Jews of the film world, who left in search of the kind of success that blessed Miloš's friend, the actor Hugo Haas, who went all the way to Hollywood. Others at Barrandov reacted like scared quislings. The famous director Leni Riefenstahl, who worked periodically at Barrandov, and who shot the final scenes of *Tiefland* there in the autumn of 1944, later recalled that her rapport with the Czech stagehands was 'amazingly good. Not a word was uttered about war or politics.'[1] Fearing the worst or directed by envy, some locals even spoke out positively in favour of Nazification. 'We shall continue our work,' commented an article in the magazine *Filmový kurýr*, 'for we share the Führer's belief that Prague will flourish and will enjoy long-lasting peace. We also share our President's sincere hope that even within the new form of statehood our nation can realize a peaceful and successful existence and can accomplish great prosperity in the future.'[2]

[1] Leni Riefenstahl, *The Sieve of Time. The Memoirs of Leni Riefenstahl* (London, 1992), p. 297.
[2] Cited in *Prague in the Shadow of the Swastika*, op. cit., p. 154. The article appeared in *Filmový kurýr* (24 March 1939).

Then there were the locals who tried to ignore the whole dirty business by living a life of champagne jollity and good sex. The Prague colony of pin-up stars, many of whom fantasized they were already living in Hollywood, and who bathed in luxury villas with swimming pools, fanzines and fashionable parties, certainly fell into this category. A few of them – sitting on the lap of Lída Baarová, the Czech film star who had an affair with Goebbels even before the Nazis conquered Prague – even found fascism fascinating.

Then there were many others, among them Uncle Miloš, who were disgusted by fascism. He was dead against emigration – which probably would have meant internment in Switzerland. He instead worked hard, often diplomatically behind the scenes, to ensure the survival of Czech cinema – without soiling either his own or its reputation by manufacturing propaganda. The choice required him to tread a dangerous highwire. Miloš reasoned that not only his, but hundreds of workers' jobs, and the survival of their families, were at stake. So too, he told his friends privately, was the 'national spirit' and language of the Czechs, whose slow death by strangulation would otherwise be the probable effect of 'the great concentration camp of the German Protektorat'.[1] And when the war and Nazi occupation ended, as surely they would, post-war reconstruction would require a vibrant Czech film industry, which could not easily be built from images alone.

His reasoning yielded fruits of questionable sweetness. Miloš's stubbornness meant that several dozen of the best Czech film talents – including the writer (and later the first Czech to win the Nobel Prize for Literature) Jaroslav Seifert, actor Karel Höger, the writer Vítězslav Nezval, the director František Čáp, the actress Nataša Tánská – were spared from having to work directly for the Nazis. The Havel studios at Barrandov were also spared, even though during the occupation the output of Czech feature films steadily declined, from thirty-two films in 1939 to nine in 1944. Over three dozen films altogether appeared during the Reichsprotektorat. Easily the most popular was *The Grandmother* (*Babička*), based on Božena Němcová's classic nineteenth-century novel about a

[1] Quoted from the letter of Miloš Havel to the Minister of Information Václav Kopecký, 9 July 1945, reprinted in *Mé vypomínky*, op. cit., pp. 93–94.

wise and powerful heroine who brings up her grandchildren as good, devout Czechs – a film which pictured Czech identity as threatened constantly by foreigners, for instance by an invading Hungarian soldier, who rapes a young Czech girl, who becomes pregnant and goes mad.

It was also an achievement that no openly pro-Nazi film was ever produced by AB Studios, although some scenes from the anti-Semitic epic *Jud Süss*, whose final scenes of vengeance against the victim proved rousing for German audiences in Prague, were shot there. Miloš knew of course that there were official restrictions on what could be made at the studios. Escapist entertainment was acceptable, but the Reichsprotektor's office was clear about the fascist *noblesse oblige*: Barrandov was allowed to survive and thrive so long as it accepted the indisputable guidelines laid down by the Führer. Historical dramas were forbidden from scorning the Habsburg Empire. Jews were not to be represented favourably. Student life had to be ignored. Any visual representation of groups or individuals suspected of 'anti-German' behaviour was strictly forbidden.

The task of saving what could be saved forced Miloš personally to swim in ice-cold waters. Trouble began immediately after the Nazis poured across the Czechoslovak border. The day after Hitler checked into the Prague Castle, AB Studios was visited twice by a Reichsprotektorat agent guarded by a squad of patriotic Czech fascists (*gajdovci* – supporters of an errant Czechoslovak officer, Radola Gajda). They bore the news that the Barrandov facilities now belonged to the 'National Fascist Community'. Miloš threw them off the premises. The Gestapo responded by searching his flat, confiscating documents, including his passport, and taking him away for interrogation. Miloš was then summoned before Herr Glesgen, the Reichsprotektorat Commissioner of Film, who told him that AB Studios was 'a Jewish enterprise'. Miloš had anticipated the charge. He quickly won the consent of his friend Osvald Kosek, the only Jew on the board of AB Studios, to step down from 16 March 1939 – the day he was first honoured with a visit by Nazi agents. When Miloš coolly explained his actions to Commissioner Glesgen, he grew angry. 'We're therefore going to have to change the Jewish law because of you, so that it will have been in effect from 15 March 1939,' Glesgen snapped. He added, red-faced, with a cold laugh: 'We shall call it *lex Havel*.'[1]

So the law was backdated. Rough treatment of Miloš followed. He was offered 'peace and quiet' and a handsome pay-off in Reichsmarks if he sold his shares in the studios. When he carried on acting like a figure of granite he was threatened with homelessness and consignment to a concentration camp. The Reichsprotektor, dispatching a trustee (*Treuhänder*), Herr K. Schulz, to run the business, soon acquired a majority share in AB Studios by fiddling the value of its share capital through the courts. Miloš then had no option but to lease back AB Studios from the Reichsprotektorat, and to dig deep into his own pockets to pay his employees. The Nazis meanwhile employed a favourite tactic: publicizing the false information that Miloš had joined the cultural section of the National Czech Council, a front organization of the League Against Bolshevism.[2] He threw the letter officially informing him of his Council membership into the wastepaper bin; instructed his secretary, Eva Svobodová, not to reveal his whereabouts to strangers; and, using a secret radio transmitter, sent a message for help to the exiled Beneš government in London.

From there on, his world at Barrandov, like the rest of society, was prey to terror. Miloš became frightened, especially after Heydrich's assassination. On the day after, he recalled being at home in his Barrandov villa, sitting with Venoušek's father, glued with fear to the wireless as it warmed up, listening to news of the revenge executions. 'Many of our friends met with this fate, among them Dr Veleslav Wahl and his brother. It was a beautiful day, but for us the atmosphere was stifling. On the River Vltava, we saw a large punt sailing towards Prague, carrying something like gallows on its stern . . . We didn't know how they executed people.'[3] Shortly afterwards, his trusted lawyer, Dr Jan Hochmann, was carted off to a concentration camp. Paul Thümmel, otherwise known as Dr Holm, an agent of the London-based Czech intelligence service who had earlier protected Miloš from the Gestapo, was arrested and sent to Theresienstadt. Miloš was enveloped as well in the stench of suicides – of Lucerna administrators like Mr Sedláček, who found

[1] *Mé vzpomínky*, op. cit., p. 92.
[2] See the account of his attempt to rebuff the false information, ibid., pp. 90–91.
[3] *Mé vzpomínky*, op. cit., p. 65.

the terror of total power too much. And there were executions. Among the murdered was František Stejskal, the same good friend who had appeared beside young Venoušek's stroller, rattle in hand, dressed in the suave style of Adolf Hitler. Also murdered was Miloš's architect friend Vladimír Grégr, who designed his Barrandov villa, in whose elegant wooded garden (surviving photographs show) his nephew Venoušek and his young brother Ivan liked to play hide-and-seek.

Miloš feared he would be next, that only time stood between him and his crushing under what he called 'the wheel of the German inquisition'[1]. From one day to the next, he never knew whether an informer or an imprudent remark would earn him a final visit from the SS. He continued to believe in the eventual defeat of the Nazis. But the fact was that the secret police now had him in their sights. Death chalked crosses on his doors and ravens flew overhead. All exits were blocked. Only the defeat of Nazism and the advent of peace in Europe – whatever that meant – seemed capable of saving him from paying the supreme price for failing quietly to rescue what could not be rescued.

[1] Miloš Havel to the Minister of Information Václav Kopecký, 9 July 1945, reprinted ibid., p. 94.

COLD PEACE

9 May 1945: the day after the beast War has been pronounced officially dead in Europe. Angels with trumpets play tunes of peace to heaven and earth. The politicians, flanked by journalists, formally declare the wings of violence to have been clipped. Men of religion remind the faithful that peacemakers are blessed, and that where there is peace there is God. Moralists agree that peace is the elevating and healing face of the world. Philosophers add: peace is liberty with tranquillity. But seated at his desk at his parents' country house at Havlov, near the Moravian village of Žďárec, a little boy trembled.

The boy gripped his pen. In his neatest handwriting, eight-year-old Václav Havel recorded on paper that the day of general jubilation was for him filled with scenes of panic, slaughter, destruction. 'On the 9th of May in the morning,' he began, 'Žďárec was bombed because German troops who had not surrendered were still there.' He continued: 'After the air raid many residents of Žďárec came to our house to seek shelter. In the afternoon, we experienced a stampede of German troops near us and shooting at them. They left behind a lot of ammunition, wagons, cannon, horses. Russian shells almost landed on Havlov.' The young boy added: 'We children were afraid (and I think the grown-ups were as well). At that moment I wanted to be in Australia and little Ivan pooed himself.'[1]

For the past year, the Havel family had shivered through the cold dawn of peace. They had been gripped by the feeling that peace would be war in masquerade – that the earth and skies of middle Europe would continue to be convulsed by men slaying each other like wild animals. Talk of peace had begun to seem like words in the wind, thanks to a miscalculation by the Americans. Early in the afternoon of St Valentine's Day, 1944, a squadron of American bombers lost its way in thick cloud and strong winds over Czech territory. Thinking Prague was Dresden, the pilots roared from the direction of Jinonice through the city centre, dumping a deadly cocktail of high-explosive, incendiary and phosphorous bombs as they passed over the Jirásek Bridge. More than 500 people were killed and many others wounded. Extensive damage was caused to several hospitals and to the bridge itself. Many residential buildings

[1] From an undated two-page report, written by Václav Havel and entitled, 'Konec války na Havlově', reprinted in *Václav Havel '97* (Prague, 1998), pp. 124–125.

were wrecked, including a block on the Vltava embankment. In
the middle of the afternoon, young Václav, together with his little
brother and parents at Havlov, huddled around the wireless to listen
to a special report from Prague about the bombing raid. An hour
later, Uncle Miloš telephoned with bad news. The apartment next
door to the Havels' flat had been hit directly. Fire had spread to
their apartment, destroying its roof and top floor. 'Our house
is now uninhabitable,' reported Miloš. 'Mr Hartvich and a few
other employees from Lucerna rushed there to rescue whatever
they could. You must stay at Havlov.'[1]

The misdirected 'bloody February' assault on Prague was not
unexpected, since the allied air forces had been in a position
to bomb the Protectorate from bases in Italy from late 1943.
From the summer of 1944, Prague could be reached as well
from airfields in France. Partly for humanitarian reasons, the
Czechs were spared destruction until the autumn of that year.
Prague was first deliberately bombed in the late autumn of
1944. Damage was officially declared as light – the phrase 'light
bombing' is insulting to its victims – for a total of five stray bombs
hit a suburban electricity station, killing four and injuring thirty
people. The following year's raids were considered 'heavier': for
instance, during the miscalculated 'bloody February' attack, and
again on Ash Wednesday, 25 March, when American bombers
targeted the Böhmen und Mähren engine works, which manu-
factured self-propelled guns for the Nazis. The bombs killed
another 500 Prague residents and left the city in a thick pall of
black smoke.

By German and British and Russian standards, these attacks
resembled nuisance encounters. But for many Prague citizens air
raids meant weeks of screaming sirens, the wails and grunts of
men, women, and children helter-skeltering into railway tunnels,
coal cellars, and basement apartments, their faces and spines chilled
with the fear of ending up underneath a mountain of choking,
crushing rubble. As a young boy – a child born six months
before the Franco–Hitler assault on the Basque town of Guernica
– Havel twice tasted one of the twentieth century's foulest technical
inventions. He never forgot them, and it is unsurprising that several
of his earliest notebooks, completed around this time, contain

---

[1] *Mé vzpomínky*, op. cit., p. 65.

crayon and black-and-white sketches of fighter planes, as menacing as those drawn by Otto Dix.

The air raid was especially terrifying for children. It was technical power at its most destructive. Once upon a time, technical methods of killing others in war were clumsy. Read, for example, how Carthaginian elephants were used in the concluding cruel moments of the first Punic War to trample mutinous mercenaries to death.[1] Compare the twentieth-century masterpiece of finishing off the enemy with mechanical power. The air raid: a new and improved form of mechanized power over human beings. From great heights, its potential victims look faintly absurd. Reduced to ant-like figures in the far distance below, they scurry for shelter, if they can. The young are swaddled, dragged, cajoled. The old hobble, fall, and are collared and hauled to safety. There is great tumult and much confusion. Nobody wastes time. Everybody's ears ring with sirens, screams, shouts. It is as if each person is suspended in time and pinned down in space. It is almost as if they don't exist. Hearts thump. The hunted feel both weightless and leaden. Their existence now depends upon architecture. And technical error. Or survival is a matter of instinct, or pure luck.

The airborne masked raiders: looking down from their flying machines, armed like Jove with thunderbolts that can be hurled from the sky, the bombers' hearts beat equally fast, but for different reasons. The attack is the perfection of technical power in the face of danger. The attackers zoom and turn and zoom again, and yet again. Their mission involves cleverly dodging their opponents – if there are any – so as to hit their target. The prize is obliteration. Armed with the means of burning and levelling everything, and killing everyone below, the attackers buzz over their victims, delivering their sting with anonymity, and impunity. Then they roar away, at high speed. Clouds of smoke rise. The attackers vanish. Hidden from their eyes are wrecked and burning buildings, maimed and dying and dead victims. The raiders' ears are meanwhile deafened by the roar of steel machines. Below, the air bursts with groans and screams and pitiful whimpers. Roofs collapse. Metal carcasses burn. Human victims lie as still as stone. Dogs sniff and lick at their wounds. Crows peck and tear at their limbs.

[1] See the fragments from the years 301–60 B.C. by Diodorus Siculus, *The Historical Library* (London, 1700), pp. 752–753, book XXV.

RED DAWN

(1945–1956)

RED STARS

The terror of the air raids for peace omened the end of the Nazi occupation. But terror also paved the way for the rapturous welcome given to the columns of Soviet tanks bearing red stars as they rumbled through the torn-up streets of Prague in May 1945. Out from under their turrets leapt weather-beaten, sandy-haired young men bearing machine guns. Young women in nylons posed before cameras, sitting on gun barrels laced with flowers. Crowds cheered, threw hats in the air, kissed the soldiers, invited them to their homes, offered them gifts, bore their children. The good-humoured Russians laughed and brought out their accordions. People chatted about a new and happy life in a free, democratic, truly people's Czechoslovakia. They danced, drank, and sang. Fragrance and joy filled the cobbled streets of Prague. From every lamp post and window the Soviet flag flew beside the red, white and blue colours of free Czechs.

The air raid and the rumbling tank: two key symbols of the killing power of the twentieth century. Though nobody yet knew, they were the midwives of a new system of government that would corrupt and deform the lives of Czechs for at least forty years. The basic elements of the new regime were detectable in the organized political attacks on Havel's Uncle Miloš at the start of the cold peace. On the last day of June 1945 – a day bathed in brilliant Prague sunshine – the new Minister of Culture, Václav Kopecký, freshly back from exile in Moscow, accepted an invitation to address a gathering of film-industry workers and others on the restaurant terraces at Barrandov. It was a charity event to raise money for families whose loved ones had died at the hands of the Reichsprotektorat. Kopecký seemed irritable. He used the occasion to hurl insults, threats and warnings at all those in the industry who had 'collaborated' with the Nazis. Later that day, when introduced to Miloš for the first time at a meeting of the National Committee for Prague District 16, Kopecký kept up the class-war offensive. 'I've heard some unpleasant things about you,' he said in a loud voice, not shaking hands. 'Since I am an outspoken person, I shall tell you these things to your face.'

It was a bad start for Miloš and the rest of the family. In front of other members of a Prague branch of the resistance organization of Communists and non-Communists, Kopecký went on to accuse 'that film-industry Havel' of associating with senior Nazis, like Karl Hermann Frank, the Higher SS and Police Leader in the Reichsprotektorat. Kopecký repeated the Nazi claim that Miloš had willingly joined the Cultural Section of the Czech National Council. And he insisted, pointing a finger at Miloš, that anybody who owned capital in either the First Republic or the Reichsprotektorat – and then made money off the Nazis – must be politically suspect.[1] Miloš later denied each of these charges in a carefully worded letter to Kopecký. No reply was forthcoming. Kopecký's aim was to discredit Miloš as a 'class traitor' and to expel him from the soon-to-be nationalized film industry. He succeeded – using well-tried Bolshevik methods. Rumours, even bigoted remarks about his homosexuality, continued to circulate. A network of informers was set up around him. Attempts were made to recruit his chauffeur at Barrandov studios. Elaborate secret-police files on him were built up. Miloš was soon carted off for interrogation by the Commission for Internal National Security.[2] During the month of October 1945, the Communist-dominated Senate of the Disciplinary Council of the Union of Czechoslovak Film Workers voted to expel him from the film industry.

Hemmed in by methods of harassment that sometimes resembled those of the Nazis, Miloš (reported his brother, Václav's father) began to suffer a 'great disillusionment'.[3] Many of his former friends, now concerned about their careers, their children and their lives, abandoned him. There were even family friends – like the father of Václav Havel's good friend Radim Kopecký – who said privately that they considered Miloš to be a collaborator.[4] And some former colleagues, like Otakar Vávra, atoned for their co-operation with the Nazis by becoming Communists and pitching in with their own denuciations of him. During the first week of March 1948, he and his brother were informed that the Lucernafilm company would be nationalized and renamed Czechoslovak State Film. Their appeals to have the

[1] Kopecký's allegations are carefully listed in the letter of Miloš Havel to Václav Kopecký, 9 July 1945, reprinted in *Mé vzpomínky*, op. cit. pp. 88–95. Kopecký told Miloš Havel (ibid., p. 93) that he had written a paper on the negotiations with the Nazis of 'those Havels'; unfortunately, its existence remains unproven, and its whereabouts are unknown.
[2] See Miloš Havel's 'Report Dated 24 April 1946', reprinted in ibid., p. 100.
[3] *Mé vzpomínky*, op. cit., p. 66.
[4] Interview with Radim Kopecký, Prague, 5 November 1998. Radim Kopecký, son of the former Czechoslovak Ambassador to Switzerland, was unrelated to Miloš Havel's enemy, Václav Kopecký.

decision reviewed were rejected, as was their own free-standing plan for nationalization. Miloš was then offered a job by the Israeli envoy in Prague to help set up film studios in the nascent state of Israel. His application to emigrate to that country was personally refused by Václav Kopecký, without any proffered explanation.

Shortly afterwards, on the last day of March 1949, the penniless and haggard Miloš was picked up by the secret police, charged under the Law for the Protection of the Republic, and put in Prague's Pankrác prison for three months. While awaiting trial, he tried to escape across the border to Austria. But a Russian patrol nabbed him, and handed him back to the secret police in Budějovice. He spent the next two years in the dreaded Bory prison and in a labour camp near Ústí nad Labem. Depressed and ill, his face covered in a 'glassy look, the look of a hunted man who had lost faith in human justice'[1], Miloš finally returned home to stay with Václav's family for Christmas 1951. It was a mixed homecoming. His sister-in-law, Václav's mother Božena, concerned to protect her sons from political trouble, told him that he couldn't stay indefinitely. 'We've had enough troubles already because of you,' she reportedly said.[2] Meanwhile, young Václav, now fifteen years old, sobbed over the state of his loved uncle. So too did his brother Ivan. They were last together with Miloš at Havlov, where one summer's afternoon, chatting while sitting on a log, he gave them each 500 crowns. Václav had the distinct impression that his favourite relative was saying goodbye. He was right. During the first week of September 1952, he and his parents heard over the wireless from Radio Free Europe, which broadcast from Frankfurt am Main, that an 'important refugee, Miloš Havel', travelling under the name of 'Karel Stránský', had been helped by American troops to escape through Vienna safely to the Federal Republic of Germany.

[1] *Mé vzpomínky*, op. cit., p. 72.
[2] Interview with František Novák, London, 7 February 1997.

COUP DE PRAGUE

The Communist savaging of Havel's uncle – and the subsequent harassment of the rest of the Havel family[1] – foreshadowed the fate of many other Czechs. Following the military defeat of Nazism, they found themselves once again flung back into the laboratories of power. They experienced something new: a semi-constitutional seizure of state power, backed by street demonstrations, secret subversion and threats of armed force, the combined effect of which was to abolish the old constitutional and state structures to produce a one-party state that governed its subjects' lives for over forty years. It was later to be called the *coup de Prague* – in honour both of its geographic locus and some similarities between this type of seizure of political power and that of its predecessors.

Talk of *coups d'état* echoes from the depths of early modern European political history. The term was first used to baptize a reality that had hitherto been without a name. It first gained currency in works like Gabriel Naudé's *Considérations sur les coups d'état* (1632). Here the term *coup d'état* was used to describe an 'extraordinary' measure taken by the sovereign for the sake of the public good. The idea that an organized group – for 'reasons of state' – could legitimately plot to use the state to protect itself by wielding blows against its opponents survived well into the nineteenth century. The sixth edition of the *Dictionnaire de l'Académie Française* (1823) tells us that a *coup* is 'an extraordinary and always violent measure to which a government resorts when it deems the security of the state to be in jeopardy'. The definition is interesting because, under the impact of the terror of the French Revolution and the strengthening pressures for democratic power-sharing, the term *coup d'état* begins to accentuate its violent character. It comes to signify intrigue, manipulation, illegality, illegitimacy, bloodshed. In so doing, the term casts doubt on the 'public-spirited' motives of those who seize power. The suspicion grows that their talk of the public good is *maquillage*, that justifying power-grabbing with reference to *raison d'état* is an alibi, that power games of this sort are

---

[1] See *Mé vzpomínky*, op. cit., pp. 72–73: 'Miloš's escape cheered us, but it brought us hard times. By October 15th, we had to move out of our flat [on the Vltava embankment] where we had lived for forty-seven years. We found out as well that Havlov was sealed. The StB [secret police] in Brno wrongly presumed that Miloš was a co-owner of Havlov.' Until Havlov was reopened, Václav and his family had no option but to stay in Prague in the fourth-floor studio apartment previously owned by his maternal grandfather, who had died two months earlier.

undemocratic. The *coup de Prague* undoubtedly helped to tarnish the reputation of calculated and violent seizures of state power. It did so for a reason that was understood by eleven-year-old Havel and helped dramatically to complicate his teenage years. Simply put, the *coup de Prague* had totalitarian effects. This is how it happened:

According to the Košice programme proclaimed by the new Czechoslovak government on 22 March 1945, the restored republic was to be a state of Czechs and Slovaks based on the principles of the rule of law and power-sharing. It was supposed to be governed by a coalition of parties called the National Front, which, unlike its counterpart in Yugoslavia, was not supposed to function as a single monolithic organization. Yet from the moment of its birth, the new republic contained a central contradiction. Its protection of formal liberties to share state power extended opportunities to foxes to hunt down chickens. The Communists, who were familiar with the theory of the 'contradictions' of 'bourgeois democracy' and the need to 'smash' it, took full advantage of the opportunity provided them. Manipulating with great skill the Front structures, they craftily worked to transform it into a one-party system. Their struggle to control the Ministry of Agriculture, which controlled the distribution of land seized from 'collaborators', was a vital case in point. So too was their control of the Ministry of Interior, which allowed them to command the police and to penetrate, from the top downwards, the National Security Corps (SNB). The Party also manoeuvred a prominent Communist intellectual and biographer of T. G. Masaryk, Professor Zdeněk Nejedlý, into the post of Minister of Education. And the Communists gained control over the Ministry of Information, which was responsible for Prague Radio and the Union of Czechoslovak Youth (ČSM).

So the Communist Party started out as a strong force in the fledgling republic. But at the first parliamentary elections, held in May 1946, its hand was massively strengthened within the governing coalition of independent parties. Uncontaminated by the betrayal at Munich, proudly claiming solidarity with the glorious Red Army that had liberated the country from Nazi rule, the Communist Party registered big electoral successes. The results were especially striking, not only because they were obtained without widespread rigging – both local and foreign observers confirmed that the elections were freely conducted by

secret ballot – but also because of the size of the Communist vote.[1]
Support for the Communists was especially strong among Czech
workers, and it also received hearty support from the peasantry,
who were among the beneficiaries of land confiscated during the
previous twelve months by the Communist-controlled Ministry
of Agriculture from the German and (in Slovakia) Hungarian
minorities and other 'collaborators' immediately after the defeat
of the Nazis. The scale of the expropriation was considerable: in
the space of just over a year, nearly 2¼ million Germans alone
were expelled from the Czech lands, enabling nearly the same
number of Czechs to move in. Little wonder that they voted
for the Communist Party in droves. Most were formerly peasants,
landless labourers, and smallholders, and many of them, thanks
to Communist Ministry patronage, acquired well-functioning
German farms with excellent equipment and livestock.

The expulsions were officially declared ended by October
1946. Inevitably, they resulted in confusion, hardship and violence against the German-speaking Czechoslovak citizens. Official
responsibility for some measure of the whole bloody process –
and the political advantages it gave to the pro-Soviet Left – is
traceable to the Communist-controlled Ministry of the Interior,
which together with the Ministry of Agriculture began to function
as a state within a state. The Communist Party naturally attracted,
like rats to rubbish, fellow-travelling opportunists and hangers-on
from all classes, who saw that the Communists could help them
climb ladders of opportunity. That expectation translated into
votes in the May 1946 parliamentary elections. It also fed the
widespread presumption that the Communists, backed by the
great Soviet Union, were the up-and-coming political party.

It would have been possible for the Communist Party to
seize power in the spring of 1945, had it so wished. But in
politics the cultivated art of waiting is often critically important,
and in accordance with that rule the Party, under the leadership of the Moscow-trained Klement Gottwald, cunningly chose

---

[1]The Czech National Socialists won 18 per cent, the People's (Catholic) Party 16
per cent, and the Social Democrats 13 per cent; and the Slovak Democrats, who
won a clear majority (61 per cent) of the votes cast in Slovakia, gained an overall
14 per cent. But easily the lion's share of the aggregate vote was captured by the
Communist Party, which won 38 per cent of the poll (40 per cent in Bohemia and
Moravia and 30 per cent in Slovakia). See Hugh Seton-Watson, *The East European
Revolution* (New York, 1961), p. 182.

to wait. This had the immediate benefit of maximizing his reputation as a 'patriotic and moderate' leftist, thus ensuring that at some later point in time the Communists could seize everything, and claim to be doing so legitimately. So they waited for their moment, which came in the summer of 1947, just before Václav Havel's eleventh birthday. On 7 July, an invitation was accepted by the Czechoslovak government to attend a preliminary conference in Paris on the Marshall Plan. The next day, in Moscow, Stalin told a Czechoslovak government delegation led by Gottwald, the Foreign Minister Jan Masaryk, and Minister of Justice Prokop Drtina, a friend of Václav Havel's father, that they must decline the invitation. Stalin's ultimatum posed the question of whether the country 'considered the Pact of Friendship and Mutual Aid between our countries valid, or preferred to go to Paris'. Gottwald immediately telephoned Prague. The government reluctantly accepted Stalin's point. Soon after, on 10 July, it issued a declaration that sealed the geopolitical fate of the country for the next four decades: 'Czechoslovak participation would be accepted as a deed aimed against friendship with the Soviet Union and the other Slav allies.'[1]

The rejection of the Marshall Plan signalled the beginning of a permanent political crisis within the People's Front government. The Communists tried all manner of political trickery, beginning with a sensational attempt, by Gustáv Husák and others in November 1947 in Slovakia, to implicate prominent members of the (majority) non-Communist Slovak Democrat Party in an alleged 'conspiracy' linking fascist elements and Slovak émigrés, especially the former quisling Foreign Minister, Ďurčanský. The Prague Communist Premier Klement Gottwald backed the Slovak conspirators, and together they tried to take advantage of the ensuing rumpus about suspected fascist takeovers by calling an emergency meeting of the National Front, to which Gottwald invited representatives of the Communist-controlled trade unions and the Czech Farmers' Association. Several of the governing parties objected strongly to the proposed cynical favouring of

---

[1] See the accounts provided by Karel Krátký, 'Czechs, the Soviet Union and the Marshall Plan', in O. A. Westad, *The Soviet Union in Eastern Europe 1945–1989* (New York, 1994), pp. 9–25; Karel Kaplan and Vojtěch Mastný, 'Stalin, Czechoslovakia, and the Marshall Plan: New Documents from Czechoslovak Archives', *Bohemia*, volume 32, 1 (1991), pp. 133–144.

their 'class friends'. And loud voices were raised against the unconstitutional attempt of the Communists to transform the governing National Front structures into an instrument of the Communist Party's will by inviting non-party-political organizations, who had no business being there.

The tactic of producing political confusion and deadlock through concocted conspiracies of imagined 'class enemies' was a sobering lesson to sections of the Czechoslovak political class. During the same month of November, at its congress held in Brno, the Social Democrats voted by a majority to replace their chairman, Zdeněk Fierlinger, who several months earlier had struck a secret co-operation deal with the Communists, with the more independently minded Bohumil Laušman, who still believed in the need to keep the National Front intact. Friction between the Communists and others worsened. The Communists played every trick in the handbook of those plotting a *coup d'état*. Irresponsible demagogy: the Communists publicly proposed a 'tax on millionaires', supposedly to pay compensation to peasants hard-hit by the preceding summer's severe drought, but whose key purpose in fact was to create a climate of fear among those loyal to the republic and arouse bullish resentment among the potentially disloyal. The Communists tried to shout down opponents of the proposed tax, who pointed out that the revenues to be generated would nowhere near compensate the peasants, and that the tax was a 'political' contrivance. Sabotage of markets: the Communist-controlled Ministry of Trade unfairly accused some leading Prague shops of hoarding textiles (when in fact it had earlier forbidden them to sell their stocks until the lists of new prices – subsequently never delivered – were issued). Amidst a storm of protest, the Minister then proceeded to accuse the owners of sabotage and to close their shops. Sowing seeds of incivility: within the cabinet, permanent aggravation surrounded the agitation for a new land reform led by the Communist Minister of Agriculture, Ďuriš. He was repeatedly accused of using his department unashamedly to favour Communist Party clients. He responded by calling a mass meeting of delegates of the Communist-controlled Farmers' Union, to be held in Prague on 29 February 1948. Agitation from the streets: a tactic used to frustrate the pay increase for all state-sector workers proposed by the Social Democratic Minister of Food, Majer. The Communist trade-union leader Antonín Zápotocký, who had plans to purge and award certain civil servants, summoned a congress in Prague of delegates of factory councils, to be held in Prague on 22 February. It was as if he knew by heart Machiavelli's stricture that whenever a party of men residing in a city call in outside support, something is wrong in its constitution.

The timing of the two mass meetings summoned revealed the Communists' planned desire to consign others to the dustbin of history. But the decisive crisis was unplanned. It was generated by a string of rows about the precious republican principle of public control and monitoring of police powers. With new elections due in the early summer of 1948, there were many calls publicly to ensure that the police did not tamper with basic civil liberties, such as freedom of public assembly and freedom of the press and radio. Nosek, the Communist Minister of the Interior, ignored such 'bourgeois' advice and merrily carried on stacking the police force with his own men. He even did battle with the Ministry of Justice, whose investigations showed that the Olomouc branch of the Communist Party was responsible for dispatching letter bombs to the Minister of Justice himself, Prokop Drtina, as well as to the National Socialist vice-Premier Zenkl, and to the Foreign Minister Jan Masaryk. The Communist press replied with heavy abuse. Nosek, backed by the Communist premier Gottwald, meanwhile instructed the police to delay or refuse action. Class justice had to be done, and seen to be done.

On 21 February 1948, after repeated warnings to Nosek, some part of the cabinet – comprising twelve ministers from the Slovak Democrat and Czechoslovak People's and National Socialist Parties – resigned in protest. Here was the moment that proved that miscalculation is ultimately the key player in the drama of a *coup d'état*. In moments of power struggle, miscalculation reveals weakness. Weakness slakes the thirst of those wanting power. It provides them with enough energy to make the last climb to the summits of power. So climb the summits the Communists did – vigorously, and without procrastination. Their opponents were ill-prepared and short-sighted. They committed the initial mistake of missing the chance of enforcing a constitutional solution to the crisis. By failing to ensure that the Social Democrats resigned along with them, the outgoing ministers made the fatal error of voting themselves into a minority. They also failed to win over

ailing President Beneš to their side. Since liberation, Beneš had
enjoyed immense popularity as a patriotic defender of the Czechs.
Despite poor health – he had suffered a major stroke the previous
summer, and was still physically tired and seriously ill – he tried to
defuse the mounting crisis by acting even-handedly. The resigning
ministers thought that they had had an understanding with him.
They supposed that he would refuse to accept their resignations,
and would then either enforce a more favourably balanced cabinet,
or call for elections earlier than the scheduled May date. Beneš
indeed warned against the 'split of the nation into two quarrelling
halves'. He insisted that the new government must be based on
the political parties of the National Front, and led by their
recognised leaders. But the Communists bombastically refused
discussions with the old leaders. At the same time, they insisted
that the working class 'with absolute unanimity and indignation
condemns the policy of these parties'. Beneš hesitated, especially
because he was anxious to avoid a quarrel with the Soviet Union,
which (like many across the political spectrum) he considered the
principal defender of Czechoslovakia against the German phoenix.
The Western powers stood by in silence.

   The Communists knew well that on the eve of a putsch fine
words butter no parsnips. They proceeded to arm squads of
factory workers and to parade them under Communist leadership
through the streets of Prague. The tactic went unchallenged, and
indeed was helped along by General Svoboda, the pro-Communist
Minister of Defence, who ordered his troops to remain strictly
neutral. That was the signal for Communist gangs to enter the
offices of the ministries and party headquarters of those ministers who had just resigned. In one extraordinary scene, the
headquarters of the Social Democratic Party were occupied by
Communist toughs so that the left-wing minority led by Zdeněk
Fierlinger could seize control of the party machine. Throughout
the country, like attractively red-coloured poisonous mushrooms,
Communist-dominated 'action committees' sprang up to replace
the all-party people's committees. Their job was to prepare for the
final push to power, aided and abetted by the Communist Minister
of the Interior Nosek, who warned public officials everywhere
to co-operate with the action committees. Gottwald helped out,
on 22 February, when he addressed the long-planned congress of
factory councils. The mood of the congress quickly grew militant.

Hell-bent on destroying the old political class, it passed resolutions condemning the ministers who had resigned; insisted that they should never again be allowed to hold office; and demanded a programme of nationalization that was far more sweeping than that of 1945.

Three days later, under immense pressure from all directions, Beneš caved in. The moment of the *coup d'état* came on the morning of 25 February 1948, when Beneš agreed to the formation of a new government dominated by the Communists.[1] The trade-union leader Zápotocký became vice-Premier, the pro-Communist Social Democrats were well represented, while for appearance's sake the other parties each had a 'representative' chosen for them by the Communists. Among them was the charming and good-natured democrat Jan Masaryk, who agreed to stay on as Foreign Minister. He knew that Beneš was a broken man, and that the President's attempt to act as a bridge between East and West had failed. Yet Masaryk accepted the post avowedly to attempt to blunt Communist ruthlessness, and especially to help citizens to escape the country into exile.[2] Despite the political tragedy that had now befallen the country, he tried to keep his dignity. He also retained his razor-sharp sense of irony, manifested for instance in his private remarks about how he didn't mind working with Communists in the Foreign Ministry, simply because they expedited business considerably, and certainly saved on telephone calls to and from Moscow.

Masaryk was the last surviving male member of the family of the 'President-Liberator', and he had a considerable following within and without Czechoslovakia, especially in the Anglo-Saxon countries. None of this mattered. According to the once-standard story, a fortnight after accepting his post Masaryk fell deeply into depression, especially after visiting his father's grave and (after seeing Beneš for the last time on 9 March) realizing that the President had no plans and had already lost the fight to control the future. So Masaryk had committed suicide by jumping from a window of the Foreign Ministry building, the Černín Palais. According to others – the relevant documents, including the Masaryk archives,

[1] Hubert Ripka, *Czechoslovakia Enslaved* (London, 1950) provides a detailed account of the events from the losing insider's point of view.
[2] *Foreign Relations of the United States*, volume 4 (US Department of State, Washington, DC, 1948), pp. 741–742.

were carted off to Moscow, and are still incomplete – the official story doesn't add up. Masaryk after all left behind no last testament. Those who knew him well also suspected, as did the Soviets and some local Communists, that he was preparing to flee the country. This would have been so embarrassing to the new government that Masaryk's plans had to be thwarted and an alternative plan devised, at any cost. Thus – according to the alternative view – the new Communist authorities decided upon making it look as if the last icon of democracy was after all a coward who had finally conceded with his own suicide that the age of bourgeois democracy was over. So during a moment when he was unattended, they arranged for his arrest within his apartment in the top floor of the Foreign Ministry building. His murderers then suffocated him without leaving marks on his body, and then shoved the corpse out of a small bathroom window into the courtyard below. There he lay, sharing the fate of parliamentary democracy, a harbinger of the coming purges, the new Soviet-style constitution, and President Gottwald, standing proudly before the rising sun of Czechoslovak socialism.

FLYING SPLINTERS

Strong mother, strong son: such was the formula by which Václav Havel survived the onset of Communist rule. Powerful his mother Božena certainly was. She was the daughter of Hugo Vavrečka, who had been co-editor of *Lidové noviny*, a keen ceramics collector, Ambassador to Hungary and Austria during the First Republic, and (briefly in 1938) Czechoslovak Minister of Propaganda.[1] Everyone who made the acquaintance of the journalist diplomat politician's daughter – even those who didn't warm to her snobbishness and supercilious kindness – noted her self-confidence, her tendency to impatience with low standards, her methodical approach to everything she took on.

These qualities were certainly applied to her first-born son's education, for which she took charge. Shortly after the assassination of Heydrich, and a month before his sixth birthday, she had arranged for young Venoušek to attend his first school near Havlov, where the family spent most of the wartime and early post-war periods.[2] Throughout those years, not unusually for his class background, a good deal of his early education was carefully conducted at home. Božena closely supervised him, helped along by a succession of au pairs, whose names were Hana, Eva, and one whom Havel respectfully called 'Slečna' (Miss). Božena introduced her son to a wide variety of intellectual challenges. Before getting married, she had studied the applied arts, and had begun writing a thesis on footware styles of the medieval Czech nobility. She was a keen artist, and especially tried to get Václav interested in watercolours and drawing – with good success, as the surviving examples in his first scrapbooks show.

Božena also believed in books. The family library was small, but it contained a wide selection of titles, including for instance a six-volume, nicely bound history of the twentieth century in Czech. Václav had a natural curiosity, read much, and sometimes talked to his young brother Ivan about exciting discoveries, like the strange-sounding word 'metaphysics'. At Havlov, at the age of ten, he read with great excitement a biography of the famous

---

[1] See Nina Pavelčíková, 'Pozoruhodná osobnost Hugo Vavrečky', *Lidové noviny*, 6, 129 (6 June 1993); and Hugo Vavris, *Život je spís román* (Ostrava, 1997), especially part 1.

[2] Some background details are drawn from my several interviews with Václav Havel's brother, Ivan Havel, especially the one conducted in Prague, 23 April 1996. His brief account of the primary school is found in 'School for the Curious', in *Open Eyes and Raised Eyebrows*, manuscript (Prague, 1997), part B, pp. 92–94.

Czech historian, František Palacký, who (Havel noted) read the whole Bible when he was only five years old.[1] Like Palacký, Havel proved to be the family bookworm. While young brother Ivan loved to play outside, or stalk through the woods, or play with his parents or the governesses, Václav would sit in his room, reading literature and philosophy.[2] He was also enthusiastic about poetry, especially (he told his father) after the day, aged ten, dressed in a navy-blue suit, he had recited before his class a little poem about seasons and politics:

> If I were a little boy
> I'd bring snowdrops and
> the first violets
> that bloomed in hiding
> and I'd say:
> 'Take them, Mr President, I
> bring you greetings of spring.'[3]

He was encouraged to supplement his bookworming with conversations with friends of the family, like the philosopher Josef Šafařík. Václav's mother also tried to interest him in foreign literature and foreign languages – she spoke French and German from her childhood, and started on Russian and learned good English during the Reichsprotektorat period. She liked to use such skills in front of the children, and after 1945 she took out subscriptions to *Time* magazine, *The National Geographic* and *Illustrated London News*. She encouraged her children to look at the pictures, to learn to recognize foreign words like 'the', and told them of stories and news from afar, for instance descriptions of the first Univac I computer, which – young Václav was amazed to learn – could recognize its own errors and, like a proto-human robot, confess them automatically by means of a flashing red light.

A few months before the Communist putsch of February 1948, at the age of eleven, Havel was transferred by his mother to a small private boarding school located at Poděbrady, a spa town straddling the River Elbe thirty miles east of Prague.[4] The King George

[1] *Story* (Prague), 30 September 1998, p. 7.
[2] Interview with Ivan Havel, Prague, 24 September 1997.
[3] Václav Havel to his father, Havlov, 9 March 1947.
[4] The following details are drawn from an interview with Havel's classmate at Poděbrady, Alois Strnad, Prague, 28 September 1997.

School of Poděbrady was the brainchild of its Director, Dr Jahoda. When in Dachau concentration camp, he had made secret plans with several other prisoners to set up a new type of school aimed at educating a cosmopolitan elite of future leader-citizens who would strive to repair the damage done to a Europe ravaged by war, totalitarianism, and social injustice. Named after a fifteenth-century Bohemian king famous for having written a tract outlining the building of peace in Europe, and housed in his draughty old castle, King George School was a boys-only institution, mainly for boarders. It was sometimes likened to Eton. The eighty boys who had been admitted were by definition special. The school emphasized ruggedness, resilience, high intellectual standards, the ability to survive extremes of temperature, and discipline by severe whippings handed out on long benches in the boys' toilets. The pupils were pushed hard by their teachers, who included an English teacher, Miss Henry. Stress was placed upon academic excellence, including the learning of languages (Czech, English, Latin, Russian). Failure was frowned upon – poor performance was subject to expulsion – and rule-breaking was not tolerated. Havel never forgot the bellowing that came his way one morning for wanting to go to the toilet before early-morning exercises, which was strictly forbidden. Equally memorable was the moment when he exceeded his quota of detention points and ended up nursing a bruised and bleeding bottom.[1] And there was also the day, following a minor misdemeanour, when a petty-minded master forced him to transport a large pile of heavy stones, one by one, across a fast-flowing stream, then to return them to their point of origin, one by one.

Havel the boarder had exeats once a fortnight, but (unlike his younger brother Ivan, who joined him later at the school for a brief, homesick six-month period) he seemed not to mind the separation from his parents. Although his grades were below average – several classmates remember him being near the bottom of his class – he adjusted to the limited free time and strict schedules. There was obligatory study time in the evenings, heavy loads of homework, and rigid lights-out rules supervised by dormitory monitors, who were boys (like Miloš Forman) several

---

[1]The scene is recalled in Paul (Pavel) Fierlinger's animated autobiography, *Drawn from Memory* (Acme Filmworks, PBS American Playhouse, 1998), in which voice-over commentary by Havel himself is used.

years older than those in their charge. Various extra-curricular activities were offered, including drama (at which Václav showed some early talent), typesetting, book-binding, cabinet-making, and metal-working. Sports like ping-pong, volleyball, canoeing, and bicycle-riding also featured. The chubby and bandy-legged Havel wasn't much good at any of them – his classmates never forgot the day the short-legged, panic-stricken Havel careered recklessly out of the school gates on to an open road on a bicycle whose pedals he was unable to reach[1] – and indeed his nickname from this time was *chrobák*, a type of cumbersome beetle. So Havel concentrated on other extra-curricular activities, like onanism. 'Mr Havel,' Dr Jahoda said stiffly to him one day, 'it's been brought to my attention that you've been immoral with yourself'[2]. There were the boy scouts, which he joined and whose activities in the 'Arrow' group (trips to the mountains, first aid, camping, general-knowledge quizzes) he enjoyed. After the Communist coup, scouting was banned – one of his scout-leaders, Dagmar Skálová, was subsequently jailed for sixteen years[3] – and the school troop was forced to operate secretly under the leadership of a master named Mr Hoffhans, nicknamed 'the long man' (*Dlouhán*). Havel admired him, and began, for the first time in his life, correspondence with him during the summer holidays. Unfortunately, the carefully composed letters he wrote to Hoffhans from the age of twelve appear to have been lost.

Before its closure by the Communists for 'class bias' – never mind that the school had a policy of funding itself by mixing the fee-paying well-to-do with wartime orphans and a few local village pupils who received free tuition – King George School turned out some prominent people. Among them were not only Havel's mathematician and philosopher younger brother, Ivan; the film-makers Miloš Forman, Ivan Passer, and Jerzy Skolimowski; the *Sesame Street* animator Pavel Fierlinger; the politician and General Secretary of the Czechoslovak Socialist Party Jan Škoda; Ctirad Mašín, who took up arms against the local Communists, and then made a daring escape through East Germany to the United States; the chairman of the Czechoslovak

[1] Miloš Forman and Jan Novak, *Turnaround: A Memoir* (London and Boston, 1994), pp. 55–56.
[2] Ibid., p. 57.
[3] *Lidové noviny*, 1 April 1998, p. 4.

Olympic Committee, Milan Jirásek; and Alois Strnad, a successful businessman whose father had been carted off by the Nazis and then the Communists to concentration camps. Havel was to join the list of future distinguished Poděbrady boys. But his academic or career prospects didn't seem at all bright in the spring of 1950, when he was expelled from the school after a mere two and a half years there. The reason was made clear by a secret-police agent who visited the school: the building of socialism necessitated the levelling and clearing of forests of privilege, and that meant that some were bound to suffer the punishment and pain of flying splinters.

Labelled officially for the first time as a member of the privileged 'bourgeoisie', condemned therefore as an enemy of socialism, Havel was forced to attend several state schools in Prague, in the neighbourhood of the family's rebuilt home on the Rašínovo (renamed Engelsovo) embankment. There was to be no respite in the Party's class struggle against his origins and attitudes – against his subjective and objective class treachery, as was said by the Stalinists of the time. His early teenage years began to feel like a merry-go-round of class defeats and expulsions. Alois Strnad, his classmate from Poděbrady who had been expelled from there and (also like Havel) subsequently from several Prague schools, explained that 'Václav simply couldn't settle down at school or take the classroom seriously. Formal education, the target of Stalinist reforms and expulsions, resembled a bad joke.' No doubt, this was why he never completed the first phase of secondary school, and why the two friends hung out in cafés and (prompted by Havel's mother) went along to dancing classes and balls, where Havel learned to quickstep, waltz, and foxtrot.

For a time, he worked as an apprentice carpenter. *Chrobák* suffered from dizziness, so his mother, worried that he might slip from a ladder and that the job would reinforce his tendency to coast intellectually, took measures to educate her son in unofficial ways. In 1951–1952, through a friend of the family named Otto Wichterle, the inventor of contact lenses, his parents found him a job as an apprentice laboratory assistant at the Institute of Chemical Technology in Prague, which Wichterle had just founded. They reasoned that working in a tertiary-level institution might give him a taste for further study. They encouraged him as well to apply for night school at an institution in Štěpánská Street, just off Wenceslas Square, and for several years, four hours a night and five nights a week, he worked towards his final matriculation [*maturita*] examinations. Not only did he come to consider himself a practising scientist with a serious interest in chemistry, on which he wrote an early paper that proposed an alteration of the Periodic Table. It was at night school that he also came to talk philosophy and politics, thanks to his friendship with a fellow student of equally bad class origins named Radim Kopecký, an apprentice blacksmith/ironmonger and son of a former politician and ambassador to Switzerland, who had been arrested by the Communists, and was at that time still behind bars.

After passing his matriculation exams at night school – his grades were good, but not as good as those of his younger brother Ivan – the eighteen-year-old Havel made two attempts to get into Charles University, but he was rejected, both by the Arts Faculty and the Film and Drama Faculty. He settled eventually for a place at the Technical University in the Economics Faculty to study urban transport. It was not what he wanted to do, but it allowed him to lead a double life.

From around the time he was seventeen, Havel was tutored privately in philosophy by J. L. Fischer, a friend of the family who had helped Václav's father found the Barrandov discussion group.[1] Born in 1896, Fischer is not well remembered today, but his influence on young Václav was considerable. Fischer was an inspired teacher and story-teller. He told Havel that after studying with Masaryk at Charles University, his university teaching career had given him the freedom to play the role of a democrat with a social conscience. So, during the First Republic, he had publicly criticized the policies of Rašín (even after his assassination), which he considered socially divisive, and inimical to the interests of the little man and the middle and lower classes. For that outburst, Masaryk had him transferred to a regional university in Olomouc, where he won a reputation as a gifted teacher with high ('Oxford-style') standards. He published furiously, read widely and deeply in several languages, and was the joint editor of the cosmopolitan and most highly respected academic journal in the human sciences, the *Sociologická revue*. His best-known work (published just after he had pushed himself to the point of physical exhaustion and a nervous

---

[1] Interview with Viola Fischerová, Prague, 26 September 1997.

breakdown) was the two-volume *The Crisis of Democracy* (*Krize democracie* [1933]). He was an honest and independent thinker who published brave attacks on the Stalin trials. He was also a constant target of Communist surveillance.[1]

During the Reichsprotektorat, fearing for his life, he fled to Holland, helped materially by a generous going-away gift from Havel's father of a box containing gold, platinum and other precious metals. Fischer left behind a family and flat in Brno. It was repeatedly searched during his absence, although (he told Havel) he later learned that the Gestapo stopped visiting only after one of its officers, rummaging through his library in search of something on Schopenhauer, discovered with joy the very book he had been hunting. Fischer also told the young Havel – it was among his favourite stories – how the Nazis treated him less bookishly in Holland. Bearing down on the frail Czech intellectual wanted for questioning in the Reichsprotektorat, the Gestapo hunted him to the port from which he had planned to sail that day across the Channel to England. He hid for five hours in a barn, crouched and crammed into a barrel of hay. During the search, a Gestapo officer reported that there was nothing inside after poking with his bare hands the top of the barrel of hay in which he was hiding. Later that day, sheltered by a local Dutch family, in the middle of a massage to relieve the painful cramps caused by confinement in the barrel, Fischer heard the same Gestapo officers pounding down the door of the house where he had crawled to hide. They ransacked the house, and before leaving thrust bayonets into a curtained wall behind which he was hiding – stab, slash, stab – narrowly missing Fischer's body in three places.

Upon returning to Czechoslovakia in 1945, he told the young Havel, his social conscience had led him to join the Communist Party – he liked in conversation to distinguish between Lenin and Stalin – but immediately after the *coup de Prague* he had handed in his Party card, which cost him the rest of his university career. As the sun of socialism brought dawn to the country, Fischer continued his quest for synthesizing his various thoughts, likening the process to the difficulty of constructing a Gothic cathedral. He also remained gregarious, and was often visited by former students, who

---

[1] See the StB file mentioning 'the very damaging ideological activity' of Professor J. L. Fischer, in František Koudelka, *Státní bezpečnost 1954–1968* (Prague 1993), p. 146.

sometimes brought him gifts of his favourite forest mushrooms. Yet Fischer's philosophical interests changed. He focused more on the natural sciences, and at one point worked hard to develop a fourth law of thermodynamics. He also became preoccupied with philosophical categories. He was particularly interested in the possibility of overcoming modernist preoccupations through a new emphasis on quality, for instance through the development of a 'quality democracy'. Fischer practised the quality he preached. He expected much from his pupils, even though during these Stalinist times he had compulsorily lost all but one of them. Whenever Havel visited him, sometimes in Brno for advice and tutoring, Fischer would present the teenage boy with a long list of books to read, including titles in German philosophy. 'But, Professor, I don't know how to read German,' confessed the young Havel during one session. 'Well, young Mr Havel,' replied Fischer, 'you will just have to apply yourself to learn that language.'

TRIALS

D own below, in the penumbrae of state power: young people like Václav Havel imaginatively rescuing a philosophical heritage. Up above, at the grisly summits of totalitarianism: men in grey suits plotting to murder each other. The absolute contrast was not immediately evident, not even to those caught up in the business of murder. On 31 July 1951, in the form of a telegram, President Klement Gottwald sang a hymn of high praise to the General Secretary of the Czechoslovak Communist Party, Rudolf Slánský, on the occasion of his fiftieth birthday. 'Honoured comrade!' began Gottwald's greeting. 'You were always an effective fighter for the promulgation of the Bolshevik line against all opportunist saboteurs and traitors and for the forging of a Bolshevik party.' And so he steadfastly remained, Gottwald continued. 'Our whole party, our working people, salute you as their faithful son and warrior filled with love for the working classes and with loyalty to the Soviet Union and to the great Stalin.'[1]

On exactly the same day that Gottwald sent his telegram, in the basement cellars of Ruzyně prison in Prague, Soviet teachers (as advisers from the motherland were called by their Czechoslovak colleagues) were hard at work torturing their victims into spluttering concocted evidence and spewing false confessions that would soon be used to bring Slánský's life to a gruesome ending. Such were the paradoxes of socialism that its faithful son and warrior certainly knew and approved of the Soviet and Czechoslovak torturers, who had been busy for at least two years nurturing a climate of terror in the ruling circles of Czechoslovakia. The dirty business of Communists liquidating Communists by means of Communism had begun in the Soviet Union itself, where, against the backdrop of the onset of the Cold War, Stalin's creeping paranoia, and the Soviet–Yugoslav split, show trials were already an integral feature of Stalinism by the time of Slánský's fiftieth birthday. The Soviet Union, conforming

---

[1]Cited in Josefa Slánská, *Report on My Husband* (New York, 1969), pp. 4–6. The following account draws upon several works of varied quality, including Miriam Šlingová, *Truth Will Prevail* (London, 1968); Karel Kaplan, *Die politischen Prozesse in der Tschechoslowakei 1948–1954* (Munich, 1986); Artur London, *The Confession* (New York, 1971); and the two works by Eugen Loebl, *My Mind on Trial* (New York, 1976) and *Die Revolution rehabilitiert ihre Kinder* (Vienna, 1976). An important source, originally published in English, is Jiří Pelikán, *The Czechoslovak Political Trials, 1950–1954: The Suppressed Report of the Dubček Government's Commission of Inquiry, 1968* (Stanford, 1971). I have also consulted the transcript of Prague Radio broadcasts in the files of Radio Free Europe, *Trial of Rudolf Slánský* (Munich, 1952).

to the rule that big powers always strive to become even bigger powers,[1] now controlled all of Europe east of a line drawn from Stettin on the Baltic Sea to Trieste on the Adriatic. Led by the United States, the Western powers, fearing further expansion of Communism westwards, pursued a geopolitics of 'containment'.

The Cold War intensified. American strategic support for the Royalists in the Greek Civil War in 1946 was widened the following year into the Truman Doctrine, which offered economic, political, and military assistance to any state threatened by Communism, and the announcement of the Marshall Plan to rebuild Western Europe so that it could resist Communism from within. Then during the month of June 1948 two significant Western moves were made to counter Stalinism. The Western powers decided to build up a strong, anti-Soviet West Germany, thus preparing the way for the transformation of the Brussels Union into NATO, so completing the job of ring-fencing the Soviet Union with a global network of strategic military bases. In the same month, President Truman announced that the brief of the newly established Central Intelligence Agency (CIA) would be broadened to include covert operations against the Soviet Union and its satellites in the fields of 'propaganda and economic warfare; preventive direct action including sabotage; subversion including assistance of underground resistance groups; and support for indigenous anti-Communist elements'.[2]

Stalin ensured that all national roads to socialism were blocked. The western satellites of his empire were now subject unconditionally to the exclusive validity of the Soviet example. The onset of Cold War was interpreted in terms of the 'growing intensity of class struggle' in the transition from capitalism to socialism. According to this interpretation, vigilance against class enemies became of paramount importance, since it was to be expected that the enemy, beaten and cornered, would resort to desperate and devious measures to conspire against socialism and its people's democracies. Class enemies and agents of imperialism would certainly try to infiltrate the Party, which is why, in the spring of 1948, the paranoid suspicions of Stalin found a convenient validation in the Stalinist Tito's rebellion against Stalin's own

---

[1] Hannah Arendt, *Essays in Understanding, 1930–1954*, ed., Jerome Kohn (New York, San Diego, London, 1994), p. 157.
[2] National Security Council directive NSC 10/2 (May 1948).

attempts to turn Yugoslavia into a subservient client state. The purges would undoubtedly have taken place without Tito's antics, but the fact that they occurred confirmed the principle that the most dangerous class enemy was the one who held a Party card and occupied a high-ranking position in the apparatus.

The purges that followed in the Soviet Union were not a replay of the Great Terror of the 1930s.[1] In those power struggles, the victims were first selected and the necessary script written afterwards. This time round, the script was first written and then the victims were selected. The point was to produce a 'theatrical masterpiece'[2], broadcast live from the courtroom and given the widest possible publicity. The identity of the player-victims was also different. Arthur Koestler's tragic hero and victim, Rubashov, talked and acted like Bukharin and wore Trotsky's pince-nez and represented the entire Bolshevik old guard, Lenin's comrades-in-arms brutally destroyed by Stalin's thirst for absolute power.[3] Now, fifteen years later, it was the turn of the young guard of the Communist leadership to be annihilated. These were men and women who were most definitely not opponents of Stalin. No less devoted to the policies of Moscow than their executioners, they simply had the misfortune of having been chosen by their master to serve him as victims, according to the rule: genuine Communists were required to distrust pseudo-Communists.

The ageing paranoiac Stalin applied this rule by accusing Molotov, Zhukov, Beria, Voroshilov, Mikoyan, and even his personal secretary Poskrebyshev of being English spies. Some of their relatives were arrested; even their wives and children were thrown into prison as traitors. Chief Party ideologist Andrei Zhdanov was forced into early retirement and died suddenly under mysterious circumstances. Stalin, who was probably responsible for his death, reacted by accusing the top Jewish physicians in the Kremlin of his murder by a 'doctors' plot'. Many thousands of prominent Soviet Jews were liquidated. Plans were drawn up to deport all remaining Jews to Birobidjan in Central Asia.

[1]See Roy A. Medvedev, 'New Pages from the Political Biography of Stalin', in Robert C. Tucker (ed.), *Stalinism. Essays in Historical Interpretation* (New York, 1982), pp. 212–223.
[2]H. Gordon Skilling, 'Stalinism and Czechoslovak Political Culture', ibid., p. 269.
[3]Arthur Koestler, *Darkness at Noon* (New York, 1961). On the Soviet trials see Hannah Arendt, *The Origins of Totalitarianism* (New York, 1951); Roy Medvedev, *Let History Judge* (New York, 1971).

In the so-called 'Leningrad affair', which was closely related to Zhdanov's death, virtually the entire staff of Leningrad's Party apparatus, the local Komsomol and Soviet executive committee, as well as teachers, professors, factory managers and scientific personnel, were arrested. Many thousands were executed. Even Stalin's chief weapon of terror, the security service headed by Lavrentii Beria, was torn apart by accusations of spying, arrests, and plans to liquidate Beria himself.

From the Soviet Union, the terror spread, first to Albania, with the secret proceedings against the fallen Albanian Minister of the Interior, Koci Xoxe; into Bulgaria, in the form of the Kostov trial; and then to Hungary, where the trial of Lászlo Rajk served as the prelude of the terror in Czechoslovakia. The spreading pattern of terror in Havel's own country was virtually formulaic. The executioners wasted no time with the victims. They certainly had their methods of humiliating class enemies in civilized ways. Diets were improved, espresso was offered in proper cups, calcium shots were administered, and waiters brought sandwiches and wine into prison cells. Concerned doctors healed tortured bodies. Kind interrogators handed out cigarettes, promised light sentences and helped their prey to rehearse their memorized confessions, which sometimes changed in accordance with the latest Party lines. The pampered victims suffered terribly. In a matter of weeks or sometimes only days, Communists who were physically and psychologically tortured were robbed of their clear-headed humanity, transformed into helpless clumps of inhuman flesh. Comrades beat comrades with rifle butts and rubber truncheons. The victims' nails were ripped out. They were then denied food and drinking water and forced to drink the piss and eat the shit of their captors. They were dragged unconscious into cages in which they could only crouch; submerged in electrified water baths; threatened with the arrest and disposal of their children and spouses. The world-historical point was to humiliate them, to teach them the meaning of class struggle. The methods were mostly failsafe . . . except when overzealous comrades, acting out the laws of history, tortured their comrades into insanity, or plunged them into the deep night of death.

During the long period of terror that raged for five and a half years in all, rotating the whole time on the narrow axis of the Slánský trial, the prisons of Pankrác, Koloděje, Leopoldov, and

Ruzyně were stuffed full of class enemies. More than a hundred people were murdered. Tens of thousands were jailed or deported, and – the figures apply to a country with a population of only 14 million – more than 136,000 souls, Communists, fellow travellers and non-Communists alike, were victims of the terror in one way or another. Although, as Havel's private schooling at this moment illustrated, the terror did not penetrate every nook and cranny of Czechoslovak life, its scope was considerable. Since its epicentre was the Party – according to one interpretation – the large footprint of the terror should not be surprising.[1] Prior to the outbreak of World War II, this view supposes, the highly industrialized parliamentary republic of Czechoslovakia had (after Germany and France) the third largest Communist Party in non-Soviet Europe. Its supporters had been prominent as volunteers in the International Brigade during the Spanish Civil War. Most of its cadres and leaders had fled from the Nazis to France and then England, where they worked with the Czechoslovak government-in-exile. From the point of view of the post-'48 terrorists, therefore, Czechoslovakia contained the largest nest, on the western margins of the Soviet empire, of Spaniards, Westerners, Trotskyists, Titoists, Jews, and other unreliable – and exterminable – elements.

Large numbers of potentially 'objective' enemies of socialism cannot alone explain the frenzied terror during Havel's teenage years. Nor can the terror be understood by means of explanations that refer symptomatically to 'personality cults' or the frenzied paranoia about 'bourgeois nationalism' or 'imperialism' or 'Trotskyism' or 'Titoism' or 'Zionism'. The depurators' detailing of 'class enemies' and their crimes in this way was obviously a key feature of the terror. But to say that it was caused by paranoiac labelling is merely to redescribe the metaphors mobilized by men and women who were dragged from their beds at night into a laboratory of power organized by the rule that politics could do anything. The belief in the necessity of conducting politics as a vicious, life-or-death struggle between friends and enemies no doubt stemmed partly from the deracination and consequent dehumanization of significant parts of the Czech and Slovak

[1]George H. Hodos, *Show Trials. Stalinist Purges in Eastern Europe, 1948–1954* (New York, 1987), p. 73.

political classes by nearly two decades of international betrayal, Nazification, total war, zoologism, and a Communist *coup d'état*. During the Terror phase of the French Revolution, it was noted by Germaine de Staël that the prior breakdown of social bonds fed the irritability and mutual jealousy of actors who were consequently inclined to humiliate one another.[1] During the Czechoslovak terror this same pattern of incivility was at work. But it was fed as well by the key actors' belief in the possibility of human regeneration through power politics.

Actors like Gottwald and Slánský thought of themselves as waging a struggle for universal human emancipation. The point was to change the world through revolution. This meant that it was imperative to recognize the gap between the facts of life as it was currently and the wished-for goal of a classless society without state power. That gap between facts and vision could not be denied or overlooked without abandoning the principles of the revolution itself. So the revolution dictated only one alternative: if Communist society was not yet a fact, then this was because there were enemies who stood in the way. Fashioning the human condition in unprecedented ways thus required everybody to realize that the revolution was endangered, that its enemies had precipitated an emergency situation which could only be resolved by cunning political action aimed at liquidating such enemies. The stage of revolution was thick with wilful actors divided between those with pure intentions and others with evil plans. No power was innocent, no will beyond suspicion. The only certain thing was that the impure should be purged from the body politic – by actors arrogating to themselves what had once been a divine monopoly, that of creating the human world by redesigning it. Insofar as perverse wills still stood like logs on the road to socialism, politics had to eliminate all opposition. This was the ultimate purpose of the terror: to frighten and then do away for ever with the adversaries of history. The show trial was its necessary propaganda arm: its immediate purpose was to personalize class enemies, to put them in the dock in flesh and blood, to put a face on abstract,

---

[1] Anne Louise Germaine de Staël-Holstein, *Considérations sur les principaux événemens de la Révolution française* (London, 1818), book 2, chapter 15, p. 118: 'Because the various classes of society had almost no relations among themselves in France, their mutual antipathy was stronger . . . the irritability of a very sensitive nation inclined each person to jealousy towards his neighbour, towards his superior, towards his master; and all individuals not content to dominate humiliated one another.'

'objective' political crimes, to give the world one last look at the scoundrel enemies of history before their physical liquidation and political murder.

THIRTY-SIXERS

W hile the Party was terrorizing itself, Havel, actively encouraged and organized by his mother, drew together during
the autumn of 1952 a remarkable literary circle of friends and
acquaintances who were all his age, and whom he soon began to
call the Thirty-Sixers. The name was thought up by the son of
the jailed former Ambassador to Switzerland, his good friend from
evening gymnasium, Radim Kopecký. It seemed appropriate, not
only because participation was restricted to people born in that
year, but because 1936, Havel noted at the time, was 'the characteristic year of our accursed [postižená] generation'.[1] Aside from
Kopecký, whose father was serving a life sentence for 'anti-socialist
behaviour', the circle included schoolfriends like Miloš Dus,
the imprisoned industrialist's son, Stanislav Macháček, his friend
František Pecák, Libuše Ryglová, the enthusiastic young philosopher of pragmatism, Ivan Koreček, and an acquaintance from
Poděbrady, Honza Škoda, who first nicknamed Havel 'chrobák'.
There was as well a chapter formed soon afterwards in Brno.
The key link in the invisible chain stretching between Prague
and Brno was the ill-at-ease, constantly fidgeting, highly talented
poet Jiří Paukert (who later wrote under the name of Kuběna).
Others active in the Brno circle included two woman writers,
Marie-Luisa ('Pipka') Langrová and Alena Wagnerová; the tall
and lanky essayist and prose fiction writer Pavel Švanda; the
talented pianist Petr Wurm; and the young poet and daughter
of the philosopher J. L. Fischer, Viola Fischerová.

The circle of the accursed came together in a variety of
unplanned ways. After returning from Poděbrady, for instance,
Havel got together with a childhood friend named Ivan Hartmann,
who went to Prague's French gymnasium. The sixteen year olds
liked to spend their Sunday afternoons going on long walks
round the romantic old Prague district of Malá Strana, pondering
philosophical problems. The peripatetics convinced the two boys
of the need somehow to keep their conversation going; Havel
took a step further by completing, in the quiet of his bedroom at
the embankment, a draft of a short book on philosophy, which he
called A First Look at the World. The evening gymnasium located

[1] Po roce sochařské práce (After a Year of Sculptural Work [August, 1953], and dedicated
to 'the Thirty-Sixers on the occasion of the first anniversary of their activity'), p.
7. See also the interview with Havel in Antonín Liehm, The Politics of Culture (New
York, 1968), pp. 379–380.

in Štěpánská Street was another source of Thirty-Sixers. A largish group met regularly outside the school gates after classes ended at 9 p.m. The group of young women and men felt a common bond based on official disapproval of their 'bourgeois' origins. Academic achievement was important to them: they thought of knowledge as power, the power somehow to survive and perhaps even succeed in life, despite living in a one-party regime. The group called themselves 'the young ones', and they often walked together all the way from the gymnasium in the direction of Vinohrady, where most of them lived, towards Mírové náměstí (Peace Square), where individuals then began to split off in the direction of their homes. They debated on the move, and did so both light-heartedly and passionately, Havel recalled.

There were as well individuals who burst into the circle. An example was Milan Kalous, a friend of Ivan Hartmann's from the French gymnasium, a highly intelligent young man with sparkling eyes and a sharp tongue capable of debating for hours on end. Havel found his opinions remarkable, if repugnant – 'a fanatical worshipper and devotee of Nietzsche, an admirer of the cult of power and the individual, even a preacher of fascism'[1] – but Kalous's provocations didn't last long. He soon quit the group, leaving them to feel a bit sorry for him, convinced that this passionate, highly-strung, almost hermit-like loner would one day become a great philosopher, or end as a suicide statistic.

Then there was Jiří Paukert, who at the time lived in Brno. Havel learned about him through Kopecký, and corresponded with him – each week 'in characteristic round hand, full of harmony, in green ink'[2] – for nearly a year before meeting him for the first time in Prague at the end of the summer of 1953. It so happened that Kuběna had to change trains at the Woodrow Wilson Station *en route* to a hop farm, where his gymnasium class, like so many others, was required by the authorities to help bring in the harvest in time to meet socialist beer-production targets. He had a few hours to spare and decided without warning to see

[1] *Po roce sochařské práce*, op. cit., p. 14.
[2] This and the following details of the relationship between Paukert and Havel are drawn from the radio broadcast written and presented by Paukert under his *nom d'emprunt* Jiří Kuběna, *Z mého orloje* [*From My Astronomical Clock*] Czech Radio (Prague, 1997), programmes 5 (entitled 'Přítel z poštovní schránky' ['Friend from a Mail Box']; 6 (untitled); and 7 (entitled 'Havlov Revisited'); and Jiří Kuběna, *Krev ve víno. Výbor z díla (1953–1995)* (Olomouc, 1995), pp. 583–584.

if his 'unknown, old good friend' Havel was at home. At around eleven in the morning he rang the doorbell at the embankment flat. Božena came to the door. 'She was so unbelievably young and cheerful, as if she wasn't his mother, but his older sister,' recalled Paukert. Božena ushered him towards her son's back den. Paukert never forgot the moment he first set eyes upon Havel – lying in bed. 'I had imagined him as a dark-haired Eugene Onegin type,' said his new friend for life. Instead there lay 'a plaster-white-faced, reddish-tinged, blond-haired Ilya Ilyich Oblomov, fatally hesitating to decide whether or not it made any sense at all to get out of bed, just as noon approached.'

First appearances were deceptive. Jiří Paukert soon spoke in superlatives about 'Vašek', whom he described as 'an art-loving soul . . . a free spirit open to everything . . . beautifully broad-minded, even though in the corner of his soul there lurked a natural scientist who had respect for all aspects of reality, natural as well as social'. He remarked that Havel was endowed with 'a thirst for philosophy', a tendency to synthesize (rather than to analyse), and a good sense of seeing and judging things disinterestedly. Paukert also noted his new friend's 'intellectual agility, quick and sharp thinking, his spiritual clear-sightedness'. He didn't overlook Havel's 'great personal charm', as well as what he considered to be perhaps his strongest quality: that 'this apparently shy boy', someone who at first sight looked nearly like a 'simpleton', in fact resembled 'a young sovereign' (*vladař*) who had the remarkable capacity of using his good brain to 'gather around himself crowds of friends, as if he lived only to think about others and the general good'.

The strong feelings were mutual. Paukert turned out to be one of Havel's favourite friends. He was highly intelligent, had a deep love of poetry, and was deeply committed to the Thirty-Sixers. It was also significant that Havel's mother adored him. She was especially keen to put him at the centre of the meetings that she hosted and catered for at the spacious embankment flat. Her idea of forming a circle was first successfully floated during a gathering of Havel's friends at Havlov in August 1952, and the group first met formally at the embankment flat in early October that same year. It was followed by another twenty or so meetings at the embankment during the course of the next two years, culminating (during the second week of August 1954) in a

memorable week's residence at Havlov. Hosted by Božena, the
meeting (according to everybody who attended) was marked by
mirth, earnest discussion, photography and poetry competitions,
long breakfasts on the patio, sunrise and sunset dips in the
swimming pool, and by Jiří Paukert's openly displayed crush
on Václav's young brother, Ivan. Counselled by Božena, Paukert
soon came out.

The Prague group was sometimes (at Havlov, for instance)
joined by members of the Brno chapter, and sometimes they
all met elsewhere: at Charles University, in cafés like Pasáž and
Tatran, and especially in the smoke-filled, riverbank Café Slavia,
where practically every Saturday at noon the group gathered at
the 'headquarters' of the circle, as Havel described it. During
the winter of 1952–1953, after their meetings, they often went
walking as a little group through snow-covered Prague. Sometimes, out of curiosity, they attended the round-table discussions
and literary matinees organized by the Writers' Union. The circle
was preoccupied with literature, and it learned, as teenagers, the
enjoyable if disorientating art of criticizing and being criticized in
turn – to concede, as Havel put it at the time, that 'it was finally
necessary to disclose, to reveal oneself, and to look at oneself as
well through the eyes of others'.[1]

The circle loved to discuss forbidden books such as Kafka's *Der
Schloss*, the works of Herman Hesse and Anna Akhmatova, and
debated such questions as whether Karel Čapek or F. X. Šalda was
more important for the survival and growth of twentieth-century
Czech literature. They read works by Masaryk and the memoirs
of Beneš. An old family friend, the engineer and philosopher
Josef Šafařik, author of *Sedm listů Melinovi* (*Seven Letters to Melin*),
came to talk about his views on modern technological civilization.[2] Havel himself ploughed through a Czech translation of
Marx's *Das Kapital*. He and Paukert also liked to draw up tables
of dozens of writers and poets for the purpose of evaluating
their work on a scale of 1 to 5; they agreed at one point
that the highest possible score ('1') should be awarded to two
officially approved writers, Vítězslav Nezval and Konstantin Biebl,
and three writers 'neglected by official culture': Jiří Kolář, Josef

[1] *Po roce sochařské práce* op. cit., p. 4.
[2] Václav Havel, *Do různých stran*, edited and introduced by Vilém Prečan, (Prague,
1986, 1990), pp. 274–76.

Palivec, and Vladimír Holan.[1] The circle of Thirty-Sixers took an active interest in French and American literary trends, dug around in second-hand bookshops, and borrowed and circulated among themselves books from libraries. They also published two magazines: a poetry review called *Stříbrný vítr. básnická revue 36* (*Silver Wind*); and *Rozhovory 36* (*Discussions 36*), a few hand-made copies of which were lovingly prepared and typed by Havel, with the artistic assistance of his mother. Only one issue of *Silver Wind* seems to have appeared. It contained two short poems by Havel: a page-long 'Gold Coins of Faith' (*Zlaťáky víry*) and a three-page piece entitled 'In the morning when' (*Když ráno*). The first issue of *Rozhovory* appeared in October 1953. Five more numbers appeared before the next summer. Each had the feel of a *samizdat* publication: unsanctioned essays, polemics, literary criticism, and (as Paukert put it) 'the main discipliner of youth: poems, poems, poems'.[2]

Havel quickly established himself as the group's unrivalled convenor. The others found him enthusiastic, confident, out-going and a good diplomat, who usually greeted people with a wide smile, shuffling feet, stooping shoulders and bobbing head movements that resembled those of a wooden duck. Havel was also good at offering advice and 'a born organizer'. Some group members were amused at his ability to 'stage-manage situations'.[3] He was certainly quick to issue orders, for instance by providing detailed instructions to each member of the group to read this book, to go to see that film or play, or to organize a visit to meet this or that previously unknown person, like the poet and painter Jiří Kolář. Havel was often impatient, sometimes even bossy. He wanted results. 'Now! Now! Go on!' he told Viola Fischerová as she found Kolář's number after nervously searching the Prague telephone book. She got through straightaway, explained that she and some friends wanted to meet the poet, which they did two days later, only to find that Kolář was the very same man near whom they had often sat at the Café Slavia.

Just how much he was a born organizer – and not the shy,

[1] From *Z mého orloje*, op. cit., programme 7 (entitled 'Havlov Revisited').
[2] Ibid., programme 6 (untitled).
[3] Interview with Viola Fischerová, Prague, 26 September 1997; Pavel Kosatík, '*Člověk má dělat to, nač má sílu*'. *Život Olgy Havlové* (Prague, 1997), p. 58.

self-conscious diffident that he later tried to project publicly – is revealed in recently discovered correspondence from this period. Towards the end of the first year of the Thirty-Sixers – the circle had met twenty times – he wrote a twenty-eight-page assessment of its performance. The report, *After a Year of Sculptural Work*, contains a striking contradiction. While it emphasized that the Thirty-Sixers were 'a circle of good friends, whose aim is no manifesto or commonly declared summary', a group based on 'voluntary discipline, concord, serious discussion', the report reads a bit like the carefully composed memorandum of a (potentially) domineering party-political whip urging his comrades to raise their consciousness, to work harder and more efficiently.[1] So, with a sharp eye for power relations within the group, it systematically surveyed their range of individual concerns. 'Ivan Hartmann always makes his presence felt with a cogent reminder,' wrote the leader, in a typical passage, 'he follows the discussion with his illuminating sense of logic. He chips in mainly if art is being talked about, also when Ivan Koreček and Miloš Dus (if he's present) have the floor. Both the Ivans repeatedly give accounts of their abundant *oeuvre* in the field of art; Ivan enthusiastically composes music. Perhaps the best results in poetry are achieved by our "corresponding member" from Brno, Jirka Paukert.'

Havel's report also mapped out the ways in which, during discussions of ethics, the group dynamics split into 'two main camps' – despite the fact that he had come to the group armed with a carefully prepared 'ethical system' that he called 'optimalism'.[2] The ethical doctrine had been concocted in advance with the help of his friend Radim Kopecký, and it amounted to a simple species of rationalistic liberalism. 'Optimalism' supposed that individuals strive rationally to calculate and to fulfil their own personal needs. Havel described how it proved untenable when confronted with the unbridled criticism of good friends. Radim Kopecký was adamant that Havel was too sentimental about terms like morality and humanity, that Havel was unprepared to admit

[1] Václav Havel, *Po roce sochařské práce*, op. cit.

[2] Further evidence of the tension is found in the previously unrecorded correspondence between Radim Kopecký and Havel. See especially Kopecký to Havel (Prague, 16 December 1952); Havel's reply (Prague, 17 December 1952); and Kopecký to Havel (Prague, 28 December 1952).

competition outside the intellectual field, and that especially in matters of economics he failed to grasp the importance of material competition. Sixteen-year-old Havel denied the charges. Man is not a beast but a 'thinking creature', he insisted. And that meant that man does not simply apply 'his reason as an animal for the sake of merely satisfying his needs'.[1] He rejected the philosophical conviction that life is 'an eternal struggle, tough, even cynical, and merciless egoism'. Havel soon reasoned himself into the philosophical counter-conclusion that egoism in the human condition is muted by sympathy for others. He considered himself a 'soft humanist' (others in the group presumably thought this about him too). He confessed that he had become 'a devotee of Masaryk in ethics, combining it with some sort of conception of socialism and with Hegelian pantheism in metaphysics'.

Finally, and most revealing of all, is that Havel's end-of-year report recommended stern measures against some of the dozen-or-so participants who showed signs of 'passive resistance'. Havel mentioned no names, but he referred to 'boys' who 'sat and occasionally uttered their "I agree" or, less frequently, "I disagree", to keep up appearances'. These young men, who 'came, puffed away at their cigarettes, and then left', or who 'showed interest in another area' or 'looked down on the Thirty-Sixers', had to be excommunicated, 'in as decent and as tactful a form as possible', Havel insisted. The language sounded almost Bolshevik at certain points. What Havel called 'our congenital Czech Švejkian behaviour' had to be exorcized through a 'great intensification' of all individuals' active involvement with the Thirty-Sixers. 'To work actively is, after all, nothing to be ashamed of!' he wrote. No one should 'hide any more behind the curtain of collective discussion'. It needed to be made clear to everybody that the group needed 'quality people'. And why? Because each Thirty-Sixer should see that they had 'founded some sort of cell which could become the crystallized core of a future movement, the work of the young, a political and cultural movement!'.

Such proto-Bolshevism was perhaps expressive of the hormonal exuberance of youth, but it also revealed something of the ambitious and power-conscious character of this particular

[1] Havel to Kopecký (Prague, 17 December 1952).

sixteen year old. What is also interesting about Havel's little-known memorandum is not that his puerile dreams of an emergent 'political and cultural movement' went unrealized, but that the document prefigures, in clear outlines, his later principle of empowering the powerless by living responsibly in the truth. On one reading of the memorandum, the Thirty-Sixers represented a remarkable example of what Masaryk called 'small-scale work' (*drobná práce*). Better, it was an attempt to create what the French political thinker Alexis de Tocqueville long ago called a *corps intermédiaires*. Positioned between the individual and the state, civil associations of this kind were commonplace during the First Republic. They had been badly weakened in Czechoslovakia by fifteen years of appeasement and political demoralization, invasion, fascist occupation, total war, geopolitical uncertainty, social fragmentation, enforced exile, Communist takeover, and Stalinization. The Thirty-Sixers glimpsed the importance of renewing group solidarity. It was for them an effective means of making friends, having fun, tasting the joy of acting together, widening horizons, learning how to recognize and regulate differences at close range, and of putting down roots in the present and thinking about the future by reconnecting with the past.[1]

The formation of the Thirty-Sixers was certainly an act of re-membering – especially the remembering of literary traditions that were under threat of destruction by a decade and a half of fascism, total war, and socialism. Havel was among the most vigorous historians of the group. He and Paukert conducted what they called 'raids' (*výboje*) on various cultural figures, in other words, purposeful visits to cultural figures linked directly with the First Republic, like Eduard Valenta and Karel Čapek's widow, Olga Scheinpflugová; painters old and new, such as Libor Fára, Karel Souček, and Jan Koblasa; and actors and film-makers like Eduard Kohout and Václav Krška. Havel, playing the role of the bourgeois rebel unhappy with his bourgeois origins, liked to carry out his raids well into the night, much to the annoyance of his disapproving mother. Undaunted by her chiding, the subject of occasional meal-table rows, he tried hard to relive the atmosphere of some of the famous bars of the First Republic – especially

---

[1] These and other functions of intermediary associations are discussed at greater length in my *Democracy and Civil Society* (London and New York, 1988), and *Civil Society: Old Images, New Visions* (Oxford and Palo Alto, 1999).

Olympie in the Smíchov quarter, and the Old Town's Sherry Club, where the legendary pianist Jiří Eliáš had once played. Accompanied sometimes by Paukert, he liked to stay out late before returning home to his den, slightly drunk, to plates of sandwiches lovingly prepared by his disappointed mother.[1]

Through his father's contacts, and accompanied on one occasion by Miloš Forman, Havel also had several audiences with the man who would later be the first Czech to win the Nobel Prize for Literature, the man considered widely to be the greatest Czech poet of the twentieth century, Jaroslav Seifert. Havel showed the poet some of his own earliest poems, and the two spent time discussing Seifert's work: his earliest Proletarian Poetry, in which the poet, like a prophet, sings revolutionary songs on behalf of the downtrodden; his later use of jolly verbal and visual jokes, in which the poet rather resembles a clown who talks much of love; and the work he was soon to publish, the rather sentimental *Maminka* (*Mummy*, 1954). Havel also found his way to Seifert's friend, the prolific poet, novelist, and dramatist Vítězslav Nezval, who had just been removed from his post as head of the Ministry of Information's Film Department. Old family photographs show young Venoušek sitting on Nezval's knee. Two decades later, Havel was struck by Nezval's capacity for free association, his mastery of rhyme and rhythm. He noted as well his unlimited *joie de vivre* – Nezval still adored the modernized epicurism of brightly lit cafés, excursions, intoxicating drinks, spa promenades, teeming boulevards – and his sickly odes to peace, Stalin, and President Gottwald.

Then there were the visits to see Vladimír Holan, to whom Havel had been introduced by Seifert. 'I was terrified by the thought that somewhere in Prague, living and available to me, was the physical person of this great poetical sorcerer,' Havel later remarked.[2] Too shy to go alone to Kampa, where Holan lived with his wife and daughter in an apartment tucked away next to the medieval Charles Bridge, in the heart of old Prague, Havel asked for the moral support of Miloš Forman. 'He hasn't stepped out of his apartment in years,' Havel explained to Forman on the way. 'He just won't set a foot out so long as other poets are sitting in

---

[1] *Z mého orloje*, op. cit., programme 6 (untitled); interview with Ivan Havel (Prague), 23 April 1996.
[2] Václav Havel, *Disturbing the Peace* (London and New York, 1990), p. 25.

jail in this country.'[1] The two young men shook with fright. The unsmiling raven-faced poet, squinting at the bright spring day as he opened the door, ushered them into a room with closed shutters, lit by a single lamp that cast expressionist shadows. Wine was poured, Holan soon loosened up, even expressing interest in the young men's work. Havel plucked up courage to ask the poet to read from his works. For two hours Havel and Forman were treated to Holan's neologisms, cryptic metaphors, distorted syntax, and obsolete, recondite and twisted expressions. Havel visited Holan regularly thereafter, on average once a month, always armed with Moravian wine. He was fascinated by Holan's striving after a coldly cerebral and deliberately unorthodox poetic style. But Havel cared neither for his anti-Semitic talk nor Holan's most recent – fellow-travelling – poetic homages to the Red Army, his protests against imperialism, and his cheap cracks against the Naziphilia of Pope Pius XII. Still the two men got along well. Holan sometimes invited other poets to their gatherings – including Jan Zábrana, who was the first to tell Havel in detail of the existence of the banned poet and collagist Jiří Kolář and his Group 42.

Havel found the meetings on Kampa exciting. They provided him with a map and compass with which gradually to piece together the fragments of the alternative Prague literary scene, much of it by now buried under the rubble of socialist realism. The teenager grasped for the first time that an intellectual (as he later put it) is a person 'who perceives a broader interconnection of phenomena than others and feels a broader responsibility'.[2] He also observed at close range older men who were no longer allowed to climb the road to Parnassus, but who were literary survivors nonetheless – men who quietly cursed political power, avoided theatricality and bombast, and who simply loved literature and spirited their poetic talk with free-flowing wine. 'I even celebrated his fiftieth birthday with him,' Havel later said, recalling his invitation as an intrigued nineteen year old to Holan's half-century celebration. 'We got drunk on wine that had been sent to him, clearly out of a guilty conscience, by the Writers' Union.'[3]

There was certainly plenty of undisciplined carousing within the circle of Thirty-Sixers, and what is striking in retrospect

[1] *Turnaround*, op. cit., p. 56.
[2] Václav Havel, *1992 & 1993* (Prague, 1994), p. 99.
[3] *Disturbing the Peace*, op. cit., p. 25.

(even to those who remember their involvement well) is just how little the members considered their activities dangerous. Certain precautions, like not writing up circulated minutes or reports of their meetings, were deliberately taken, but generally they didn't worry their heads about official punishments. 'When I think back on it,' Havel reflected, 'my hair stands on end: if we'd been five years older, we'd have almost certainly ended up in Mírov labour camp; in those days, you could easily get twenty years for that kind of thing.'[1] Havel and his poet friends certainly lived a paradox. In the 'damned birdcage of Bohemia' (as Seifert later described the scene), they survived daily under a canopy of Stalinist repression and cruelty. And yet they enjoyed considerable civil freedom, right under the noses of vicious apparatchiks, to write and discuss their poems and essays, then to fling them to the wind, as if they were launching gifts from the living to the not yet born. Given the generally repressive atmosphere in Prague, the group naturally had a touch of daring about it, symbolized by Paukert's openly flouted homosexuality after coming out in front of Václav's brother, Ivan. There were also jibes at the authorities, for instance the favourite joke about one of their high-school teachers, a disagreeable Bolshevik character, who one Friday afternoon, at the end of a week of intense speculation about possible reform of the Czechoslovak currency, had insisted before his pupils that since the Party had said that there would be no currency reform then there would be no currency reform. The teacher mockingly told his pupils of a friend who, sceptical of the Party's assurances, had searched Prague's shops for a suit of armour, which would serve as a valuable collector's item that symbolized the need for protection against monetary devaluation. The whole class laughed. Next day a major currency reform was announced. On Monday morning, the teacher, looking sheepish, asked the class whether they would rather discuss chemistry or current events. 'Comrade teacher,' barked a spindly boy with a deep voice, 'I think we ought to discuss current events.' The teacher asked the same boy to begin. 'Well,' he said, 'you know that friend of yours with armour? At least he's got armour and we've now got fuck all.'

The Thirty-Sixers thrived on ribaldry and individual members saw each other socially. There were no affairs, although dark-eyed

---

[1] *Disturbing the Peace*, op. cit., p. 24.

Viola Fischerová, who complained often to the boys about their bad habit of seeing her as body and not as mind, was close to Václav, whom she trusted and whose intellect she respected. She didn't fancy him. None of the women in the group did. They liked his brain, but felt that he 'had about as much sex appeal and sex awareness as a bear cub'.[1] Rumours nevertheless circulated that Božena feared that her son would get involved with Viola, and that she disapproved, perhaps (the evidence is unclear) because of maternal jealousy, or because she thought Fischerová was not good enough for him.

Václav nevertheless persisted in seeing her, as if he were practising the art of rebellion against his strong mother. One scorching summer's day, Viola went swimming with Václav in a public pool on Prague's Žofín island, accompanied by kid brother Ivan. There was nothing to slake their thirst with except beer, so the three began to drink their fill, during which time a bronzed stranger came and sat down in their midst. As the curious Václav began politely to ask him about his profession – under socialism, lazing about in the sun was politically incorrect and therefore discouraged, except for some privileged holidaymakers – the stranger interrupted. 'You are Václav Havel. I know, because I knew well your Uncle Miloš, who would have had no time for all this riff-raff here.' The stranger embarrassed the three friends. They had been raised by their parents in the democratic spirit of the First Republic, so they blushed when the stranger continued to rant in old bourgeois language for some minutes about the noisy chaos of the swimming pool. After the bronzed stranger had said goodbye, Havel couldn't resist a squiffy, sarcastic remark. 'Now there's a man who understands the meaning of the Great October Revolution!' The three revellers laughed loudly, drank more beer, and staggered back home. There a chiding mother helped dizzy young Ivan to the toilet, with a calm father standing in the background, exclaiming in a quiet drawling voice, 'Václav, Václav . . . You have got your brother Ivan drunk again.'[2]

---

[1] Correspondence from Dr Louise Mares (née Marie-Luise Langrová), Sydney, Australia, 11 November 1998.
[2] Interview with Viola Fischerová, Prague, 26 September 1997.

ASHES ON ICE

On 20 November 1952 – at the moment when the strongly mothered sixteen-year-old Havel was beginning to fancy himself an intellectual – there began the week-long 'Trial of the Leadership of the Anti-State Conspiratorial Centre led by Rudolf Slánský'. Comrade Slánský and his thirteen co-defendants were led handcuffed into the courtroom of Prague's Pankrác prison and seated before the chief prosecutor, Josef Urválek, the hand-picked members of the court, and the counsels for the defence. Pre-printed copies of the trial script, complete with questions and answers, were on hand. Everything was pre-planned. Nobody was allowed to forget their lines, which was unlikely since Security Minister Karol Bacílek had arranged beforehand the taped filming of a dress rehearsal of the trial, with the interrogators acting the role of the judges, just to ensure that on the day no defendant retracted his confession. And so that everybody of note could relax in the certainty of the trial's outcome, the tape of the dress rehearsal had been screened privately a few days beforehand to an audience consisting of Gottwald and chosen members of the inner Party leadership.[1]

This was no ordinary kangaroo court, but instead a bizarre exercise of totalitarian power. The particulars of the alleged crimes were incidental to the proceedings. The individual defendants themselves were of no significance as individuals. It is true that here stood men with rich biographies. For a moment or two longer they would remain high-ranking Communists. Once, some had risked their lives on the battlefields of Spain. Others had served in the French Resistance. There were those who had fought with the partisans in the forests and mountains of Slovakia. Still others had endured the hell of Nazi prisons and concentration camps. None of this mattered, for now their time had come to be reduced to nothingness – to be transformed into inert molecules in a crazed experiment in the arts of legalized terror.

According to the surviving trial transcripts and press reports, Slánský and his comrades were police informers, imperialist spies, Trotskyite traitors, ultimately agents of a bourgeois-nationalist-Titoist plot to murder Klement Gottwald and overthrow the government of Czechoslovakia. Slánský was accused of conspiring with the arch-criminal Konni Zilliacus, a left-wing British Labour

[1] *The Czechoslovak Political Trials, 1950–1954*, op. cit., p. 111.

Member of Parliament, 'with the aim of detaching Czechoslovakia from the Soviet Union and from the camp of the people's democracies'. Slánský was implicated as well in what the indictment called the work of the 'Fascist-Tito clique'. He in fact confessed in his deposition to a meeting with Moša Pijade, who gave him Tito's order to step up the counter-revolutionary struggle in Czechoslovakia. Slánský admitted that 'the anti-state conspiracy centre followed a line similar to that of Tito'. Then came the anti-Semitic abuse. The Jewish ancestry and habits of Slánský and the other defendants were repeatedly emphasized. One of the witnesses reported that Slánský had developed contacts with the spies of 'international Zionism'. Another described him as 'the son of a wealthy Jewish family, the great hope of all of the Jews within the Communist Party'. Yet another prattled on about Slánský as an agent of Zionism, and Zionism as an agent of American imperialism in its fight against the Soviet Union and the people's democracies. 'Under the pretext of helping the Jewish emigration to Israel,' he added, 'Slánský assisted the illegal flight of a great number of capitalist elements who fraudulently smuggled out of the country large quantities of gold, silver, and jewellery.'

Trials peppered with words like these were commonplace throughout the courts of the country. The show trials even gathered momentum *after* news of the death of Stalin reached Prague during the first week of March 1953. Stalin may have expired; his body could no longer breathe or move, but in Czechoslovakia his nails continued to lengthen. Within the Soviet Union, the death of the butcher led almost immediately to the issuing of some closure notices on the whole bloody business of slaughter. The Jewish physicians arrested in connection with the alleged 'doctors' plot' were released from their Moscow prison cells. The first groups of intrepid survivors of the Gulag archipelago were released. Khrushchev ordered the arrest and execution of Beria and other administrators of the apparatus of terror. The stage-managers of the show trials in central-eastern Europe, former State Security Minister Abakumov and General Byelkin, were shot. So too were the two main Ministry of Internal Affairs (MVD) advisers in the Czechoslovak purges, Generals Likhachev and Makarov.

But in Czechoslovakia the incarceration and killing by show trial gathered pace. Even the death of Gottwald, one week after returning from the funeral of his master in Moscow, failed to bring the terror to a halt. The committee led by Gottwald's successor, Antonín Zápotocký, who was assisted by such people as Václav Kopecký, the personal enemy of Miloš Havel, actually worked hard to step up the terror. The political reason was clear: since they were the ones whose political careers were deeply entangled in the terror, and certainly responsible for the torture and trial and disposal of their comrades, any reprieve would most probably have resulted in their own arrest, torture, and killing. So *tu quoque* terror claimed its victims. A number of high-ranking diplomats and officials of the Ministry of Foreign Affairs – Pavel Kavan from the embassy in London; Eduard Goldstücker, former envoy to Israel; Karel Dufek, chargé d'affaires in Turkey – were given long-term sentences and packed off to prison. There were six secret trials of key officials in the Ministry of the Interior. Among them were the head of its security department, Osvald Závodský, a former International Brigade commander in the Spanish Civil War; and the Deputy Minister of the Interior, Josef Pavel, who was sentenced to twenty-five years in a concentration camp. Shortly afterwards, there were another six secret trials of senior army officers. There was also the trial of the 'Trotskyist Grand Council', which comprised seven second-rank Communist apparatchiks who were sentenced to a total of 103 years in prison. This was followed by the major show trial of Slovak Communist leaders, including the 'Slovak bourgeois-nationalist' Gustáv Husák, who retracted his confession in court and was sentenced to life imprisonment.

The whole project of terror during this period was a considerable technical achievement. Hundreds of high-ranking Communists of Party and state had to be rounded up, interrogated, tortured, imprisoned, executed, disposed of. Thousands of trial witnesses had to be primed, only later to be arrested and brought into the dock in connection with things they had or had not said. There were in addition tens of thousands of lesser Communists who had to be sentenced summarily to long spells in prison or shipped off to concentration camps on elaborately prepared fictitious crimes of sabotage, espionage, Zionism and bourgeois-nationalism. Many of them had to be kept under surveillance in prison for two or three years before their cases were heard. During that time, Party security agents had to organize their signing of revised versions of their confessions, in accordance with the latest changes in government policy.

The terrorists huddled around Antonín Zápotocký had their hands full in supervising the sorting of victims into the proper groups, dictating their statements, preparing their show trials, and administering their punishment. Yet at no point did they ever overlook their important task of finishing off the high-ranking apparatchiks who (for reasons of time and showcasing) had not featured in the earlier trial of Slánský. So they set upon heads of the regional organizations; members of the Central Committee, most of them Jews; and a key defendant, the Secretary of the Central Committee of the Czechoslovak Communist Party, Marie Švermová, for whom the prosecutor had asked the death penalty, but who was sentenced merely to life imprisonment. She was lucky, if a reprieve from death by terror can be called luck. On 27 November 1952, the hapless Slánský and ten of his co-defendants, tranquillized into indifference with pills and staring fixedly straight ahead, were handed the prearranged verdict of the Pankrác prison court: death. Six days later, on a chilly but bright 3 December, each was hanged. The bodies were immediately cremated, the ashes shovelled into sacks and scattered on an icy side road in the outskirts of Prague.[1]

---

[1] Karel Kaplan, *Dans les archives du Comité Central* (Paris, 1978), p. 212.

STALIN'S SHADOWS

(1956–1968)

THE PUBLIC POET

Those who heard him speak publicly for the first time swore they saw him shake while shuffling towards the podium. Tense-faced, clean-shaven, dressed in a brown check suit and matching tie, blond hair neatly parted and combed, looking the part of a public-transport student, or perhaps more like a chubby sportsman about to receive an award, the twenty-year-old Havel laid down his notes on the carved oak lectern, quivered, glanced up at the smoke-filled conference hall of Dobříš Castle, and began, looking down and slow-drawling the compulsory salutation, 'Distinguished Comrades!'

The young rebel who fancied himself a poet had risen early that morning. Wanting to calm his nerves before breakfast, he had walked briskly through the thickly timbered castle grounds, alone, wrapped in a heavy coat and scarf, early winter mist biting his ears. The setting of the 'writers' home' – a confiscated eighteenth-century château sitting atop a hill in a little town a few kilometres south of Prague – felt intimidating; it was as if he were the peasant guest of a prince. It was 9 November 1956, the second day of a three-day meeting of young Czech and Slovak writers, gathered together by the Party journal for young writers, *Květen*, to discuss the past, present and future of art.[1] The first day had been dominated by dry discussions about art and everyday life. Havel had sat silently in the smoke, listening carefully, paralysed by the feeling of being encircled by famous people. 'The place was literally swarming with them,' he later recalled. They came in various shapes and sizes – short and tall, round and slim, garrulous and reserved, drunkards and teetotallers, bookworms and womanizers – but all of them nomenklatura men and women. Over there was Pavel Kohout, best known for his recent collection of verse mourning the death of the Stalinist President Gottwald, *A Time of Love and Struggle* (*Čas lásky a boje*), and for his socialist-realist drama, *The Good Song* (*Dobrá píseň*), which justified the show trials by suggesting that anyone who betrays their beloved is prone to betraying their country. Next to

---

[1] The proceedings are reported in four articles in *Literární noviny*, number 48 (1956), p. 7. One of them, presumably based on his own contribution, is written by Václav Havel and entitled 'Program a jeho vyjádření' ('The Programme and its Expression'). Havel's later account of the Dobříš conference is found in *Disturbing the Peace*, op. cit., pp. 28–33. A thorough search of the Czechoslovak Writers' Union record groups stored in the state archives in Staré Hrady, near Jičín, uncovered no new material, except traces of weeded files.

him stood the Central Committee member and novelist Jan Drda, the well-known author of a collection of sentimental stories about Czechs resisting Nazification and a novel, *The Wanderings of Peter the Liar* (*Putování Petra Sedmilháře*), which carefully mixed realism, whim, optimism and fairy-tales to tell the story of a boy who concocts fantastic stories about himself and his unknown father. Standing behind Kohout and Drda were distinguished guests like Jiří Hájek, the editor-in-chief of *Mladá fronta* publishers, and Marie Pujmanová, a founder of Czech socialist realism and well-known Stalinist. Next to them were the editors of *Květen*, chatting to the elderly novelist Marie Majerová, whose earliest writings, touched by feminism and anarchism, underwent heavy self-revision just before the Communist take-over, leaving her reputation hanging on socialist-realist novels like *Ballad of a Miner* (*Havířská balada*) and a Communist Utopian novel about overthrowing the capitalist state by sabotaging a reservoir, *The Dam* (*Přehrada*). Havel wasn't much impressed. There was something odd about such company, he later said. People like this divined out of him a strange respect for the famous and, at the same time, the feeling that they were unworthy of admiration, that they were Party hacks and time-servers, and that he was on his own, an utter outsider.

The first day's proceedings had begun with short addresses by Antonín Jelínek and Vítězslav Kocourek on the subjects of poetry and prose. Dull skirmishes ensued. The atmosphere was stiff and theoretical. Some participants sided with the view that art is or ought to be a testimonial to life, a midwife to the facts of everyday life. They thought of art as a recording angel. Others took issue with this view, insisting that art is a hanging judge. Artists are not spectators, but co-creators of reality, and therefore the best art is thoughtful, enthusiastic, self-sacrificing – and well equipped to pass definitive judgements on everyday life.

The call for *art engagé* had quickly produced a second, much livelier discussion about 'progressive art'. Should art be 'progressive' and, if so, does that mean that it is indistinguishable from modernism? Some participants proposed definitions of modernity and modern art, with others insisting that 'progressive' art, which for them was synonymous with the struggle for socialism, was quite different. This discussion spilled over into the second morning, and was sharpened unintentionally by a short speech by *Květen*'s editor-in-chief, Bohuslav Březovský. A good Communist who was nearly twice the age of most participants, Březovský rambled through remarks about the role of the journal, the young artists listening in silent half-concentration. After Březovský sat down, a string of comrades stood up to emphasize the danger of art losing touch with young workers and young farmers. Along similar lines, others warned against the pitfalls of 'intellectual exclusivity' and pointed to the limits of 'the passionate need to theorize about art'. A political twist was given to the discussion by Milan Schulz, who shortly afterwards published an account of the meeting. 'Something important and new has appeared in our midst', he reportedly said to a sea of silent faces. 'There are clearly now great differences among people who are thirty, those who are twenty-five and those who are twenty.' Havel, in the latter category and one of the youngest artists present, froze. Schulz continued: 'One should not play up general differences, of course. But the representatives of these different generations who are here look at the world around them in completely different ways. They do the same with the past, which for some of them was a time of maturing and for others a time of childhood. One cannot overestimate the influence of even five years – nor ignore the warning signals produced by the literary efforts of the youngest, who are inclined to be apolitical.'

The words chilled the spines of the audience, who understood well the wider webs of power in which their own narrow discussions were operating. Schulz's remark served as a chilling reminder, especially to those who harboured political illusions, or who had drunk too much or slept badly the night before, that in matters of culture things were not going well. The unveiling of a giant granite statue of Stalin on the banks of the Vltava River on May Day, 1955 signalled the intention of the Czechoslovak Party to resist any local attempts to loosen the ties of Stalinist Communism now that Stalin was dead. The Party closed ranks. It refused to find a senior sacrificial figure like Malenkov, who had been pushed from power in the USSR. Slánský was not rehabilitated, although the slanderous charges of Zionism and Titoism against him were muffled. Following the strong criticisms of Stalin at the CPSU's Twentieth Party Congress in February 1956, the Czechoslovak Party made mere noises about the cult of personality. Gottwald, dead for three years, was spared. Especially after a series of meetings and demonstrations of students and young

writers in Brno and Prague in April and May – six months before
the Dobříš meeting – the Party authorities and their newspapers
adopted a hard line against cultural dissent. The attack on the
cultural policies of the Party by the distinguished poet Jaroslav
Seifert at the Second Congress of Czechoslovak Writers at the
end of April – Seifert called on writers to act as 'the conscience
of the people' – was denounced in tough terms. And at a Party
conference in June, amidst mouthed slogans about the importance
of the 20th Party Congress, the leaders Novotný and Zápotocký
sideswiped abstract 'bourgeois' concepts of freedom in the name
of waging the class struggle. The charges made by writers, students
and others were viciously attacked. The Party would keep its grip
on national life. It would move ahead with a new Five-Year Plan
(1956–1960) that emphasized heavy industry and the completion
of collectivization. Liberalization was not to be permitted. It was
not even a word to be used.

Then there were the current events in neighbouring Hungary.
At the very moment that Havel and his young fellow artists
were listening to talk of 'progressive art' and warnings about
'exclusivity' and 'apolitical' attitudes, Hungarian youths with only
their bare hands were fighting the Soviet tanks crashing through
the rubble-strewn streets of Budapest. A fortnight earlier, in the
same city, the cornered Hungarian Communist Party's Stalinist
Secretary and head of the secret police, Ernö Gerö, had called
for Soviet military intervention to save his skin. The Red Army
had bashed its way into Budapest and then retreated, and it
seemed for a few days as though a peaceful compromise had
been struck. The Soviet Ambassador and later First Secretary
of the CPSU, Yuri Andropov, dumped Gerö and approved his
replacement by János Kádár, a loyal Communist and former victim
of Stalinist persecution. The forces of reform, gathered around
the Prime Minister, Imre Nagy, were heartened by the appointment of several non-Communist ministers into his government,
and by the release from prison of Cardinal Mindszenty. Joyous
demonstrations followed. The short-lived Communist monopoly
on power seemed to be crumbling. Revolution was on the
cards. In quick succession, the hated security-police building
was attacked, Budapest came to be run by popular councils, and
the Nagy government announced Hungary's withdrawal from the
Warsaw Pact, at the same time calling on the United Nations

for help. Unluckily for the revolutionaries, the Western powers were preoccupied with the presidential election in the United States and with resolving their serious differences over the Suez crisis. Four days before the beginning of the Dobříš conference, Moscow removed its velvet gloves. Supposing that political power springs from the barrels of guns, Soviet tanks smashed their way back into Budapest against their street-fighting opponents. There were hundreds of casualties. The job of replanting the tree of Communism in a puddle of blood had begun.

The young outsider paused. He began, first with a nervous cough, then by praising in stiff words the journal *Květen* for having grouped together like-minded writers:[1] 'It is an important phenomenon in our literary life,' he said, 'because here for the first time in a long time writers are finally recognizing that a shared basic attitude towards the creative efforts of today does not necessarily require it to be the complete ideological unifier of the artistic front. The bearers of this shared attitude can be people of very different artistic means and ends, and it is not at all unhealthy for our culture if people who are artistically close come together, either around journals or directly within groups.' It was a plea for pluralism, admittedly in convoluted words. But then Havel bit back at the hand currently feeding him. Pluralism necessarily implied the recognition of differences of opinion, he argued. Consider *Květen* itself. 'No matter how healthy the central idea of *Květen*'s programme, that does not mean that its current theoretical formulation and concretely poetic form in *Květen* has reached maturity, or that it is the only possible way of helping our literature to perform its social and human role.'

The young Havel was only minutes into his headstrong speech. The nomenklatura began to twitch. Havel didn't let them relax. He criticized *Květen* for pursuing theoretical ideas that were generally 'unclear and inconsistent'. Its concern with artistic practice rated no better. It contained 'many mistakes and much confusion'. Havel also pointed out that *Květen*'s programme resembled the work of the explorer who persisted in discovering lands that had already been mapped. Why had the editors so far been silent

---

[1] Compare the different views of the achievements and limitations of *Květen*, especially Zdeněk Pešat's mention of Havel, in Bohumil Svozil (ed.), *Časopis Květen a jeho doba: Sborník materiálů z literárněvědné konference 36. Bezručovy Opavy 15–16. 9. 1993* (Prague and Opava, 1994), pp. 13–16.

about earlier Czech aesthetic trends, like the once-respected modern realist movement in poetry originating in the circle around Skupina 42 (Group 42), including modernist poets like Josef Kainar, Jiří Kolář, and Jiřina Hauková? Why had they so far said nothing about the important notion of the heroism of everyday life crystallized in the pre-World War II publications of the anti-romantic Czech dramatist, prose writer and columnist Karel Čapek? What were their opinions about his argument that individuals comprised many potential selves, that prudence was to be preferred over the potential 'inhumanity' that resulted from self-sacrifice, daring, dogmatism, and flaunted sexuality, and who, on the basis of doubting all absolutes, championed the virtues of down-to-earth 'ordinariness'? And finally, why had the editors so far dodged basic questions about the essence of 'socialist art' and its relationship to modern art? Why the continuing ambiguity about 'the basic driving motives, the means, ends and significance of art'?

Havel's cloudburst of questions was daring, but even his sympathizers must at this point have hoped, for the sake of prudence under difficult circumstances, that he would thank the comrades, pick up his notes, step down from the podium and let others run with the argument. He didn't. Sweating but now relaxed, he began to hammer away at the presumption that art and truth are a happily married couple. Alluding to the earlier discussion about whether art is a recording angel or a hanging judge, Havel pointed out that both sides were secretly agreed that art lives in the Temple of Truth. This amounted to saying nothing, he continued, for the brutal fact is that virtually every artist can in principle say that their work is an expression of the truth. Why would they ever want to do otherwise? Surely it would be ludicrous for them to insist that their art is an expression of falsity? The key philosophical point, argued Havel, is that 'knowledge of the truth is the fruit of discussion', from which it followed that the editors of *Květen* should not presume that they somehow had a monopoly on the process of defining truth. On the contrary, the editors needed to be more humble. They should realise that there are 'positive forces that are appearing increasingly in the literature of young people on a variety of fronts', and that *Květen* could be a 'journal richer in ideas and artistic successes'. The final criticism was tough. 'Because there is still no forum or journal other than *Květen* for expressing

young writers' different currents of thinking about art, it is clear
that it should become such a forum for diversity, which means that
it cannot rigidly limit itself to the opinions and established taste of
a handful of its collaborators.' *Květen* was full of people who had
been 'spoiled and pampered by power from the very first lines
they wrote'. These were people who had had 'audiences with the
President at twenty', who were 'used to the limelight', and who
had been 'decorated with state prizes for literature'. Things had
to change. The implication was diamond clear. Poets shouldn't be
Party sutlers. 'After the Twentieth Congress of the CPSU and the
Second Writers' Congress, it is obvious that all restrictions on the
freedom to develop different opinions and to express reality can
only burden our cultural and national life with the repetition of
past mistakes and negative results, in every sense.'

The odd thing about Havel's dare-devil speech is that its
published version contains an ill-fitting paragraph about socialism.
After defending the principle of the indivisibility of art and
freedom of expression, Havel went on clumsily to acknowledge
the need for placing limits upon that freedom. 'At the same
time, however,' he wrote, 'the unifying condition of the most
diverse efforts consists, of course, in a positive attitude towards
the basis of our socialist system.' He added: 'And it is mainly
young authors who can never be allowed to be satisfied with
themselves and left to assume that they have attained the ultimate
and absolutely irrefutable truth of some matter – anyway, that is
clearly contradicted by the dialectical conception of things.'

Did Havel actually utter these words about socialism and
dialectics at the Dobříš gathering? Were they merely added
by him in the subsequently published report? Voluntarily, or
under pressure from the editors of *Literární noviny*? We do not
know. Years later, Havel recalled that, after his speech, over
drinks and into the wee hours of next morning, he had debated
the nature of art and truth with comrades who, 'as they got
drunker, would alternately heap ashes on their own heads and
accuse me of betraying socialism'. Perhaps. But what is clear is
that Havel's first public performance as a young man of letters
produced explosions. Marie Pujmanová, herself a tough-minded
Stalinist from rich bourgeois stock, in effect called Havel a traitor.
She expressed astonishment that a young upstart could arrogantly
witter on about long-forgotten Czech poets when at that very

moment socialism was fighting for its life and bleeding in the
streets of Budapest. From the floor, Havel replied by saying that
he simply couldn't understand how such an elaborate and costly
conference on poetry could be held without discussing Czech
poets like Čapek and Skupina 42. This won him some sympathy
from the audience, some of it in the form of coded encouragement
to throw more stones. 'Do you realize,' said the satirist Jiří Robert
Pick, 'that those who sit here represent at least two generations –
the over-politicized generation that is now around thirty years of
age, and the apolitical generation that is already twenty years of
age? Well, on behalf of the thirty-year-old grandfathers I'd like to
tell our "youngsters": we've already "experienced" a thing or two
of what you've discovered here, but we don't say it.'

    This roused others (reported Havel) into open praise for his
'daringly critical' and 'courageous' speech. Still others launched
aggressive rebuffs, of which Miroslav Červenka's was the most
sophisticated. Červenka had already jousted with the young Havel
in the pages of *Květen*.[1] Some time before the Dobříš conference,
in the second issue of the journal, Havel had responded to the
editors' call for comments on the journal's promotion of a type
of poetry – 'a poetry of everyday life' – that aimed to express daily
human experience. He was astonished when the editors invited
him to Dobříš and then published his poorly written, one-page
piece – his first-ever publication. In it he rebuked *Květen*'s
'theoretical inconsistency and lack of systemization'. Although he
had sympathized with the launch of the journal after the Second
Congress of Czechoslovak Writers, it struck him as a bundle
of dimly expressed contradictions. He accused it of silencing
alternative views about the nature of poetry, and warned that,
whenever there is ideological and institutional favouritism, damage
is necessarily done to the whole of art, including alternative views,
which are 'automatically pushed aside to the fringes of the current
generation and its literature'. Havel again cited the wartime group
Skupina 42. Why was their work being passed over in silence, he
had asked? Was this because the editors were secretly attached to
the view that modern art was 'bourgeois'? Were they supporters
of the socialist-realist view that Josef Škvorecký had already shown

[1] See Václav Havel, 'Pochyby o programu' and the reply by Miroslav Červenka, in
Květen, 2 (1956–1957), pp. 29–30.

to be absurd when applied to the work of great writers like Walt Whitman? Then Havel cheekily asked the editors the embarrassing key question: were the editors remaining silent about socialist realism because they presumed its tenets to be true, or rather because they were 'simply afraid to say that today they can no longer agree with all its postulates'?

In his written reply to 'Comrade Havel' in the second issue of *Květen*, Červenka had dodged the question and issued a denial as smooth as a pebble: 'It is pointless assuming that my friends or I have wilfully avoided any question whatsoever, perhaps even because we were calculating or afraid.' The key criterion of artistic truth, he had added vaguely, was art's 'noetic stance' – its relationship to reality, including its basic emotional and intellectual attitude towards life. At Dobříš, Červenka now had a chance to elaborate his disagreements face-to-face with Havel. Poetry indeed needs facts, he argued from the floor of the conference hall, quoting the Czech immunologist, poet and essayist, Miroslav Holub. But Comrade Havel was utterly mistaken in thinking that the poet is just an 'ordinary civilian' distinguished from other people only by an unusual capacity to write on the basis of 'a stronger sensation of existence'. Poetry is not merely the recorder of everyday facts. It 'grows out of indignation and desire: out of indignation at everything which weakens life, and out of desire for a united harmonious humanity'. What is metaphor, Červenka asked, if not a basic instrument for shaping objects and situations through the mental images and judgements of the poet? And what else is the subtext of a poem than a certain mood produced by the juxtaposition and jostling of words? 'The meaning that results from the connection of two words is different from the sum of their individual meanings,' he added, quickly acknowledging to the other comrades that of course the criteria of 'socialist humanism' serve ultimately as the 'court of final appeal' in matters of artistic truth.

In the ensuing discussion, this kind of argument proved vulnerable to two strong, if conflicting objections. First, within the socialist system, understood merely as a 'court of final appeal', did it not license poetry with a bit too much 'civil' freedom to define its own metaphors and subtexts? And, secondly, didn't Červenka's argument rather arbitrarily, or at least offhandedly, specify the criteria of 'socialist humanism'? What was so special about these criteria? Were they really true? Hadn't Červenka at one point in the discussion described himself as a romantic? Wasn't he obsessed with the inner life of the poet and the ideal of the poet as a harbinger of human harmony sensitive to the sweet fragrances of the world? What did any of that have to do with socialism? And didn't the young Havel secretly agree with the anti-socialist thrust of this view?

The debate on the conference-hall floor gradually turned nasty. In the end, Havel later recalled, power-broking Jiří Hájek stood up and played the role of peacemaker. Delivering a long-winded sermon in the delicate art of dialectics, he faintly praised Havel for having triggered a lively debate of fundamental importance. He then turned on Havel by stressing that Czech literature could never allow itself to be robbed of its partisan socialist qualities. 'Dear comrades,' he concluded, 'although we all still have much to learn, the most important thing to remember is: the task of art is to create.'

STALIN'S CARCASS

The unlucky sculptor named Otakar Švec discovered in grief that the times were more lunatic than these fine comradely words implied. His work of creative art – the World's Biggest Statue of Josef Vissarionovich Stalin, flanked by eight Soviet and Czechoslovak peasants, intellectuals and workers wielding flags and guns – had just been unveiled. Whether or not it was artistically 'creative', the statue certainly made him larger than life. Residents of Prague swore that he 'could be seen from everywhere', recalled Otakar Švec's co-worker.[1] The monument was to dominate the Prague skyline for seven years. Rumour had it that Švec had halfheartedly entered the compulsory competition for the monument design, and only then after one afternoon's work of modelling, washed down with two bottles of vodka. He had presumed that the competition would be rigged, and that from the ranks of the fifty-four entrants a Party-approved leading architect like Karel Pokorný would get the job. It is probable as well that he privately doubted the motives of the Party, which likely wanted something imposing, since they understood well the time-honoured law that all political rulers struggle to define and to control space in their honour; that is, to inspire devotion among their subjects by making the exercise of power seem unblemished – and unchallengeable – by carving out places and stamping them with the symbols of their own power.

Perhaps indeed Švec had been worried about prostituting his talents. Although the gifted pupil of the famous Czech sculptors Josef Václav Myslbek (the creator of the Wenceslas monument in Wenceslas Square) and Jan Štursa, Otakar Švec had tried his hand at imprinting power on public places several times before: a proud T. G. Masaryk for a town square; a bulky statue of the fourteenth-century religious dissenter Jan Hus for another square; and on yet another site a blustering sculpture of Franklin Delano Roosevelt. The Nazis saw to it that the first two were demolished, while the homage to the American New Deal was scrapped following the *coup de Prague*. So checkered by previous paymasters was Švec's career that, understandably, he felt reticent about serving yet a new set. 'Švec was a pessimist from

---

[1]Švec worked together with Jiří Štursa and his wife, Vlasta. The remark is cited in Marcela Kašpárková, 'Udělal Stalina, chtěl taky Masaryka', *Magazín Dnes + TV*, 14 October 1993, p. 9.

the beginning,' remarked one of his assistants.[1] Little wonder, considering that, when the surprise announcement came that he was the winner of the statue competition, the judges ordered him to make the figure of Stalin bigger, and considering as well that as soon as construction got under way bags of anonymous hate mail began to arrive. The commonplace accusation that he was unoriginal, even a plagiarist, was tolerable. So was the popular joke that the statue resembled a queue for scarce meat. More worrying were the insinuations of declared Stalinists who criticized him for demeaning their master by placing him on the same plinth as ordinary proles – and even committing the crime of lining them up behind him in such a way that the whole structure looked like a catafalque. Others said the same thing by accusing him openly of 'Trotskyism'. Still others – scribbling from a variety of standpoints – berated him for legitimating and actively promoting the 'murder' of the Czech nation.

Švec began to be shadowed by the secret police. President Antonín Zápotocký, a former stonemason, personally urged him to stand firm for socialism, but the sad fact was that the razzmatazz caused by the statue broke its creator's heart. He started womanizing and drinking heavily; his wife was so depressed that she locked herself in her kitchen and turned on the gas; a year later, and only three weeks before the unveiling of the statue, Otakar Švec did the same thing. The suicide pact spared him the ordeal of having to come to terms emotionally with his most imposing creation. Mounted on a huge concrete plinth high above the Vltava River, on the clifftops of the Letná Plain, the 12 metres-wide and 22 metres-long granite statue stood 15 metres high, dominated by a faintly smiling Stalin, dressed in a greatcoat, right hand on heart, left hand clutching a book, presumably a volume of the collected works of Marx and Engels. The sheer scale of the 6,240-ton monument, which took five years to build, using 8-cubic-metre blocks of granite quarried near Liberec, left everybody breathless, especially those who witnessed its unveiling on the evening of May Day, 1955. Václav Kopecký – Uncle Miloš Havel's foe – the Deputy Prime Minister and the hyper-Stalinist overlord of film, art, and public propaganda, otherwise known as the Minister of Information, even bragged in his pompous unveiling speech

[1]'Udělal Stalina, chtěl taky Masaryka', op. cit., p. 8.

that the statue was proof positive that socialism was winning the struggle with capitalism.[1] He made no mention of Švec. He was silent about the workers who had lost their lives in accidents during construction. Comrade Kopecký spoke only of the need to recall that this was the tenth anniversary of 'the glorious liberation of Czechoslovakia' by Generalissimo Stalin. He lambasted 'German fascism' and Western 'imperialism' and reminded his listeners of 'the strong friendship which today binds the Czechoslovak and Soviet peoples'. 'It is a granite-strong friendship!' he added, without a grain of irony. He went on to express, on behalf of the Czechoslovak people, 'our unconditional loyalty and our burning love for our brotherly Soviet Union, our great ally, our powerful support, and our shining example'.

The hand-picked crowd assembled at the foot of the floodlit statue waved flags and cheered as Kopecký declared the monument open with a string of slogans. 'Glory to the Soviet liberators of our country!' he shouted into the evening spring air. 'Glory for ever to the memory of Generalissimo Josef Vissarionovich Stalin! Long live the strong and growing eternal friendship of the nations of Czechoslovakia and the nations of the Soviet Union!' After quick follow-up speeches by the Czech-speaking Soviet Ambassador and the Mayor of Prague, cannon fired into the night against the backdrop music of the Soviet and Czechoslovak anthems. Régime poets like Vítězslav Nezval were ecstatic. 'He, the victor, standing tall above Letná, will succour Prague for ever', he wrote. 'For ever he will stand guard over the happiness of humanity living in peace. For ever he will be among us, he will be ours.'[2]

A bitter irony: at the very moment that Prague was wrapping Stalin in eulogies, Moscow was busily derobing the cult of the personality. So that when the Czechoslovak Party finally decided to get in step again by issuing a demolition order, The Thing, full of the arrogance of the vain survivor, brought nothing but headaches to its deconstructors. Given the fanfare at its unveiling, the matter of its dismantling seven years later was sensitive. The whole affair was potentially embarrassing to the Party, and it was therefore unsurprising that the constant stream of interested citizens who

---

[1] See the text of the speech, and other details of the unveiling, in *Rudé právo*, 2 May 1955, p. 3.
[2] Cited in Zdeněk Hojda and Jiří Pokorný, *Pomníky a zapomníky* (Litomyšl, 1996), p. 213.

went to take a look with their own eyes at the hushed-up
preparations had to be shooed away by plainclothes policemen.[1]
But keeping private the public destruction of the Biggest Stalin in
the world was only one battle to be fought. The far bigger problem
was technical in nature. The Party liquidators were informed by
engineers that one big bang would directly damage parts of the Old
Town of Prague and likely cover it under a scree of clifftop rubble
produced by the blast. So the fireworks master Jan Příhoda decided
to wrap the monument with pipes and blast by numbers.

Poor old Stalin and his comrades were first loosened up on
17–18 October 1962, just before the Month of Czechoslovak–
Soviet Friendship. The writer Bohumil Hrabal noted that after the
first remarkable show of flashing lights, clouds of smoke and flying
pipes the statue 'stood untouched, seemingly stronger and bigger
than ever before'.[2] Some wags claimed that Stalin's smile had
widened. But the truth was that the first round of mini-explosions
transformed him and his comrades from socialist-realist icons into
rather modernist figures. There were further blasts a week later.
They left the statue looking like a grotesque carcass sculptured by
Giacometti. Workers meanwhile beheaded Stalin, then smashed
into the stump of the statue with heavy steel sledgehammers in
preparation for the final blasts, which commenced (here there was
a sweet irony unknown to the Czechs) on Guy Fawkes Day, 5
November. Stalin and his supporters were no more. The rubble
was then cleared, and the concrete plinth on which The Thing
had rested was repaired, eventually, for lovers and strollers and
skateboarders to frequent, under the shadow of a huge metronome,
a symbol of the passing of time.

The trouble was that clock time and political time refused to
hold hands. Many observers – Havel included – wished secretly
that the demolition of political Stalinism could have proceeded as

[1] Information provided by Milena Janišová, Institute for Contemporary History,
Prague, 26 June 1998. Other useful background material includes Berthold
Unfried, 'Denkmäler des Stalinismus and "Realsozialismus" zwischen Ikonoklasmus
und Musealisierung', *Österreichische Zeitschrift für Geschichtswissenschaften*, 5, 2 (1994),
pp. 233–258; Marcela Kašpárková's interview with Jiří Štursa, one of the assistant
architects of the monument, in 'Udělal Stalina, chtěl taky Masaryka', *Magazín
Dnes + TV 4* (4 October 1993), pp. 7–9; Josef Škvorecký, *Talkin' Moscow Blues*
(London and Boston, 1989), pp. 37–38; and 'Vykřičník století aneb "Čechy krásné"',
Reality Public Reportáž, 7–8 (1996), http://www.capitol.cz/tisk/public reality/1996
0708/page2.html.
[2] From Bohumil Hrabal's short story, 'Betrayal of the Mirrors', cited in *Pomníky a
zapomníky*, op cit., p. 205.

swiftly as the destruction of Švec's monument. It was not to be. After Stalin's death in March 1953, the Czechoslovak Communist Party demonstrated in words and deeds that it was not for turning. It pursued a tough line against liberalization, or what elsewhere was being called 'de-Stalinization', mainly because its whole identity — above all, its power — had been shaped by the hammer and sickle of Stalinism. After coming to power through a *coup d'état*, the Party consistently undertook the most ruthless purges and trials in central-eastern Europe, quickly developing in the process a reputation as the most dogmatic sergeant in the socialist barracks. And so although it is customary to describe 1956 as the year of the beginning of the thaw within the Soviet empire, the year zero in which de-Stalinization and Malenkov's 'New Course' began, no such development took place in Havel's homeland. Frightened that disturbances of the Hungarian kind might spread to their own territory, the Party tightened the screws of political repression. At home, it lashed out with all fours against 'mistakes' and 'incorrect opinions', as if the whole population was potentially or actually guilty. In the world of geopolitics, the Party gave strong backing to the goal of holding the fort of Soviet hegemony throughout central-eastern Europe. It hit out at 'National Communism' and 'revisionism' in both its Yugoslav and Polish form. It loudly backed Kádár and the new Hungarian regime, and naturally it took sides with Moscow in the emerging conflict with Peking.[1]

There were admittedly some changes that followed the death of Josef Vissarionovich Stalin. The Party hierarchy began to stress the importance of collective leadership. There were signs of restraint in the public praise for Stalin. Many imprisoned during the show trials of the early 1950s were released. For a brief period during 1956 — as Havel's public performance at Dobříš demonstrated — a minor thaw occurred in the frozen world of official culture. Forceful speeches were made. Bold articles and suppressed manuscripts were published. Greater Slovak autonomy was promised. At the Second Congress of Czechoslovak Writers, in April 1956, reformists managed to gain control of the union. On May Day, during their traditional *Majales* (May Festival) parade, students in

[1] See Galia Golan, *The Czechoslovak Reform Movement. Communism in Crisis 1962–1968* (Cambridge, 1971), part 1; H. Gordon Skilling, *Czechoslovakia's Interrupted Revolution* (Princeton, NJ, 1976), pp. 30–42; Edward Taborsky, 'Czechoslovakia's March to Communism', *Problems of Communism*, 10 (March–April 1961), pp. 34–41.

Bratislava and Prague even chanted slogans and unfurled banners calling for liberalization: freedom of speech, access to the West, and freedom of assembly.

Such scattered resistances were exceptional interludes within a neo-Stalinist immorality play. From the death of Stalin until the eventual demolition of the tyrant's statue on the banks of the Vltava River, nine years later, the Party did everything within its power to ignore Malenkov's New Course, to treat it as a boring comedy that could be 'sat through', sniggering. After the death of Antonín Zápotocký in November 1957, Novotný inherited the supreme Party and state posts of First Secretary and President without a power struggle. The man who triumphed by working his way up through the apparat, contributing to the Slánský trials along the way, insisted publicly that 'the ambiguous word "de-Stalinization"' was a synonym for 'the idea of weakening and giving way to the forces of reaction'.[1] And so the Party closed ranks. No Khrushchev-style figure emerged at or near its summits. No 'revelations' or purges were allowed to surface. Treading the path cut by the Barák commission, which reaffirmed the guilt of Slánský in October 1957, no new Czechoslovak 'scapegoats' were allowed. Even Gottwald was spared. A militant purge of state organs got under way. The cardinal principle of the leading role of the Party was fostered in every nook and cranny of life. There was a vigorous and harsh new drive towards collectivized property and industrialization. Religious believers, journalists, writers, dramatists, Slovaks, academics, youth were constantly accused of 'mistakes' and 'false opinions'. The students were told that from here on they were banned from holding their festival. At Party conferences and at Writers' Union gatherings, organized attacks were launched on 'deviationists' of 'bourgeois' and 'liberal' persuasion.

The whole trend was confirmed by the bold optimism of the special Party conference of July 1960. It approved the Third Five-Year Plan (1961–1966) and agreed the text of a new constitution. Framed in 'the spirit of the scientific world outlook, Marxism-Leninism', the 1960 constitution declared Czechoslovakia to have passed the threshold of socialism *en route* to full Communism. Novotný welcomed and summarily defended the legal blessing

[1] *Rudé právo* (29 January 1957).

given to the victory over modern capitalism. Aping the previous
year's announcement in Moscow – where it was said that the
struggle for socialism had been completed, and that the transition
to Communism had begun – Novotný declared that socialist
Czechoslovakia had taken a giant's step upwards and forwards in
the world-historical route-march towards Communism. Capitalism had been consigned once and for all to the dustbin of history.
But there were still some remaining obstacles along the path to
Communism. The new constitution, he concluded, was designed
to 'cleanse our state of various "birthmarks", comprehensible in
a transitional period'. The overtaking of the West – that meant
capitalism – required above all that the whole socialist bloc draw
together more tightly the threads binding the Party and the state.
The Party must be respected as the leading force in all policy
matters. One particularly ugly 'birthmark' therefore needed to be
erased urgently: what Novotný called 'liberal pseudo-democratic
principles of the division of power'.[1]

[1] *Rudé právo*, 17 April 1960.

TO BARRACKS

H avel was among those who clung to the old-fashioned 'bourgeois' principle of power-sharing, but throughout his teenage years he managed, protected by the political privilege of youth, to escape the direct hand of the state. It first clawed at him during the year 1957, when he was drafted for two years into the Czechoslovak army. Going into uniform was not foreordained – against his mother's wishes, Havel deliberately gave up being a laboratory assistant and studying chemistry at the Technical University in Prague[1] – but whatever unhappiness that resulted from his declining interest in the natural sciences was not washed away by army life. After completing induction and basic training, he was assigned to a regiment of sappers within the Fifteenth Motorized Artillery Division, based in České Budějovice, south of Prague. As a black sheep of 'bourgeois' origins – a 'member of old Prague's dynasty'[2] – the crew-cut Havel found himself among other young men branded with various black marks. The point of the assignment – that they were considered by the officer class as dregs and potential cannon fodder – quickly dawned on each of them. The Czechoslovak army 'borrowed from the Soviets the tradition of sending the less worthwhile elements of the population to serve with the sappers', said Havel later, 'because in any action the sappers go in first and lose a higher percentage of men'.[3]

The realization that others thought him dispensable, coupled with his intense dislike of boondoggling – lugging around a bazooka, barracks routine, petty discipline, and the meaningless tomfoolery of mess-hall culture – prompted Havel to complain bitterly about army life, especially to his trusted girlfriend, vivacious and beautiful Olga Šplíchalová. The pair had first met in 1953, thanks to a mutual friend named Zdena Tichá, at the well-known Prague writers' hangout on the embankment, the Café Slavia. Havel was struck by her natural beauty and was attracted as well to her mature confidence – she was three years older than him – and to her self-taught interest in the arts. She had already tried her hand at co-writing a television script version of Jane Austen's *Pride and Prejudice*. She was interested in the history of painting, liked to go to the cinema and to read novels (her

---

[1] Interview with Radim Kopecký, Prague, 5 November 1998.
[2] Pavel Kosatík, '*Člověk má dělat to, nač má sílu*', *Život Olgy Havlové* (Prague, 1997), p. 53.
[3] *Disturbing the Peace*, op. cit., p. 37.

favourite authors were Hemingway, Steinbeck, and Faulkner), and
she loved and lived for theatre. At the time Havel laid eyes on
her, she was taking private acting lessons with the drama teacher
Ludmila Wegenerova, and was soon to make her stage debut – as
the lead role of Cinderella in a performance for children at the Máj
Theatre in Vinohrady. For her part, Olga was especially attracted
to the seventeen-year-old Havel's way with words. She thought
him impractical, yet the chubby, blond-haired, boyish-looking
young man seemed highly educated and immensely clever, and
she was most impressed that he was already writing poems, one
of which he dedicated to her. It redescribes their place of first
meeting:

Beyond the window of the café sleet is raging
We are silent with the desired cigarettes, I don't know
how one could imagine us without them.
It is hard to explain
what we're observing in ourselves without defences.
It's growing dark, on the lookout tower a red star shines,
for lovers in happy moments

Words join to express his feelings of mystery, exoticism, strangeness in Olga's presence:

Your soul is a suburb full
of smoky roads, muddy paths,
walls, cemeteries and telegraph poles
full of life's dramas
of people living somewhere on the edge of our
strange era. You read verse,
you'd like to be an actress and you say
that you're as cruel as the scourge of God.

And strangeness put more directly, but in hope:

It took half a day before we could really communicate.
You, Žižkov's daughter, I, still an inexperienced
habitué of writers' cafés. The two of us,

somewhere on the edge of spring.

Yet not quite springtime. More like unconsummated desire:

Day is dawning, the frogs in the pond at your place
are croaking furiously, quiet, not a soul anywhere.
We're standing by the wall, which is set
with shards of glass
to make life difficult for thieves.
I'm struck by comparisons with myself – a thief,
and with your face – a wall with shards to make
the way to your soul more complicated for me.[1]

Havel's comparison of himself to a burglar and Olga to a wall
covered in broken glass was perhaps understandable, given that
when they first met she was seeing someone else, so that it took
him three years to pluck up the courage to ask her out. Alas,
the times were such that not even serious romance was safe
from the clutches of arbitrary state power. Havel's bellyaching
to Olga about life in the army brought her instant trouble.
Strolling one day down Wenceslas Square, Olga was telling a
girlfriend just how 'awful' Václav was finding his treatment. All
of a sudden, out of thin air, a man began to chase them, calling
out menacingly, 'Comrade, what did you say? What was that?'
They ran as fast as they could, and fortunately managed to give
him the slip.

   When Havel heard this story from Olga, he was uncowed.
Olga toughened his views. Born in Žižkov, one of the roughest
working-class districts of Prague, Olga Šplíchalová was a strong
woman with radical views that harboured no sympathy for Communist nonsense. As a young girl, she had refused to join the
Pioneers and the Czechoslovak Youth Union and, from the early
1950s, Olga always referred to the Communists as 'Bolsheviks',
and as 'cheats' and 'criminals'. She had been raised by her mother,
to whom she was so close that fiery disagreements between them
were common. The fires were fuelled by the fact that Olga's

---

[1]'On the Edge of Spring' (cycle of poems), published originally in samizdat form
in Josef Hiršal and Jiří Kolář (eds.), *Život je všude* (Prague, 1956). Translated by
Derek Paton.

mother had joined the Party immediately after the military defeat of the Nazis. As a strong-headed sixteen year old, Olga quarrelled with her about the trainload of gifts dispatched by Prague workers to Stalin in 1949, in time for his 70th birthday. Olga also found repugnant her mother's shy defence of the execution, during the following year, of the former member of parliament, Milada Horáková, whose trial on trumped-up charges of 'leadership of the subversive conspiracy against the Republic' was broadcast live over street amplifiers in Prague. The biggest row followed her mother's decoration of one of their flat's window-ledges with metal portrait reliefs of Beneš, Stalin and Gottwald. One morning, during an argument, teenage Olga took aim with a hammer and knocked all the great men down. Her mother grew so furious that she threw every bit of Olga's clothing out the window into the courtyard below. Olga retaliated by locking herself in the toilet for the rest of the day.[1]

Havel meanwhile began planning another act of 'dissidence', as it would later be called. He fought back quietly against barracks discipline by banding with an army buddy named Karel Brynda. Both privates were interested in literature and one evening, over beer, it occurred to them that it just might be possible to lighten their parade-ground and training duties and cheer themselves up by writing about the absurdity of their army lives. The regiment had a theatre troupe, which was pretty second-rate. Both men were also aware that there was something of a tradition, or at least a precedent for, plays being written for and about army life. So during the first year of service, Brynda and Havel got permission from the regiment commander to cut their teeth on a staged performance of Pavel Kohout's *September Nights* (1955). Set within the army, itself seen as a microcosm of the contemporary Czechoslovak regime, the drama tracks the fate of Major Cibulka, the officer in charge of political affairs. He is a well-meaning, dull-witted ideologue whose efforts to manage men result in the serious demoralization of the whole regiment. He has some potential officer rivals, including the ambitious First Lieutenant Škrovánek, played by Havel, but the interesting thing about the play is its break with socialist stereotypes. The officer rivals for Cibulka's post are not pictured as class enemies, which

---

[1] '*Člověk má dělat to, nač má sílu*', *Život Olgy Havlové*, op. cit., p. 26.

leaves the audience free – for a time – to question and judge the characters' motives and even to wonder whether the system itself fails to recognize merit and so produces incompetents like Cibulka.

Havel and Brynda's version of *September Nights* retained Kohout's scripted resolution of the drama by introducing the *deus ex machina* figure of Colonel Sova, a wise man who in his capacity as Cibulka's superior has the good sense to recognize the damage he is inflicting upon the regiment and to sack him from his post. Sova could have been seen by the audience as something of a Good Man Khrushchev or a Good Communist Novotný, or perhaps both. In this respect, Havel and Brynda's production trod a difficult path between praise and criticism of the system, but the odd thing was that Havel himself aroused the suspicions of his company commander, who accused him of playing the role of Škrovánek so convincingly that he had revealed his own personal designs on the post of company commander! Havel was demoted on the spot to a mere footsoldier. He was amused by the absurdity – and delighted to relinquish his bazooka, which was in any case heavy and needed to be cleaned every Saturday.

The demotion gave Havel more idle time, which he put to good use sketching fragments of a play in preparation for an all-army theatre-festival competition, to be held in Mariánské Lázně, a town west of Prague, on the German border. With the assistance of Brynda, he wrote and staged his first-ever piece, called *You've Got Your Whole Life Ahead of You* (*Život před sebou* [1959]). The script produced by the two budding playwrights – Brynda recalled – was simple and entertaining, but carefully constructed for a purpose. 'That ridiculous little play was simply what we army boys called a piss-take (*vychcanost*),' he said. 'We did it to be cheeky to the authorities. It was a reaction to the stupid situation we found ourselves in, and nothing more.'[1]

Set within a small regiment, the amusing drama centres on Private Pavel Maršík, who falls asleep one night while on guard duty after having been out on the razzle. He is rudely awakened by gunfire. An intruding civilian lies on the ground, wounded by shots fired from the rifle owned by Maršík. He is suddenly in trouble: asleep on duty and without possession of his weapon,

---

[1] Telephone interview with Karel Brynda, Jihlava and Prague, 5 November 1998.

which had been mistakenly taken by the officer on duty, Corporal
Jan (Honza) Kubeš, who actually did the shooting. The two men
secretly agree that it is in their mutual interest to cover each
other's backs. Maršík is quickly rewarded for his duplicity. He is
written up in the local newspaper, congratulated by his officers,
and promoted to lance-corporal. But undeserved success gnaws
at his conscience, even though his mates try hard to convince
him that everything means nothing and therefore anything goes.
'Is it really such a big deal, getting promoted to lance-corporal?'
sneers a buddy. 'Or do you mean that little item in the newspaper?
Hmm. Today they write about you, and tomorrow there'll be an
article about a milkmaid and the day after tomorrow about the
guy who slops the pigs. You don't really believe anybody reads
that, do you?' The same buddy threatens blackmail. That makes
Maršík fret and fume, but his moment of reckoning soon arrives:
he is asked to join the Party. He accepts, following the company
commander's reminder to him that his whole life is in front of
him, and that he should not ruin it through senseless posturing.
In the final scene of *You've Got Your Whole Life Ahead of You*
the induction meeting is convened. Lavishly wooden speeches
supporting Maršík's candidacy are given. He then begins his
acceptance speech . . . during the course of which he surprises
and embarrasses everybody gathered by slowing down, falling silent
and staring into the distance. Maršík has refused temptation. His
reputation is probably ruined, but his future is now wide open. He
has made the essential gesture of resistance to untruth, amorality
and duplicity.

    Although the commanders of Havel's regiment were not them-
selves experts in matters of theatre, they shared a native dislike of
the play, initially because they could not accept that Czechoslovak
soldiers, even rookies, fall asleep on duty.[1] Behind their disapprobation stood the suspicion that this was army theatre with
a difference, which it most certainly was. The play is simply
structured, so simply in fact that it is easy to discern within
it some of the standard theatrical tropes for which, within a
few years, Havel would become a world-famous playwright. It
is true that the dozen or more plays that Havel subsequently

---

[1] The authorities' reaction is described by Havel in *Václav Havel: A Czech Drama*,
op. cit.

wrote during the next thirty years can be clumped into several different categories. There are plays that are nominally based on, and in content redolent of, other plays written earlier by others. The *Beggar's Opera* (*Žebrácká opera* [1975]) is an example of his rather conventional attempt to use well-known plays as a vehicle for Havelian ideas. So is his last-ever script, *King Lear* (1989), which examines the extent to which the world of powerful people collapses when they are driven from their positions of power.

Then, at the opposite extreme, there are plays which are written so as to be unperformable. Like *The Mountain Hotel* (*Horský hotel* [1981]), they are an exercise in twisting and stretching the conventional structures of theatre into something entirely unrecognizable, even at the risk of bringing theatrical forms to breaking point. These are plays which are so abstract that they resemble formal experiments that have little or no chance of being staged successfully. In between is a variety of plays that are 'political', in that they take a stand against the dominant power structures by raising uncomfortable questions about how lives are malformed and misshapen by those structures. Some of these political plays concentrate on the deeply personal aspects of unequal and dominating power relationships. An example is *Audience* (*Audience* [1975]), a treatment of a fictional character, a brewery worker named Ferdinand Vaněk, whose drunken conversations with his beer-swilling, burping, bullshitting, belligerent, bosom-buddy boss have much that is perspicuous to say about inequalities of power in 'the world as it is'. Other plays within this political category concentrate more on the structures through which power is exercised over individuals. *The Garden Party* (*Zahradní slavnost* [1963]) falls within this group. It is a play that concentrates especially on the power effects of language, including the structural mechanisms – of syntax and vocabulary – that enable distorted language to colonize and deform the lives of individuals. The same theme is central to *The Increased Difficulty of Concentration* (*Ztížená možnost soustředění* [1968]) in which a computer named Puzuk displays a good deal more emotion than any human being.

Through these different – arbitrarily defined – categories run several threads that are common to the plays that Havel wrote from the time of his days in the barracks. The plays normally probe the tortuous world of some bureaucratic organization in order to uncover its vastly complex, but standardized, patterns of interaction. The organization usually resembles two worlds fused into one: the world of Franz Kafka, choking on metaphysical anguish, and the world of Jaroslav Hašek, populated with low-life clowns.[1] Few, if any, references are made to the world outside, but rather like the plays of Harold Pinter, which also confine themselves to a single setting, a whiff of threatened violence – as in *You've Got Your Whole Life Ahead of You* – is constantly in the air. The organizations being probed are barren – like Beckett's stage – and oppressive. Like Kafka's buildings, these functional organizations are purposeless, even though they exercise immense power over the lives of those who live and work within them.

Havel's probes into the world of pointless bureaucracy, in which everything is 'just the way it was planned'[2], poke fun at its fastidious rituals, its confusions, dark sides, neurotic compulsions, and its hidden and open conflicts. The language games played within it are the special target of Havel, who has been described, correctly, as a 'master juggler of words'.[3] Conversation between characters – as in *The Memorandum* (*Vyrozumění* [1965]) – is reduced to mechanical phrases, as if language were now computerized clichés. Behind Havel's mockery of vacuous bureaucratic language (*kecy*) there usually stands the plight of the Ordinary Individual, normally a man, who finds himself caught up within, and struggling against, a vast spider's web of power and intrigue.

The struggle for identity, for recognition and power, resembles life – the struggle is endless, full of setbacks, and usually doesn't succeed – except that it is worth noting that in Havel's plays the divided and dominated individuals never band together in groups to resist and overcome their powerlessness. Like the Chief Censor Aram in *The Conspirators (Spiklenci* [1970]), an official who compulsively munches sandwiches with monstrous punctuality, individuals are alone, very often twisted and deformed by the power that is exercised over them. Havel dispenses with the masks and costumes of classical tragedy. His characters are obviously in an

[1] Martin Esslin, in his introduction to *Three East European Plays* (Harmondsworth, 1970), p. 16.
[2] Václav Havel, *Vernisáž*, in *Hry 1970–1976*, op. cit., p. 276.
[3] Klaus Juncker, in the documentary film by Karel Prokop, 'Z Dramatika prezidentem', Česká televize (Prague, 1995).

advanced state of confused disintegration. Havel usually develops this depressing point at length, and in so doing tries to prevent his audiences from prematurely taking sides, for or against a would-be hero. His plays in fact contain no heroes because they desist from all forms of moralizing and political propaganda. Havel describes himself as a 'sarcastic critic of all arrogant explainers of the world'.[1] He therefore rejects as mistaken all ideas of so-called 'political theatre'. He explains that 'the theatre shows the truth about politics not because it has a political aim. The theatre can depict politics precisely because it has no political aim.'[2] The techniques of emplotment of the plays try to ensure this by relying upon liberal uses of irony, the parroting of almost identical clichéd words and phrases, often in entirely different contexts, and of inverted repetition. And Havel's characters – unlike Beckett's, for whom there are questions without answers – provide answers without being asked any questions.

The combined effect of these techniques is to work against the immediate and 'automatic' bonding between play and audience. Audiences are rather encouraged to see the absurdity of normal situations. Havel's aim is to make the play exceed its author, so that it is 'cleverer than he is'[3], so that through the mediation of the play – no matter what Havel was consciously intending – audiences come to grasp some deeper truths about their times. The feeling of absurdity experienced by the audience, says Havel of his plays, results from the sense of estrangement (*ozvláštnění*) which 'turns into nonsense that which made sense before, it denies the given situation, reverses and negates it'.[4] So spectators are held back from identifying easily with the action on stage, and this has the paradoxical effect, or so Havel intends, of increasing the 'involvement' of the audience with the play. Theatre should 'provoke the audience, stimulate their fantasies, put questions before them, force them to find their own answers – to motivate them into not forgetting everything about the play by the time

[1] *1992 & 1993*, op. cit., p. 20.

[2] Václav Havel, 'Politics and the Theatre', *Times Literary Supplement*, 28 September 1967, p. 879.

[3] Václav Havel, 'Light on a Landscape', in *Three Vaněk Plays* (London and Boston, 1990), p. viii.

[4] Václav Havel, 'Anatomie gagu', *Protokoly* (Prague, 1966), pp. 126–127. Note that the English word 'estrangement' (Bertolt Brecht's '*Verfremdung*') is a poor substitute for the Czech word used by Havel – *ozvláštnění* – which connotes 'distant', 'alien', and 'strange'.

they reach the foyer'.[1] The audience are not patronized as idiots incapable of judging for themselves what the play or its particular characters 'mean'. They are not on the receiving end of sermons delivered from the playwright's pulpit. Audiences instead find themselves drawn into the intrigues of the open-ended, puzzling, sometimes riotously funny plot, in consequence of which they are gently but surely forced to become active *interpreters* of the webs of stories that comprise the play. They are themselves cast in the role of co-determiners of its meaning. It might even be said that they become part of the play – that they not only understand but *overstand* the play, thereby transforming the physical place of the theatre building into a shared public space, within which basic questions about the contemporary human condition are raised, worked through, but not easily answered.

[1] From a conversation with Jan Grossman, filmed during 1965 at the Theatre on the Balustrade.

SOCIALIST REALISM

Havel's whole approach was at right-angles to the official aesthetic dogma known as 'socialist realism'. After the *coup d'état* of 1948, this dogma became part of the arsenal of the organized attempts to turn the theatre into a political instrument of Marxism-Leninism. The stage was required to defend the new totalitarian order, initially by discrediting the power and ideology of its 'class enemies', the 'bourgeoisie', whose agents were seen to be operating both within and without the country. The theatre was required as well to propagate positive images of the present and future. Its job was to help spread the Truth of Marxism-Leninism, to endorse specific policy decisions of the government, and above all to sing praise to the Party and its world-historic hero-leaders.

In practice, the official cultivation of socialist realism required the education and re-education of new dramatic cadres untainted by 'bourgeois' prehistory. They were required to see that artistic criteria were nothing: Communist principles were everything. The time frames of the plays varied. Some plays concentrated on the 'bourgeois' past. Vojtěch Cach's *The Viaduct at Duchcov* (1950) featured the bloody confrontation between striking workers and the Czechoslovak militia during the Masaryk period of bourgeois 'pseudo-democracy'. Other plays concentrated on the present. An example was Otto Šafránek's *The Honour of Lieutenant Baker* (1950), which tracked the fate of an American pilot who had been on board the fighter plane from which the atomic bomb had been dropped on Hiroshima. Shortly after leaving the armed forces, Baker had become unemployed, the sharp experience of which opened his eyes to the evils of capitalism and the necessity of Communism. During Havel's teenage years, the title of many of the most respected socialist-realist productions — Jaroslav Nezval's adaptation of President Zápotocký's *When the New Warriors Will Rise* (1949), Ilja Bart's *Coal is Mining Man* (1950) and Karel Stanislav's *Built by Bricklayers* (1950) — give a flavour of what was expected by the commissars of culture. The model play of this period was usually about a project important for the building of socialism, in which a worker or the working class were as a rule treated positively as heroes standing up for socialist virtues. The stage was filled with shirt-sleeved men, women clad in bright-red dresses, singing and chortling children. Usually a 'class enemy' or two stood in their way. And the plot was often thickened by the presence of foreign spies and conspirators. The drive towards socialism was sometimes seen to fall into difficulties. This was not because of saboteurs or divided and twisted characters, but due to insufficient morale among some workers. But it was supposed that even they grasp that all problems are ultimately solved by the wise application of the scientific homilies of Marxism-Leninism. So they ultimately rise to the occasion, leaving the play to work towards an obligatory happy ending that again proves the triumphant march of socialism into the world. All this is typically a cause for celebration. As the plot unfolds, audiences are encouraged to split their sides in laughter. The standard-formula socialist-realist play was a comedy, since this genre best reflected the official optimism of the Party about the march of history upwards and forwards into the future.

For Havel, socialist realism was no laughing matter. The whole genre of socialist realism was tedious and tiresome – and philosophically mistaken. So he set about proving that it was possible to sustain a different – more exciting, unpreaching – genre of theatre that could both expose the limits of socialist realism and push beyond its narrow horizons, so as to enable theatre to speak to its audience in radically more concrete and vibrant ways. The whole aim was to do theatre well without taking itself too seriously. This at least was the instinct that developed during his army days, so that while still in uniform Havel decided to sit the entrance exams to allow him to study dramaturgy at the theatre department of AMU. Required to write under examination conditions an analysis of a play called *The Eccentric*, by Nazim Hikmet, Havel produced a well-written hyper-Marxist interpretation that concluded that the narrative contained the basic laws of dialectical materialism. It was a skittish attempt to practise the art of deception, but it failed. The admissions board smelled a rat and rejected him.

So Havel had no choice but to fall back upon family connections to find his way into the official world of theatre. His father was an old friend of the performer, entertainer and playwright Jan Werich. Werich, who was about to retire, offered him a job as a stage-hand at Prague's ABC Theatre. Built in 1928 by the architect O. Polívka and situated in a labyrinth of passages that linked up with the Lucerna complex that was once owned by the Havel family, the ABC Theatre was the site of Havel's emotional conversion to the stage. He dropped the commonplace prejudice that a theatre is the mechanical sum of its plays, booking office,

ushers, actors, auditoriums, toilets, and audiences. 'It was there I
came to understand,' he later reflected, 'that theatre doesn't have
to be just a factory for the production of plays.' His time with
Werich was inspiring. He adored watching Werich perform –
the famous dialogues (forbíny) between Werich and Horníček in
front of the curtain during intermission Havel found unforgettable
– so much so that they convinced him that the theatre could be 'a
place for social self-awareness, a vanishing point where all the lines
of force of the age meet, a seismograph of the times, a space, an
area of freedom, an instrument of human liberation. I realized that
every performance can be a living and unrepeatable social event,
transcending in far-reaching ways what seems, at first sight, to be
its significance.'[1]

Each evening at the ABC Theatre, Havel eagerly pitched in
with the practical work of creating the special magnetic field that
develops around a successful playhouse. In his spare time he also
wrote a few theoretical articles for the theatre magazine *Divadlo*.
He turned his hand as well to writing another play, initially
for himself. It was crafted in the style of Ionesco and called
An Evening with the Family (*Rodinný večer* [1959]). Although it
wasn't performed at the theatre, it was good enough to land him
a job offer, in the summer of 1960, at Prague's Theatre on the
Balustrade (*Divadlo Na zábradlí*). A converted former warehouse
located just near the River Vltava in cobblestoned old Prague, the
Balustrade had been founded two years earlier by Ivan Vyskočil and
Jiří Suchý following a split that developed among the organizers
of another small theatre called Reduta, which had until then been
the pioneering small theatre in the Prague scene. The Balustrade
Theatre was typical of the small theatres springing up at the time,
and although (as Havel wrote in a letter to Werich) he had been
profoundly satisfied by his time at the ABC, he instantly felt more
at home at the Balustrade. He liked the head of its drama section,
Ivan Vyskočil, who was a multi-talented 'hands-on' figure who
did everything from playwrighting to acting and directing. The
people working at the theatre were also closer in age to Havel;
and he found that they were less interested in reviving plays from
the past than in creating something new.

Something of the spirit of the early Balustrade is evident in

[1] *Disturbing the Peace*, op. cit., p. 40.

Hitchhiking (*Autostop* [1961]), the first-ever Havel play written (with the help of Vyskočil) and performed there. It is an absurdist satire of the automobile, which is represented as an icon of the burgeoning conspicuous consumption of modern societies, both of the capitalist and socialist variety. In effect, the play tries to plant the idea that what Marx called the fetishism of commodities is not just a chronic feature of 'bourgeois' societies, but of socialism as well. The play contains three loosely related parts. *Hitchhiking* uses a variety of absurdist verbal gags to explore the theme of the obsession with owning a car, which was a prominent and growing status symbol in Czechoslovakia in the late 1950s and early 1960s, that is, during and after the official declaration that the country had at last achieved socialism. The play tells of the good fortune of an unadventurous and pudding-headed young man who wins an automobile in a lottery and is catapulted overnight into a sought-after society idol. The theme of the second part of the play is strikingly similar to Ionesco's *Le Salon de l'Automobile* (1953), in that it relies on the device of bringing inanimate objects to life to the point where they come to dominate and deaden living human beings. Ionesco tells of a buyer riding away in a newly acquired vehicle that is female, and that he decides to marry. Havel shows how people obsessed with owning or driving cars begin to speak in sounds resembling their engines. Human feet start to look like car wheels. Some individual car-lovers are even transformed into cars. In contrast to the grotesque and dark atmosphere within many Ionesco plays, *Hitchhiking* is rollicking fun. For those who don't find it so, or don't get the point, a university professor (originally played by Vyskočil himself) steps into the car-crazed culture to deliver a mock lecture on the historic transformation of people into automobiles. The didacticism grows during the last part of the play, when the degree and scope of the reigning automobile craze is tested scientifically according to the criterion of hitchhiking: the reaction of individual car-owners when asked for a lift reveals the degree to which they have been either dehumanized or retain a few sparks of humanity in an age of commodity fetishism.

GARDEN PARTY

Hitchhiking was the accomplished work of a talented twenty-four year old. But like another short play called *The Best 'Rock' Years of Mrs Hermanová* (*Nejlepší Rocky paní Hermanová* [1960]), co-written with Miloš Macourek and performed the following year, the satire on the automobile was very much a 'transitional' work. Both plays revealed the considerable – but temporary – influence at the Balustrade Theatre of Vyskočil.[1] He was its *spiritus movens* during its first several years. He encouraged collective authorship of plays and he appeared to favour satirical theatre – the blending of a literary text with improvisational acting, loosely connected by the story of an allegorical character – very much in the style originally championed by Voskovec and Werich ('V + W'). Vyskočil strongly emphasized as well the importance of engaging audiences not by means of 'plays' but by posing questions, conflicts, and problems in need of urgent consideration. The distinctive feature of the Balustrade Theatre, he used to say to Havel, was its reliance upon the 'appeal' (*apel*) to the gathered public to enter into a silent dialogue with the performance during or after its staging. 'The theatre of "appeals" does not wrap a problem in the confines of a story or of an image but restates it in such a way that it directly confronts the spectator's experience,' he once wrote. By asking questions, theatre tries to 'engage the intellect and the imagination of the spectator who is then forced to agree, disagree, compare and view a subject from various angles.'[2]

The principle that plays should be open-ended dialogues was to make its mark permanently on Havel's understanding of drama. But the departure of Vyskočil from the Balustrade Theatre during 1963 made room for Havel to experiment with dramatic form. Under the new leadership of the famed critic and dramaturg and director Jan Grossman, the small theatre quickly developed a European-wide reputation as the showplace of the so-called 'drama of the absurd', both foreign and domestic. For the first time, all within the year 1964, Prague audiences were shown Eugène Ionesco's *The Bald Prima Donna*, Samuel Beckett's *Waiting for Godot* and Alfred Jarry's *Ubu Roi*. It was an exciting period for

[1]See Vladimír Justl, 'Po piatich rokoch', *Slovenské divadlo*, 11 (1963), pp. 489–505; and Paul I. Trensky, *Czech Drama Since World War II* (White Plains, 1978), pp. 104–106.
[2]Ivan Vyskočil, 'Poznámky k Autostopu', in *Autostop* (Prague, 1961), p. 1727.

Havel. He was now sure that the theatre was for him, and so all remaining thoughts of pursuing formal education were finally abandoned. While his mother wasn't pleased, Olga was. She actively supported his judgement, even making the big decision herself to harmonize her life with his by working nights at the Balustrade Theatre as an usherette. She was serious about their relationship. Having a daytime job with nights off would have meant permanent separation from Havel – and would have left him alone to the temptations of the theatre dressing rooms.[1]

Havel reciprocated by accepting Olga's proposal of marriage, knowing full well that their decision would spark his mother's further resentment. Božena was already upset about her older son's 'bohemianism'. For years, he had developed the bad habits of staying out late and keeping company with friends of questionable social background. He had failed to excel academically . . . and now, he was marrying a tough-minded, chimney-smoking, spirit-drinking girl from working-class Prague. 'Miss,' said curt Božena to Olga during a visit to see Havel when he was still in service, 'I wish you could mix dumplings as well as you shuffle cards [to mix dumplings and to shuffle cards is the same verb in Czech, *míchat*].' Olga gave as good as she got. Although she was very fond of Havel's father, she found Božena stuffy, obsessed with keeping alive bourgeois culture in her household, despite the painful fact that the Havel family had lost most of its property since 1948. Olga occasionally went out of her way to remind class-conscious Božena – 'Mrs Havlová' she called her – that she already had a mother, and didn't need another.[2] So on 9 July 1964 – two days before Olga's thirty-first birthday – the two theatre-lovers married in secret in a civil ceremony held at Žižkov Town Hall. Olga was unveiled, carried no flowers, and the couple didn't exchange rings with their promises. Accompanied by the official witnesses – Jan Grossman and Libor Fára – they went to lunch afterwards at the Moskva restaurant, ate and drank well, then returned that evening to work at the Balustrade Theatre.

The newlywed Thespians threw themselves eagerly at the experiment that Grossman had launched. He was down-to-earth

---

[1] Interview with Olga Havlová, in Eva Kantůrková, 'Olga Havlová', *Sešly jsme v této knize* (samizdat 1980 [Prague, 1991]), pp. 6–15.

[2] Pavel Kosatík, '*Člověk má dělat to, nač má sílu*'. *Život Olgy Havlové*, op. cit., pp. 71, 91.

and highly skilled at motivating others. Under his guidance, the tiny Balustrade Theatre on Anenské Square became renowned for its experimentation and excellence. Although the authorities left the theatre alone – probably because it was full of young people, who were assumed to be unthreatening to the regime – everyone at the Balustrade Theatre, like the characters in Ivan Klíma's play *Games*, soon found themselves to be treading not just on a theatre stage, but on political ground. The atmosphere was egalitarian and fearless. After queuing for tickets, audiences gathered in the open-air courtyard for a drink or entered a smoke-filled foyer decorated (stylishly for this period) with fake-leather armchairs and formica-topped, metal-legged tables. The popular drinks were cola (*kofola*) and a fizzy soft drink called *amara*, both served with rum for a few extra hellers. The theatre itself felt a bit like a living room in an apartment block: the stage was only 4½ metres wide, the audience's chairs were tightly packed together, and in winter they were kept warm by a coal-fired heater. It was a youthful place in which fresh thinking was encouraged, personal rivalries discouraged, audiences were warmly welcomed, and in which the rehearsal and production of plays – *The Times* of London noted in March 1965 – was considered an act of co-operation. 'Each stage performance is discussed in detail and carefully prepared by all members of the group, from director to usherette, long before the first rehearsals. Everyone is engaged in stage performance. Hierarchical divisions of roles don't exist, as in the case of other theatrical groups. Grossman actually leads, rather than fights, with the talented people with whom he's surrounded himself. He's simultaneously a catalyst and generator of ideas.'

Grossman thought highly of Havel, and gave him enough space and resources to enable him to become the theatre's most important resident playwright – and a star of the Prague scene. The arrangement quickly resulted in *The Garden Party*, whose première during 1964 marks the beginning of authentic absurdist drama in Czechoslovakia. *The Garden Party* has been described above as an 'unperformable' play, in no small measure because the story it tells lacks a story. That made it all the funnier. Audiences at the Theatre on the Balustrade typically chuckled through the whole performance – which was very rare at the time.[1] The

[1] 'Rozhovor s Janem Nedvědem o Tváři (Druhá část)', *Střední Europa*, 9, 30 (May 1993), p. 92.

action, although the right word might be inaction, centres on a young good-for-nothing man named Hugo Pludek. His ambitious father is so perturbed by his son's wistfulness that he arranges for him to land a respectable job at the Liquidation Office by making contact with one of its chief officials, who happens as well to be an old acquaintance. Hugo is supposed to meet him at a Liquidation Office garden party, but the official doesn't show. The young good-for-nothing Hugo nevertheless rebounds by taking advantage of a developing rift between the Liquidation Office and the rival Inauguration Office. He curries favour with the Liquidation Office officials and soon finds himself appointed to the post of liquidator of the Liquidation Office.

At this point, Pludek's career takes off. After working his way skilfully into the rival Inauguration Office, he becomes head of a brand-new, all-powerful body called the Central Commission for Inauguration and Liquidation. His rapid rise to power takes its personal toll by transforming Pludek into an unlimited conformist. He is an unbreakably plastic character. He seems able to adapt to any situation, to the point where in fact he wilfully becomes a nobody. Not even his parents can recognize him any longer. The personality of the good-for-nothing turned careerist constantly slips out of gear. He has no personality. He is a self-less creature incapable of speaking, judging and acting for himself – he is what the ancient Greeks would have called an *idiot*.

The theme of the decomposition of Pludek's character (contrary to literal-minded interpretations of the play) does not prove that Havel had a 'pessimistic vision of modern society'.[1] *The Garden Party* in fact parodies more conventional narrative versions of the same psychodramatic theme, so that it is not, say, a variation on Kafka's *Metamorphosis*. Like absurdist playwrights before him – Havel was especially familiar at this point with the works of Ionesco and Beckett – *The Garden Party* develops the theme of depersonalization *ad absurdum*. It does this by encouraging the audience to concentrate upon a spectacle of words that drown out any real plot, or conflict, or psychodrama. The play is about nothing else but words – words that do not play the role of 'neutral' conduits of meaning, that is, of expressing the ideas and emotions of characters interacting on a stage. Precisely the

[1] Paul I. Trensky, *Czech Drama Since World War II*, op. cit., p. 108.

opposite role of language is highlighted. The characters, Pludek in particular, become the deformed medium of a deformed and deforming language.

Havel's aim here is not to repeat the point – which has become heavily clichéd since Lord Acton's *Historical Essays and Studies* (1907) coined it in this way – that power tends to corrupt individuals, absolutely so when they exercise absolute power over others. *The Garden Party* works up the more profound point, sometimes in riotously witty ways, that *language can corrupt and disempower* the individuals who speak it, and that *corrupted language corrupts and disempowers them absolutely*. Havel, playing the role of parodist playwright, experiments in various ways with underlining and then flinging back the debased language into the faces of the audience. There are moments in the play, for instance, when the language of the so-called characters degenerates into dry-as-dust, pseudo-precise, belaboured bureaucratic memoranda. Consider the exchange about facilities between the She-Secretary and the He-Secretary, two Liquidation Office employees, who are seated at the entrance to the garden party at a desk covered with rubber stamps and heaps of paper:

SHE-SECRETARY: You are at present at the main entrance B13. You can buy here a general admission card, one which will provide you with the right of free movement throughout the entire topographical extent of the garden as well as with the right of visitation to all attractions organized within the framework of the garden party of the Liquidation Office –

HE-SECRETARY: There is, for instance, the discussion with the Chairman of the Development Department concerning liquidation methods, which is conducted in the area of the Little Pond.

SHE-SECRETARY: An entertaining Quiz Programme on the history of the Liquidation Office, conducted in Pavilion No. 3 –

HE-SECRETARY: Or the programme of humorous stories from the liquidation practice of Section 5 that were recorded and will be narrated by the Head of Section 5.[1]

---

[1] Václav Havel, *The Garden Party*, in *Selected Plays 1963–83* (London and Boston, 1992), pp. 11–12. The translation by Vera Blackwell loses something of the bureaucratic stiffness of the original. Compare the original version printed in the collection of Havel's plays, experimental poetry and essays, *Protokoly* (Prague, 1966), p. 21.

The so-called dialogue elsewhere in the play is no less counterfeit. Mechanical repetition is common, as when there are verbal duels between speakers repeating identical words or phrases. Purely grammatical combinations of words – an example is the tedious extended conversation between the Director of the Liquidation Office and the She-Secretary, using derivatives of four words: delimitation, liquidation, form and norm. Then there are the nonsense proverbs, which upon closer examination turn out to be mere slag heaps of semantically unrelated words. 'Dear son! Life is a struggle!' says Pludek's father, as if he were a speaking automaton. 'Stone walls do not an iron bar! To be or not, aye there's the rub! Consider the lilies of the valley, they spoil not, neither do they tin. You are my son!'[1] In such instances, language seems to be destroyed not only by otherwise grammatically 'correct' sentences that unfold randomly. The meaning of the language is also destroyed from within: the proverbs have all the formal characteristics of proverbs, including the right intonation and rhythm, but the bizarre combinations and sequences of words are merely mechanical. *The Garden Party* also contains plenty of nonsense disputes, as when an absurd disagreement erupts over whether the Large Dancing Floor is larger than the Small Dancing Floor.

The bizarre language that is burlesqued in these exchanges among individuals reveals that their capacity for communication has nearly been destroyed. The destruction is much more radical than in a drama by Chekhov, say. In Havel's hands, people do not communicate with each other. They do not even understand each other. They simply have nothing to say. They no longer even think. True, they talk at each other in prefabricated clichés that are repeated over and over again and sometimes twist and intertwine. They stride around the world, cushioned by words. Pludek even acts confidently in the world: his posture is self-assured and his carefully crafted sentences seem to be living proof that he trusts in the observations he makes and the ideals he espouses. He is the sort of character (as the director Andrej Krob says[2]) who not only is a master of chess, but probably knows all the world's

---

[1] *The Garden Party*, op. cit., p. 10.
[2] Andrej Krob, 'Pokus o aktuální přemýšlení o jednom zdánlivě neaktuálním dramatikovi', in *Milý Václave . . . Tvůj. Přemýšlení o Václavu Havlovi* (Prague, 1997), p. 83.

telephone directories by heart. Lacking an identity, he possesses absolute certainty about everything. He even knows the craft of saying something at odds with what he really thinks.

The trouble is that Pludek's decency is a synonym for stupidity. He is self-nullifying. He is everybody and nobody. Not only does he say nothing. His language, thanks to Havel's touch, is so hyperbolized that it is utterly absurd. Bureaucratic terminology, mechanical repetition, prefabricated platitudes abound. It is little wonder that nonsense proverbs and nonsense disputes result. Equally disturbing is the way in which false syllogisms and circular illogic abound to the point where the so-called conversations lose their veracity and spiral into nothingness. Its low point is the absurd autobiographical monologue – which rather resembles a lecture that lampoons Marxist-Leninist dialectics – delivered by Hugo during his homecoming. 'Me! You mean who I am?' he begins: 'Now look here, I don't like this one-sided way of putting questions, I really don't! You think one can ask in this simplified way? No matter how one answers this sort of question, one can never encompass the whole truth, but only one of its many limited parts. What a rich thing is man, how complicated, changeable, and multiform – there's no word, no sentence, no book, nothing that could describe and contain him in his whole extent. In man there's nothing permanent, eternal, absolute; man is a continuous change – a change with a proud ring to it, of course! Today the time of static and unchangeable categories is past, the time when A was only A, and B always only B is gone; today we all know very well that A may be often B as well as A; that B may just as well be A; that B may be B, but equally it may be A and C; just as C may be not only C, but also A, B, and D; and in certain circumstances even F may become Q, Y, and perhaps also H.'[1]

[1] *The Garden Party*, op. cit., p. 50.

THE CRISES

E quations suggesting that A may be B as well as A, and that A is B and C . . . as well as D were meanwhile appearing in the force-field of Czechoslovak politics. Despite the official declaration that the world-historic phase of socialism had been reached, and that the final struggle for Communism had begun, the Communist Party slowly lost its grip upon power. Signs of crisis within the regime began to appear everywhere.[1] 'Crisis' is admittedly a strong word that has been polluted of late by overuse, especially within the worlds of advertising and everyday life. There it pops up regularly to describe everything from having a flat tyre and losing one's wallet to the resignation of a football coach or a government minister. The more precise – originally Greek – meaning of the term refers more narrowly to an extended sequence of events disfigured by self-paralysis. A crisis is a turning point, an interregnum during which what has existed for some time begins to fade, or to die away. Everybody caught up within the crisis feels (and is) less powerful. Their capacity to act is impaired. They live together in the subjunctive tense. They know that things could soon be otherwise, that everything in future depends on what now happens. That is why some, not surprisingly, summon up courage to act to resolve the crisis in positive ways. But the crisis also makes many others feel enervated, and in consequence some others react morbidly.

The morbid symptoms of crisis appeared in force in the Czechoslovak system during the years 1963 and 1964, when for the first time since the *coup d'état* the regime began seriously to malfunction, to the point where the world seemed out of joint and nobody seemed confident enough to diagnose, let alone heal, the problems. The feeling of growing powerlessness in the face of this self-paralysis was compounded by the multiple roots of the crisis, all of which were however traceable in one way or another to the totalitarian state structures. The 1960 constitution had codified the leading role of the Party – Czechoslovakia was the first regime in the world to do so – which had the effect of legitimating the undesirable concentration of power within the

---

[1]The following accounts of the crisis-ridden process of liberalization before 1968 proved useful when preparing this vignette: *The Czechoslovak Reform Movement*, op. cit; *Czechoslovakia's Interrupted Revolution*, op. cit., part two; Kieran Williams, *The Prague Spring and its aftermath. Czechoslovak politics 1968–1970* (Cambridge and New York, 1997), chapter 1.

upper echelons of the Party led by Novotný. Reliable maps of
the pyramidal structure of decision-making power are hard to
draw, but estimates suggest that most of the 300,000 members of
various Party committees from the local level upwards had little
power to determine anything except local supplies and deliveries
of goods and services. These Party members – the nomenklatura
– naturally were privileged by comparison with the huge majority
of the population who remained outside the Party structures. But
the reality was that state power was overwhelmingly concentrated
in the hands of the 8,500 employees of the national Party apparatus;
in the hands of the 750 apparatchiks who ran the Party at its very
centre; and above all in the hands of the supreme organ of the
Party, the Presidium.

The privileges – related to such resources as sex, luxury goods,
vacations, and housing – accorded those who clung to the pinnacles
of state power are legendary. Less well known are the administrative burdens that so enveloped the ruling oligarchy that even they
began to sense the need to 'offload' the piles of paperwork on to
others, and to call it decentralization of power. Whereas in the
year of the *coup d'état*, the average Presidium meeting dealt with a
handful of items, by the early 1960s paperwork business emanating
from the Party's Central Committee, government ministries or
research teams had increased four-fold. Each week, the average
Presidium member received some 500 pages of briefing materials
relevant for the scheduled Tuesday meeting. Whether intended
or not, paper in this quantity had an intimidating effect upon
Presidium members, who uttered platitudes or simply kept their
mouths shut for fear of making themselves look like the ignorant
idiots many of them were. So as each item on the agenda of
the Tuesday meetings was concluded, the First Secretary tried
to take account of every speaker's point by verbally proposing
a compromise resolution (*usnesení*). No vote was subsequently
taken to confirm the proposed decree, and indeed the final written
version, which was drafted afterwards by the First Secretary and his
staff, often bore no relationship at all to what had been discussed
and verbally agreed.[1]

---

[1] See Karel Kaplan, *The Communist Party in Power: A Profile of Party Politics in
Czechoslovakia* (London, 1987), pp. 54–101; Archive of the ČSFR Government
Commission for Analysis of the Events of 1967–1970, R131, cited in *The Prague
Spring and its aftermath*, op. cit., p. 14.

The disempowerment and overburdening of officials in the alpine regions of the Party was compounded during this period by the sense that all was not well in the green fields of state investment, production, trade and consumption.[1] It is misleading to speak of 'the economy' as an independent source of crisis within the Czechoslovak socialist regime, simply because an economy in the strict sense didn't exist.[2] Everything from wage rates and international trade to the price of bread and condoms and bananas, or even whether they were obtainable at all, was decided by the Party-dominated institutions of the state. The state's elimination of an independently functioning 'economy' certainly confirmed the principle that socialism would abolish commodity production and exchange, but the price that had to be paid was high. Right at the beginning of the third Five-Year Plan (1961–1965), the robust industrialized production system that had hitherto been the showcase of the Communist world began to fall apart. The Sino-Soviet dispute and the dramatic confrontations in Berlin and Cuba meant a downturn in exports. There was a string of poor harvests. Capital equipment (like factory machinery) and office administration were often of poor quality and, above all, investment policy and management decisions were frequently senseless. The disturbing result, especially from the point of view of the trumpeters of Communism, was that during 1963 alone national output declined by at least 2 per cent. The Five-Year Plan was by then scrapped, the inflated presumption that the transition to Communism would accelerate the onset of material abundance was pricked, and Czechoslovakia, which had been ruthlessly exploited by its Comecon partners by making it dependent upon heavy industrial exports to pay for its fuel, foodstuffs and raw materials, found itself tightening its belts.

The resulting squeeze on the population was aggravated by the lack of intermediate groups and self-help organizations standing between the individual and the Party-dominated state. When

[1] Good accounts of this trend include Jiří Kosta, *Abriss der sozialökonomischen Entwicklung der Tschechoslowakei, 1945–1977* (Frankfurt, 1978); Martin Myant, *The Czechoslovak Economy, 1948–1988: The Battle for Economic Reform* (Cambridge, 1989); and Judy Batt, *Economic Reform and Political Change in Eastern Europe: A Comparison of the Czechoslovak and Hungarian Experiences* (London, 1988); and Karel Kaplan, *Sociální souvislosti krizí komunistického režimu v letech 1953–1957 a 1968–1975* (Prague, 1993).

[2] Ference Fehér et al., *Dictatorship over Needs. An analysis of Soviet societies* (Oxford, 1983), p. 25.

times are hard, such social organs sometimes mean the difference between life and death, or between comfort and misery. *Corps intermédiaires* – free trade unions, charitable organizations, self-help circles like the Thirty-Sixers – are barriers against the destruction of people's identities and, conversely, vital conditions of their ability to act in and on the world. Their absence in Havel's homeland was striking – it was a determinant feature of the totalitarian system – and it meant that, when frustrations began to build, as they did during the early 1960s, individuals had virtually nowhere outside their households and district Party headquarters to turn. There were no spaces in which, even in the face of adversity, they could feel themselves more or less free. Such *prostory*, as the Czechs call them, had been badly damaged by the Reichsprotektorat and total war and the post-war disruption and hardship, but the 1948 *coup d'état* and totalitarian rule that followed had a devastating impact upon the patterns of social self-organization, whose roots were often traceable back to the First Republic, and beyond.

The Communist seizure of power effectively demolished the rural and urban middle classes along with their associations, so that for instance in the decade after 1948 the number of craftsmen's studios and privately owned shops declined dramatically from 250,000 to a mere 6,553.[1] The shocking effects upon the whole social structure were compounded by the systematic uprooting and disorientating effects of state policy, which used every means possible to prepare the way for 'socialism'. After the *coup d'état*, thousands of 'bourgeois' professors and students were hounded out of the universities. The Augean world of newspaper and radio journalism was scrubbed clean.[2] At least 300,000 people of the wrong class background – the young Havel, as we have seen, was one of them – were immediately kicked downstairs, or sideways into other official institutions. They were replaced by over a quarter of a million mostly young working-class people aged between twenty-five and thirty. These nomenklatura, whose ranks soon swelled, were hastily trained and promoted within the dominating power structures, even though they were only there thanks to Party patronage. Managerial competence was

[1] Jindřich Pecka, Josef Belda and Jiří Hoppe (eds), *Občanská společnost, 1967–1970. Emancipační hnutní Národní fronty, 1967–1970* (Brno, 1995), p. 8.
[2] Peter Hruby, *Fools and Heroes: The Changing Role of Communist Intellectuals in Czechoslovakia* (Oxford, 1980), chapter 1.

in short supply: by the early 1960s, it is estimated that nearly half a million men and women of the nomenklatura occupied key decision-making positions, particularly in the management of enterprises, for which they were formally unqualified.[1]

The combined consequence of these various structural problems of the socialist state – unqualified leadership, administrative bottle-necks, economic stagnation, the absence of social 'shock-absorbers' – was to encourage a faction of the ruling oligarchy to embark on a dangerous journey called liberalization.[2] At first there was no detailed or coherent programme, only random policy suggestions and an emerging sentiment that the present wasn't workable, that something needed to be done, and that the rulers themselves might well have to defer to experts and clients to find solutions. Power relations within the regime consequently began to feel less totalitarian – a regime of command and obedience in the grip of a Party monopoly – and more like an approximation, so it was said officially, of the ideal of power as a property of the system as a whole, as the making and use of authoritative decisions by the Party to mobilize commitments and obligations for the purpose of furthering the effective pursuit of collective socialist goals, without conflicts of interest, coercion and the use of force.[3] It was exactly this momentary faltering in the onward march of socialism, its attempt to switch from bossing to persuasive bargaining, that provided a breathing space in which official ideas and initiatives in favour of liberalization could be proposed and tried. In theory, the Party was from here on supposed to win the trust and loyalty of the population – to earn its leading role – by persuading others, setting examples, and compromising for the sake of building socialism. In practice, the proposed reforms,

[1] Jacques Rupnik, 'The Roots of Czech Stalinism', in Raphael Samuel and Gareth Stedman-Jones (eds.), *Culture, Ideology, and Politics: Essays for Eric Hobsbawn* (London, 1982), p. 312.

[2] On the process of 'state-led liberalization from above', see Guillermo O'Donnell et. al., *Transitions from Authoritarian Rule* (Baltimore and London, 1986); and *The Prague Spring and its aftermath*, op. cit., especially part 1.

[3] It is ironic that the new socialist understanding of power mirrored the new 'functionalist' understanding of power defended by Talcott Parsons, the high priest of American academic sociology, and a figure not known to be sympathetic to socialism. See Talcott Parsons, 'On the Concept of Political Power', *Proceedings of the American Philosophical Society*, volume 107, 3 (June 1963), pp. 232–262, especially p. 243: 'The power of A over B is, in its legitimized form, the "right" of A, as a decision-making unit involved in collective process, to make decisions which take precedence over those of B, in the interest of the effectiveness of the collective operation as a whole.'

and the resulting hopes and fears and confusions they generated, lifted the lid on the public expression of dissatisfaction – along with ballooning popular expectations. By early 1967, noted Alexander Dubček, the Party leadership had 'learned from reports of the district Party committees that the public mood in both Slovakia and the Czech lands was increasingly impatient and in favour of change.'[1]

Isolated group initiatives had actually begun to spring up well before then. There was active discontent in Slovakia, directed especially at alleged Czech bigotry and the under-representation of Slovaks within the trade unions, cultural associations and other state institutions. Many students voiced dissatisfaction with poor dormitory conditions, restrictions on foreign travel, and the compulsory boredom induced by courses in Marxism-Leninism. Within the artistic field, theatre for instance, the centre of gravity moved during this period from large established state organizations towards smaller experimental institutions. Similar pressures for innovation became evident in the field of publishing, as was evident in the feverish tensions that built up during 1966–67 within the Writers' Union. Denounced by one of its senior apparatchiks as a 'bourgeois brat', Havel spent much time lobbying and petitioning and pestering officials in support of the goals of liberalization. He was heavily involved in the case of the writer Jan Beneš, whose arrest and conviction for sending articles to the Paris-based *émigré* journal *Svědectví* (*Witness*) resulted in moves to expel him from the Writers' Union. According to its by-laws, the case was cut-and-dried: a member convicted of anti-state activity was expelled automatically. At a rowdy all-day meeting lubricated by beer, the members eventually voted by a big majority in favour of Beneš's expulsion, but only after one of the most devoted Party members angrily exclaimed, 'Comrades! If you do not expel this Beneš, I will cancel my membership of the Union.' In a tiny minority, Havel raised his hand and voted against, with a few other writers like Josef Škvorecký abstaining.[2]

The prelude to these battles was the controversy hovering over the monthly magazine for young writers, called *Tvář* (*The Face*).

[1] Alexander Dubček, with Jiří Hochman, *Hope Dies Last: The Autobiography of Alexander Dubček* (London, 1993), p. 112.
[2] Josef Škvorecký, 'Ten buržoázní spratek', in *Milý Václave . . . Tvůj*, op. cit., pp. 52–53.

Havel was invited on to its editorial board in the spring of 1965, just as it was about to be threatened with closure. For a while, the controversial contents of the journal – a translated excerpt of Heidegger's in the first issue, pieces by T. S. Eliot, Eugène Ionesco, and Alain Robbe-Grillet in the fourth, for instance – had seemed to escape official disapprobation from the Writers' Union. Everything initially was played out behind the scenes, after the fact. The Party censors made it known that they objected to 'non-socialist' foreign translations and previously banned Czech authors, like Jan Hanč from the Group 42. Soon the Party's slow-footed censorship found its stride. The editors got hell for what was about to appear. Then they were not allowed to print certain things. Then, in June 1965, the Writers' Union moved to shut down the whole journal.[1]

The editors decided to fight the decision by circulating among people in the arts a petition against the ban. After enough signatures had been collected in Bohemia and Moravia, Havel, accompanied by the editor, voluteeered to take it to Slovakia. The trip was eventful from the moment they set off from Wilson Station, where two Party writers, Antonín Brousek and Jiří Gruša, tried unsuccessfully to stop them physically from climbing aboard the overnight express to Bratislava. Havel and Nedvěd talked their way through the blockade, to arrive next morning in good time for a meeting to discuss the matter convened by the Union of Slovak Writers. 'Václav went there [alone] and turned the meeting upside down,' recalled Nedvěd, 'and returned from it with some important signatures.'[2] For the next few days, the two young rebel writers flitted like butterflies from flower to flower, usually – but not always – with success. They tried to get in touch with the dramatist and novelist, Peter Karvaš, who lived in a villa surrounded by a tall fence. For some reason, his doorbell wasn't working, so it was up and over the fence the hard way. Chubby Havel, complaining that his trousers were 'too modern', got stuck during the climb. Nedvěd eventually bunted him over,

[1] See the graphic accounts provided in 'Rozhovor s Janem Nedvědem o Tváři', Střední Europa, 8, 29 (1993), pp. 133–145, and 'Rozhovor s Janem Nedvědem o Tváři (Druhá část)', Střední Europa, 9, 30 (May 1993), pp. 92–102. Nedvěd notes (p. 139) that he was informed at the time that Milan Kundera, a member of the top organ of the Writers' Union, voted in favour of the decision to liquidate the journal. According to Kaplan (p. 50), Kundera abstained. Either way, Havel must have not been pleased with Kundera, with whose literature and politics he subsequently did not see eye-to-eye.
[2] 'Rozhovor s Janem Nedvědem o Tváři', Střední Europa, 8, 29 (1993), p.141.

to be greeted by a surly dramaturg well known for his two recent plays, *The Scar* (1963) and *The Great Wig* (1965). The conversation with the intruders started badly, and didn't ever improve. Karvaš refused to sign.

Havel's politicking in support of what he affectionately called 'the tiny oasis of *Tvář*' was the opening round in a battle with the Party state that lasted nearly a quarter of a century. His editorial work for the journal was certainly important. It kept him abreast of current literary trends, and confirmed his dislike of ideological prejudice in literary matters. *Tvář* was intolerant of Marxism, but it was so exactly because its editors objected to the principle and practice of judging literature according to some ideological line or another. The later vicious attack on Havel by *Trud*, the Soviet trade-union newspaper, understood well what was at stake. Havel was indeed working for the depoliticization of culture, that is, 'full freedom for any views, including anti-socialist ones, and no obligation on writers to defend proletarian ideology'.[1] *Tvář* also proved to be a forum in which he could experiment with the art of essay-writing, as evidenced by the success of the well-crafted 'Notes on Being Half-Educated', which generated considerable discussion of its insistence that the younger generation deserved tough criticism for failing to educate itself properly.[2]

So the literary importance of *Tvář* to Havel was clear. Of greater significance was the fact that the petition taught him several political lessons. Vigilance in the face of dirty tricks: likening himself to the poor Gascon gentleman d'Artagnan (in Alexandre Dumas's *The Three Musketeers*) who comes to Paris in the reign of Louis XIII, only to be persecuted by him for duelling with some of his musketeers, Havel made duplicate lists of the signatures before returning with Nedvěd to Prague from Bratislava, just in case he was caught. His concern about police harassment was not misplaced. Shortly afterwards, he found a wad of anti-state leaflets stuffed in his home mailbox. He was convinced they were bogus, and perhaps even printed by the state authorities themselves. He reacted swiftly by telling his friends of the trap that had been set and reporting the whole matter to the local police station. He was rewarded with a secret-police file that listed him as 'an anti-socialist

---

[1] *Trud* (Moscow), 21 June 1968.
[2] Václav Havel, 'Poznámky o polovzdělanost', *Tvář*, 9–10 (December, 1964), pp. 23–29.

collaborator'. [1] And he was savagely criticized in the official media, for the first time, by the Head of the Ideological Department of the Central Committee of the Communist Party of Czechoslovakia, František Havlíček, who denounced him as a 'bourgeois' writer whose family had owned various businesses, including the Barrandov studios.[2] Temptation: at one point in the struggle between the editors of the journal and the Writers' Union, Havel was taken aside by the boss of the Cultural Department of the Party's Central Committee, Pavel Auersperg, and secretly offered the chance of starting up his own magazine, with the editorial right to commission pieces from the editorial board of *Tvář*, which was earmarked for redundancy. Havel had heard that Auersperg, behind his back, had described him as 'a dangerous fellow', which drove home the point that Auersperg's offer was a clear attempt at *divide et impera* by a Party hack. Not wanting to 'get mixed up in back-room wheeling and dealing', and feeling that 'a new and fresher wind was blowing'[3], Havel flatly rejected the offer. There was also a lesson in civic initiative: the petition was so successful – over 600 signatures were collected – that a plan was hatched to widen the basis of support for *Tvář* by creating a group of people around the journal, who would seek to shield it from further harassment. Leadership: the resulting supporters' network was named the Young Persons' Action Group, with Havel as its first chairman. He was an obvious choice, especially after delivering a swingeing attack on the 'evasive thinking' of the delegates attending the conference of the Union of Czechoslovak Writers – and getting roundly applauded by the very same delegates whom he accused of not 'defending the right of literature to be literature'.[4] Criticism: Havel agreed to act as the mediator between the editorial board and the Writers' Union. Several times during 1965 he negotiated a compromise position with the Writers' Union, only to be rebuffed for his plasticity by the majority of the board, led by Emanuel Mandler. Havel later

[1] Interview with Andrej Stankovič, Prague, 10 November 1998.

[2] František Havlíček, 'Nepřekročitelná hranice' *Nová mysl* number 12 (1965), pp. 1374–82.

[3] *Disturbing the Peace*, op. cit., p. 83.

[4] The Writers' Union conference had been convened to celebrate the twentieth anniversary of the 'liberation' of Czechoslovakia. The speech, entitled 'On Evasive Thinking', was delivered in Prague on 9 June 1965 – exactly twenty years after he wrote his account of the air raid on Havlov. It is reprinted in Václav Havel, *Open Letters. Selected Prose 1965–1990*, ed. Paul Wilson (London and Boston, 1991), pp. 10–24.

claimed that *Tvář* had its dogmatic 'inner sanctum', and that its
sectarianism proved the truth of Eugene O'Neill's famous maxim:
'We fought so long against small things that we became small
ourselves.'[1] Whatever the truth, Havel's perceived mishandling of
the negotiations caused acrimony within the board, so that at one
point a mutual acquaintance, the playwright Pavel Kohout, was
asked to sort Havel out. He did – by arranging to pick Havel
up in his Volga one afternoon, and then driving around Prague,
all the while trying to drum into Havel that there should be no
retreat, and that he and others must never give up.[2] And failure:
although the whole action seems to have prolonged the life of
Tvář for about six months, the Party rounded on it at the end
of 1965. The tenth and final issue, which included contributions
by the German social psychologist Erich Fromm and the century's
greatest Czech philosopher, Jan Patočka, appeared in December
of that year.

Then there was the experience of learning to live with defeat:
various members of the circle of supporters of the banned journal,
including Havel, were profoundly impressed by their reading of
Dietrich Bonhöffer's famous prison letters[3], and it is therefore
not surprising that the spirit of resistance pervading those letters
steeled the *Tvář* group in fighting for its life. Havel and others –
including some of his friends like Věra Linhartová and Josef Topol
– continued for the next eighteen months or so to meet regularly,
in defiance of the authorities, at various venues, including (it
was a standing joke) the loft of the building of the Union of
Soviet–Czechoslovak Friendship.[4] These and other sweet ironies
of defeat were appreciated by everybody who was involved, and
this in turn reinforced the fun and games that were played
throughout the whole saga of the banning of *Tvář*.

Shortly after its closure, Havel and other members of the editorial board organized a wake. It took the form of a drunken crawl
through a handful of Prague's night-clubs. From several, Havel
and his friends were thrown out for being improperly dressed,
so they moved on eventually to the Kravín wine bar, where they

[1] *Disturbing the Peace*, op. cit., pp. 87–88.
[2] 'Rozhovor s Janem Nedvědem o Tváři (Druhá část)', *Střední Europa*, 9, 30 (May 1993), p. 94.
[3] Ibid., p. 101.
[4] Interview with Andrej Stankovič, Prague, 10 November 1998.

spent a good part of an evening. On their way home from there, lurching down Vinohrady Street, they stumbled into the grounds of St Ludmila's Church, where they happened upon a pile of freshly cut Christmas trees. They naturally helped themselves to the collective wealth produced by socialism and, each with a tree in hand, resumed their journey towards Karlovo náměstí. They were suddenly stopped by a police patrol. 'Where are the receipts for these trees?' a stern officer asked. Of course, Havel and the rest of the group had none. But just at that moment someone in the group (Jan Lopatka) pulled out a press pass. The officer studied the pass, and then replied: 'You mind your business, and we'll mind ours!' And so Havel did – but not for long.

THE MEMORANDUM

The Party's decision to liquidate *Tvář* was officially justified as an exercise in 'improving the journal'. The hypocrisy was typical of the times, as Havel had emphasized in his attack on 'evasive thinking'. It was epitomized by a recent tragi-comical incident in Prague's Vodičkova Street, where a loose stone window-ledge happened to fall below on to a woman pedestrian, whose instant death caused a local scandal, which was then reported officially as proof that socialism was making enormous progress.[1] That is to say, the combined effect of the pressures from above and below to liberalize the crisis-ridden regime led by President Novotný was to produce much confused double-talk, especially so within the thawing alpine regions of the Party hierarchy. The criticisms and reform proposals of the liberalizers – 'the antidogmatics' Havel called them – were for instance still normally labelled by their defenders as 'socialist'. They were mainly articulated through the mainstream official channels, which meant that – just like their 'establishment' opponents – they carried the birthmarks of inflexible and intolerant ideological thinking. And the reform proposals often came from the very same lips of journalists, scholars and writers who, not much more than ten years ago, had sung sweet songs of praise to Stalin and did everything they could to hound 'bourgeois' opinion out of the ranks of the nomenklatura.[2]

The air was so ripe with whiffs of confused hypocrisy that Havel decided to make it the target of his wonderfully absurdist satire *The Memorandum*. The ribald two-part, twelve-scene drama unfolds within the offices of a large department that is somehow connected to a larger, undefined, bleak bureaucracy. The stage set of Jan Grossman's first production of the play at the Theatre on the Balustrade included special fire extinguishers with removable coats of arms, one for each new director; filing cabinets containing nothing but clerks' cutlery, wrapped in plastic bags, withdrawn and replaced with chronometric precision; an empty can, front stage, into which water drips with deadening regularity; and contrastingly loud snatches of bouncy music, resembling some terrible mixture of *Nabucco* and *Lohengrin*, designed as a counterpoint, to make the audience

<hr>

[1] 'On Evasive Thinking', in *Open Letters*, op. cit., pp. 10–11.
[2] *Fools and Heroes*; op. cit., p. xv.

laugh.[1] Laugh it certainly did when the department director, Josef Gross, discovers in his morning mail a memorandum written in a strangely jumbled language. He is surprised to find that his subordinates already know that the language exists. It is called Ptydepe. So Gross tries to have the memorandum translated, without success. His secretary hasn't yet grasped the grammar of Ptydepe, while his other subordinates haven't been authorized to attempt the translation. Entangled in red tape, feeling ever more isolated, Gross slowly realizes that he has been disempowered within his department, that there has been a plot behind his back, and that his deputy, Baláš, is responsible for the introduction of the strange new *lingua franca*.

The bewildered Gross, hanging on for dear life to his director's post, finds that the stated aim of the newly circulating language is to improve the efficiency and effectiveness of the organization by eliminating imprecision of meaning. Whereas the old natural language produced misunderstanding and inaccuracy, the new language of Ptydepe is supposed to usher in transparent communication. Its grammatical rules are straightforward. It is said to be a 'strictly scientific . . . thoroughly exact' language blessed with an 'unusually broad' vocabulary and a grammar constructed with 'maximum rationality'. Similarity among words is purposefully minimized. Professor Perina, the organization's language expert and teacher, explains that 'words must be formed by the least probable combination of letters'. Here the so-called principle of 60 per cent dissimilarity comes to the rescue. 60 per cent of the letters in any word in Ptydepe must be different from any other word of the same length. The vocabulary of Ptydepe is built on another logical principle as well: the more commonly used a word, the shorter it is. In Ptydepe, the word for wombat has 319 letters. At the other extreme, a word like 'whatever' – a favourite of amoral cynics – is the second shortest word, 'gh'. The 'f' word, we are told, is being held in reserve, just in case science should discover a term more commonly used than 'whatever'.

It is easy to see that *The Memorandum* is a satirical attack on an imaginary world – a world only a few notches away from

[1] See the account provided in Andreas Razumovsky, 'Der Mechanismus von Feigheit und Macht', *Frankfurter Allgemeine Zeitung*, 5 August 1965.

Havel's current reality – defined by the absence of communicative interaction and the complete destruction of freely expressed public opinion, that is, a pure totalitarian order in which the exercise of power no longer needs to be legitimated because nobody is capable of speaking and interacting with others. Ptydepe's rules of vocabulary and usage are based ultimately on the principle that language itself should become obsolete in human affairs. 'The greater the redundancy of a language,' says the wise professor, 'the more reliable it is, because the smaller is the possibility that by an exchange of a letter, by an oversight or a typing error, the meaning of the text could be altered.' Ptydepe is more than a super – new and improved – synthetic language. It is an anti-language, for it seeks to reduce its speakers to mechanical creatures who have neither ethical self-awareness nor even the capacity to distinguish between the language itself and the context in which it is embedded.

Little wonder, then, that throughout the play Gross's secretary sits at her desk, props up a mirror on her typewriter, and combs and teases her hair; or that Gross is constantly precluded from communicating with anybody else, or that the secretary of the Translation Centre has no contact with the outside world except for her shopping trips in search of lemons, melons and onions, and the continual ironing of the Chairman's underwear. Ptydepe is admittedly a rigorous language. It is designed to eliminate the need for communication. From here on, says the deputy director, no one will be led to think that being injured is the same as being helped. But it has several disadvantages. First reports received from the pilot projects where it had already been introduced showed that the trouble with Ptydepe was that it soon began to assume some of the degenerate characteristics of a natural language: various imprecisions, ambiguities, emotional overtones. Then there was the close-to-home difficulty of figuring out its grammar and vocabulary. Although Ptydepe classes had been set up for the employees, almost everybody found it utterly baffling. Only the departmental teacher and the staff of the Translation Centre understand its intricacies – although even the Head of the Translation Centre confesses that progress is slow, and that he's only on his second translation.

During the first part of the play, Gross – who resembles a Communist of the 1948 generation and repeats several times that he'd like to be a little boy again so that he could live his life differently, and claims as well that he is unfriendly towards Ptydepe because he is a humanist believer in Man – suffers defeat at the hands of the amalgam of words called Ptydepe. Gross, who received at the outset a text from the authorities in Ptydepe explaining their ruling that the language was from here on the official one, is victimized by the authorities' supplementary ruling that no person can be granted a translation of a memorandum in Ptydepe text until his or her own memorandum has been translated. Gross is subsequently kicked downstairs to the post of staff watcher.

Yet towards the end of the second part there is an apparent reversal of power relations within the organization. Havel here uses the circular structural pattern typical of absurdist plays to drive home the point that everybody in the play is caught up in the amoral tumble and scramble of the organization. The authorities order the liquidation of Ptydepe. A new and improved synthetic language called Chorukor is invented. Its aim is to put a stop to the unreliability of communication caused by Ptydepe's strenuous pursuit of words as dissimilar from each other as possible. Chorukor tries to achieve this through the – opposite – rule that the more similar words are, the closer their meaning. So Monday in Chorukor is 'ilopagar'; Tuesday is 'ilopager'; Wednesday is 'ilopagur'; 'ilopagir' is Thursday; Friday is 'ilopageur', while Saturday is 'ilopagoor' and Sunday is 'ilopagor'. But won't words intermingle, or get mixed up? And won't confusion result? The recipe is flawless, the consequences quite predictable, Professor Perina says reassuringly. Perfect interaction will result. And if a typist asked to arrange a staff meeting makes a mistake, then no harm will result. In typing 'ilopager' instead of 'ilopageur', all that will happen is that the meeting takes place earlier than expected – on Tuesday, rather than on Friday – so allowing business to be worked through well ahead of schedule.

SUMMER FRIENDSHIP

T he early hot spring and summer of 1968 meant various things to different people, but for Havel it was a time of being surrounded by friends. It all began with a delicious surprise. On his way from Prague to New York in early May, accompanied by his wife Olga, he had a scheduled two-hour stopover at Charles de Gaulle airport in Paris.[1] Taking advantage of the political thaw in Prague, Havel had telephoned in advance a man named Pavel Tigrid, who lived in Paris as editor of the most important Czech *émigré* literary quarterly journal, *Svědectví* (*Witness*). Havel yearned to greet him for the first time. Not only did he want to talk face-to-face with the editor to whose magazine he had contributed some pieces in recent years. Havel was also busily collecting material for a series of radio programmes on Czech *émigrés*, and Pavel Tigrid was an important part of the story of the tragic scattering of Czech talent around the world by twentieth-century power politics. The editor of *Svědectví* had not only seen a good deal of life on both sides of the Iron Curtain. His life was coterminous with the twentieth century. Born in 1917, he had grown up in the new Republic of Czechoslovakia, only to witness its destruction while studying at Charles University. He first went into exile during the Nazi occupation, to Britain, where in London he spent the war years working as a radio journalist for the BBC. Tigrid – affectionately codenamed 'the old man' (*nestor*) by Havel in their subterranean correspondence – returned home in 1945, to become editor of a national weekly. But in 1948, after the *coup de Prague*, he moved to West Germany, then to the United States, and then finally to Paris, the base from which he devoted his time to spinning the precious gossamer threads connecting otherwise isolated writers who represented what remained of independently-minded Czech and Slovak literary culture. KGB agents described him as a 'reactionary American agent'; naturally, they kept him under their magnifying glass.[2]

Havel had no knowledge of the geography of Charles de Gaulle airport. Nor did he have a visa to allow him to exit into the main terminal building. The wise Tigrid had promised Havel

[1] The following material is drawn from my interview with Pavel Tigrid, Prague, 18 September 1996.
[2] See 'KGB Report on the "Counterrevolutionary Underground" in Czechoslovakia, October 13, 1968', in Jaromír Navrátil, ed., *The Prague Spring 1968* (Budapest, 1998), p. 515.

on the telephone that he would do everything to ensure that they met. He had instructed Havel to stay in the transit lounge. 'Make yourself visible to people waiting in the arrivals section of the airport, and keep your eyes open,' he had said. And suddenly there he stood. Thirty metres away, separated by security barriers, immigration officials and thick plate-glass windows, the short, greying, bearded editor smiled and waved, his delighted eyes fixed on the denim-jacketed, long-haired young playwright. The pair briefly put on a mime show, with the desperate Tigrid gesturing to the Havels to stay put. He then hurried to the nearby Air France sales desk, to join a queue of ticket-purchasers.

Time was preciously short. Only one hour before the Havels were to set off for Prague, perhaps never to return. Tigrid acted fast. He had brought enough cash to buy a ticket to ride – out of the country to nearby Brussels, or to Amsterdam, or Zurich. The destination was irrelevant. So was the price. It was not even a question of paying a price worth paying. Friendship was after all at stake. There is a saying that a friend in the market is better than money in the chest, which is to say that friendship is more and other than a monetary matter. Genuine friendship does not know the rules of selfish calculation. Friends have no interest in profit. Friends prove their friendship in times of need. They share all things in common. Friends are sincere with each other; they are a second self; they are generous; their requests do not wait until tomorrow to be satisfied; they are not vain. Friends are certainly a source of disagreement, sorrow, bitterness. But friendship ends when those qualities triumph; that is to say, friendship is an elixir of civility. Friends are non-identical, pure equals. Friendship is a relationship of mutual empowerment. It is not built on unequal power. 'Friends are an aid to the young, to guard them from error,' wrote Aristotle, 'to the elderly, to attend to their wants, and to supplement their failing power of action; to those in the prime of life, to assist them to noble deeds.'[1] And all this is chosen. Relatives are bound together by nature and saddled with fate, but friends make themselves by choice. Friendship is a form of public freedom.

Tigrid moved towards the head of the queue. He would have to explain quickly, cut the chortle, race through immigration,

[1] Aristotle, *Nicomachean Ethics*, Book 8, Section 1.

and make a mercy dash to the transit terminal, with luck into the arms of strangers. Imagine then his bewilderment when, at precisely that moment, the officials behind the Air France desk slapped a 'Closed' sign on the counter and began turning off lights, locking doors, picking up bags, and walking off the job. So did all the other officials in the nearby airport departments. Even the immigration section stopped guarding the arrival and departure gates. Suddenly the barriers between East and West collapsed. Travellers and well-wishers alike were magically free to move wherever they liked. Borders were meaningless. Identity papers were obsolete. Surveillance was just a word. Nobody asked questions. The distinction between citizen and alien, between insider and outsider, was struck down. Everybody was equal. Havel and his editor were free to lock together in a warm embrace. It was a meeting whose time and place were to be noted and never to be forgotten. It was the early morning of Monday, 13 May in the international transit lounge of Charles de Gaulle airport. It was the first day of a half-planned, half-spontaneous general work stoppage organized by the left-wing parties and such trade unions as the CGT, the CFDT, and the FEN (National Federation of Education). The glorious May Days had begun.

During the next few days, as guest of Tigrid and his wife, Havel breathed the spring air of free and independent Czech culture in exile. It was thrilling to discuss Kafka and Čapek and Seifert in exotic circumstances. Paris was in a state of pre-revolutionary upheaval, and through their hosts' eyes, and with their help as translators from French into Czech, the Havels witnessed breathtaking scenes and events, mainly on television. On the afternoon of their arrival, between 600,000 and 1 million demonstrators (the estimates were always contested politically) marched their way across the city. At various rally points, speaker after speaker denounced the government's deaf ears and heavy hands and accused the riot police of provoking the worst street-fighting witnessed by Parisians this century. There were graphic descriptions of the use of toxic grenades, of innocents torn from their cars and from cafés and beaten, of several women raped by police in the streets. Speakers described how, in recent days, students had fought back by building the first barricades seen in Paris since 1944, and by forming thousands of *comités d'action*, whose aim was to establish counter-institutions of grassroots democracy outside the existing political structures. The huge crowds jeered when speakers quoted the week-old words of the Minister of Education, who had claimed that the disorder was caused by 'students playing at revolution'. Mention in public of the ORTF (the French equivalent of the BBC) produced scowling talk of ignorance and bias. There was wild applause at the announcement that its technicians had just joined the general strike. But – this reaction on the streets was telling of the wider mood of insurrection – the loudest hoots of irreverent laughter were reserved for the oft-repeated words of Georges Pompidou, the Prime Minister. Two days earlier he had addressed the country: 'I ask everyone,' he had pleaded, 'and in particular those who are leaders of representative student organizations, to reject the provocations of a few professional agitators and to co-operate.' He had added: 'For my part, I am ready for peace.'

That evening, as the Havels feasted on a home-cooked meal of venison, red cabbage and dumplings with their new friends, students armed with red flags settled into their occupation of the Sorbonne, which was declared open to the people, no longer a hierarchical institution, a place where 'labourers and workers are invited to come and discuss their common problems with the university students'. From this time the Sorbonne became the shop window of the uprising. It was the front line (as Daniel Cohn-Bendit said) against the France of Aunt Yvonne – enclosed, conservative, unable to understand that the world around it was changing. The Sorbonne housed many of the action committees set up by the general assembly of students, which met nightly in the courtyard to take decisions. Permanent teach-ins, debates and entertainment were organized. The style of action soon spread. During their week in Paris, the Havels witnessed the occupation of nearly every university in the country. Many university administrators threatened to resign unless the government stopped interfering and guaranteed full university autonomy. Two-thirds of *lycées* in Paris went on strike. Many regional towns experienced the first-ever demonstrations since the Liberation. *Comités d'action* were set up in the Renault plants, Citroën, Air-France, Rhône-Poulenc and the RATP (Parisian underground). Some workers and trade-union branches began to prepare for a long strike, and street battles with the police became commonplace. The École Nationale des Beaux-Arts and

the Conservatoire Nationale de Musique in Paris were occupied.
For the first time, the ORTF workers voted for a total strike
against government interference and in support of the principle
of public-service broadcasting. And (Havel noted) the Odéon, the
national theatre, was occupied by demonstrators who declared it
open to the public for discussion and cultural expression and as a
meeting place for artists, students, and workers.

Despite the near-paralysis of public transport in strike-bound
Paris – the government and CGT-led crackdown on the rebellion
was yet to come – Pavel Tigrid managed to get his friends safely
to the airport in time to catch their Czechoslovak Airlines flight
on to the United States. It was a tearful ending, succoured only by
the thought that friendship is more easily kept than it is made. Then
came New York. There he walked the streets, listened to 'beat
music', grew his sandy hair, sported an 'Elect Robert Kennedy'
badge, and made more friends. In Jackson Heights, he was invited
to the apartment of the famous pipe-smoking Czech journalist,
Ferdinand Peroutka. They argued about the Prague Spring –
Peroutka advised Havel to go slowly, and not to irritate the
Russians[1] – and attended the première of Havel's *Memorandum*. He
also gave an interview to *The New York Times*, in which he called
for Czechoslovak legislation 'to remove censorship and guarantee
freedom of speech and freedom of assembly', and reportedly said
that 'swift political action by liberals in Czechoslovakia is necessary
now, while the opportunity exists to make the country more
democratic'.[2] He followed up these remarks in London a few
weeks later in an impressive BBC *Late Night Line Up* interview
with Joan Bakewell. Dressed in a turtleneck jumper, looking well
fed and squeaky-clean, he told her that for him personally it was
a good period, and that more freedom – probably – was coming
to his country.[3]

Havel returned to Prague during the last week of June, in
time for an address to the Fourth Czechoslovak Writers' Congress, during which he praised the 'supreme, self-reliant poise'

[1] The taped conversation, recorded in Peroutka's apartment in mid-summer 1968,
was passed by Havel to Czechoslovak Radio, whose archivists subsequently lost or
miscatalogued the material.
[2] See the report by Stephen Klaidman, 'Czech Writer Here, Sees Opportunity for
Liberals', *The New York Times*, 5 May 1968.
[3] 'Václav Havel – Czech Writer: An Interview with Joan Bakewell', *BBC Late Night
Line Up* (London), 26 June 1968.

of Alexander Solzhenitsyn and warned that 'instead of uttering a thousand bold words, of which a hundred are later gradually retracted, it is always better to utter only a hundred, but to stand behind them to the bitter end'.[1] Havel was clearly exhilarated, both by his taste of the West and his return to the East. But he was exhausted by his travels, which is why he wanted most of all to spend the rest of the summer relaxing in the countryside. The previous year Havel had bought a house and some land in the village of Hrádeček, near Trutnov, near the Polish border, 130 kilometres north-east of Prague. Hrádeček took its name from the nearby ruined small castle called Břecštejn. The village comprised a dozen or so houses. The ethnic Germans who had originally lived there were cruelly removed during the pogroms that swept through the country following the military defeat of Nazism. Among the new, Czech occupants was Mr Kulhának, who by 1967 wanted to sell the farmlet, where for four decades he had raised rabbits and goats for local sale. Through Andrej Krob, Kulhának's next-door neighbour, the deal was struck – with Havel, for the relatively modest sum of 24,000 crowns, some part of which probably was paid out of his foreign-currency earnings.

Havel was keen (perhaps to keep the authorities off his back) to hang the sign of modesty on his new purchase. He always subsequently spoke of his new purchase as a 'cottage', but the small castle in name was in reality grander than that. It rather resembled 'a little country estate' (said his good friend Jan Tříska, who spent the whole summer of 1968 there). Havel employed a live-in servant, a simple young man named Karel Švorčík (nicknamed Kešot), who looked like a bearded Russian peasant, drank rum by the litre, and worked quietly as a handyman, sous-chef, waiter, and loyal Czech bodyguard.[2] The little estate also included an orchard, which yielded good crops of apples, plums and pears, and a large stand of century-old beech trees, some of them measuring three hands in circumference. The main house, which included Havel's study that opened out on to the orchard, was flanked by a robust barn and a good-sized stable, and the whole property was surrounded by rolling wooded hills and, during summertime, meadows carpeted

[1] The address is partly reprinted in *The Prague Spring 1968*, op. cit., pp. 9–10.
[2] '*Člověk má dělat to, nač má sílu*'. *Život Olgy Havlové*, op. cit., p. 53.

in blackberry and gooseberry bushes, burdock and sweet-smelling flowers.

Hrádeček needed some immediate refurbishment, and that summer, after planting some front lawn with Olga, Havel himself carefully designed and built a flat-stone pathway leading through the garden from the front door – even working by torchlight well into the night so as to complete the job before new guests arrived from Prague. A multitude of friends there was that summer. Friends came as individuals and in groups, in all shapes and sizes, sometimes overlapping so that the property bulged with housewarming well-wishers. Each person arriving was welcomed with a blast from the Hrádeček hi-fi set of the Bee Gees' love song 'Massachusetts'. It had been a big hit in America and England, and Václav adored its soft guitar and classical sounds and carefully crafted vocals; perhaps its sentimental talk of love, hitching a ride to San Francisco, and coming home also convinced him to use it as a stirring anthem for the new summer retreat. Havel – the compulsive dramatist – played the role of a generous and charming host who attended to the *mise-en-scène*.

For some guests, the daily routine began at sunrise. Others preferred to sleep in, and then, encouraged by splendid weather, to sit lazily in garden chairs in front of the house, in the shade, sipping cups of black tea, or coffee, or morning glasses of Pilsener beer, story-telling, laughing, and discussing philosophy, art and politics. During the daytime, there was plenty of tomfoolery. Havel and Tříska, for example, spun elaborate jokes about the fact that their idiosyncratic fathers had each owned a thermometer containing three scales (Fahrenheit, Celsius, and Réaumur); and they decided to found the International Organization for Rescuing René Antoine Ferchauld de Réaumur from the Abyss of Condemnation by Science, with Havel as its elected president. The new incumbent (Havel) jokily pressed the point that Réaumur had been hard done by. 'Just because water boils at 80 degrees on the Réaumur scale is no reason to discriminate against him,' he would say, all the while cautioning against conspiracy theories. 'Celsius was Swedish. Fahrenheit was a German born in Poland. And our Monsieur Réaumur was French. So there's no reason to suspect that he was the victim of an extreme nationalist plot . . .'[1]

---

[1]Cited by Jan Tříska in *Milý Václave . . . Tvůj*, op. cit., pp. 68–69.

There was reportedly much serious interaction as well. Conversations were 'sharp, competent, inspiring, noteworthy, even educational'.[1] And there was tranquillity. Olga would often appear later than the rest. She would wander outside silently, aloof from the others' good mornings, unlit cigarette and box of matches in separate hands. During the day, friends chatted with the Havels, helped tidy up, odd-jobbed around the property, played music – a large collection of LPs had been brought back from America and England – drank wine, went swimming in local ponds or walking in nearby woods, or made love quietly in some tight corner.

The evening dinners – Havel called them 'jolly parties' (*veselé večírky*) – were definitely the highlight of the day. Havel did most of the cooking – Olga always confessed her preference for theoretical cooking and reading recipe books – and by all reports he tried to show off by preparing 'interesting' dishes. Grilled chicken was always popular; his penchant for spicy food, like devil's goulash and tangy sauerkraut, was the source of some jesting and quipping. There was usually a banquet setting, with a large lace tablecloth, candles, frivolous dressing and mock speeches. The cellar at Hrádeček was stocked full of luscious Moravian wine, and so naturally was the dinner table. There was polite conversation, gossip, loud laughter, drunken prattle, seduction, talk of art. And the guest named politics naturally dined at the table.

After several hard years of writing and literary politicking, Havel felt like a rest from official politics that summer. It wasn't to be. He shared in the widespread hope that the Czechoslovak Communist Party would show its human face, and, political animal to the core, he was therefore naturally reluctant to ignore the dozens of political stories and rumours delivered first-hand from Prague. He suspected (and top-secret records subsequently showed) that he was under surveillance, that along with Milan Kundera and others he was being described as a conspirator in an 'underground anti-Party group' that was hell-bent on undermining the foundations of socialism in the ČSSR, and turning 'the country gradually on to the path of capitalist development'.[2] The description resembled the most wooden of lines from one of his absurdist plays, which is perhaps why he found it impossible that summer to

<hr/>

[1] *Milý Václave . . . Tvůj*, op. cit., p. 67.

[2] 'KGB Report on the "Counterrevolutionary Underground" in Czechoslovakia, October 13, 1968', in *The Prague Spring 1968*, op. cit., p. 515.

ignore the political thunderstorms that became world-wide media events. 'We were self-confident, rebellious and intensely happy . . . everything seemed so simple'[1], recalled his principal guest. But it so happened that this summer of 1968 was the moment of birth of a global public sphere that linked together, for the first time, by means of jet aircraft and print and electronic media like the telephone, radio and television, millions of unrelated people in many different countries. This fledgling public sphere moulded them into interested witnesses of spectacular media events. It endowed them as audiences with the feeling that they were living in the subjunctive tense. It made them feel that the existing 'laws' of society and power politics were far from 'natural'. It even convinced some of them, Havel included, that the future shape of the world was dependent at least in part on current public efforts to contest and refashion it, according to new and different criteria.[2]

Havel's sense of living suspended in the subjunctive tense had been reinforced by his travels to France, America and England. It was confirmed by the nightly broadcasts of Radio Free Europe and the BBC World Service. Through these channels, he learned at least some details of the violent disturbances that swept through the United States following the earlier shooting dead in Memphis, Tennessee of Martin Luther King, the man whose funeral eulogy stressed that he 'gave his life for love'. There was the gathering global controversy produced by the vicious fighting in Vietnam following the NLF Tet Offensive against American forces and their South Vietnamese allies. There was the aftermath of *le joli mai* in France and continuous stories from London, cast as a sensual, exotic playground where artistic extremes were initiated and driven forwards by an uneasy alliance of hippies, artists, students, youth, rock musicians and political activists, united in their fight against a collective enemy – the supporters of the war in Vietnam. There were also the widely circulated images that quickly turned into clichés: long hair and blue jeans; Dionysian talk of turning on, tuning in, and dropping out; clenched fists at rock concerts; and apprehensive hippies tentatively offering flowers to impassive policemen. There were love-ins and die-ins; Jimi Hendrix waving high his 'freak flag'; the street chants of 'Ho,

---

[1] Jan Tříska, in *Milý Václave . . . Tvůj*, op. cit., pp. 65, 66.
[2] See my 'Structural Transformations of the Public Sphere', *The Communication Review*, volume 1, number 1 (1995), pp. 1–22.

Ho, Ho Chi Minh! We will fight, we will win!' Then there was 'Jumpin' Jack Flash', the mid–summer smash hit by the Rolling Stones. Stories of John Lennon living in India, learning the art of transcendental meditation and composing the song 'Revolution'. Bob Dylan. The Pope's public refusal of concessions to liberal opinion on birth control. The first anniversary of the Six Day War between Israel and its Arab neighbours. The death of Senator Robert F. Kennedy, shot by a Palestinian Arab immigrant, Sirhan Sirhan, only hours after winning the California primary election. And there was Prague.

MID-SUMMER'S NIGHT

T he lush Prague spring and early summer of 1968 seemed to unfold naturally, in harmony with the local soil, seeds, trees, birds and animals. There were no flowers of evil, only the flowers of Strahov, the chestnuts of Žofín, the gulls hovering over Jirásek Bridge – and the rebirth of socialism. Socialism with a human face, it was called, especially by Dubček and the new group of Communists who had arrived, with no blood on their hands, at the top of the Party hierarchy. The change had begun on 5 January 1968, amidst sensational rumours of the uncovering of a 'hostile faction' within the Party. There was talk of the need for drastic intervention, perhaps by Moscow, or by the Czechoslovak armed and police forces, whose officers, interestingly, had just received a 1,000-crown bonus.

After an all-night, bad-tempered struggle within the top echelons of the Czechoslovak Communist Party, Alexander Dubček was voted in unanimously to replace Antonín Novotný as First Secretary. A vain man for whom power was an aphrodisiac, Novotný had for months resisted the proposal to split off his office of Party First Secretary from his other, combined positions as President of the Republic, Supreme Commander of the Armed Forces and Commander of the so-called People's Militia (armed units of the Party, known as the 'iron fist of the working class'). At the last minute, he changed his mind. Novotný calculated that the election of the Slovak Dubček would produce a backlash among the Czech members of the Central Committee. Some would say that Dubček's candidacy was 'inappropriate'; others that he was too radical; still others would denounce him as a weakling unsuited to resolving the crisis. So the dispute would drag on, providing cover for Novotný supporters' further manoeuvring. Alas, comrade Novotný miscalculated. The red-eyed Central Committee unanimously elected Dubček, who proceeded to give a short speech of thanks. In it, he highlighted the need for 'all-round reinforcement of relations with the Soviet Communist Party and the parties of the other countries in the socialist camp'; he stressed as well that he would personally 'exert every possible effort to work towards the aims which the Central Committee has always held under the leadership of comrade Novotný'. After concluding business, reactionaries and reformers rose together to sing The Internationale. An early summer of tragic ironies had begun.

Although Havel could not be described as a Dubček man in

any simple sense, ever since his election to the post of First
Secretary Havel often brimmed with enthusiasm for what the
new leadership was achieving. It was symbolized that year by the
May Day parade in Wenceslas Square, Prague's historic avenue.
Havel was there to witness the endless procession of people,
flags and enthusiastic chants. 'Of our own free will, for the first
time!' read a prominent banner. 'Our Party draws its strength not
from its power, but from the truth,' read another. A thrilled
Dubček perched on a rostrum watched the glorious procession, occasionally improvising a loudhailer with his hands to
respond to well-wishers. 'Carnations, roses, tulips, sweet-smelling
sprigs of lilac and lily of the valley were thrown at the rostrum,' reported *Rudé právo* next day. 'This is the spring of
our new existence.'[1] Havel shared similar feelings. 'Just think
of it', he said later. 'Suddenly you could breathe freely, people
could associate freely, fear vanished, taboos were swept away,
social conflicts could be openly named and described, a wide
variety of interests could be expressed, the mass media once
again began to do their proper job, civic self-confidence grew:
in short, the ice began to melt and the windows began to
open.'[2]

From the time Dubček was elected as First Secretary, Havel
had been struck by the contradictoriness of the reforms. Havel
said that he had 'agonizing doubts and hesitations' about the
shaky entitlements of the non-Communist majority of the population, especially because the Party leadership, which still believed
that Communists were always right, refused to put into question the principle of the leading role of the Party. The related
principle of political pluralism, he noted, 'was simply beyond
the leadership's power to comprehend'.[3] And nobody in the
Dubček group had yet dared to grasp the twin nettles of the
immovable masses of Stalinists in the state security forces and
the possibility of military intervention ordered by the Kremlin.

Above all, Havel worried about the schizoid reactions of the
Party leadership. They were clearly in a good mood, as he
discovered first hand when attending a lively public meeting –

[1] *Rudé právo* (Prague), 2 May 1968.
[2] *Disturbing the Peace*, op. cit., p. 94.
[3] *Disturbing the Peace*, op. cit., p. 96.

a question-and-answer session organized by 'the men of January' – held at Prague's House of Slavs. 'Suddenly these people were enjoying spontaneous support and sympathy, something none of them had ever experienced before, because the only kind of support they had ever known was organized from above,' he commented. But popularity bred fear, he added. The Party leadership felt itself to be swamped by the rising tide of social expectations that otherwise kept it afloat. It didn't understand its various currents of opinion, let alone the wider sea, whose rising waters it tried hard to dam up for the sake of a brighter socialist tomorrow. There were moments when watching the Party leaders cope with their own confusions made Havel feel a strange sadness. 'Again and again they were caught off guard, because things began to happen and demands began to be made which were sometimes incomprehensible, even terrifying, given how far they overstepped the limits of the "possible" and the "admissible".'[1]

Havel summarized these various points in a widely discussed essay 'On the Theme of an Opposition', which appeared in a Spring 1968 edition of *Literární listy*, the successor to *Literární noviny* and the most influential weekly at the time in Czechoslovakia.[2] Beginning from the premise that 'power only really listens to power', the essay argued that the combined democratic tasks of keeping a government on its toes, improving its performance, and making it conform to certain ethical standards required permanent public threats, not only to its reputation – through the free expression of public opinion – but also periodically to its very existence. The essence of democratic government is that organized public opinion can help kick it out of office at election time. Democratic government 'assumes the existence of at least two commensurable alternatives,' he wrote, 'that is, two autonomous and mutually independent political forces enjoying equal rights and the equal opportunity to become the leading force in the country, should the people so decide'.

Havel's reasoning was not especially original, being a familiar

---

[1] *Disturbing the Peace*, op. cit., p. 95.

[2] Václav Havel, 'On the Theme of an Opposition', *Literární listy*, 4 April 1968, translated in *Open Letters*, op. cit., pp. 25–35. The middle-of-the-road position staked out in Havel's argument is revealed in H. Gordon Skilling's good account of the debate about pluralism during this period, in *Czechoslovakia's Interrupted Revolution*, op. cit., pp. 356–363.

axiom of modern political thought in the Atlantic region, and
certainly in Czech political culture during the First Republic;
and despite its warning against the dangers of 'suprapersonal
categories' in political life it still clung dogmatically to the old
First Principle of 'the people' and its sovereign power. In the
context of the Prague Spring, it is true, his reasoning served
as a canny but sympathetic critique of the ideal of 'socialism
with a human face'. A two-party system was now required in
Czechoslovakia, he concluded. Did that require the Communist
Party to lose its leading role, his readers might have asked?
Well, yes and no, he replied. The activities of the Communist
Party should be supplemented by a new 'democratic party',
which would revive the 'Czechoslovak democratic and human-
istic tradition'. That would then enable a 'moral reawakening
of the nation' and help along the task of 'redefining human
dignity' and placing emphasis on such values as 'conscience,
love of one's neighbour, compassion, trust, understanding'. At a
minimum, this would require a 'comprehensive rehabilitation' of
all non-Communists 'who were made to suffer for years because
they knew certain things before the Communists got around
to figuring them out'. The Communist *coup d'état* of February
1948 would need to be put behind everybody. The two parties
would then function as partners in a coalition. Their respective
names, conjoined, would symbolize the 'two poles' of the global
political project facing the country: 'the creation of democratic
socialism'. There was only one catch. Since classes had been
abolished, Havel argued, the two parties by definition would
not compete and clash along class lines. That implied as well
that they should work to preserve the 'socialist social structure',
and that both parties should therefore enter a legally binding
pact containing 'an agreement on the basic outlines of their
common goal, which would be the humane, socially just, and
civilized self-realization of the nation on the way to democratic
socialism'.

It is unclear whether Havel's patriotic democratic socialism was
heartfelt. He had certainly absorbed from his father a principled
affection for freedom, social equality and solidarity. In the spring
of 1968, along these lines, he signed a declaration issued by the
Club of Committed Non-Party Members (KAN), in support of
the task of combining 'the socialist system, the democratic exercise

of power, and freedom of the individual'.[1] But it is puzzling that at precisely the moment when the iceberg of Bolshevism had begun to crack and thaw he was arguing the formula, Social Justice + Individual Freedom = Communism. It is most likely that he had not thought through deeply enough the *social* preconditions of political democracy. 'Political programmes,' he did admit, 'are not born at writers' desks, but only in the everyday political activity of those who carry them out.' It is also likely that his call for a 'democratic party' was principally a tactical manoeuvre designed to consolidate the process of liberalization – and perhaps even a move to make a name for himself as a writer by angling for the political middle ground among the intellectuals.

Whatever the case, he had a chance to air these same ideas at his one and only meeting with the new leaders of the reforms. Shortly after his visit to the West, in early July 1968, he was invited by Premier Černík to a drinks party at Prague's ornate Hrzánský Palace, organized by the Party for the purpose of bringing together its new leadership and young artists who were stirring passions in the burgeoning world of independent art. Havel eagerly accepted. He wasn't disappointed. The Renaissance beauty of the Palace setting was matched by a mid-summer spirit of friendliness; the cheese and canapés (*jednohubky*) were delicious; the wine and spirits flowed freely. And since the literati and apparatchiki had another thing in common – their late-night staying power – guests mingled unhurriedly with the 'men of January' until just before dawn. Everybody who counted was there, including leading writers like Josef Škvorecký, Pavel Kohout and Ludvík Vaculík, and such key politicians as First Secretary Dubček, Premier Černík, the Minister of Culture Galuška, and a quiet man named Gustáv Husák.

After plying himself with a cognac – this was the first time he had met heads of government – Havel sidled up to the First Secretary, Alexander Dubček, to tell him personally a few things.[2] On a terrace bathed in the light of a mid-summer's moon, the floodlit stars-and-stripes flag of the nearby American Embassy fluttering above the tree tops in the warm breeze, the unhurried Havel and

---

[1] The manifesto was issued on 13 May 1968 and later published as 'Manifest Klubu angažovaných nestraníků', *Svobodné slovo* (Prague), 11 July 1968, p. 1.
[2] The following account draws upon an interview with Josef Škvorecký, Toronto, 17 November 1996, and *Disturbing the Peace*, op. cit., pp. 99–100. The scene is fictionalized in Josef Škvorecký, *The Miracle Game* (Toronto, 1990), pp. 149–156.

Dubček chatted about the future of socialism. Havel performed the old art of *ketman* (from the Arabic: *kitman*, concealment): simulating adherence to a prevailing political doctrine which conflicted with much of what he believed to be true, all the while taking some self-mocking pleasure in practising the techniques of concealment. Seated on a low wall, surrounded by a cluster of admirers, the First Secretary did most of the listening.

'I assure you, Mr Secretary,' said the long-haired, denim-clad playwright, 'practically everybody who lives in this country supports socialism.' 'Do you think so?' replied the small First Secretary with a large nose tailor-made for caricaturists. He seemed for an instant to twinge with the discomfort caused by the unfamiliar 'Mr' and by the smart new silver-patterned summer suit chosen for him by his advisers. 'Most certainly!' continued the playwright. 'Look at me, for example. My father was a millionaire, and some might therefore say that I would gain a lot from the restoration of capitalism. But believe me, Mr Secretary, I've never ever had such thoughts. I'm not interested in accumulating property. I'm a man of the theatre – and theatre, potentially at least, fares better under socialism.'

The frowning First Secretary's attention seemed to fix on the souvenir dangling around the playwright's neck, a brass peace symbol on a leather chain acquired during the recent trip to America. 'Are you really sure that socialism has such support?' he asked again, adding: 'Perhaps it seems so to you because of your talents. You find full satisfaction in your work, and so do I. But not everyone can or does. You and I believe in socialism. The fundamental question is whether others do as well. Even those who have no artistic talent.' Sucking up, the playwright grew more emphatic. 'An absolute majority believes!' he said. 'Socialism is the *epitheton constans* of the modern world.' 'Do you think so?' asked the First Secretary, for the last time.

A POLITICIAN OF RETREAT

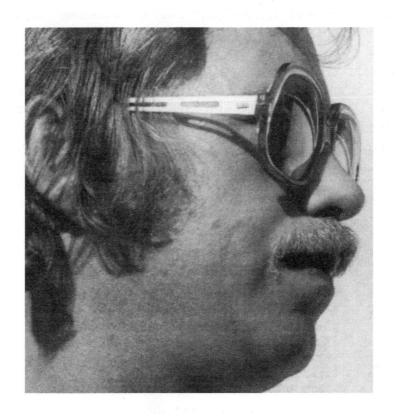

A mini-skirted waitress resembling a Carnaby Street mod, juggling drinks and snacks on a platter, cut short the conversation, but years later Havel still recalled being impressed by Dubček's capacity to listen and to ask questions. Such openness, he said, 'is not at all common among politicians, especially Communists, because they are too busy churning out their own phrases and clichés to listen to anyone'.[1]

Uncommon the First Secretary was, but arguably the flattered young playwright's enamoured description of him was a trifle too simple. Dubček was indeed a rare species of political animal – a *politician of retreat*, let us call him.[2] To understand him well involves taking issue with the dominant habit within modern political philosophy to concentrate either upon the arts of capturing and maintaining the key resources of power (examples include Machiavelli's *Il principe* or Carl Schmitt's *Die Diktatur*); or upon the process of limiting, controlling, and apportioning state power (an example of which is *The Federalist*, drafted by James Madison and others). Although the two standpoints remain indispensable to mapping and measuring the mechanics of power, they are in fact complementary, since each presumes that the lust for political power is both polymorphous and universal. Edmund Burke expressed this conventional point succinctly in *A Letter to a Member of the National Assembly*: 'Those who have been once intoxicated with power, and have derived any kind of emolument from it, even though but for one year, can never willingly abandon it.'[3] In the century before, Thomas Hobbes's *Leviathan* put the same point more pithily: 'Kings, whose power is greatest, turn their endeavours to the assuring it at home by Lawes, or abroad by Wars: and when that is done, there succeedeth a new desire; in some, of Fame from new Conquest; in others, of ease and sensuall pleasure; in others, of admiration, or being flattered for excellence in some art, or other ability of the mind.'[4] The flipside of such reasoning was well put three centuries later by

<hr/>

[1] *Disturbing the Peace*, op. cit., p. 100.

[2] John Keane, 'The Politics of Retreat', *The Political Quarterly*, volume 61, 3 (July–September 1990), pp. 340–352.

[3] Edmund Burke, 'A Letter to a Member of the National Assembly, in Answer to Some Objections to His Book on French Affairs', in *The Works of The Right Honourable Edmund Burke* (London, 1859), volume 4, p. 11.

[4] Thomas Hobbes, *Leviathan, or The Matter, Forme, & Power of a Commonwealth Ecclesiasticall and Civill* (London, 1651 [1968]), part 1, chapter 11.

the Czech humorist and friend of the Havel family Jan Werich. The struggle against the stupidity of those who exercise power, he liked to say, is the only human struggle that is as futile as it is permanently necessary.

What such modern commentaries on power have failed to grasp is that there are political contexts defined mainly by the logic of *retreat from power*. Dubček was one of a crop of political leaders during the second half of the twentieth century – a century, it should not be forgotten, dominated by various kinds of state-enforced 'moral projects' – whose chief role is to have contributed to the (temporary) *dismantling* of a despotic political system. Latin American observers long ago recognized the importance of 'state-led liberalization from above',[1] but in European political thinking this process has rarely been discussed, despite a succession of political figures who have tried their hands at de-concentrating power: Adolfo Suárez, who forced through a democratic constitution upon becoming Spanish Prime Minister after Franco's death; János Kádár, who survived the fall of Khrushchev and eventually helped prepare the way for market reforms and a multi-party system in Hungary; Constantine Karamanlis, who with high-ranking military support facilitated the dismantling of the 'regime of the colonels' in Greece; Wojciech Jaruzelski, who eventually colluded with the formation of the first Solidarność-led government in Poland; Milan Kučan, the protagonist of constitutional reform in Slovenia; Mikhail Gorbachev, who walked in the footsteps of Nikita Khrushchev, the first leader to attempt to dismantle the Soviet system from above; and the man who tried to wear Khrushchev's shoes, Alexander Dubček, the chief symbol of reform Communism and 'socialism with a human face' during the 1960s.

Like all politicians of retreat, Dubček had been schooled in the arts of conventional politics. His career began in the corridors and committee rooms of state power. Born on 27 November 1921 at Uhrovec, a tiny village in western Slovakia, he spent his early years in the Soviet Union with his father, a joiner, who was among the first members of the Czechoslovak Communist Party. Dubček himself joined the Slovak Communist Party when he was eighteen, and after fighting for a partisan brigade in

[1] *Transitions from Authoritarian Rule*, op. cit.

western Slovakia, and living as a manual labourer and regional Party organizer, became a full-time Party official in 1949. Shortly after Stalin's death, he was drafted to the advanced Party school attached to the Central Committee of the Soviet Communist Party in Moscow, to perfect himself politically. After spending three years there and returning home his promotion was rapid. In 1960 he was elected to the Secretariat of the Czechoslovak Communist Party; in 1963 to the Presidium; and in 1963 he replaced the Stalinist, Karol Bacílek, as First Secretary of the Slovak Party.

Despite his irresistible rise to power, Dubček was not a strong-willed, charismatic and (potentially) iron-fisted figure – like, say, Woodrow Wilson, Mussolini, Roosevelt, Churchill, Stalin, Hitler, Adenauer, and de Gaulle before him. Everybody who knew him well commented upon his tendency to indecision, a quality quickly branded as weakness in conventional politics. Immediately after he had replaced Novotny as head of the Czechoslovak Communist Party, it became an open secret in the Presidium of the Party, in the Secretariat and the Central Committee, that Dubček was an 'innocent', a 'hesitater', a 'decent fellow who does not like drastic measures', while Jiří Hendrych, Novotný's right-hand man, said that 'Dubček is an honest man, but he is indecisive'.[1] Such remarks pointed to the fact, especially evident after becoming First Secretary, that Dubček was not to devote his remaining life and political career to the task of preserving or expanding his state's integrity at home and abroad.

It was not that he was a weak leader. It was rather that he – like Suarez, Karamanlis and Gorbachev who followed him – was caught up in a bundle of contradictions related to the politics of retreat. As a *Communist*, he criticized, with enthusiasm, the Communist creation for which he continued to stand; he worked for the liberalization of a regime that in his youth seemed to be the pride of anti-liberal forces in the world; and he tried to breathe life into 'bourgeois' principles, like freedom of expression and assembly, that he once spoke of as mere 'bourgeois relics' of a bygone era. Such contradictions normally dog politicians of retreat. Rather than being driven by lust for power or visions

[1]Pavel Tigrid, *Why Dubček Fell* (London, 1971), p. 13.

of grand victories through conquest, Dubček was instead forced, by dint of circumstance and choice, into becoming a practitioner of the difficult art of unscrewing the lids of despotism. He withdrew and retreated from unworkable political positions. He worked hard to forge new compromises between state actors and their subjects. He thereby enabled the growth, out from underneath the edifices of state power, of the first tender shoots of social life.

Dubček learned this art belatedly, when the process of dismantling in which he was embroiled had already begun. This is unsurprising, since the art of retreat, as von Clausewitz explained in his essay 'Vom Kriege',[1] is the most difficult of all political skills to learn. It requires an ability to know the difference between foolishness and magnanimity. It entails knowing how to spot jiggery-pokery and when and how to blow the whistle on (potential) opponents; it demands the guts to abandon untenable positions, and to slip through the loopholes of retreat. It sometimes necessitates surrendering the middle ground and it always requires mettle, acumen, nerve, toughness, and patience. The politics of retreat is naturally a delicate and dangerous process. As Dubček quickly found, its protagonists get trapped in quicksands. He risked his career and life at every step, surrounded at all times by enemies lurking in the shadowy corners of state power. Ingratitude of his rivals and subjects was to be his ultimate fate. Although his well-known unshakeable faith in socialism sometimes got the best of him, and even though he was therefore not among the wisest politicians of retreat, Dubček eventually learned that he had to be ruined for the good of others.

That ruin stemmed partly from the fact that, unlike early modern enlightened bureaucrat reformers who aimed to strengthen society without initiating political reforms, he was a politician of retreat who worked for the disintegration of the existing Stalinist regime. He therewith threatened certain individuals and groups whose power base lay within the *ancien régime*. Dubček, like other politicians of retreat, suffered unpopularity in the ruling Novotnyite and Brezhnevite circles because he insisted

---

[1]Karl Philipp Gottlieb von Clausewitz, 'Vom Kriege', in *Hinterlassene Werke über Krieg und Kriegführung* (Berlin, 1832–1834), Books 1–3.

on doing without certain privileges or customary routines –
like unconditional observance of the principle that Communists
were never wrong. Certainly, his actions helped dramatically to
widen the political spectrum, even to the point where public
opinions, independently formed, began to be expressed. But
this was not to everyone's liking, or full satisfaction. Not only
did Dubček's actions breed the uncertainty, disorientation and
confusion typical among people who have just come from prison –
what Havel later called 'post-prison psychosis'. Politicians of retreat
like Dubček usually do not offer immediate positive benefits to
their supporters. Although they know one thing best – that
despotic regimes can die from swallowing their own lies and
arrogance, and that fear and demoralization cannot govern for
ever – they tend to speak the language of future gains, described
in abstract terms.

Politicians of retreat also often lead a tenuous – and usually
short – existence because their actions have the unintended
consequence of fostering the growth of *social* power groups
acting at a distance from the despotic state which they help
to dismantle. In helping to disarm the Leviathan, the politicians
of retreat encourage the growth of a self-organizing civil society,
whose chattering, conflicts and rebellions unnerve them. They
learn too slowly that effective government requires winning
the trust of citizens, and that this involves more than dismantling or scheming, rapacity, peacockery, and shouting orders.
For all these reasons, but especially because they play the role
of midwives of civil society, the politicians of retreat typically
sow the seeds of their own downfall. Comrade Tito, who was
given a tumultuous public welcome in Prague in early August,
warned Dubček privately of this. He spoke from experience. In
domestic matters, he said, the Czechoslovak leadership should
advance cautiously towards its goal of decentralization so as not
to 'weaken the influence of the Party'. Decentralization required a
'strengthening of the centre from which all power emanated'. He
reportedly gave examples. Abolishing pre-publication censorship
was a step in the right direction, but the Party had to be
sure that its men and women were in charge of news and
entertainment; and although a resolute fight against conservatives
and hardliners was necessary, Tito warned Dubček, the 'excesses
of the reformists' and 'the danger of "social-democratism"' should

never be underestimated.[1] Tito was right, if for the wrong reasons. In the end, Dubček proved a poor match at home for the political and social forces which he had helped to unleash. Like all politicians of retreat, he fell victim to his own success.

Some politicians of retreat suffer bitter disappointment when their reforms prove to be stillborn. Others have the cold comfort of knowing that their experiments with the status quo lead to consolidated reforms. Some politicians of retreat find that their efforts breed revolution. Dubček was less lucky, for his liberalizing reforms resulted in a full-scale military crackdown, the dramatic force of which he had not anticipated. In his heart, the First Secretary had never believed in the possibility of an outside military invasion of a friendly socialist country; he was convinced Communists would never commit that kind of treachery. During the summer of 1968, besides, the Dubček group did everything it could to behave itself in the company of geopolitics. Its so-called Action Programme, presented by Dubček to the Central Committee on 5 April as a working blueprint for 'our socialist homeland', bowed and scraped to the Soviet Union.[2] And as tensions mounted within the country, Dubček and his friends consistently played their strongest card: since January, they insisted, Prague's foreign policy hadn't changed; her loyalty to the Warsaw Pact, Comecon and the Soviet Union remained steadfast; and no future changes would take place. Even Dubček's speeches were peppered with attacks on 'imperialist reaction', calls to fight 'neo-Nazi and revanchist tendencies' in the Bundesrepublik, and other run-of-the-mill phrases from the lexicon of Novotný.

Moscow was not much impressed. Brezhnev and others there correctly spotted that Prague's stated allegiance to the hammer and sickle was contradicted by developments *inside* the country. The point was simple: regardless of whether or not it was viable, a 'new model of socialism', the realization of Dubček's final vision of a more open and just system, was ultimately impossible without revising Czechoslovak relations with the Soviet Union. There was mounting evidence of this, Moscow observed. There were clear signs of the public contestation of the 'leading

[1] Cited in *Why Dubček Fell*, op. cit., p. 94.
[2] *Action Programme of the Communist Party of Czechoslovakia*, printed as a special supplement of *Rudé právo* (Prague), 10 April 1968, pp. 28–29.

role' of the Party (meaning its absolute power). Czechoslovak newspapers, radio and television were spreading reports 'both incorrect and outside Party control'. A mid-summer's purge of the Soviet security forces – many of them kicked upstairs and paid not to do their quisling jobs – was being carried out by the Minister of the Interior, Josef Pavel. And the Soviet marshals were uneasy about parallel reforms being carried out by General Dzúr in the Czechoslovak army. So it was concluded that the Soviet trap had to be set, leaving enough room to catch the mouse.

The open-ended July manoeuvres of the Warsaw Pact armies on Czechoslovak soil opened the trap. The exercises were designed to exert pressure on the Dubček leadership, even to get the population used to foreign occupation, which lifted only after a conference resulted in the signing of the Treaty of Bratislava on 8 August. The mouse was drawn into the trap at these talks at the railwaymen's clubhouse in the eastern Slovakian border village of Čierna nad Tisou, where the Soviet delegates, led by Brezhnev, arrived on the morning of Monday, 29 July in a special armoured train with bullet-proof glass and its own radio link. The Soviets (to recall Hegel's description of Napoleon) acted like history on horseback. They instantly went on the attack, beginning with Brezhnev's abusive four-hour monologue, in which he issued sour-faced denunciations of various 'counter-revolutionaries' and quoted extensively from the Czechoslovak media to prove that Dubček was losing control of the situation. Much of the four-day meeting resembled a dialogue of the bad-tempered deaf, who sat as two teams on opposite sides of a long table, refused to dine with each other, interrupted, spoke excitedly out of turn, and exchanged insults. The worst moment came when Aleksei Kosygin – who had earlier grunted that 'if we wanted to, we could occupy your entire country in the course of twenty-four hours' – grilled one of the Czech delegates. 'Who is this Kriegel? Is he a Czech at all? Is he not a Galician Jew?' František Kriegel politely enquired why he was objectionable. The Ukrainian Petr Shelest shouted: 'You just *are* – we don't have to explain why!' Dubček instantly stepped in, banging the table with his fist and shouting in Russian: 'You're not going to treat *us* as underlings, comrades!' 'You'll get used to it, Alexander,' snapped his friend, the Czechoslovak President

Ludvík Svoboda. 'Marshal Koniev treated me as an underling all through the war.'[1]

Throughout the Čierna talks, the Soviets tried to prove that political power ultimately grows from the barrel of guns. The railwaymen's club, located 150 metres from the railway station, was surrounded by Soviet guards with hand-grenades in their pockets; a division of Soviet troops was on standby 5 kilometres from the frontier, on Soviet territory; each night, the Soviets in their special train pulled back across the border, 300 metres away, on to Soviet territory. Although the Čierna talks ended with an agreement and a one-day summit meeting in Bratislava, the Czechoslovak delegates were made constantly to feel trapped. Even their private telephone line to Prague was bugged by the Russians. The point is that it would have been possible to arrest and kidnap Dubček and his team in Čierna, but the Soviets prudently waited, all the while carefully preparing the final details and assessing the risks of intervention.

They did not wait for long. Hours after the Dubček leadership published (on 10 August) draft Party statutes guaranteeing such principles as the separation of state and Party power, a Party 'controlled by the people', the protection of minority opinions, and limited tenure of offices, the final decision to invade was taken.[2] Havel happened during that period to be in the northern Bohemian town of Liberec, visiting friends. During the warm, sleepy night of 20–21 August, he was awakened by the steady noise of low-flying planes. Lights went on in the town and his telephone started to ring. Unmarked soldier-loaded trucks, tanks and armoured cars were pouring across the border with the German Democratic Republic, he was told. One caller described the tank column wending its way through the streets of Prague, guided by a Soviet Embassy car, bound for the building of the Central Committee of the Czechoslovak Communist Party. Another rang to tell of the occupation of Prague airport, where huge Antonov transport planes were landing at sixty-second intervals.

At four-thirty on the morning of 21 August, Havel heard Radio Prague confirm the invasion and call upon citizens not to resist. As the Czechs say, the truth had prevailed, but this time in cruel and

---

[1] *Why Dubček Fell*, op. cit., p. 84.
[2] Robert Rhodes James (ed.), *The Czechoslovak Crisis, 1968* (London, 1969), p. 29; Philip Windsor and Adam Roberts, *Czechoslovakia, 1968: reform, repression and resistance* (London, 1969), pp. 60–61.

surprising ways. Five Communist countries wielding twenty-nine divisions, 7,500 tanks and 1,000 planes had begun the invasion of a sixth Communist country in the name of 'international proletarian solidarity'. The beautiful summer that had begun early in May 1968 had ended abruptly. Yet something new had been conceived; the present was now pregnant with a different future. Thanks to the Prague events, the arrows of socialism, like those of Nimrod, had been hurled at the sky, only to fall back to earth, stained with infamy and blood. The Soviet empire was now fated to suffer terminal decline; the word 'socialism' was soon to be discredited; and Havel's career as a world-class playwright would collapse, ironically leaving him free to become a serious political essayist and to fight his way into political life, equipped with an entirely new vision of the Czechs' – and the other Europe's – place in the world.

LATE-SOCIALISM

(1969–1989)

NORMALIZATION

The invading armies soon smashed their way into the town of Liberec. Hours after the Prague Radio announcement, Havel witnessed unforgettable scenes of violence. Warsaw Pact tanks crashed through arcades near the main square, burying several people under the rubble. Trucks, weaponry, heavy equipment, jeeps, troops felt omnipresent. And, at one point, a tank commander, armed with a sub-machine gun and perched on his turret, opened fire into a crowd, badly injuring several people. The situation – guns, tears, dust, diesel fumes – felt hopeless. Grown men cried. Women wailed. Children had fear etched on their faces. Protest was out of season. It seemed imperative that everybody observe the maxim, reportedly formulated by Favorinus when yielding to the Emperor Hadrian, that it is ill arguing with the master of thirty legions.

Havel barricaded himself in the local 'free' radio station with Jan Tříska. The building was protected against the invading troops by the efforts of local workers, who moved swiftly to ring the site with huge transport trucks loaded down with massive cement blocks. Disguised in blue overalls, unshaven, and carrying a fake identity pass supplied by the manager of a local factory concerned to help him escape from any personal danger, Havel worked for a week as a resistance journalist. He and Tříska appeared on local television, in a studio rigged up on nearby Ještěd Hill. Working into the wee hours of the morning, Havel also ghost-wrote speeches for the chairman of the National Committee, and crafted as well declarations for various organs of the Communist Party. Havel listed involvement in the town's National Committee, the District Committee of the National Front, the Communist Party's District Committee and its District National Committee, for each of whom during that week he prepared poster material that was pasted up on the walls of Liberec, or for whom he wrote commentaries broadcast to the local population over street loudspeakers.[1]

Havel also wrote at least five radio commentaries that were read out on air by Tříska, who later described Havel's texts as 'inflammatory' and his own performances as 'tongue-tied' and 'jabbered'. 'The country is brimming with thousands of lads from

[1] Among the documents in my possession are 'Výzva spolobčanům!' (Liberec), 22 August 1968, and 'Všem občanům!' (Liberec), 26 August 1968.

the Ukraine and Kazakhstan who aren't quite sure what country they're in, don't understand the local language, and can't figure out why it is that, wherever they go, people are shaking fists at them', ran one Swiftian broadcast, which then added, cheekily: 'Mr Brezhnev is sitting in the Kremlin over a glass of vodka and is fuming.' Another resembled a message in a bottle tossed with a prayer into stormy seas. It appealed for support from a long list of literary figures, including Kingsley Amis, Samuel Beckett, Günter Grass, Eugène Ionesco, Arthur Miller, John Osborne, and Jean-Paul Sartre. Still another, likening the resistance to that of David to Goliath, spoke the language of anarchism: 'Search for new ideas about how to fight! Organize yourselves, ensure contact between each other, establish action cells and co-ordinate their activity, establish a network of contacts, approach things in an organized way. Join forces!' Throughout, the broadcasts called for the triumph of 'conscience' and 'humanity' over 'beastliness' and 'the pistol'. They also forecast possible cloudbursts of violence: 'We could lose our free transmitter any moment. So we can't allow ourselves to lose contact with each other. Any minute, soldiers with machine guns might be walking through the town square, firing at anybody from the town who is wearing the tricolour. Any moment they could arrest our principal city politicians and the head workers in the factories.'[1]

It was what might be called a Greek experiment – an exercise, attempted in classical Greece, in the political art of using public words against the power of violence. After Soviet agents and Czech conspirators shut down the country's transmitters on the night of the invasion, in order to put on air a more powerful propaganda station called 'Vltava', thousands of clandestine radio and television studios, calling themselves 'free' and 'legal' stations, sprang up. They had a single aim: not to let an army of a quarter of a million men kill the spoken, written, and televised word. The studios' calls for help were on air twenty-four hours a day. They may have bordered on the editorially primitive and improvised – surviving transcripts and secret-police records show – but they propped up an extraordinary seven days of government by microphone. For

---

[1] 'Člověk má dělat to, nač má sílu'. *Život Olgy Havlové*, op. cit., p. 104. Compare Havel's account of the occupation of Liberec in *Disturbing the Peace*, op. cit., pp. 106–109. The direct quotations are from radio transcripts in my possession, dated from 23 August 1968.

the first time in the history of modern telecommunications, spirited broadcasts of the Liberec kind assumed all the normal functions of a clandestine 'government' bent on waging non-violent resistance to an occupying power. 'The mass media,' Havel recalled, 'outwitted the occupiers and moved and mobilized the entire society against the powerful will of the aggressors and some of their helpers at the time. The country simply refused to pay attention to the occupation.'[1] The new media government's appeals for help – spread by transistors, television sets and word of mouth – brought prompt responses; its orders were swiftly executed. The townspeople of Liberec, responding to 'free' radio appeals, actively resisted the invading 'fraternal' armies. Wrong directions and information about the town's buildings were given systematically, helping to foil the invaders, forcing them to retrace their steps, and even on one occasion to fire on themselves. Secret-police cars were immediately identified and permanently tailed. Within the town, a long-haired youth group called the Tramps volunteered for civic duties. During the first night of occupation, they carefully removed all street signs and neatly stacked them in front of the town hall. The group was subsequently invited by the mayor to wear armbands of the auxiliary guard, and to provide extra protection for civilians by accompanying the local policeman on duty. The town hall, a key symbol of the local civic resistance, was protected by sentries twenty-four hours a day. At one point, Havel recalled, the mayor's own office was guarded by the long-haired Tramps. These 'troops' wielded guitars and sang the Bee Gees' 'Massachusetts', against a backup band of revving tanks.

For a brief while, government by microphone proved immensely popular. It again demonstrated to Havel, as it had done in Paris in May '68, the importance of a form of power that is often underestimated: what is sometimes called people power. Roman political thinkers referred to *potestas in populo*, by which they meant that without a people or group there can be no power. The old insight remains important, for there are times – the Czechoslovak people's reaction during the first week of the Soviet invasion is exemplary – when it becomes clear that the power to act in and on the world is primarily not the property of an individual, or the isolated leaders of an institution like an army or government

---

[1] Václav Havel's preface to *The Prague Spring 1968*, op. cit., p. xvi.

bureaucracy, and that power derives instead from the group which acts in concert for some felt or stated purpose. In these circumstances, it is people's support or resistance that empowers or disempowers others – military generals, politicians, administrators – and forces them, without using guns or shouted orders, to take note of their external dependence upon others. Those 'in power' are compelled to recognize, if only for a fleeting moment, that whatever power they have to act in fact derives from others, in whose name they are empowered to act. This is what was meant by a host of eighteenth-century political thinkers (James Madison, David Hume and others) when they remarked that all governments rest on opinion.

As if they had grasped this rule, the residents of Liberec stuck together. They tried to demonstrate that the resort to violence can result in a loss of power, that guns alone could not decide things – or, as Talleyrand famously remarked, that armies cannot expect to rest their weight upon their own bayonets. The strong display of public solidarity in Liberec, Havel recalled, 'showed how helpless military power is when confronted by an opponent unlike any that power has been trained to confront; it showed how hard it is to govern a country in which, though it may not defend itself militarily, all the civil structures simply turn their backs on the aggressors'.[1] He was right. Liberec locals showered their new disc jockey with flowers, food, medicine, and good wishes. Whenever broadcasts were temporarily stopped because of transmission problems, fatigue, or lack of material, hundreds of telephone callers inundated the station to find out if Havel and Tříska were all right. Olga pitched in as well. Her speciality each day was to keep up the radio station's morale by raiding the local bakeries and fetching biscuits and sweets.

But popular power under difficult circumstances has its limits. A week after the Soviet armies invaded Czechoslovakia, the spontaneous resistance from below began to falter. Like many other activists, Havel began to feel exhausted – even to feel that the resistance wasn't working, as if the summery world of nature was totally indifferent to the wintery despair felt by Czechs and Slovaks. It was the beginning of the end of ideals, especially socialist ideals; decay from disillusion and inefficiency would destroy the

[1] *Disturbing the Peace*, op. cit., p. 109.

felt need for solidarity, leaving behind only the common-sense conviction that from here on the 'powerless' were in the jaws of the all-powerful. Things were not helped by the lame reactions of the Dubček government. The full-scale military invasion forced it to live a daily contradiction: it was compelled to serve its masters in Moscow while demonstrating at home that it remained loyal to its citizens. Paralysis resulted. Since it had believed all along that the application of military force by Moscow was an improbable option that in any event could be averted by last-minute negotiation, the Dubček government initially dithered. 'I, who have devoted my whole life to collaboration with the Soviet Union, now they do this to me!' stuttered Dubček, as if struck by lightning from a blue sky. 'This is the tragedy of my life!'[1] It vaguely followed that his country had no choice but to decide against resisting a vastly superior aggressor. He thus began to think that it was imperative to avoid battles that it would surely lose in advance. The decision came slowly. During the first few hours of the invasion, the Czechoslovak armed forces remained without orders; not until one o'clock in the morning of 21 August did the Presidium finally instruct the armed forces to remain in their barracks.

Just imagine the extended political farce that followed: a group of former Communist revolutionaries, once the representatives of the supreme power in their own country, now trapped in a dire emergency, in a state of permanent shock and resentment at the betrayal by 'class friends', attempting to come to terms with military occupation by convening meetings of the National Assembly, of the government, and of the Central Committee. During the first few days of occupation, it is true, the tactic of handling the crisis exclusively in a legal-democratic way seemed to wrong-foot the occupying forces. When the Soviet Ambassador Chervonenko went to Prague Castle to persuade the President of the Republic to nominate a new 'revolutionary workers' and peasants' government' so as to 'avoid the worst', President Svoboda sent him packing. He refused to negotiate, and asked politely that he leave the building at once. Then at midday, still on the first day of occupation, a general strike began. An hour later, 'free radio' broadcast a declaration, signed by a clear majority of government members, condemning the occupation

---

[1] Cited in *Why Dubček Fell*, op. cit., p. 102.

and calling for the rule of law. Meanwhile, Soviet agents failed to win control of the Ministry of the Interior, thanks to 'free-radio' broadcasts of their car registration numbers that led quickly to their detection and arrest. And the Fourteenth Extraordinary Congress of the Czechoslovak Communist Party, meeting in best James Bond-style in a factory at Vysočany, confirmed that there was no split in its ranks. By the evening of 22 August, Brezhnev, sitting at the end of a telephone in Moscow, was forced to recognize that successful military occupation was producing political defeat, and that something dramatic had to be done.

The whole country watched and listened breathless next morning as news leaked out that the holders of power had been kidnapped and brought by plane to Moscow to be taught a lesson in international workers' solidarity. The Czechoslovak leadership, including President Svoboda and First Secretary Dubček, received a grand reception. They were promptly whisked away in polished black cars to the Kremlin, behind whose closed doors their smiling hosts quickly turned into fanged interrogators. At such talks at a 'summit level', the Soviets were experts at the art of sickling their opponents to pieces and then hammering them into the ground, like small wooden stakes. A key member of the Czechoslovak Presidium, Josef Smrkovský, confessed later that he would rather commit suicide than repeat the Moscow experience of being 'humiliated and insulted'.

Dubček told friends that after being wrapped in handcuffs and abducted to Moscow, he gave up all hopes of returning home.[1] On the verge of a nervous breakdown, he fainted twice during the interrogations. Like the others, he was cut off from outside information, kept isolated, the aim being to break his and his comrades' wills, to make them pliable in the hands of power, shatter their nerves, reduce their capacity for making shrewd political judgements to mere fawning capitulation. During the four days and nights of bullying, letters and telephone calls to and from Prague were banned. The delegation saw nobody except their interrogators. Not even Khrushchev – who emerged from retirement and came excitedly to the Kremlin on the second day to urge Brezhnev not to compromise or use half-measures against his victims – was allowed to see them. Any thoughts among the

[1] *Why Dubček Fell*, op. cit., p. 116.

kidnapped that they might at some point be able to escape back
to Prague, even to have an agreement ratified by the government
and the National Assembly, were crushed with threats and insults.
'We have already got the better of other little nations, so why
not yours too?' Brezhnev shouted at one point, vodka in hand,
quickly adding a reference to class enemies like Havel. 'As for
the intellectuals,' he burped, 'put your minds at rest, in fifty years
there will be a new generation, healthier than this one!'

At midnight on 26 August 1968, after four torturous days and
nights, the capitulation document – later called the Moscow
Protocol – was signed by the Czechoslovaks, with only one
dissenter: 'the Galician Jew', František Kriegel. He was missing
from their delegation as it assembled on the tarmac at Vnukovo
airport, and for two hours Dubček and his friends refused to
board any aircraft until the Soviet partisans of Aryan purity backed
away from their plan to keep him in reserve for a possible
show trial of 'Zionists' and other Czechoslovak 'deviationists'.
The Soviets capitulated, reluctantly, so permitting the whole
delegation to arrive back in Prague at dawn, incognito. No
crowds, no journalists, no officialdom awaited the capitulators,
who retreated directly to the Prague Castle, where they rested
for a few hours and worried their heads about who would say
what and when to the country.

Mid-afternoon that same day, the official radio broadcast a
communiqué on the Moscow agreement. After the voice of
a frail President Svoboda sounding like Hácha speaking about
the Munich disaster came on air, it was Dubček's turn. His
speech was among the unforgettable moments of the twentieth
century. Punctuated by long lapses and loud sobbing, Dubček's
words moved millions to tears. They managed to conceal the
worst possible news in the optimistic assurance, repeated again
and again in the rambling sentences of a man verging on a
nervous breakdown, that the Moscow agreement was based on
the 'progressive withdrawal of the five countries' troops from our
territories'. 'Our ultimate aim,' he said, 'is the complete retreat of
these troops, to be effected as quickly as possible.'

Although it seems improbable that Dubček deliberately lied
to his audience, there is no doubt that his chronic Communist
optimism got the better of him. It concealed the bitter truth: the
fifteen-point Moscow Protocol legitimated exactly the opposite

outcome. The top-secret document stated that the recent Fourteenth Extraordinary Congress was 'invalid', and that a new congress would be convened when the situation in the Party and the country was 'normalized'. The document left no doubts about the meaning of 'normalization'. It confirmed both parties' commitment to purging from office everybody who failed to promote 'the imperative task of reinforcing the leading role of the working class and of the Communist Party'. The communications media were singled out for harsh criticism of their 'openly anti-socialist standpoints', and the Bolshevik question of what was to be done was answered in pure Bolshevik terms. 'A re-allotment of leading posts in the press, radio and television is inevitable,' it said. As for the matter of the socialist troops in socialist Czechoslovakia, it was not quite true that the parties agreed to their 'progressive withdrawal', as Dubček claimed. The agreement made it clear that the withdrawal was utterly conditional on satisfying other criteria. It could begin only when 'the threat to socialism in Czechoslovakia and to the security of the socialist countries has passed'. The agreement also emphasized the thorny problem of securing the country's border with the Federal Republic of Germany, the front line of 'aggressive plots of imperialism'. And it highlighted the primacy of rebuilding and maintaining what it described as 'Soviet–Czechoslovak friendship'. The final clause of the document – by implication – left no doubt that the troops might be there for quite a while. 'Both sides pledged in the name of their parties and governments to promote all efforts of the Soviet Communist Party and the Czechoslovak Communist Party and the governments of their respective countries to intensify both the traditional friendship between the peoples of both countries and their fraternal ties,' it read. It added just two final words: 'for eternity'.

LATE-SOCIALISM

H avel, along with millions of other Czechs, was pushed sideways and downwards by the pledge to retain socialism, if necessary by armed force. Perhaps that is why the surviving fragments of his life during the first twelve months or so following the occupation suggest hesitation, even incoherence. Whereas before and immediately after the invasion he had been a driving intellectual force by calling for an opposition party and citizens' involvement in political opposition, he now began to react with some uncertainty about what to do. The key political question was whether to submit to 'realism', or whether the process of normalization required and even facilitated greater political radicalism. 'Realism' meant accepting whatever measures the invading power and their quislings decided upon, hoping perhaps that the restoration of order might take the foreign heat off the country, and thus enable a further phase of liberalization to take place, as appeared to be happening in neighbouring Hungary under the leadership of Kádár. The option of 'radicalism', by contrast, supposed that no good could come from the invasion. The pacifiers had to be resisted non-violently – through strikes, petitions, protest letters, street demonstrations – for that was the only way that the liberalizing achievements of the Prague Spring could be rescued, and perhaps developed further.

There were fleeting moments – around the time (17 April 1969) that Gustáv Husák was appointed as First Secretary of the Central Committee of the Communist Party – when Havel may have thought that the 'realist' option of getting rid of Dubček, the politician of retreat, was necessary for promoting much-needed political order. The secret-police claim to have recorded a conversation in which Havel observed that 'the situation in the state needed a firm hand. Dubček wasn't up to it, because he is a dreamer and a lyric poet.' Havel apparently went on to favour Gustáv Husák, who was at the time (because he worried about a split in the Party) posing as a friend of the Prague Spring, and whom Havel considered to be the only person 'who has a genuinely firm vision and can lead the people out of this crisis situation'. In an interview around the same time, he suggested that Husák's appointment was 'not a bad thing' since it would clarify the lines of power and subordination. He made it clear that Husák was no friend. 'He will rule dictatorially,' he said.[1]

---

[1] This, and the following quotations, were kindly supplied in a letter from Professor Adam Roberts (Oxford), 25 May 1998. The StB transcript is available in Prague's Archive of the Ministry of the Interior of the Czechoslovak Socialist Republic, H 3–2, i.j. 46, č.j. N/Z-0079/69.

Then there were moments when Havel seemed to waver, and bend back towards the option of supporting Dubček, in the hope that he might speak out actively for resistance to the occupation – and for continuing liberalization. A few days before Dubček's dumping, Havel addressed a huge meeting at the Arts Faculty of Charles University, attended by about 1,200 students. Turning to several members of the Central Committee who were also on the podium, Havel urged everybody to stand behind Dubček. 'We must ask for progressive members to fight harder – to fight on small issues as well as big ones,' he said. Two weeks before the first anniversary of the Soviet invasion, he wrote a private letter to Dubček appealing to him to walk out from 'this dark and tangled wood into the light of what we might call "simple human reasoning". To think the way every ordinary, decent person thinks.'[1] Havel said that he feared that the ruling authorities were preparing to pressure Dubček into making a public confession in favour of occupation. It would be a set-piece speech, in which Dubček acknowledged the failings of his leadership, fully endorsed the Soviet view of things, and confessed that with hindsight he had come to realize that the Soviet leadership should be thanked for their 'fraternal assistance' in sending planes and tanks to preserve socialism against counter-revolution.

Havel warned that if Dubček gave such a speech, then it would deal a terrible blow to the population's morale – by fostering the collective depression, indifference and cynicism that would be required for Soviet-style 'normalization' to succeed. It was therefore imperative, argued Havel, that Dubček take a moral stand. His stated support for democratization might well be misused by the ruling authorities to justify further repression. So be it, for the moral significance of taking a stand in support of the highest ideals of the Prague Spring would be threefold. The 'prestige of Czechoslovakia's struggle in the eyes of the world' would be enhanced. The stand would keep alive the ideal of democratizing socialism, which Havel described as 'one of the more positive aspects of the Communist movement'. Above all, Dubček had the chance of acting as an ethical mirror before the eyes of the population. His words of support for continuing

[1] Václav Havel to Alexander Dubček, 9 August 1969, reprinted and translated in *Open Letters*, op. cit., pp. 36–49.

democratization would have immeasurable ethical significance. 'People would realize that it is always possible to preserve one's ideals and one's backbone,' wrote Havel. They would be reminded 'that one can stand up to lies; that there are values worth struggling for; that there are still trustworthy leaders; and that no political defeat justifies complete historical scepticism as long as the victims manage to bear their defeat with dignity.'

It cannot be ruled out that the letter to Dubček was Havel's first calculated move towards assuming leadership of the moral opposition to the abnormalities of normalization. The thought may not have occurred to Havel, certainly. But equally certain is that the letter initiated that effect. The tone and content established a pattern that was to be repeated often during the years to come. The letter was notably tough on Dubček's doings prior to the invasion. 'I must say,' Havel wrote, 'I am convinced that you must share some of the blame for your present situation.' He especially laid into Dubček for signing the Moscow agreement, whose effect was to provide the illusion of success when in fact they merely postponed the decision explicitly to say 'yes' or 'no' to intervention – thus failing to take advantage of the other fact that the Soviet leadership was initially wrong-footed and embarrassed by the local (if uncoordinated) resistance to invasion. What is also interesting about Havel's letter was its anticipation of Dubček's skulking off into the oblivion of silence. Havel noted that if Dubček behaved like Švejk and pretended that he could fool everybody by quietly slipping unscathed out of the crisis, then Dubček would draw fire from both sides. The Party would quickly get rid of him. The population would dismiss him as a schmuck. That of course is precisely what happened. Dubček gave up without a fight, and a month after Havel sent off the letter, he was removed from the Presidium and then, in January 1970, expelled from the Communist Party.[1]

Dubček's capitulation confirmed Havel's hunch about the importance of long-term moral resistance. The need for such resistance had surfaced some months earlier in a public tussle with Milan Kundera, whose strange essay called 'The Czech Lot'

---

[1] In *Disturbing the Peace*, op. cit., Havel later wrote about Dubček's non-decision: 'He disappeared rather quietly and inconspicuously from political life; he didn't betray his own cause by renouncing it, but he didn't bring his political career to a very vivid end either.'

(*Český úděl*) had aroused much controversy after its publication in mid–December 1968.[1] Kundera suggested that the long–term significance of the Czechoslovak autumn would outweigh that of the Czechoslovak spring. The two periods, despite appearances to the contrary, were on a positive continuum. The attempt to build humane socialism was now being reinforced by the dignified – and successful – resistance to the invasion. The reform policies and their underlying principles remained intact, and no police state had been installed. Everybody should cheer up. Those who had fled the country, or who remained abroad after the invasion, should return. 'People who are today falling into depression and defeatism,' he wrote, 'who are commenting that there is an absence of guarantees, that everything could end badly, that we might again slide into a marasmus of censorship and trials, that this or that might happen, are simply weak people, who know how to live only in the illusions of certainty.'

Writing in February 1969, Havel strongly objected to Kundera's view that things weren't so bad. It rested upon the mythopoeic presumption that the small nation of Czechs was fated to be the creator of big values, not a nation of exploiters. Kundera's position, he argued, exuded a form of typically Czech passive patriotism that served to rationalize away a disaster as a moral victory. It also suffered from a typically nostalgic form of Czech myopia, argued Havel. It was easy to celebrate imagined past glories – imagining 'how good we were before August and how marvellous we were in August (when those bad guys came to get us)' – all the while forgetting about present–day needs. Kundera could accuse him of 'moral exhibitionism'. He could insinuate that Havel was suffering from the 'illness of people anxious to prove their integrity'. Yet the harsh reality was that there was now an urgent need 'to examine what we are like now, who among us is still good and who not at all, and what must be done so that we are true to our previously earned merits'.

[1]Milan Kundera, 'Český úděl', *Listy*, volume 1, numbers 7–8. (19 December 1968), pp. 1, 5. Havel's reply, 'Český úděl?' *Tvář*, 2 (1969), pp. 30–33, is printed in Václav Havel, *O lidskou identitu* (London, 1984), pp. 195–196. Kundera's reply to Havel, 'Radikalismus a exihibicionismus', appeared in *Host do domu*, volume 15 (1969), number 15, pp. 24–29, and was reprinted in *Svědectví*, 74 (1985), pp. 343–349. The two writers subsequently made amends. See Kundera's homage to Havel, 'A Life Like a Work of Art', *The New Republic*, 202 (29 January 1990), pp. 16–17, and Milan Kundera's letter to Havel, 24 October 1986.

The defiant tone of Havel's remarks was foreshadowed a few weeks earlier in tough replies to the questions put by a journalist from *Svět v obrazech* (The World in Pictures).[1] He criticized the current government's reassurances that the 'springtime of politics' would mature into summer, despite the arrival of thousands of Warsaw Pact troops. He noted that the government's talk of democratizing the system was contradicted by the reintroduction of censorship. He said he feared that the ethos of the springtime was suffering liquidation, and that therefore stiff civic resistance was required. In a democracy, said Havel, the aim of citizens should be to 'make life more complicated for its government' by expressing their opinions openly about its aims, methods, and policies. 'I am for democracy,' he said in the old spirit of Dobříš, 'and so I am also for a maximum amount of freedom of information, because such freedom is the first condition of democracy: in order that people truly keep tabs on their government and influence it, they must perforce know what the government is doing and why, and they must have the right to express themselves freely about what it does.' Havel said he intended to use responsibly to the full the existing freedoms. He was currently working with Jan Němec on a screenplay on the theme of the swindling of 'ordinary people' by 'the international establishment'. He also reported that he was sketching a new play called *The Wedding* (*Svatba*). It was to be a portrait of a convivial wedding reception. At one point during the celebration, one of the newlyweds' relatives suddenly interrupts the chatting and laughter with a straightforward burst of honesty about the marriage. The relative is pounced upon and beaten up by her husband. Nobody comes to her rescue. Everybody feels sorry for her. But then she falls silent, and everybody resumes their feast of small talk, sprinkled with laughter.

The Wedding ended up in the dustbin. A script written with Jan Němec and called *Heart Beat*, about the international mafia trade in human hearts, went unfilmed. Under the weight of military occupation, Havel instead wrote the dark and depressing play *The Conspirators* (*Spiklenci*). It proved not to be among his favourites. He later complained, harshly, that it was the first of his plays to be 'forbidden', that it had been conceived in times suffering from

---

[1]See the interview conducted by Jiří Nožka, 'What He's Thinking About', *Svět v obrazech*, 48 (14 December 1968), reprinted in ibid., 1 (5 January 1990), pp. 4–5.

'lack of air and senselessness', and that the play consequently felt (to him) 'lifeless, over-organized, bloodless, lacking humour as well as mystery'. It resembled 'a cake that has been left in the oven too long and has completely dried out'.[1] Posterity may draw that same conclusion. Yet *The Conspirators* reveals – in fifteen precisely structured scenes – Havel's ongoing preoccupation with the subject of political power, and its corrupting effects. A revolution erupts. Student demonstrators in Concord Square call for freedom and justice, above all for the immediate release of a political prisoner, Alfred Stein, an individual loved for his honesty, his passion for philosophy, his desire to live quietly with his cat. Public joy floods through the streets of the capital. Cries of 'Long live the revolution!' signal the end of the bloody despotism of Olah. But behind the scenes, four conspirators set to work. Parroting slogans like 'Freedom and Democracy!', warning of the 'evils of anarchy' and the need for 'unifying action', they jostle for control over the revolution. Like swine before slop, their greed before power proves limitless. Two conspirators – the weakling Commander-in-Chief of the Armed Forces, and the Chief Censor Aram, an idiot who can only think after denouncing others – are quickly shoved out of the way. That leaves two figures locked in a Hobbesian struggle for state power: Chief Prosecutor Dykl and Chief of Police Moher. As menacing crowds gather in Concord Square, this time to demand the return of the exiled despot Olah, the much-loved political prisoner, who has been tortured into making diametrically opposed confessions of guilt, commits suicide in his cell. The two conspirators try to outmanoeuvre each other, without success. Incapable of absolute victory, they end their struggle in stalemate. So Chief of Police Moher gets to the point. 'My friends, let us finally stop beating about the bush! After all, everyone knows that one man is capable of establishing order here, to return the nation to the path of disciplined work . . . and a future of genuine freedom and democracy.' He continues, in twisted logic: 'Seriously, my friends: if we do not want the leadership qualities of this man to be misused against the people, why could we not also use them for the benefit of the people?' The soliloquy is interrupted by a phone call from Monte Carlo. The curtain falls – with the Chief of Police striding towards the

---

[1] Václav Havel, 'Dovětek autora', *Hry 1970–1976* (Toronto, 1977), p. 307.

telephone, to invite back the despot to take charge of the new revolution.

Legislative Measure Number 99/1969 turned *The Conspirators* into a 'forbidden' work. On the late afternoon of 22 August 1969, as street battles raged in several cities, especially in Brno, the Presidium of the Federal Assembly passed legislation by this name. It was presented by Gustáv Husák and signed by three of the principal proponents of the Prague Spring, including Alexander Dubček, who later claimed (typically) that he did so only because he had his arm twisted.[1] Passed in the absence of the Federal Asembly, Legislative Measure 99/1969 in effect cleared the way for a permanent state of emergency. It provided for steep fines and imprisonment for those involved in public disturbances. Crimes of a political nature, including defamation either of the Republic and its representatives or of any state in the international socialist system and its representatives, were from here on punishable with increased sentences. Criminal proceedings related to political violations were to be expedited: pre-trial proceedings were scrapped, one-man tribunals were introduced, the right to defence was limited, and the maximum period of detention without trial was extended from forty-eight hours to three weeks. The legislation also took aim at trade unions and other (potential) civil associations by restricting or disbanding volunteer and other organizations. And it prepared the way, within such bodies as schools, universities, theatres, the academies of science, and the state ministries, for mass purges of 'untrustworthy' individuals suspected of having 'disturbed the socialist social order'.

Born of street protests crushed by water cannon, truncheons and firearms, Legislative Measure 99/1969 contained the basic elements of the late-socialist regime of power all Czechs and Slovaks would have to live with for the next twenty years. Late-socialism admittedly had older roots – traceable to the Bolshevik Revolution, and deeper still to the practice of party discipline, the calculated use of promotions, demotions and expulsions, and the life-and-death struggles for organizational control within the oppositional socialist parties of the nineteenth and early twentieth

[1] Oldřich Tůma, 'Dubček and Legislative Measure No. 99', paper presented to the One Day Colloquium on Alexander Dubček, held at the Slovak Embassy, London, 7 November 1998.

centuries. Late-socialism – as Havel himself was to point out – also preserved certain characteristics from the regime built from the *coup de Prague*. But the type of state that was born of the military invasion was nevertheless a new and distinctive system of power. Although the Communist Party continued to rely ultimately upon government by fear and brutal repression, it did so in considerably more anonymous, selective and calculated form. Violence was from here on 'targeted' against the unlucky few who 'disrespected public officials' or engaged in 'acts against the Republic'. Big show trials became a thing of the past. The Party's utter disregard for efficiency, characteristic of the delirium of the Stalin period, was also abandoned. Especially in matters of administration and production, much emphasis was given to innovation, productivity and the need for permanent reform. There were novelties as well in the field of communications. While the Party still attempted to contain everything that was said within an ideological tent of words and images covering the past, present and future worlds, almost nobody – probably not even senior Party apparatchiks – believed any longer in their pantomime of ritualized claims. Finally, the late-socialist regime abandoned the old totalitarian formula, *L'état, c'est nous*. The state no longer strived to control fully the bodies and souls of its subjects, to embrace everything in depth, to magnetize everyone so as to produce a single will, focused upon the Great Leader. Late-socialism was instead largely content with the regulation and control of *apparent* behaviour. So long as its subjects forgot the past, quietly conformed and merely grumbled among themselves, they were probably safe.

To this list of novelties of late-socialism should be added another: the painful disruption caused to many Czechs and Slovaks during the drastic transition to late-socialism during the years 1969–1971. Among the paradoxes of late-socialism was the fact that it was able to tolerate the quiet conformity of its subjects only after it had rummaged through their personal and working lives to an unprecedented degree. In the name of eliminating 'right-wing' and 'anti-socialist' forces, a mass purge of the population was carried out. The Communist Party of Czechoslovakia was designated as the major force of cleansing and regeneration, but the key problem was that the Party was internally divided, with a clear majority of its members and officials opposed to winding back the political clock. So the Party had to be rebuilt – around what was called the 'sound core' of Communist officials and members who believed that the most dangerous enemy was to be found within its own ranks.

The scale of the autumn cleaning was inversely proportional to the defeats inflicted on Party unity in the spring years. During the two-year period following Legislative Measure 99/1969, at least three-quarters of a million citizens of the country, or about 2 million people if their households are included, lost their jobs or were demoted or seriously discriminated against – rarely with a punch in the mouth, usually with a frown or a warning, and quite often over a cup of coffee, or with a smile or a shrug of the shoulders, or a handshake from the perpetrators. The 'civilized violence' of the purges was felt in every nook and cranny of the regime.[1] Far-reaching changes in the supreme legislative bodies were enforced. Three-quarters of the ministers and all of the premiers (including Dubček) of the federal and two national (i.e., Czech and Slovak) governments were dismissed. The same proportion of leading diplomats was replaced. The entire top team at the Czechoslovak General Prosecutor's Office was sacked. There were sweeping changes as well in the field of production and commerce. The whole management of the major banks – the State Bank and the Commercial Bank – was removed. More than two-thirds of directors of national enterprises and foreign trade corporations were dismissed. More than a third of a million management officials were screened at least once, while workers' councils, which had sprung up during the Prague Spring, were entirely liquidated. 'Normalization' in the trade unions meanwhile meant the total reorganization of their committees and councils and the dismissal of 125,000 officials. In the field of education the story was much the same. Hundreds of headmasters and their deputies and thousands of teachers at the secondary and primary levels were dismissed or removed to more remote localities and disqualified from teaching political subjects. The Union of University Students was liquidated. Some 2,000 university teachers were forced out of their posts.

The purges were especially harsh in the field of media and cultural policy. Most film and television directors, actors, camera-men, music-hall artists, script-writers, painters and sculptors were

---

[1] The following details are drawn from Karel Kaplan, *Political Persecution in Czechoslovakia 1948–1972* (Köln, 1983), especially pp. 27–40; Milan Šimečka, *Obnovení pořádku* (samizdat, 1978, and Köln, 1979).

screened and re-screened and then forced on to a long-term treadmill of persecution. 475 of the 590 members of the Czech Writers' Union were removed, while 130 writers, among them Havel, were put on the blacklist and had their earlier editions removed from public libraries. The entire management and senior editorial staff of television, radio and the news agency were booted out. Out of forty influential dailies and weeklies, thirty-seven editors were replaced. Nearly 40 per cent of all journalists were forced to resign, their jobs being filled especially by young people lured by increased salaries. The autumn purges also extended into the mass 'front' organizations which functioned like flesh on the bones of the Party. The changes were especially harsh within those front organizations considered strategically vital, such as the peace committees, the Association for Co-operation with the Army, and the organizations of youth, women, and co-operative farmers. But even the 'non-political' organizations suffered. Sackings, warnings and demotions were commonplace in such bodies as sporting clubs, the Red Cross, local fire brigades, and associations of huntsmen and beekeepers.

The fear and disruption produced by the purges was well worth it. Late-socialism became renowned world-wide as a system of state power structured by the grey and dreary principle of the leading role of the Party. Under late-socialist conditions, the Party was sovereign – it was the central nervous system of the political order, so that all important powers of making and administering decisions were concentrated in its hands. The Party organization itself was pyramid-shaped. All Party members were formally equal, but the upper echelons – the senior nomenklatura – were definitely more equal than the rest. Having carefully climbed the ladders of power within the Party, they enjoyed wide-ranging privileges, including a special kind of non-monetary wealth attached to their leadership roles.

The sovereign powers of the ruling group within the Party ran wide and deep. Leading members of the Party chose the Party membership, and also structured the outcomes of the Party Congress. Constitutional changes had to be approved by the Party leadership before going through the mere formality of acceptance by the Party-dominated parliamentary bodies. The Party executive suppressed market mechanisms by monopolizing key decisions concerning investment, production and consumption.

In matters of law, court decisions were also supervised closely by the Party executive, especially in sensitive cases, when the courts functioned as executive bodies. The army and police and secret police – the beating heart of the Party, Czechs said – were also supervised closely by the Party leadership, even with direct assistance of their Party-controlled Soviet counterparts. In the field of communications media, the hand of the Party leadership was omnipresent as well. The Party sought to entomb the whole population within an ideological pyramid of clichéd and often bizarre language. 'Socialism is a young, dynamic social order,' said Gustáv Husák at one point, typically, 'which is seeking and testing in its stride ways of making even better use of its advantages, of organizing and controlling social development most efficiently.'[1]

The monopoly powers of the Party leadership in matters of state policy-making and administration, production and consumption, communications, law and policing led unavoidably to arbitrary decision-making. It also produced a constant widening of the discretionary powers of the Party authorities. The line of the Party leadership was always correct – even when it contradicted itself, or changed course markedly. The Party had a sibylline quality. It represented itself as wise and omniscient. Its 'scientific' pronouncements were presumed to be incontrovertible, even if onlookers often found them mysterious, confused, unfathomable. The standpoint of the Party, especially its leadership, seemed synonymous with life itself.

The overall function of the Party and its leading echelons was to determine the substantive aims and formal methods to be followed by all subsidiary organizations and personnel. The upper layers of the Party aimed to penetrate, strictly subordinate and centrally unify the vast labyrinth of state ministries, which perforce had distinct chains of bureaucratic command, interact with each other at various levels, and develop and defend (partially) divergent interests. In this task of centrally co-ordinating and synthesizing the various state bureaucracies, the sovereign Party leadership was reinforced by a complex network of subordinate Party structures – trade unions, youth and women's and writers' organizations, for instance – staffed by middle- and lower-level Party members.

[1] Gustáv Husák, 'May Day Speech', in *Information Bulletin of the Central Committee of the Communist Party of Czechoslovakia*, 4 (Prague, 1984), p. 9.

The task of these ancillary Party organizations was to enforce the primary objectives of the ruling pinnacle of the Party and, thereby, to monitor, regulate and discipline each and every organization within the political order.

Their function was also to keep the Party's firm grip on each and every individual citizen. Since proportionately few citizens were Party members, the vast majority of the population were considered second-class citizens. The life chances of a young person who refused to join the Party, for instance, were extremely limited, for she or he in effect refused to accept the principle that only Party members can and should govern. That person also refused to acknowledge the converse of this principle: that the programmes and actions of the Party were always binding upon its individual subjects, who therefore had to be prevented systematically from developing alternative policies, organizations and forms of expression in matters of politics, production and culture. These policy areas were deemed the exclusive prerogative of the Party, its ministries and ancillary organizations. Their goal was 'socialism' – meaning unchallenged rule, the complete sub-ordination and incorporation of all individuals into the crystalline structures of the Party-dominated state. The vast majority of the citizenry of late-socialist regimes had no say at all – not even legally – in the decisive question of who would rule them. This question was always answered in advance. Since the Party was always right, even retroactively, it was obliged to lead, limit and teach its citizens. The one-party system of late-socialism was in this precise sense totalitarian: democratic pluralism was outlawed.

Under the conditions of post-Stalinism, in other words, the citizens of late-socialism were expected to join what Havel's friend Ivan Klíma called the 'community of the defeated', and to abide by its basic rules: that there would only ever be one governing party, to which everything, including truth itself, belonged; that the world was divided into enemies and friends of the Party and, accordingly, that compliance with Party policies was rewarded, dissent penalized; and, finally, that the Party no longer required the complete devotion of its subjects, only the quiet acceptance of its dictates. This meant that the Party emphasized discipline, caution, respectability, self-censorship, resignation, and moral flaccidity among its subjects ('far better not to know and not to think'). Conversely, the Party feared and actively discouraged independence of mind and judgement, excellence, boldness, perspicacity, courage, public commitment to democratic principles and the pagan mistrust of official jargon and bureaucratic regulations.

These basic unwritten rules of late-socialism implied that no subject was ever fully innocent before the Party apparatus. In effect, this apparatus subjected each individual to a form of permanent internment. Life was made to feel like one big grey dreary depressing prison. And since the Party was always right about everything, even retroactively, those individuals who ceased to be humble and obedient Party followers were automatically considered to be its deserters and, therefore, enemies of socialism. Citizen opposition to the Party was always regarded by its top echelons as 'decadent' and seditious, which is why the (potential) opponents of the Party were to be found not only among intellectuals like Havel, but also in every pub, café, street queue, factory, church and theatre.

BEGGARS' OPERA

A tall man with a menacing face stepped front stage from behind the drawn curtain. Artfully, in slow motion, he lit a cigarette, which glowed brightly in the darkness of the makeshift theatre. The invited audience of 300 people – painters, writers, actors, relatives, even Havel's ageing father – stilled. The speechless man carefully aimed a smoke ring in their direction, then began eyeing them defiantly. Nobody laughed. Nobody smiled. The man's face began slowly to resemble that of a psychopath. He stared coldly at each person below and beyond the stage, beginning with the first row and working his way gradually sideways and backwards, one person at a time. There followed a second puff of smoke, accompanied this time by menacing glances directed like darts at every single member of the audience in the middle distance. By the time the third smoke ring circled overhead, everybody present had the feeling that something was amiss. It seemed that trouble had entered the theatre – even that they might well each have to pay a heavy price for choosing that night to drive to Horní Počernice, on the outskirts of east Prague, and to huddle, nervous and sweating, in a pub restaurant called U Čelikovských, whose biggest room had been converted into a theatre sealed off with mattresses to hamper police entry and to muffle the roar of scruffy drunks in the adjoining bar.

The man completed his sinister inspection, then slipped silently behind the curtain. Time seemed to stop, as if fate's turn had now come. The hearts of the audience thumped. Their brows sweated, their bottoms remained riveted to the creaky chairs. The tense atmosphere was toughened by the knowledge, shared by actors and audience alike, of just how dangerous the whole performance was. The play that was about to be performed had originally been written three years earlier, in 1972, for the Činoherní klub in Prague, but the crackdown after the Prague Spring had prevented its performance. Havel's next-door neighbour at Hrádeček, the actor and director Andrej Krob – the man with the sinister face – proposed doing it by subterfuge. Havel agreed, and Krob set about pulling together a makeshift troupe of actors and stage-hands, who spent the next eighteen months rehearsing. So as not to be caught by the StB, the performers – Jan Kašpar, Lída Michalová, Jana Tůmová, Viktor Spousta among them – moved around from apartment to apartment. Krob, one of those figures who lived life seriously without taking it seriously, proved demanding. He always said, like Molière, that he'd like to die on stage.

Others regarded his despotic intensity with trepidation. 'As a person, he's wonderful,' remarked Kašpar, 'but as a director he's awful.' Lída Michalová also found him 'terrible, intolerant, selfish'.[1] Personalities aside, nobody really thought that a performance was possible, but everybody battled on, trying to improve the dialogue and to perfect the blocking and rhythm. A rehearsal was brought to Hrádeček, and soon after Havel wrote to Krob with his criticisms and advice: 'You have chosen one of the most difficult plays,' he reflected. 'Every sentence must be precise; it must have an exact meaning. It may not be important in some realist-psychological play if Nora says to Ingrid "You are evil", "You are cruel", or "Ingrid, you piss me off". But here, the whole effect stands and falls on language, its exactness, the logic of its syntax, its melody and rhythm. Every word is important, no word can be omitted or altered. If you do, the situation immediately loses its spark and becomes just a story.' Havel added a paragraph of warm praise. 'Regardless of whether you get through to the end and what the outcome is, I think it's great that you are searching together for something, that you are able to find time and energy for something which is burdensome and will not bring you any profit. It seems to me that it is something unique, good and meaningful in today's earth-bound world.'[2]

Havel and his old theatre friend Jan Grossman came to see the dress rehearsal. The two masters of contemporary Czech theatre gave their seal of approval, and young bearded Viktor Spousta, who was to play a lead role in the play, set about finding a place for the performance. It had to be accessible to the audience but inaccessible to the police. U Čelikovských, the pub restaurant in Horní Počernice, seemed perfect. Costs were covered by selling a limited number of tickets. Havel, hitherto bewildered, grew excited. He was about to see the only one of his plays ever to be performed under late-socialist conditions. Others doubted that it would happen. An hour before the performance was due to start, only a handful of relatives had taken their seats. Everybody presumed the worst: that the StB

[1] Quoted from the documentary film by Olga Sommerová, *A znovu Žebrácká opera* (*Beggar's Opera Revisited*), Česká televize 1 (Prague, 1996).
[2] Cited in *Divadlo na tahu: 1975–1995* (Prague, 1996), pp. 16, 14.

had got wind of the event and had already begun roadblocks and arrests.

A chink of light, then a curtain suddenly opening to reveal a stage, costumed actors, a table, chairs, movement, expression, and words. Catharsis: the first and only performance of *The Beggar's Opera* had begun. For the next two hours, the audience grinned, laughed and clapped its way through Havel's adaptation of John Gay's early eighteenth-century musical play. Through his anglophile friend and literary scholar, Zdeněk Urbánek, Havel had discovered some years earlier Gay's work, whose central character is Captain Macheath, a highwayman and lighthearted winner of women's hearts. Macheath falls in love and marries Polly, but her father, a receiver of stolen goods who also makes a living by informing on his clients, is not pleased. Furious at her folly, he decides to spoil the marriage by grassing on Macheath, with the aim of elevating his daughter into the 'comfortable estate of widowhood'. Macheath is arrested and sent to Newgate prison, where, awaiting execution, he manages to conquer the heart of a woman named Lucy. Polly and Lucy subsequently do battle for the affection of the swashbuckling Macheath, who shows no remorse ('How happy could I be with either, Were t'other dear charmer away!') as he makes his escape from prison.

Havel's emplotment of *The Beggar's Opera* runs a different course. There is no music and no singing – the opera form is stripped bare – and no happy or charming endings. It is nonetheless a comic treatment of a world in which each individual cheats on every other individual. Even the notion of honour among thieves is exposed as romantic nonsense. Everybody behaves selfishly. Selfishness is 'reality', and there appears to be no alternative but to act 'realistically', which means accepting that the system encourages and depends upon chronic lying, double-crossing, back-stabbing, trickery, the greedy pursuit of self-interest as it is defined at that particular moment. To act in contrary ways, for instance to embrace precepts like honesty or care for others, would amount to pure foolishness that would then simply play into the hands of others. In any event, acting according to those old-fashioned precepts doesn't occur to anybody. Individuals' power to act on the world has been reduced to pure manipulation and self-manipulation. Moral thinking as such, the habit of examining people and events in terms of means and ends, has disappeared. The small evils of knavery have become utterly banal. Language itself is corrupted. Sentences are no longer means of communication. Words have become mere tools of manipulation.

William Peachum, the boss of a thieves' network, is locked in battle with Macheath, the chief crook of a competing crime syndicate. Peachum tries everything to outsmart his rival. He is naturally delighted at the news that his daughter Polly has secretly been having an affair with Macheath. Peachum has plans for her. He also manages to recruit Harry Filch, a freelance pickpocket and former employee of Macheath. Peachum does business as well with Madame Diana, who runs an up-market brothel. She needs precious objects like silver cutlery, a few candelabras, and a few yards of brocade for some new curtains, and in return offers to supply Peachum with one of her best girls. Mrs Peachum agrees that her husband, in order to outcompete the swashbuckling Macheath, needs to improve his ways with women. For Macheath has a superior reputation in this field. He is renowned as a powerful desperado, a *bon vivant*, a physically attractive man of gall and charm and seduction. His formula for success is simple: his strategy with women is to simulate an inferiority complex because (he says) 'women love to help someone and to save someone'. Macheath, who likes to calculate gains and losses, admits that things are a bit more complex than that. Inexperienced 'nice' women, for instance, are exciting to seduce and they offer their services free. But, lacking erotic experience, they are seldom physically satisfying and, besides, their seduction sometimes takes up precious time that could be better spent making money. They also have a nasty habit of falling in love. So, Macheath reasons, prostitutes are a better bargain. 'Agreement is quick,' he says, 'shame does not prevent them from co-operating with any of your desires. And the act itself does not complicate your life with their feelings or demands.' If for any reason a prostitute does try to cling on, he concludes, getting rid of her is simple. 'Either behave towards such a person so despicably that her lingering dignity prevents her from maintaining an interest . . . Or the second possibility is simply to marry her.'

Macheath speaks from experience. It transpires that he is a bigamist and is already married to Polly, Peachum's daughter.

When he finds that out, Peachum instructs her to become his secret agent inside Macheath's organization – with the aim of liquidating it. The same thought occurs to Macheath, who soon receives a visit from Polly, who betrays her father's trust by confessing to her husband that her father is preparing a plan that will send him to the scaffold. Macheath no sooner berates her for not uncovering the precise details of his fate than he is lured into the arms of an old lover who now works at Madame Diana's establishment. The prostitute cries rape, Macheath is arrested by the police, and promptly carted off to prison. Peachum's plan has worked – with the help of the Chief of Police, Lockit.

The Chief of Police is a calculating knave and although working for Peachum tries to recruit Macheath into his own network of crime-fighting criminals. Lockit is unaware that his daughter Lucy is married to Macheath, whom she helps to escape with a hacksaw. But Macheath doesn't last long on the outside. He is arrested in Madame Diana's establishment while hiding out there, but a worse fate follows. His two wives finally catch up with him. He tries to rescue his reputation with oratory. 'No, girls, if I was to best fulfil my responsibility towards you,' he says, reminding them that in hours he might be on the scaffold, 'I could not follow other men in this matter, but had to follow my own path, maybe untrodden, but decidedly more moral – that is, the path which gives you equally the same measure of legitimacy and dignity.' On goes the duplicity. On and on. Lockit has Filch arrested and executed after he refuses to co-operate with the racketeering of the police. The key characters – Madame Diana, Peachum, Lockit, Macheath – resort ever more to clichés. So does the sleeping drunk who, appearing in several scenes, rouses himself to shout, 'Long live freedom of the press!' The amorality and bowdlerization of language intensifies. Peachum at one point protests against the whole trend. 'Do you at all understand what it is to wear two faces for such a long time, to live two lives, to think in two ways, from morning till night to guard oneself, to masquerade, to conceal some things and pretend others, to adapt yourself constantly to the world which you condemn and forswear the world to which you really belong?' Fine words – but he too eventually succumbs to the universal corruption, and in a most spectacular way. He proposes to the Chief of Police the formation of a new crime cartel. It is accepted by Macheath, in writing. Lockit is ecstatic.

'From this moment on, our organization controls practically all of the underworld,' he declares. The Chief of Police has finally become the chief swindler-in-charge – and nobody else knows, even though everybody serves him.

CHARTER 77

The miserable ending of *The Beggar's Opera* posed a funda-mental political question: How is it all possible to keep alive personal integrity in a world that pays no dues to the fine points of humanity? Andrej Krob, the director who played the role of Chief of Police Lockit, had an answer. He admitted that he was thrown forwards and upwards by the performance of *The Beggar's Opera*, despite all the technical hitches. 'For me it was a mess of fuck-ups – curtains opened poorly, slips of the tongue, sweating faces. But with the passage of time, I realize it wasn't a matter of a theatrical performance at all, but of something that managed to happen under absolutely incredible circumstances.'[1] Everybody who was there thought it a happening. Havel certainly felt triumphant. At the party after the performance, held at U Medvídků, a restaurant just around the corner from Prague's police headquarters on Bartolomějská Street, he told the troupe that the performance had brought him more personal joy than any of the foreign premières of his plays, 'from New York to Tokyo'.[2]

All hell broke loose when the surprise news of the performance reached the authorities. They went on the warpath to ensure that the one performance (as Krob put it) was the première and dernière.[3] Havel was brought in for questioning. Dozens of other interrogations took place. Ministry of Culture bureaucrats spread the word that there would be a tightening of policy towards the theatres, and that Havel should be blamed for the setback. The threats worked in some parts of the theatre world. 'Many a shallow-minded actor fell for it,' reported Havel later, 'and got very upset with me and my amateur actors for frustrating their artistic ambition, by which, of course, they meant their well-paid sprints from job to job – in dubbing, theatre, television, and film – that is, from one centre for befuddling the public to another. But that wasn't the point.'[4] The point was that the success of *The Beggar's Opera* encouraged Havel to go further. His boldly worded open letter to Husák, which was circulated underground, published abroad and broadcast back into Prague by Western radio stations, several of which likened Havel to Alexander Solzhenitsyn,

[1] Cited in Eda Kriseová, *Václav Havel: The Authorized Biography* (New York, 1993), p. 93.
[2] *Disturbing the Peace*, op. cit., p. 125.
[3] From the documentary film by Karel Prokop, *Z Dramatika prezidentem*, Česká televize 2 (Prague, 1995).
[4] *Disturbing the Peace*, op. cit., p. 125.

had also persuaded him a few months earlier that forms of resistance to late-socialism might be possible.[1] Around the same time, the completion of the one-act play *Audience* had a similar effect, even though it was not performed. But *The Beggar's Opera* had a special impact. After a seven-year interruption, it made him see with his own blue eyes that he could still write performable plays. It convinced him that he was not burned out. It gave him courage, and made him feel that he had energy for further projects.

Just around the corner, although he didn't yet know it, was the biggest and most important project of his life so far. Its beginning resembled the climax of a cheap television police drama. A rusted-out getaway white Saab, stuffed with boxes of sealed envelopes and documents and three scruffy men bound for the Federal Assembly building in central Prague, was chased into the district of Dejvice. It was then trapped in a railway underpass by a squad of police cars, screaming sirens, bright-orange lights flashing in the gloom of midday winter darkness. There was a squeal of tyres and the slamming of doors. Then followed sounds of scuffling bodies and scraping feet – the sounds of the three conspirators, the playwright-driver Pavel Landovský and his two passengers, Ludvík Vaculík and Václav Havel. The men were promptly bundled at gunpoint into separate patrol cars before setting off at high speed to police headquarters on Bartolomějská Street.

The authorities' arrest and all-night interrogation of Havel and his colleagues and the confiscation and careful inspection of their booty – which included a three-page document that was immediately stamped, in red ink, POZOR: DAKTYLOSKOPICKÝ MATERIÁL! NEVYJÍMAT Z OCHRANNÝCH OBALŮ (Caution: fingerprint material! Do not remove from the protective wrappers) – failed to suppress the story. Next morning, 7 January 1977, the day on which Havel was rearrested for a second round of questioning, the whole world awoke to hear the extraordinary news that a petition with the simple title of Charter 77 had been launched in Prague by several hundred prominent 'Czechoslovak dissidents'. The story was in the front section of newspapers like *Le Monde*, the *Frankfurter Allgemeine Zeitung* (which published the text in full), and *The Times* of London, which described the document as 'not the work of a Machiavellian secret policeman concocting evidence against

---

[1] Václav Havel, 'Dear Dr Husák', in *Open Letters*, op. cit., pp. 50–83.

dissident intellectuals', but 'a remarkable gesture of courage' signed by 'the flowers of the Czechoslovak intelligentsia', including 'Mr Václav Havel, a prominent playwright.'[1] The document was headlined by the Voice of America, and mentioned by tens of thousands of radio and television programmes scattered around the world.

The text of the appeal was short, and easy to report accurately. Charter 77 pointed to the discrepancy between law and reality in socialist Czechoslovakia. At the 1975 gathering of state representatives in Helsinki, it claimed, the Czechoslovak political authorities had signed up to both the International Covenant on Civil and Political Rights and the International Covenant on Economic, Social and Cultural Rights. Those covenants, Charter 77 pointed out, had come into force during the past year (23 March 1976), and were now in effect binding upon both the Czechoslovak Socialist Republic and its citizens. This constitutional change was to be welcomed, it said. The human rights and freedoms underwritten by these covenants were preconditions of a 'civilized life' and 'the development of a humane society' in which the exercise of power is publicly controlled. But – here the Charter used the intellectual strategy of immanently criticizing reality, using the law as an Archimedean lever against state power – these 'basic rights in our country exist, regrettably, on paper only'.

According to the Charter, tens of thousands of citizens were denied the right of free public expression and were victimized by a system of 'virtual apartheid' administered by the dominant Party, which harassed and discriminated against them simply because they held views that were out of step with those of the authorities. Hundreds of thousands of other citizens were denied the right to live in freedom from fear. Many young people were prevented from studying because of their, or their parents', views. Workers and others were unable to protect their interests through the unrestricted right to form trade unions and other organizations. The legally guaranteed right of free religious expression was systematically curtailed by various methods, ranging from direct interference with the activities of believers to constraints on

---

[1] See 'Une centaine de personnalités se réclament la garantie des exercices des droits fondamentaux', *Le Monde* (Paris), 7 January 1977, p. 3; *Frankfurter Allgemeine Zeitung* (Frankfurt), 7 January 1977, p. 5, which refers to 'the non-Party playwright Václav Havel'; and 'Manifesto Challenge by Prague Dissidents', *The Times* (London), 7 January 1977, pp. 1, 4.

religious training. The centralized control of communications media meant that 'no open criticism can be made of abnormal social phenomena', or of false accusations or unjust and illegal prosecutions. The freedom of movement of citizens to and fro across Czechoslovak borders was consistently violated, for instance through the biased system of granting entry and exit permits. The freedom of citizens from 'arbitrary interference with privacy, family, home or correspondence' was daily undermined by bugging telephones and houses, opening mail, house searches, and shadowing suspects. And networks of neighbourhood informers, often using illicit threats and promises, added to the pressures of daily harassment.

The Charter's allegations were serious. The Czechoslovak Socialist Republic, supposedly on the road to a free and classless society, was in effect a lawless Leviathan, whose subjects were permanently held hostage by an unchecked Party–state apparatus. It admitted that the responsibility for maintaining civil and human rights ultimately rested with the political authorities. But the Charter insisted that citizenship – the entitlement of all individuals to enjoy certain rights and to observe certain duties within a political community – also required the vigilance of the citizenry. Those who exercise power over others cannot be expected to exercise power over themselves. Within any state, the saplings of liberty must be watered constantly with the independent efforts of its citizens. 'It is this sense of co-responsibility,' it said, 'our belief in the meaning of voluntary citizens' involvement and the general need to give it new and more effective expression, that led us to the idea of creating Charter 77, whose inception we today publicly announce.' It went on to emphasize that Charter 77 was *not* to be understood as a revolutionary organization planning and plotting to seize state power, by cunning or strength. Charter 77 would instead aim to function as a citizens' initiative. It had been formed out of like-minded circles of friends and acquaintances, many of whom had been shaken by the recent trial of the rock band called the Plastic People of the Universe. The Charter comprised people who from here on were concerned to work for 'the general public interest'. The Charter was not an organization. And it was not – as Havel had argued successfully during the drafting process – a committee that would function as something like the Czechoslovak sister group of the Helsinki Human Rights

Group recently established in Moscow. The new initiative had no rules, permanent organization or formal membership. Charter 77 – the following words drafted by Havel would quickly become world-famous – was best considered as 'a free, informal, open community of people of different convictions, different faiths and different professions united by the will to strive, individually and collectively, for the respect of civic and human rights in our own country and throughout the world'.

The timing of the launch of the Charter during the first week of January 1977 had been carefully devised. Nine years earlier – Havel felt it to be a lifetime – the Prague Spring had begun in the month of January. It was also the start of the year proclaimed as the Year of Political Prisoners, and in a few months a potentially important conference was to be held in Belgrade to review the implementation of the obligations assumed by Czechoslovakia and other states at the Helsinki Conference on Security and Co-operation in Europe. Then there was the practical consideration that the last-minute tweaking of the document and its circulation among potential signatories was best done during the Christmas/New Year break, when cold weather, gathered families, and merry-making, even within the ranks of the secret police, made it easier to slip through the nets of state surveillance.

The schedule for finalizing the text, collecting signatures, and dealing with other remaining matters was tailored accordingly. Havel, who wrote the first draft of the declaration, worked closely with Zdeněk Mlynář to produce a redrafted version. The playwright Pavel Kohout thought up the name Charter 77. The threesome decided that the text should be anonymous. 'It didn't seem appropriate to emphasize authorship,' Havel later said, 'not because it would have been too dangerous, but because after all everyone was responsible for the Charter by signing it.'[1] Two handfuls of people, co-ordinated by Havel, did the rounds in search of potential signatories. Considering the restrictions imposed by time and secret police, the response was good, although unevenly distributed. 243 signatures were collected, of whom nearly 90 per cent were from Prague, with only 1 (Dominik Tatarka) from Slovakia, 1 from northern Moravia, and

---

[1] *Charta 77: Začátky*, part one of a two-part documentary produced by Česká televize 2 (Prague, 1996).

17 from Brno. The collection point was the Havels' embankment flat. There the signatures were put in alphabetical order, Bohemian champagne drunk and, at a meeting that followed, Havel was elected ring-leader of the two other first spokesmen, Jiří Hájek, Dubček's Foreign Minister in 1968, and Professor Jan Patočka, the country's leading philosopher.

So the struggle with the authorities began. It has been said that the petition 'generated a vibrant response in a country still deep in the slough of despondency resulting from the invasion in August 1968'.[1] Despondency was certainly widespread, but since there was no freely accessible public sphere in existence and, hence, no public opinion, it is impossible to say just how many Czechs and Slovaks knew about the Charter or, if they did, what were their reactions around meal tables, in pubs, or at work. Having launched a life-raft upon an eerie sea of silence, Havel and the other signatories could only ask themselves whether (as the best contemporary Czech historian put it at the time) the Charter would prove to be a catalyst of 'a new national and democratic revival [*obrození*]' comparable to the early nineteenth-century renaissance that ended a long period of darkness (*temno*), or whether the civic initiative would be stillborn, leaving despair and misery untouched rulers of the people's hearts.[2]

It was too early to tell, but the positive reaction of the world's press certainly buoyed the spirits of the drafters and signatories. Havel moved quickly to harness such responses. The cleancut, good-looking playwright actively tried to direct the international media's interests with upbeat soundbites and intelligent commentaries that not only turned the heads of many journalists, but also captured the ears of thousands of listeners and readers in dozens of countries outside the Soviet empire. The Charter performance was good for his political career. Slowly but surely, Václav Havel was becoming an international media celebrity, and certainly the best-known Chartist outside the country. Within the first year of the Charter's life he told a BBC interviewer that his support for the principles and moral rightness of the Charter was unwavering, and he claimed even that the initiative was beginning to have a visible impact upon the Czechoslovak population. 'We

[1] H. Gordon Skilling, *Charter 77 and Human Rights in Czechoslovakia* (London, 1981), p. 4.
[2] Vilém Prečan, *Kniha Charty* (Köln, 1977), pp. 22–23.

are no longer divided into a few habitual dissidents and the rest of the population,' he said, adding that 'society's conscience' had begun to awaken, and that 'the ice barrier of apathy' had begun to crumble.[1] A few months later, he told the Vienna daily newspaper *Kurier* that the Charter had a fundamentally moral quality, and that no matter what happened it would continue to play a vital role in the resistance to totalitarian power.[2]

The authorities acted quickly to dampen such civic enthusiasm. The text of the appeal reached the desk of white-haired, bespectacled President Husák on 8 January. He studied it carefully, and even took the trouble to underline in black ink certain passages, such as the claims about the lack of freedom of religion, the right of free speech, and the restrictions on what young people could study. The care he took was the clumsy care of the closed-minded ideologue bent on inflicting revenge, which came fast, in rough-edged dollops. Three weeks later, following his instruction that everyone had to pitch in to defeat the *Charta*, a packed Prague meeting of well-dressed and famous artists declared their loyal support for socialism. It was the solidarity of believers and those afraid not to believe. The television cameras caught glimpses of the guitarist and composer Jiří Brabec, the pop singer Marie Rottrová, and the Golden Nightingale award-winner, pop artist Karel Gott.

The cameramen couldn't take their lenses off the actress Jiřina Švorcová, who was warmly applauded by the delegates for a red-hot propaganda speech, in which she said that she was disgusted by people – Havel's name was surely on the tip of her tongue – who acted as if they were 'the chosen', but who were in fact traitors, mere isolates, enemies of humanism and peace, worshippers of money, imperialist agents, and the source of hatred among nations. After her speech, other actresses, joined by television personalities, journalists, painters, musicians and entertainers, including Jan Werich, an old friend of the Havel family, queued up to sign a declaration in favour of 'New Creative Works in the Name of Socialism and Peace'.[3]

[1] Václav Havel, 'Breaking the ice barrier', an interview on BBC, first published in *Index on Censorship*, volume 7, number 1 (January–February 1978), pp. 25–28.
[2] The interview appears in *Kurier* (Vienna), 31 March 1978. It was reprinted in *Listy*, volume 8, number 5 (September 1978), pp. 63–65; and in *Infoch*, number 5 (1978), pp. 5–7.
[3] The Prague meeting was held on 28 January 1977, and is treated in *Charta 77: Začátky*, op. cit., part one.

President Husák personally supported this so-called Anti-Charter. He went on the warpath. At a press conference held shortly after the launch of the Charter, he pointed out that vigilance was required, that nobody should underestimate its campaign to undermine the socialist countries. 'But history teaches us,' he said, 'that all campaigns based on lies and lacking links to the life and consciousness of the people will collapse, and that all the hired puppets of these campaigns will end up in the dustbin of history.'[1] Exactly one week after the launch of the Charter, the Communist Party's leading newspaper, *Rudé právo*, in conjunction with Bratislava's *Pravda*, reinforced the point by running a headline (that rhymes in Czech) about 'The Shipwrecked and the Self-Appointed' (*Ztroskotanci a samozvanci*). The newspaper started a campaign against named Chartists and began to carry stories of prominent sportsmen, artists, and other public figures who opposed the initiative. Czechoslovak television filmed workers (most of whom had never seen the text of the *Charta*) denouncing the enemies of order and socialism. The Party also leaned heavily on prominent waverers like Cardinal František Tomášek, who responded by issuing a signed declaration explaining that the representatives of the Church had not signed the Charter. The declaration called for universal peace, justice and love; expressed concern about the disturbances of the peace caused by the *Charta* initiative; reiterated that nobody else could speak on behalf of the trusted Holy Roman Church; and left readers breathless from the crooked logic of the document to ponder exactly what it might be saying.

Havel was also leaned on heavily, so heavily in fact that he issued a statement which revealed his concern that the authorities now suspected him of being 'the main initiator and organizer of Charter 77'.[2] Bugging devices began gathering evidence later used to prove that he was part of 'a counter-revolution'.[3] He was soon attacked officially from all directions.[4] *Rudé právo* denounced him as an 'inveterate anti-socialist'. He was accused of being in the

---

[1] *Charta 77: Začátky*, op. cit., part one.
[2] Václav Havel, 'Prohlášení' ('Declaration'), 21 May 1977, cited in *The Times* (London), 23 May 1977.
[3] Josef Frolík, *Špión vypovídá* (Prague, 1990 [1982]), p. 273.
[4] See for example *Práce* (Prague), 11 March 1977; *Rudé právo*, 12 January 1977; *Pravda* (Bratislava), 12 January 1977; *Who is Václav Havel?* (*Kdo je Václav Havel?*), originally broadcast on Czechoslovak Radio on 9 March 1977.

pay of the 'well-known agent of the CIA' Pavel Tigrid (his friend and editor of the Paris-based *Svědectví*) and the recipient of funds directly provided by American, West German and other intelligence services. His past was thoroughly muck-raked. Havel was described as a millionaire's son who was a second-rate poet and who had, in his plays, called into question 'the very essence of the socialist order'. He had been involved with the magazine *Tvář*, 'the voice of ideas absolutely foreign to socialism', and he had spent a lifetime fruitlessly trying to rehabilitate various reactionary 'bourgeois' ideas, such as those of Masaryk. Czechoslovak Radio chimed in with a programme called *Who is Václav Havel?* (*Kdo je Václav Havel?*), the text of which was published in full or as excerpts in virtually all the daily newspapers in the country. It described him as 'extremely conceited', as an arrogant nobody who held 'everybody around him in contempt'.

The authorities made two initial strategic mistakes in their anti-Charter campaigns. More minor was the fact that they had initially suspected that the launch of Charter 77 was the work (as *Rudé právo* put it) of anti-Communist and Zionist 'centres' in the West. This paranoia of the Party leadership about counter-revolutionary subversion from abroad granted the signatories and their spokesmen a small breathing space, an interregnum of comparatively nonviolent harassment, within which the Chartists could steady themselves. So, during the first several days after the launch of the Charter on 6 January, those who had been questioned by the StB met every evening at Havel's flat – he and Olga were temporarily resident in the district of Dejvice – to explain what had happened to them and what the police wanted to know. The sessions were attended by foreign journalists, who were thus able to act as on-the-spot reporters of the *Charta* initiative, providing it with the very global coverage that the Party most feared, and certainly had wanted to suppress.

The Party's other tactical mistake was inadvertently to give the advantage of publicity to its opponents. Low-cost modems, satellite-linked telephones, the affordable photocopier, and electronic mail were not yet available. But the Chartists certainly understood the potential power of communications media such as the land-linked telephone, radio and television to publicize their initiative. The Party did not, and not only because since the military crushing of the Prague Spring it had become relatively

unfamiliar with dealing with civic initiatives of the kind Havel
had helped to organize, helped along by his earlier experiences
stretching back to the Dobříš gathering and the Thirty-Sixers.
The Party leadership did not grasp at the outset that by 'going
public' about the *Charta* it not only provided it with free publicity.
It also placed itself on a level playing field – the battle for public
opinion through reasoned argument and rhetorical controversy –
with which it wasn't familiar, and on which it had trouble winning
against its opponents.

VIOLENCE

That left the Party with the option of using the one resource over which they did exercise a monopoly: the means of violence. In practice, late-socialist power brought to completion the monarchic state doctrine of sovereignty, according to which no human society is possible without government, just as no government is possible unless it possesses the ultimate capacity to have the last word in deciding who gets what, when and how, if need be through violent means.[1] Viewed in this way, sovereign power is necessary to protect the state against its enemies. It is ultimately indivisible. When the crunch comes, and especially when normal conditions are threatened by an erupting crisis, the sovereign decision-makers must insist that all other members of the body politic are decision-takers. 'All the characteristics of sovereignty are contained in this,' wrote Jean Bodin, among the inventors of the modern doctrine of sovereign power, 'to have power to give laws to each and every one of his subjects, and to receive none from them'.[2] Sovereign government must be supreme. Those who rule must wisely bear in mind the constant possibility of deception, cunning and violent opposition from their opponents. The rulers must be granted the plenitude of power and insist that the *maxime unum* is the *maxime bonum*. Sovereign power enjoys the *jus belli*. It is entitled to invoke all measures deemed necessary for the preservation or restoration of order, including suspension of the constitution and the liberties it protects. The sovereign state can and must act as a dictator. It must be intolerant of voluntary associations, regarding them (as Thomas Hobbes said) as treasonous, as nothing better than 'worms within the entrails' of the body politic.

The violent capacity of the state to kill off the worms in its entrails was displayed during the last days on earth of Havel's close colleague, philosophical mentor, and co-spokesman of the Charter, Professor Jan Patočka. More than 1,000 people, flanked by 100 police, paid their last respects to Patočka at Břevnov cemetery in Prague. The mourners were frisked, some friends and Chartists were turned away at the entrance gates, while

---

[1] The theory of sovereign power is discussed in my 'Dictatorship and the Decline of Parliament', in *Democracy and Civil Society*, op. cit., pp. 153–189; Harold J. Laski, *The Foundations of Sovereignty and Other Essays* (London, 1921); and Carl Schmitt, *Political Theology, Four Chapters on the Concept of Sovereignty* (Cambridge, Mass., 1985).

[2] Jean Bodin, *Les Six Livres de la République* (Paris, 1576), book 1, chapter 8.

others were detained for questioning. Police cameras filmed and photographed everybody, even at the graveside. The service was interrupted, and the priest's funeral oration drowned out, by a military helicopter circling overhead and the heavy revving of police motorcycles at a nearby racetrack. Havel's face, like most in attendance, showed signs of deep strain as two members of the band Plastic People of the Universe placed a crown of thorns on Patočka's grave.

From the time of the launch of the Charter, Havel had numerous brushes with state violence. For the first time in his life, he felt continuously gripped by the shadowy hand of the secret police. After signing the second document released by the Charter on 8 January, protesting police measures against the signatories, he was interrogated by the StB almost daily. He received threatening letters and anonymous telephone calls. His life began to feel as if it was one continuous round of threats, bright lights, padded doors, wooden desks, sliding chairs, handcuffs, truncheons that pointed to a limited future. When it became clear to the authorities that the man was not for giving up, and that the Charter activists could only be forcibly silenced, Havel was arrested, charged (under Section 98) with committing 'serious crimes against the basic principles of the Republic'. He was confined without trial 'in total isolation' for four and a half months in Ruzyně prison.

During this time, he managed to write an open letter (dated 13 March 1977) to the editors of all the newspapers that had published 'Who is Václav Havel?', calling on them publicly to issue retractions. To ward off the 'depressive emptiness and hopeless inner solitude' of gloomy Ruzyně prison, he also penned an eloquent obituary for Professor Patočka, whose modesty, penetrating philosophical intellect, quiet sense of humour and 'inconspicuous moral greatness' he praised. The obituary also contained a philosophical twist. Surrounded by violence and mourning the loss of a key Chartist and friend, Havel confessed that he was perplexed by a strange double injustice within the human condition. Not only does 'death even come to people who have spent their entire lives thinking about death', he wrote. It is also a fact that such 'people who understand so much about death and its meaning . . . seem to be the ones to whom death pays most attention, perhaps out of fear that they might finally reveal her mystery after all – she hurries to get them, often before the others'.[1]

His reflections on death provided a clue that the authorities were playing dirty, and perhaps even that he was anxious about his safety. Ignorant about the Charter's current activities – and denied even the heartening news of the daring release on 20 April of a large flotilla of brightly coloured children's balloons in Wenceslas Square, accompanied by leaflets publicly demanding his release – Havel was interrogated constantly about its organization, signatories and leadership. The indictment the authorities drew up made no mention at all of the Charter, but on the day of his release (on 20 May 1977) they issued an official statement in which Havel was reported to have said that his actions as a Chartist had 'not always been correct' and that his statements had been 'tendentiously interpreted by the foreign press and misused against Czechoslovakia'. Most importantly, it was claimed that Havel had agreed to resign as Charter spokesman. It was said that he had vowed 'to avoid all activity which could be classed as criminal' and given his word not to 'participate in any action which could be misused for a campaign against the ČSSR'.[2]

The heavy-handed tactics of detention and disinformation were the cause of trembling within the ranks of the Chartists. Havel tried to stand firm. In a carefully worded statement, issued to correct the official 'distortions', he confirmed that he was indeed relinquishing his position as Charter spokesman. But he said categorically that he would remain defiant in the face of state intimidation. He would not withdraw his name from the list of Charter signatories. He would stand by 'the moral obligation' it implied. And he would do everything within the law to come to the assistance of the victims of political injustice.[3] It was in this spirit of acting as if the rule of law existed that, ten days after his release from prison, he bravely called on the District Prosecutor's office in Prague 2 to initiate proceedings against the writer, Tomáš Řezáč, who was originally responsible for slandering him in 'Who is Václav Havel?'. In quick succession, he hosted a small celebration, with Chartist friends,

---

[1] 'Poslední rozhovor', O lidskou identitu, op. cit., pp. 152–155; the sentences cited here are slightly altered from the English translation, which appeared as 'Last Conversation', in Charter 77 and Human Rights in Czechoslovakia, op. cit., pp. 242–244.
[2] Rudé právo, 21 May 1977.
[3] Václav Havel, 'Prohlášení' ('Declaration'), 21 May 1977, cited in The Times (London), 23 May 1977.

to mark the appearance of the volume *Hry 1970–1976* (*Plays 1970–1976*), published by Zdena Škvorecká's and her husband Josef's Sixty-Eight Publishers in Toronto; gave an interview, published in London, about Charter 77 and independent culture; and (on 1 October 1977) helped demonstrate the meaning of cultural independence by hosting an autumn music festival at his country retreat at Hrádeček.[1] Exactly the same spirit of acting as if he were a citizen living in freedom under the rule of law was again displayed less than three weeks later in his concluding address to the Prague city court hearing the charge of 'serious crimes against the basic principles of the Republic'.[2]

The judge was so unpersuaded by the address that he dispensed with ceremony to sentence Havel to fourteen months, suspended for a period of three years. Havel had damaged the sovereign interests of Czechoslovakia and justice had been seen as done. Now it was to be done in fact. The secret police readied their weapons. On the evening of 28 January 1978, they carefully set a trap for him and other Chartists outside the Railwaymen's House of Culture building in the Prague district of Vinohrady. It had been a custom in Bohemia since the turn of the century that organizations arranged balls and sold tickets to non-members. Aware of this old custom, several women within Chartist circles had spontaneously thought up plans for Chartists and their friends to join the annual ball held at the Railwaymen's House. 'It's politics all the time. We have the right to entertainment too,' they agreed, without resistance, certainly not from Havel, who (as the Americans say) had always liked being shown a good time. A crumpled black-and-white photograph shows him on the way to the ball, grinning, dressed in a dinner jacket, looking every bit the dandy, or perhaps the ladies' man, Anna Šabatová draped over one arm and another woman over the other.

The evening quickly turned into an unrelaxing episode resembling the final murder scene in Dürrenmatt's play *Visit of an Old Lady*. At the entrance to the building, state security police masquerading as railway workers dressed in black politely greeted Havel and others, then announced with a snarl that they were

---

[1] See his letter dated 1 June 1977 (*O lidskou identitu*, op. cit., p. 278); and the interview conducted around the end of September 1977, later published in London, ibid., pp. 250–256.
[2] See 'Last Word before the Court' (18 October 1977), ibid., pp. 327–330.

unwelcome guests at the ball. Truncheons suddenly cracked heads. Havel and others fell involuntarily on to the frozen pavement, stunned, bleeding. Several women in evening dress were kicked, and the word 'whore' shouted repeatedly. Someone cried out for help. Uniformed police were instantly on the scene. They were instructed by the black-suited security police to take Havel and several others straight to the clinic for alcoholics, claiming in the process that the agitators who had been hit were actually dead drunk.

The uniformed police had the sense to take them instead to a casualty ward, in precariously slow time. Had Havel and his colleagues (Pavel Landovský and Jaroslav Kukal) been suffering brain damage, they may well have drawn their last breath during the journey. *En route* to the hospital, they were stopped and detained for ten minutes by another police patrol. After checking their identity papers and taking down their names, the police then tailed the threesome at every turn for the rest of the evening. Around midnight, after a doctor administering a blood test laughed in his face when asked for guarantees that the sample would not be exchanged, Havel was formally charged with obstructing and attacking a public official in the course of duty. He was carted off to Ruzyně prison, where he was to spend the next six weeks, pending a trial that never took place.

One evening just before lights-out, halfway through his ordeal, sitting upright on his bed, nursing a recurrent headache caused by crunching truncheons, Havel heard a man's voice calling out down the prison corridor. 'Is there anybody here from the committee to defend Václav Havel, Pavel Landovský and Jaroslav Kukal?' 'Yes!' replied an anonymous voice. 'Well then, do something,' said the first man's voice, 'I'm Jarda Kukal!'

COURAGE

It was obvious to the signatories and friends of the Charter that the initiative was an act of courage. Courage is a key source of citizens' power to act in the world, the necessary and indispensable propolis of citizenship, and it is therefore unsurprising – given the stresses and strains of acting under great pressure – that the meaning of courage and whether and under what conditions it could be sustained under duress quickly became a topic for debate within Chartist circles. It was the doing of one of its first signatories, the moustached, black-rim-spectacled writer Ludvík Vaculík – the author of the famous '2,000 Words' manifesto that called for faster and more comprehensive de-Stalinization at the height of the Prague Spring – who used a three-page feuilleton publicly to pick a fight with the Charter's basic principle of non-violent, open resistance against a regime that was systematically violating its own constitutional precepts.[1]

Vaculík began without mincing words. 'I sometimes wonder whether I'm mature enough for prison. It frightens me,' wrote the man who, together with Havel and others, was almost sent to prison in 1969 for writing the 'Ten Point Manifesto'. He admitted that he may be an unusually weak and fearful character, but insisted that everybody who is confronted with possible imprisonment because of their moral commitment has the duty to reflect on whether that price to pay is too high. The presumption that prison is always worth risking is peacockery, he argued, for taking a 'courageous' stand against the politically powerful is not always effective, and sometimes foolish. It is very often full of contradictions. For instance, risking prison drags friends, family and other contacts into the same magnetic field of force, regardless of whether they want to take the risk. Courage is not a trusted friend of freedom; it may even be the latter's enemy, as for example 'when someone provokes someone else to do something which they are then unable to retract without loss of pride, prestige or authority'. Vaculík also tried gallantly to stick up for the silent

[1]Ludvík Vaculík, 'Poznámky o statečnosti', dated 6 December 1978, circulated in typewritten samizdat form, and dedicated to the author Karel Pecka, on the occasion of his fiftieth birthday. See also Petr Pithart's reply dated 31 December 1978; Havel's reply to Vaculík dated 25 January 1979; and Havel's reply to Pithart dated 1 February 1979. Vaculík's early reaction to the controversy about courage is chronicled in *Český snář* (samizdat and Prague, 1990), entry dated Thursday, 25 January 1979. I have also consulted Václav Havel's introduction to Ludvík Vaculík, *A Cup of Coffee with My Interrogator* (London, 1987), pp. i–iv.

majority of non-Chartists by defending their so-called apathy. He did so by highlighting the well-known problem, facing everyone who was actually or potentially in contact with Charter 77, that those who watch others take risks easily see that the whole business of activism is so physically and emotionally exhausting that they – sanely – avoid it. The so-called uncourageous individual in fact acts cautiously and prudently by shunning so-called heroism and asking: Is it worth going through with it to the death? and looks for a way to retreat. The reason is clear. 'No psychologist or politician would expect heroism in public life from people except when the atmosphere is literally ionized by radiation from some powerful source. Heroism is alien to daily life.' That is why most of the population 'can less and less see anything in the even more heroic deeds of the declining number of warriors other than a personal hobby'. The encouraging fact, he warned, is that most people 'are well aware of their own limits and only do things whose consequences they are ready to take. Anyone who urges people when times are rough to do things beyond their capacity shouldn't be surprised if they get clobbered.' Here, down-to-earth Vaculík began to sound like the good soldier Švejk. Normal people living in unexceptional circumstances wisely 'stick to their good habits and virtues; they have irreducible standards and will stop them from being degraded. They don't like it when they see someone defiantly taking great risks, but like to say that honest work in peace is best, even if it isn't particularly well rewarded, and that decent behaviour will find a decent response'.

It also has to be said, continued Vaculík, that there are times when the sentenced are publicly forgotten before the sentence is ended, in which case taking a moral stand and flirting thereby with prison turns out to be a sad swan song. Vaculík charged the unofficial campaign, led by Jiří Müller and others, to boycott the 1972 elections with this weakness. He went on to insinuate that the Charter may well turn out to be performing a similar kind of swan song. 'Nobody can give a convincing answer to the question of whether Charter 77 has made things better or worse or what things would look like if it had not happened. In the answers we get,' he taunted, 'moral impulses seem to be out of step with political opinions, and the strongest positions arise from character rather than intellectual orientation.' And there is one final point, Vaculík wrote. Chartists should be honest enough to admit

– or mature enough to recognize – that acting with 'courage' and ending up in prison can have long-term destructive effects upon the individual's character. Courage, he concluded, is a term best applied to those who manage to survive prison and especially the painful period of self-destructive post-prison blues that inevitably follows.

So, people outside should be careful and not get themselves locked up. They should even be courageous enough to say no to so-called courage. They should be bold enough to ask the questions forbidden in Chartist circles: Are Chartists really heroes whose convictions have unfortunately landed them in prison? Are Chartists better described as fools who are taking risks for things that are not worth taking risks for? Or even as agents provocateurs of a regime that 'does not want to give publicity to any heroes' and is probably disposed to administer 'measured doses of repression'?

Vaculík is not a writer of common sense and conventional taste, a man without originality and political courage. He acts the part of a curmudgeon and in fact later willingly confessed his awareness that his own argument was intentionally trapped in a literary contradiction.[1] His 'Notes on Courage' was a courageous warning about the potential folly of courage but, like Goedel's maxim that not even mathematics can save itself from the quagmire of inconsistency, Vaculík's inconsistent argument had a stimulating effect upon its readers. Written in spare, angular prose, it was driven by the conviction that its tongue-in-cheek claims would shock and outrage quite a few Chartists, who understood him to be saying, or implying, that Charter 77 ought to cease all its activities forthwith – that it was time to quit the make-believe game of constructing what Václav Benda, a fellow Chartist, called a parallel polis. 'Notes on Courage' was vintage Vaculík: an overstated act of lyric *Verfremdung* from an old cuss intent on prodding and poking and rolling over on to its back the taken-for-granted principle of courage, for the ultimate purpose of highlighting the need to make judgements about the meaning and utility – and limits – of courage. The emphasis on judgement explains why Vaculík never assumed that his was the last word on the subject of courage, and

---

[1] Interview with Ludvík Vaculík, Prague, 23 April 1996. See also his comments in *Český snář*, op. cit.

why, under trying circumstances, he was calling in effect for more reflection and discussion of the topic. And doing so in the manner of a writer who assigns a special role to irony in an age inclined to over-seriousness.

There was certainly plenty of room for contesting Vaculík's unfashionable claims, as many Charter supporters and signatories, including Havel himself, saw quickly. Vaculík reported that 'Remarks on Courage' caused a stir. At first, he told others that 'everyone agreed with my piece and some even congratulated me on it', but his tune changed when the first criticisms reached his ears. Many others followed. Someone said that Vaculík had become demoralized. Others said that his piece relied upon the same base journalistic techniques used by *Rudé právo* against the Charter. A friend took a copy away to read, fell silent, then one day said: 'Listen, chum, some people have got serious reservations about it and quite rightly, too!' Others reported that the StB was probably monitoring the quarrels – and rubbing their hands together as they waited for the spoils. Vaculík was unrepentant. He made it known that since Chartists had defined themselves as free people by signing the Charter they should act freely – which included freely expressing their views, regardless of whether or not that pleased the secret police. As for the insinuation that he was acting as an unpaid agent of the secret police, that was worthy only of satire. 'Apparently I should not have spoken about heroes,' he said, 'but gone right ahead and said "a handful of self-appointed has-beens", and the sensible, normal people I spoke of are no more than the "honest working people led by the Party". And when I advocate "courageous honest work", what is it but the "honest co-operation" required by the state and the police . . . ?'

Others were unsatisfied, and some took umbrage. Havel was among the irritated. He wasted no time drafting a reply to Vaculík's leading question: Is anything the Charter has embarked upon worth going to prison for, perhaps for several years or more? The tone of his answers was impatient, and tough. He began by attacking Vaculík's suggestion that so-called dissidents are out to get something by cunning, as if they were potential shoplifters in an Eastern supermarket, rationally weighing up their chances of getting caught, of being punished, or of being left alone.

According to Havel, the luxury of calculating whether being arrested and punished is worth the risk was denied to Chartists.

True, they could legitimately minimize such risk by dropping out of the parallel polis, although even then they would not necessarily be rescued from the 'silent and unspectacular degradation' inflicted by the post–totalitarian regime upon 'thousands of anonymous people'. True, the act of signing the Charter was dangerous, inasmuch as it brought the individual into the front line of police activity against all 'enemies' of 'socialism'. From that moment on, there was a marked increase in the chances of that individual being followed, threatened, beaten, imprisoned, or forced into exile with nightmares in their head. But Vaculík's call for individual dissenters to weigh up their acts in terms of their consequences, especially the probability of imprisonment, was utterly misleading, Havel insisted. It amounted to the view that 'nothing is worth it'.

Chartists who chose to remain Chartists indeed put themselves on the path leading toward confrontation with the regime. But as the fate of the Plastic People of the Universe revealed, whether or not they were arrested or punished was not necessarily correlated directly with their intended doings. 'The people whom you call heroes, and suggest are eccentric,' wrote Havel, 'did not go to prison out of a desire to become martyrs but because of the "indecency" of those who go around imprisoning people for writing novels or playing tapes of unofficial songs.' The indecency of the political authorities had something of a random – terroristic – quality to it, Havel went on to argue. 'People who are decent and do not go to jail are lucky.' Consider the different fates of Vaculík's *The Guinea Pigs* (1970), which landed the author in no immediate trouble, and the award of a handsome prison sentence to Jiří Gruša for writing *The Questionnaire* (1975). 'You know as well as anyone,' Havel said, 'that the decision as to whether to imprison Gruša or Vaculík has nothing to do with who weighed up the risks most accurately, but is the result of cold and cynical calculation. At one time it might be better tactics to imprison Gruša and attempt in this way to intimidate Vaculík, at another it might be cleverer to imprison Vaculík and try in this way to intimidate Gruša.'

Havel's point was double-barrelled. Under post–totalitarian conditions, the question of whether or not to act with courage as a citizen could and should never be decided by calculations about the risks of imprisonment. Some things, as Jan Patočka had said repeatedly, were worth struggling and suffering for. But more importantly: courage itself is not subject to calculation. If the courage to act against unfreedom is boiled down to mere calculations of risk, then courage ceases to be courage. In effect, Havel charged Vaculík with misrepresenting courage – and, inadvertently, of calling upon citizens to lay down their arms, not to behave heroically, and to stay out of jail. 'To be a hero is to be unsociable,' wrote Havel in unusually sarcastic sentences: 'It is something other than that good honest work which decent people like so much and which keeps society going; it repels and appals people. In any case, heroes are dangerous because they make things worse. It is true that the people up there are well behaved when one treats them decently. Why provoke them with novels, music, or sending books abroad? Such things force these nice people to beat up women and drag our comrades into dark woods and kick them in the stomach. We must respect their prestige and not go around provocatively waving a wad of International Agreements or even insolently making copies of various writings by Černý, Vaculík, Havel, etc.'

Havel's mood was defiant. It was as if he had decided that the act of writing about courage needed to display courage, beginning with the elementary point that courage (from the Latin, *cor*, heart) is always ultimately a matter of a prior felt commitment to embark upon a certain course of action within a field of power. 'We never decided that we would go to jail,' he wrote. 'In fact, we never decided to become dissidents. We have been transformed into them, without quite knowing how, and sometimes we have ended up in prison without precisely knowing how. We simply went ahead and did certain things that we felt we ought to do, and that seemed to us decent to do, nothing more nor less.' Havel in effect insisted that, especially under difficult circumstances – war, repression, unemployment, murder, theft – this feeling of courage is a basic precondition of the individual's ability to act upon the world. Courage is the felt will *not* to be afraid of acting against considerable odds. Fear is its key enemy. Fear eats up the souls of citizens. It destroys courage by corrupting and weakening those who try to act upon the world, turning them into faint-hearted subjects. Havel grasped the converse of this rule: since fearlessness is not a naturally occurring substance, a personal effort must be made to shake it off. Fearlessness is the special ingredient of courage. It is the will to act gracefully under pressure that develops wherever victims of manipulation, lying and bullying make a personal effort to throw off the habit of letting fear dictate their actions as citizens.

Havel's tactic involved turning Vaculík against Vaculík. The agreed point that nobody wants to go to jail because imprisonment is frightening implied the need of citizens to demonstrate their fearlessness by exercising their courage against those who jail others illegally, against their will. Havel openly acknowledged that he could well understand the flagging enthusiasm of Chartist advocates of human and civil rights. 'Everyone has the right, when they have had enough, to retreat into the background, to stop doing certain things, to take a rest or even emigrate. This is entirely understandable, normal and human, and I would be the last to resent it,' he wrote. But to understand why activists withdraw from the parallel polis, to appreciate why they use their legs instead of courage, must not slide into sordid broadsides against the principle of courage. Figures such as Vaculík actually know better than to do that. 'I do resent it,' he said, sharply, 'when such people do not tell the truth, and on this occasion – don't get angry – you are not telling the truth.'

The sentiments Havel expressed sounded almost classical. After the high Roman fashion, perhaps without knowing it, he was repeating the maxims that the philosophers, playwrights and poets of ancient Greece and Rome had long ago insisted were vital preconditions of citizenship.[1] Under entirely different political circumstances, and using different words, Havel was saying to Vaculík that courage is generosity of the highest order, for the brave are prodigal of the most precious things. Courage is to be preferred to grovelling, love of riches, greed, violence, or selfish calculation. Courage shuns baseness. It avoids stupidity and irrationality. It is unselfish and unheroic. True courage does not require witnesses, even when it leavens actions destined for the public or world stage. Courage never leaves the world untouched. It transforms the individual citizen. Courage scorns death by reaching for the stars. It can even break the grip of bad luck. Courage takes the knocks, buoys the spirits, puts a new face on

---

[1] Some examples include Marcus Tullius Cicero, *De Officiis* (London, 1720) , Book 1, chapter 2, section 5 and Book 1, chapter 19, section 62; Epictetus, *Discourses* (Glasgow, 1766), Book 1, chapter 18, section 21; Plautus, *Amphitryon; or The two Socia's. A Comedy* (London, 1690), 1. 646 (Act 1, scene 2),; and Plutarch, *The Lives of Aristeides and Marcus Cato* (London, 1928), chapter 10, section 4.

everything, and even gives physical strength to the body. Courage in distress can stop armies from marching to success. Courage is that virtue which champions the cause of right. It loves mercy. It delights in rescuing others. It encourages others. Courage breeds courage. But courage is also modest. Courage in conflict is half the battle, but only half. It senses the dangers of pig-headedness and knows that victory is never guaranteed, that defeat is a companion of courage. The greatest test of courage is to suffer defeat without giving up. 'Some of us have passed the last two years, others ten years, and still others their whole life in a tough and depressing confrontation with the secret police,' confessed Havel. 'Nobody enjoys it. None of us know how long we can keep it up.' He took it as read that courageous are those who neither seek popular applause nor under pressure desert their cause. The remaining question for him personally was whether or not he could screw his courage to the sticking-place – without buckling under the weight of suspicion, surveillance, and further threats of arrest and imprisonment.

THE POWERLESS

The subject of how best to resist late-socialism preoccupied Havel after the launch of Charter 77. It was at the heart of an essay – 'The Power of the Powerless' ('*Moc bezmocných*') – that soon became one of those rare pieces of political reflection that outlive their time of birth and come to be regarded as classics.[1] Written shortly after the launch of Charter 77 and just prior to the birth of Solidarność in Poland, it was arguably among the most original and compelling pieces of political writing that emerged from central and eastern Europe during the whole of the Communist period.

The essay was the fruit of a 1978 initiative of Czechoslovak and Polish intellectuals committed to the defence of civil rights. In that year, they had prepared a joint seminar on the aims, problems and possibilities of their respective initiatives. Havel had agreed to write a discussion paper. He did so 'quickly' (he later said). The text was then made available to the other contributors, who were asked in turn to respond to the many questions raised by Havel about the potential power of the powerless under 'post-totalitarian' conditions. The whole original plan was flung into confusion by the arrest, in May 1979, of ten members of VONS (the Czechoslovak Committee for the Defence of the Unjustly Prosecuted). The original project had to be fast-forwarded, and it was decided by the authors to publish the Czechoslovak contributions separately as *On Freedom and Power*, a collection of eleven pieces introduced by Havel's extended essay. Compellingly structured and written in crisp prose, the essay probably ranks as Havel's finest literary intervention in the world of politics. It is haunted by the general feeling (shared by Milan Kundera) that central-eastern Europe was under siege, that its whole identity was being strangled slowly to death – and, more immediately, by the pain caused by the recent death of his friend Jan Patočka, to whose memory it is dedicated.

The immediate aim of 'The Power of the Powerless' was to explain the significance of Charter 77 to its (potential) supporters within Czechoslovakia, and to give courage to the opponents of late-socialism elsewhere in the Soviet block. The essay works with a fairly standard conception of power as the ability of (certain)

[1] Translated by Paul Wilson, the essay appeared in English in *The Power of the Powerless: Citizens Against the State in Central-Eastern Europe*, edited by John Keane (London, 1985). This volume includes a selection of nine other essays addressed to Havel's thesis from an original collection of Czech and Slovak responses.

humans to exercise their will over and against others, even despite their resistance, and it reveals no broader concern with surveying the kaleidoscope of previous conflicting definitions of power. Yet the striking feature of Havel's treatment of power is its lack of deference towards the powerful. It was uninterested in copying previous manuals of statecraft (like Machiavelli's *Il principe*) written primarily for rulers. It was also not a grammar of obedience written for subjects, like Thomas Hobbes's *De Cive*. And – perhaps more radical still – Havel's attitude to power and powerlessness also rejected the view that the subject of power is a lost cause, the view buried in the well-known contemporary joke about the two Czechs travelling by train from Brno to Prague, one of whom groans constantly, apparently in pain, until his companion loses patience, and erupts: 'Quiet! Can't you talk about anything else but politics?!' 'The Power of the Powerless' questions the cynicism of those whose encounter with the absurd unrealities of life leads them to abjure action, stand aside from life, and drift with the tide. Havel also questions the anti-political attitude of the wry-faced cynic, who curses that all rulers are bastards and concludes that the downtrodden should either smile knowingly into their beards, or soldier on, turn the other cheek, or cheat and lie and steal their way through life, or entertain or drink themselves into oblivion. 'The Power of the Powerless' is certainly not attracted by institutional politics, but its core idea is much more original than the standard middle-European version of anti-politics. The essay could even be called subversive. 'Men at some time are masters of their fates,' Cassius tells Brutus in Shakespeare's *Julius Caesar*. 'The fault . . . is not in our stars, But in ourselves, that we are underlings.'[1] The idea is repeated in Havel's essay. It proposes that under any circumstances the downtrodden always contain *within themselves* the power to remedy their own powerlessness, and that, consequently, they are the ultimate cause of their own continuing subordination.

The continuing intolerance of opposition, lingering insecurity, and especially the subordination produced by the late-socialist regime (Havel called it 'the post-totalitarian system') convinced him that the system was too ossified to be reformed from within – as Dubček and his supporters had tried to do in 1968 – and that

[1] William Shakespeare, *Julius Caesar*, Act 1, Scene 2.

there was consequently a need for more imaginative and radical ways of defeating it. Here the idea of *the power of the powerless* served him well. The oxymoron was not an exercise in clever writing – not a play on words by a playwright teasing an audience. It was rather driven by the conviction that all attempts to resist democratically the pressures of late-socialism have their essential beginnings in the extra-state areas of everyday life. The centre of gravity of potential resistance is what he called 'the existential dimension of the world'[1], or what Edmund Husserl, the most famous Moravian philosopher of the First Republic, called the *Lebenswelt*. Here a different life – what Havel called 'living in the truth' and would later call 'anti-political politics' – can be lived, and the self-sustaining aspects of the system, its presence within each individual, can be shaken off. In effect, Havel's call for dissent involved turning the system's basic logic of subordination against itself. 'This system serves people only to the extent necessary to ensure that people will serve it,' he wrote. 'Anything beyond this, that is to say, anything which leads people to overstep their predetermined roles is regarded by the system as an attack upon itself. And in this respect it is correct: every instance of such transgression is a genuine denial of the system.' In other words: individuals need to understand that so long as they act as if they accept the system then they will continue to confirm the system. They will continue to make the system, to *be* the system – until the moment that they decide enough is enough.

Havel's thesis necessarily involved something of a Copernican Revolution in the way that power is conceived. It upended the presumption that people who command states and therefore have at their disposal the accoutrements of power – spies, weapons, bureaucrats, propagandists, even the means of production – have things all their own way, at least if they play their cards right. Havel was adamant that those who speak of the sovereign power of the state should not have the last word in politics. Sovereignty may be an appealing word. Those who present themselves as 'realists' may sound convincing when they insist that the politically wise are those who bear in mind the constant possibility of deception, cunning and violent opposition from their opponents, that armed conflict against enemies is the ultimate political event. Those who

---

[1]Václav Havel, 'Dovětek autora', in *Hry 1970–1976* (Toronto, 1977), p. 306.

speak of the need for sovereignty also seem to have tradition on their side, beginning with Jean Bodin's classic insistence that those who rule through the state are required, especially in emergencies and periods of disorder, to make *final* decisions about what is to be done, including what is to be done against the enemies of the state. It seems plain common sense that those who rule politically enjoy the *jus belli* – the unlimited right to define the domestic or foreign enemy, as well as to fight and destroy that enemy with all the available resources of state power. What could be more obviously true than the proposition that political power confers upon its holders an awful prerogative – the unrestricted power to wage war and, hence, to rob others of their lives?

Havel rejected the originally monarchic doctrine of sovereign state power. Although he didn't quite put it this way, he was in effect saying that under certain circumstances *the powerful are powerless*. Power is certainly the process of affecting the actions of others with the help of (threatened) severe punishment for non-conformity to the wishes of the powerful. The powerful may even rule others by means of 'non-decision-making', that is, by effectively limiting the scope of decisions and by preventing certain felt grievances from developing into full-fledged disputes that call for decisions.[1] But there are times when the powerful are like the little Dutch boy with his finger in the dyke. The more real power they seem to enjoy, the less they can afford to throw it around, to exercise it over others.

The powerlessness of the powerful is traceable mainly to five related factors, or so Havel argued. To begin with, he empha- sized the fundamental inability of rulers to control the micro- movements of their subjects. In every nook and cranny of life – on the job, in the apartment, the kindergarten or school or university, in the pub or restaurant, in the fields of newspaper production, radio and television programming – the rulers of late-socialism may well reduce individuals 'to little more than tiny cogs in an enormous mechanism'. But the rulers themselves tend to be pudding-heads, stupid men with conservative instincts. Their minions are no better; working within and for a system that disallows individualism, they tend to be 'faceless people, puppets',

---

[1] See Peter Bachrach and Morton S. Baratz, 'Decisions and Nondecisions: An Analytical Framework', *American Political Science Review*, volume 57 (1963), pp. 632–642.

mere 'uniformed flunkeys of the rituals and routines of power'. Those who govern at various levels are not able to free themselves from the clutches of the unthinking obsequiousness of the system they direct, which has the effect of dulling their ability to govern the ship of state intelligently, including their ability to monitor, let alone motivate its subjects. Power over others breeds blindness and loopholes, hence, the possibility of crawling through them.

Secondly, Havel argued, this possibility is enhanced by the perverse tendency of the whole power structure to depend upon ideological rituals that are ever less credible, exactly because they are untested by public discussion and controversy. In systems that enjoy public competitions for power and office, there is naturally public monitoring of the ways in which power tries to legitimate itself before others. The tendency of power to wrap itself in alibis and false claims – declared by early modern thinkers like Niccolò Machiavelli and Thomas Hobbes as an active ingredient of good government – is potentially stoppable. Under late-socialist conditions, by contrast, there is nothing to prevent ideology from becoming ever more removed from the reality of circumstances. So ideology becomes 'a world of appearances, a mere ritual, a formalized language deprived of semantic contact with reality'. Most people take no notice of it, but they know it is there, always in the background, sometimes in the foreground, at all times serving as a reminder of where they are living and what is expected of them. This domination of ritual not only has the paradoxical effect of tempting power to believe its own rituals and thereby serve the ruling ideology, as if the ritualized ideology were sacrosanct, even at the highest levels of state. The '*diktat* of the empty phrase' also comes to be seen by the ruled as empty, as unbelievable, as a mere façade of the all-embracing system of power. Ideological ritual is sensed to be a crude substitute for public debate and controversies among parties and politicians, which are officially banned.

Here a third consideration arises: the possibility that some will call the ideology a lie and declare the emperor naked is nurtured by the *ontological* fact that 'the everyday, thankless, and never-ending struggle of human beings to live more freely, truthfully, and in quiet dignity' is ultimately not fully repressible. At least some individuals will resist, if only because their very identity depends upon it. Having become fed up with stagnation, having grown tired of years of waiting, of apathy and scepticism, they feel that they cannot live otherwise. They know (as Havel's friend Patočka liked to say) that the most interesting thing about responsibility is that individuals carry it around with them everywhere they go. Those who strive to live truthfully therefore simply refuse any longer to be watched by the police, to be humiliated by their superiors, or to put up with a constant feeling of insecurity before the law. They know that the possibility of freedom depends upon shaking off the presence of the one-party system within themselves by altering the relations of power 'closest' to them. They have grasped, as Havel put it, that 'life, in its essence, moves towards plurality, diversity, independent self-constitution, and self-organization, in short, towards the fulfilment of its own freedom'.

Fourth, the ontological check upon totalitarian power is nurtured by the fact that, among those who think about their situation, a felt need develops for serious reflection upon the nature and limits of the system. It is as if misery nips at the heels of imagination, forcing the mind towards concern with the human condition. They feel compelled to examine the deeper coherences of their situation, to consider how it came to assume the form that it has, and whether there are any ways of preventing themselves and their world from wasting away to nothing, or, like Gadarene swine, rushing headlong over a cliff into the sea. 'There are times,' Havel wrote, 'when we must sink to the bottom of our misery to understand truth, just as we must descend to the bottom of a well to see the stars in broad daylight.'

Finally, these individuals who 'live in the truth' reject the innocent fiction that power is a thing to be grasped or abolished. It is customary to say that this or that person or group or institution 'has power', which implies that power, like wealth, is a possession, which enables its owner to dictate some future goal. But, according to Havel, power is relational, not possessive or substantive. Within any regime, power relations are not reducible to the instruments of power. And certainly within the late-socialist system, power is never owned or concentrated in a single space, such as the leading echelons of the Communist Party or the ruling class. It is never imposed upon one group by another and never divided between those who have power and those who are powerless. Within the system, every individual is entrapped within a dense network of the state's governing instruments – a 'complex machinery of units, hierarchies, transmission belts, and indirect instruments of manipulation' – themselves legitimated by a flexible but comprehensive ideology, a 'secularized religion', that offers a ready answer to any question whatsoever. It is as if each individual is trapped within a tomb within a tomb within a tomb, and it is therefore necessary to see, argued Havel, that power relations within the late-socialist system are best described as a labyrinth of influence, repression, fear and self-censorship which swallows up everyone within it, at the very least by rendering them silent, stultified and marked by some undesirable prejudices of the powerful. The lines of power permeate the entire system; in consequence, every person is both its victim and a supporter – and potential opponent.

Since the lines of organized power within the system pass like low-current electricity through all its subjects, the latter can defend themselves against it only by being different in the most radical sense, that is, by insulating themselves against the system and preventing it from ruining their own personal lives. Those who choose to live in the truth effect something of an 'existential revolution'. They agree that 'there are some things worth suffering for', the words used by Professor Patočka shortly before his death, and they are prepared to say aloud and do what many others only think in silence. Their actions can take many forms – an open letter written by intellectuals, workers' refusal to work, the holding of a rock concert, a student demonstration, a hard-hitting public speech, the decision to go on a hunger strike – but in every case their actions rely initially on the courage and determination of existential choices made by thinking, acting individuals. Their effective power cannot be measured in terms of numbers of disciples or loyal voters, infantry divisions, or sizeable crowds of demonstrators. Living in the truth is a risky business. Its consequences for the individual are wholly unclear, and yet although it is something of an all-or-nothing gamble it can be surprisingly effective – like a bacterial weapon, said Havel, it can be used by 'a single civilian to disarm an entire division'. It is true that divisions of well-armed troops and other political authorities can succeed in crushing those who live truthfully, like insects undeserving of life. They can be dragged from their beds in the middle of the night, beaten silly, judged insane and carted off to institutions or treated as professional malcontents and labelled 'counter-revolutionaries', 'backsliders', and 'dissidents'. They can be murdered, even. But such tactics (Havel cited the case of the hunting and hounding of Solzhenitsyn out of Russia) prove the point: the powerless have within themselves the power to obstruct normality, to embarrass the authorities, to point to the possibility of living life differently – according to values like trust, openness, responsibility, solidarity, love.

Living in the truth operates initially and primarily at the existential level. Although it can manifest itself in publicly visible collective actions – a street demonstration or citizens' association, for instance – it is essentially local, invisible, anti-political. It is uninterested, say, in forming and leading a vanguard, or writing a new programme for a political party or working for the replacement of party-appointed officials by a government or head of state elected once every few years. The strategy and goal of living in the truth tries to be acephalous. It is concerned not to define itself too quickly into rigid and highly visible institutional forms, which can be spotted, 'decapitated', and eliminated easily by the political authorities, who are specialists in the art of eliminating competing political organizations. Under the extremely adverse conditions of late-socialism, living in the truth minimizes the likelihood of a crushing, total defeat and, conversely, it maximizes the chances of 'victories in defeat'. Living in the truth is for this reason also most ethically effective when it keeps its distance from formal politics. The powerless must understand that '[a]ny eventual political articulation of the movements that grow out of this "pre-political" hinterland is secondary'. They must grasp that a better system will not ensure a better life, that the opposite is true: 'Only by creating a better life can a better system be developed.' Living in the truth requires the cultivation of mechanisms of individuation, self-protection and co-operation in areas 'underneath' and beyond the reach of the state – within the household, among friends, at the office, within the parallel economy and sphere of unofficial culture, in citizens' initiatives like Charter 77. In a phrase, the empowerment of the powerless first and foremost requires individuals to build open, flexible structures of resistance that run parallel to and underneath the late-socialist state. This is best done from below, by means of what Tomáš Masaryk called small-scale initiatives (*drobná práce*). But such initiatives can thrive only if individuals recognize that the system has frustrated and flung Masaryk's original principle into a profound crisis, that it is now harder but therefore more imperative to take a stand and to renew daily the existential commitment to break the rules of the game, to disrupt the game as such, to expose it relentlessly as a mere game.[1]

[1]Tomáš Garrigue Masaryk's notion of 'small-scale initiatives' (*drobná práce*) referred to the importance of honest, responsible work in widely different areas of life, but contained within the existing social order. It emphasized the importance of cultivating morality and privileging enlightened education for the ultimate purpose of stimulating national self-confidence and national creativity. This notion of 'working for the good of the nation' not only supposed the availability of a framework of civil and political liberties within which citizens could get on with their work. It was also strongly wedded to a politics of *national* reconstruction, that is to say, a project of developing and defending the right of nations to govern themselves through territorially sovereign states. 'The Power of the Powerless' was implicitly sympathetic to the same goal, but Havel's silence about 'the national question' was at this stage hard to interpret. He was forced later to come clean.

THE VICTIM

It is easy to pick holes in Havel's arguments, for instance in his Panglossian confidence in the probable harmony among differing interpretations of what it means 'to live in the truth'. Havel dodged not only differences of political opinion, declaring the need to 'shed the burden of traditional political categories and habits', but also difficult questions about such tensions within the human condition as trust and betrayal, love and suspicion, faith and despair, creativity and destruction. Aside from moral appeals and exemplary actions, Havel's essay also offered little consolation to individuals who choose to live in the truth, and who suffer injuries when the sky falls down on them, as often it does. Havel simply *supposed* that, despite everything, individuals 'by nature' want to live in the truth, a supposition that mistakes ontology for history. The point is that we feel ourselves to be responsible individuals who want to keep our spines straight and live in dignity in the world thanks to the survival of tradition, for instance, because we have inherited such a disposition from Christian-influenced traditions, as his friend Jan Patočka was fond of pointing out. That point begs a series of hard questions about the problem of deaf ears and hostile minds and hearts. Havel was aware, of course, that the origins of our capacity for action in the world as individuals are necessarily shrouded in some mystery: if the existential roots of individuality were graspable, then the tender plant of individuality would die. But it has to be said that, although in particular contexts at particular points in time some people are inclined to live truthfully, we are not 'by nature' lovers of truthful living. 'The Power of the Powerless' thus failed to propose a way of breaking the hypnotic effects of a system of power that, as he admits in one passage, offers to people who feel lost and humiliated 'an immediately available home: all one has to do is accept it, and suddenly everything becomes clear once more, life takes on new meaning, and all mysteries, unanswered questions, anxiety, and loneliness vanish'.

The same point about the limits of Havel's ontological account of living in the truth can be put in a different way and with different implications. Whether intended or not, Havel's belief in the ontological principle of living in the truth encouraged the abandonment of politics – the often messy and always complicated activity of collectively encouraging individuals 'to live in the truth' and thereby to decide who gets what, when and how. Havel's account *supposed* that the good society is one that recognizes and gives expression to its most secure foundation, the individual living in truth. Expressed differently again, Havel's defence of living in the truth rests upon a species of what his Hungarian colleague György Konrád later called anti-politics.[1] It *supposed* that politics is a type of impersonal and unprincipled activity that reaches its zenith in the figure of the grey-suited Party apparatchik, generals with tinted shades, leather-jacketed secret policemen, military-uniformed bureaucrats, and other cogs in the late-socialist state; that politics is shrewdness, manipulation, unfreedom, the struggle of some to exercise power over others; that politics is inherently absolutist, in that its field of operation, human beings living together in complex societies, is infinitely deep and wide, and that therefore the hunger of those politicians who politically seduce, manipulate and subsume others is never fully satisfiable.

Havel's essay admittedly contained a few passing references to the importance of such procedural arrangements as the rule of law and the necessity of defending human and civil rights, as specified in the constitutions of particular states, the Universal Declaration of Human Rights, the International Covenant on Human Rights, and the Concluding Act of the Helsinki Agreement. But nowhere did the text mention politics as a form of collectively based speech and interaction orientated to the attainment of the good life (as in the Aristotelian tradition). The text also eschewed talk of parliaments, armies, police forces, the civil service, local government, as if these institutions were somehow unnecessary or secondary or optional or ultimately dispensable procedures, or what Havel called 'dry' mechanisms, since they cramp the truthfully-living individual. Talk of synergies between individuals and organizations should be suspected, he implied. There is always a zero-sum power relationship between subjects who think and act in the truth and their institutional environment. Havel's statement about the primacy of the individual's existence over the institutional frameworks within which they live made this point clear. 'It is of great importance,' he wrote, 'that the main thing – the everyday, thankless, and never-ending struggle of human beings to live more freely, truthfully, and in quiet dignity – never impose any limits on itself, never be halfhearted, inconsistent,

[1] György Konrád, *Anti-Politics* (London, 1984).

never trap itself in political tactics, speculating on the outcome of its actions or entertaining fantasies about the future. The purity of this struggle,' he concluded, 'is the best guarantee of optimum results'.[1]

The limitations of an ontology of individualism, and especially its strange other-worldly unconcern with the institutional *preconditions* of liberty, would later become evident in the political battles sparked by Havel's penchant for acting as a prima donna, surrounding himself with hand-picked appointees, and his maverick appeals to 'the citizens' over the heads of parliament and the courts of law. 'The Power of the Powerless' was equally unconcerned with the philosophical limits of individualism. Indeed, it concealed these limits through literary skill, that is, by attempting to divine *individual* readers' sympathy through the sheer rhetorical force of his text, for instance in its bold appeal to shed the burden of all inherited political thought and political habits, or in its comparison of living for the truth with the act of surfacing from darkness into the light of day. Its provocative summary of the significance of Charter 77 was also exemplary of its rhetorical force: 'The confrontation between a thousand Chartists and the post-totalitarian system,' wrote Havel, 'would appear to be politically hopeless. This is true, of course, if we look at it through the traditional lens of the open political system, in which, quite naturally, every political force is measured chiefly in terms of the positions it holds on the level of real power. Given that perspective, a mini-party like the Charter would certainly not stand a chance. If, however, this confrontation is seen against the background of what we know about power in the post-totalitarian system, it appears in a fundamentally different light. For the time being, it is impossible to say with any precision what impact the appearance of Charter 77, its existence and its work has had in the hidden sphere, and how the Charter's attempt to rekindle civic self-awareness and confidence is regarded there. Whether, when, and how this investment will eventually produce dividends in the form of specific political changes is even less possible to predict. But that, of course, is all part of living within the truth. As an existential solution, it takes individuals back to the solid ground

---

[1] *The Power of the Powerless*, op. cit., p. 205. Compare Václav Žák's original criticism of Havel and others for confusing 'the level of thinking about individual responsibility and the level of thinking about the operation of society', in 'Co je naše tradice' (samizdat, Prague, 1986).

of their own identity; as politics, it throws them into a game of chance where the stakes are all or nothing.'

Powerful rhetoric of this kind was eventually to move millions of people to clap and cheer Havel. Even at the time it seemed to work small wonders. Retyped by loyal fingers, it was read to shreds by hundreds, perhaps thousands who found the essay brilliantly persuasive. There were some who reacted with hostility – the little-known Charter 77 group around Emanuel Mandler fiercely criticized Havel's unrealistic defence of a political theory and strategy that set itself up as a 'moral judge' of society, served in practice to deepen the division between 'normal' citizens and 'dissidents', and thereby exposed the opponents of the regime to state repression.[1] The Czech dissident scholar Václav Černý reportedly also bitterly attacked the essay as the 'horribly superficial, shallow' work of a figure who was 'pathologically conceited, pathologically ambitious'.[2] Yet many more Czechs and Slovaks found the essay enlightening. Even dough-faced Party bureaucrats read and discussed its themes.[3] Foreign translations of the essay also sometimes caused a minor sensation, as in Italy, where the tiny Bologna publisher CSEO sold more than 30,000 copies in quick time.[4] The essay also earned handsome praise wherever it appeared in the Soviet block. The Polish reaction was not atypical. The Polish writer Stanisław Barańczak recalled how the underground translation of the essay produced 'broad-based popularity and unanimous respect' for Havel within the ranks of the opposition during the late 1970s.[5] The remark of the Polish Solidarity leader Zbigniew Bujak also captured something of the way the essay engendered the joy of 'living in the truth' among its first, otherwise deflated readers within the Soviet block. 'This essay reached us in the Ursus factory in 1979 at a point when we felt we were at the end of the road,' said Bujak: 'Inspired by KOR [the Polish Workers' Defence Committee], we had been speaking on the shop floor, talking to people, participating in

---

[1]This criticism of Havel is analysed in 'Co je naše tradice', op. cit.
[2]Václav Černý, *Paměti 1945–1972* (Brno, 1992 [1983]), p. 162. Černý reportedly added that Havel was 'utterly beside himself if a week went by without the world talking about him'.
[3]Robert B. Pynsent, 'The Work of Václav Havel', *SEER*, volume 73, 2 (April 1995), p. 271.
[4]Václav Bělohradský, 'Jubileum', in *Milý Václave . . . Tvůj*, op. cit., p. 27.
[5]Stanisław Baranczak, *Breathing Under Water and Other East European Essays* (Cambridge, Mass., and London, 1990), p. 54.

public meetings, trying to speak the truth about the factory, the country, and politics. There came a moment when people thought we were crazy. Why were we doing this? Why were we taking such risks? Not seeing any immediate and tangible results, we began to doubt the purposefulness of what we were doing. Shouldn't we be coming up with other methods, other ways?' Bujak continued: 'Then came the essay by Havel. Reading it gave us the theoretical underpinnings for our activity. It maintained our spirits; we did not give up, and a year later – in August 1980 – it became clear that the party apparatus and the factory management were afraid of us. We mattered.' Bujak added: 'When I look at the victories of Solidarity, and of Charter 77, I see in them an astonishing fulfilment of the prophecies and knowledge contained in Havel's essay.'[1]

It could even be said that the act of writing the essay was an exemplary case of the civil resistance to power – a small-scale initiative – that it advocated. Despite everything that was to follow this act of resistance, two major things were permanently achieved by 'The Power of the Powerless'. To begin with, Havel's rough treatment at the hands of the authorities illustrated to everybody with eyes that could see that the regime's propensity to violence highlighted the need to find peaceful alternatives – just as the essay had proposed. 'The Power of the Powerless' rejected Sorelian-type myths of brave and heroic violence. Havel admitted that there are times, during the build-up to the Second World War, for instance, when the use of violence must be regarded as a necessary evil. In these 'extreme situations' violence must sometimes be met with violence, for otherwise remaining passive effectively works against decency and in favour of the rule of violence. But the trouble with violence, he argued, is that it is the extreme case of the instrumentalization of concrete human beings, often for some abstract, spurious and ill-defined better future. Violence is the antithesis of living in the truth. It follows that 'a future secured by violence might actually be worse than what exists now'. Havel insisted that those who live in truth 'do not shy away from the idea of violent political overthrow because the idea seems too radical, but on the contrary, because it does not seem radical enough'.

The non-violent sentiment of 'The Power of the Powerless'

---

[1]Cited in *Open Letters*, op. cit., pp. 125–126.

resonated with the fact that the heavily armed late-socialist regime ensured that surveillance, military parades, prison and fears of random violence were constant everyday companions of the whole population, who understandably felt a deep antipathy towards the use of violence as a tactic of resistance. In opposition to the traditional left and right, the essay associated bravery not with heroic acts of violence, such as terrorism, assassinations or kidnappings, against perceived enemies. Bravery is rather seen as the civilized patience of citizens who seek to live decently in an indecent regime and, therefore, remain unmoved by acts of violence directed against them. Havel supposed an inner connection between violence and state-centred politics, and he therefore (implicitly) rejected Marx's well-known view that 'violence is the midwife of every society pregnant with a new one'. According to Havel, violence is the enemy of all societies, old and new. Compared with the (calculated) impatience of revolutionaries and revolutionary politics, Havel's account of power was imbued with a fundamentally different sense of time. It rejected fantasies of apocalyptic revolution because it supposed that 'living in the truth' requires citizens to acquire the art of patience. It further supposed that acts of living in the truth could not succeed in days, weeks or months; that there is no such thing as total defeat; and that, if necessary, citizens must wait a very long time and be prepared to endure harsh setbacks. In short, Havel envisaged a peaceful abolition of the late-socialist system by means of a *slow fermentation* of opposition underneath, and in opposition to, the edifice of state power.

The proposed theory of living in the truth was more than simply an attack upon late-socialism. From under the rubble of that system, it was something of a parable about the dangers of all forms of concentrated power. It therefore necessarily involved a challenge to the whole of modern political thought's preoccupation with the sovereign power of the territorial state. Without saying so in exactly these words, Havel's essay proposed lopping off the head of sovereign power. It breathed new life into the maxim that the struggle against stupidity is the only human struggle that is always in vain, but can never be relinquished. More than that – this was its second major achievement – the essay proposed a new practical solution to the age-old problem of finding a remedy for the hubris of political power.

The problem of *hybris* was first formulated by classical Greek thinkers and historians like Herodotus and Thucydides, for whom the ambitious desire to have more than one's share of power is a necessary feature of political life and one that inevitably produces disastrous effects. From Thucydides and others, there is no good news for us. The Greek analysts of power warned that power breeds overconfidence and imprudence. *Hybris* is the progeny of high position, as Euripedes explained, in a famous passage in the *Suppliant Women*, where it is said that the conqueror 'is like a poor man who has just become rich: he commits *hybris*, and his *hybris* causes him to be ruined in his turn'. *Hybris*, we are told, is also fed by the need of the powerful to shield themselves against the aggression of the powerless, whose oppression breeds fear. Power is sometimes despised by those who don't have it and those who exercise command over others become the object of fear and hostility or even hatred, which is why the powerful tend to act imprudently. They are prone to paranoia, plotting and flattery of their subjects, which prompted Pericles to say that he feared before everything else the city of Athens' arrogant mistakes, such as refusing the offer of peace during the time of Pylos, acting cruelly against other cities, and initiating new conquests, especially in Sicily. Finally, our Greek ancestors warned, *hybris* breeds *hybris*. Power leads to increases in power because powerful rulers have to act that way. As things plummet out of control, the path of prudence, the acquired skill of judging 'what is best', as the Greeks loved to say, gets ever narrower . . . and it becomes narrower still, as Isocrates, Demosthenes and Pericles in his Epitaphios all emphasized, because of the decline of civic morality among both rulers and ruled, the final effect of which is discord, *stasis*.

The originally Greek idea that *hybris* and its dangerous effect are rooted in the very nature of power over others survived into modern times – think of the various accounts of the rise and fall of the Roman empire by writers such as Polybius, Livy, Sallust, Florus, Montesquieu and Gibbon. The theme of *hybris* left a bad taste in the mouths of all those who knew that modern forms of state power were prone to corruption. Unfortunately, the analysts of *hybris* gave a Greek gift to the modern world, in that they provided no permanent remedy for the dangers of *hybris*, except for the thought that it is punishable by the gods, who so hate the wish to have more than a fair share of power that they arc prone to turn against mortals, as Herodotus reports Artabanus to have warned Xerxes before he finally made the decision to attack Greece: 'You see the biggest creatures, how God crushes them with his thunder, and doesn't allow them to make a show of their great size. But the small ones don't trouble him. You see how he always directs his blows towards the highest houses and the highest trees. God indeed abases anything that grows above the rest . . . For God doesn't allow high-mindedness in others but himself.'

Except in millenarian circles, warnings about divine intervention against the powerful ring hollow in our times, and so it can be said, from the perspective of the ancients, that we moderns have been bequeathed what might be described as an *aporia*, an extremely difficult perennial problem that seems virtually insoluble. The problem is this: given the tendency in the world of politics towards *hybris*, how can its disastrous effects be overcome? How, in other words, can citizens be liberated from the permanent dangers of corruption and the infernal rise and fall of states? Can human beings find other ways of organizing power that would release them from *hybris*? Or must we reckon with the ultimate impossibility of containing *hybris*? Is life nothing more an endless struggle for power that comes to rest only at the point of death? Or can only divine intervention now rescue us from the trials and tribulations caused by our own hubris?

In 'The Power of the Powerless', interestingly, Havel's response to these questions cross-referred to the German philosopher and critic, Martin Heidegger. In a famous interview with *Der Spiegel* published only after his death, Heidegger discussed the problem of whether any political system, including democracy, can reverse the hubris of our technological age.[1] The essence of modern technology is its imprisonment of Man within a Frame-Work (*Ge-stell*) that puts men and women in their place, assigns them tasks, and calls them to order, all the while crushing their existent individualities by means of abstractions, thus rendering them powerless. 'I don't know whether you're frightened,' Heidegger remarked to his interviewers. 'I am when I see TV transmissions of the earth from the moon. We don't need an atom bomb. Man has already been uprooted from the earth. What's left are purely technical relations. Where man lives today is no longer an earth.'

So what is to be done? Is there any solution to this problematic

[1]*Der Spiegel*, 23 (31 May 1976), pp. 193ff.

hubris of modern times? Heidegger's reply is as striking as it is unsatisfactory. 'Only a God can save us now,' he says, using words that Havel's 'The Power of the Powerless' repeats, with a twist. Heidegger's polemics against the modern world led him to urge others to step away from the 'noise' of the world, to withdraw so as to allow individuals in their concrete being-there to listen thoughtfully to the call of Being. Concrete individuals should actively strive to be passive, that is, to engage in the contemplation of the present, to prepare expectations or, as Heidegger puts it, 'to prepare to be prepared for the manifestation of God, or for the absence of God as things go downhill all the way'.

In broad outline, Havel accepted Heidegger's diagnosis of the crisis of modern technological society. Late-socialism is seen by Havel to be a thoroughly *modern* regime which, contrary to being a regression or mutant, is in fact both 'an inflated caricature of modern life in general' and the possible shape of things to come. Late-socialism was the most complete and devilish expression so far of modern attempts to transform citizens into subjects who are compelled to act as if they were mere casts of extras in a fully politicized stage performance directed from above. The Soviet-type system of late-socialism is 'a kind of warning to the West, revealing its own latent tendencies'. Havel also acknowledged Heidegger's observation that there appears to be no way out of the powerlessness produced by modern regimes of power. We seem to be condemned to look on helplessly at the coldly functioning organizations that engulf us by tearing us away from both our natural habitats and fellow human beings. 'We have no idea and no faith, and even less do we have a political conception to help us bring things back under human control.' That leaves only one possible earthly weapon against hubris. Heidegger missed it: the cultivation, from below and against all odds, of institutions that can develop 'the independent life of society' and thereby empower the powerless, even preventing them from ever becoming new masters of others. Tentatively, and in clumsy language, Havel called this new and desperate possibility 'social self-organization'. With greater confidence and precision – and political implications of the most dramatic type – it would soon be called *civil society*.

PRISON

T he StB came for him at five o'clock in the morning of 29 May 1979. The swoop was quick and quiet. He was bundled, half-asleep in a state of controlled panic, into the back of a van, handcuffed, clutching only his favourite bundle of belongings – an emergency kit containing a toothbrush, razor, nail clippers, deodorant, brush and comb, a few sticking plasters. As the sun rose he was unloaded into the sable corridors of Ruzyně prison and, along with ten other members of the Committee to Defend the Unjustly Prosecuted (VONS), charged under Article 98 of the Criminal Code for 'subversion', a crime against the state that carried a penalty of up to ten years' imprisonment.

So began a desperate personal experiment in the related arts of improving his physical health, steadying his nerves, and breathing meaning into his own existence. Havel initially spoke of it as a struggle for 'self-consolidation'. He likened his imprisonment, minus the drama and deep religiosity, to the inner commitment and outward struggle of Dostoevsky's heroes, as they go off to prison, to be themselves in a better way. Havel refused easy solutions, bolting for the emergency exits of false confessions or emigration, for instance, and he was confident that his refusal would give him the permanent strength of knowing that he had not shied away from the basic task of self-improvement. It was as if he wanted to follow the script outlined in 'The Power of the Powerless', as his first letter to Olga from Ruzyně prison on 4 June of the year 1979 records: 'It appears the astrologers were right when they predicted prison for me again this year and when they said the summer would be a hot one', he wrote. 'As a matter of fact, it's stifling hot here, like being in a perpetual sauna. I feel sorry about the many complications my new stint in jail will probably cause you . . . I don't know, of course, how long this trip will last; I'm not harbouring any illusions, and in fact I hardly think about it at all.' He concluded: 'Prison, of course, is a terrible bore; it's no fun staring at the walls day after day, but with each stay I find it easier to bear because a lot that I once found disturbing no longer surprises or upsets me.'[1]

In fact, Havel's time in prison proved a good deal more personally threatening than the phrases 'living in the truth' or 'self-consolidation' implied. His stint in prison is better described

[1]Václav Havel, *Letters to Olga*, op. cit., pp. 23–24.

as a power struggle of the most primordial kind: a struggle against the inevitability of powerlessness. He was fated to suffer a profound crisis of identity – the same profound crisis of identity represented within virtually every one of his plays – in which his own sense of self began to crumble, leaving in its trail the rubble of everything that endows human existence with a meaningful sense of order, continuity and change. Under prison conditions that resembled a 'pure' or 'concentrated' form of late-socialism, he was forced to battle with the realization of just how fragile and contingent and destructible the human personality is.

The human personality, Havel had always argued, has no guaranteed, fixed essence. It is 'a large set of possibilities, potentials, perspectives, relationships, demands, opinions and anticipated responses; it is something open, always actual'.[1] The personality resembles an unfinished play but, like all plays, its attempted or actual completion and production may end in failure. Havel, drawing on the language of existentialism, called this 'nothingness', a condition in which the human personality is virtually dissolved into its surroundings. 'If nothingness wins out,' he wrote, 'man surrenders to apathy, and faith and meaning exist only as a backdrop against which others become aware of his fall.'[2] Prison threatened him with such decline and decay into 'nothingness' – into a 170-pound lump of organic matter – and posed to him the only other realistic alternative: the struggle, against great odds, to establish (here Havel drew on Patočka) a self capable of acting responsibly in the world.

Prison hammered into Havel's hide the painful realization that responsibility is the key to human identity. 'The secret of man is the secret of his responsibility,' he concluded.[3] By this he meant that individuals' faith in their own power to live in the world is constitutive of their capacity to thrive in the world. Conversely, the disintegration of the human personality always entails the destruction of the power of the individual to carry on in the world. Responsibility is the centre of gravity of the self. It has a relational quality, in that it requires the existence of a person who is responsible and someone or something for whom or for which that person is responsible. Responsibility orientates the self within

[1]*Letters to Olga*, op. cit., p. 138.
[2]Ibid., p. 153.
[3]Ibid., p. 145.

an infinitely wider and longer landscape. It endows that self with
the power to confer meaning on its relations with the wider world.
The substance of the meaning so conferred can be and usually is
multiplicitous. Some interpret responsibility in terms of love and
sacrifice; others see it as a matter of instinctual self-preservation; still
others consider responsibility as a relationship to the sacred; some
treat it as a phantom from past times when people still feared gods.
In each case, however, responsibility ultimately makes possible the
creative 'separation' of the self from the world by enabling the self
to become an independently thinking, judging, acting being. That
means that the struggle to establish and cultivate responsibility is
a life-and-death struggle to survive as a human being. Life is
constantly threatened by nothingness. Responsibility is thus the
prize in the contest between the individual and the world; the
power of individuals to survive in the world, their ability to fend
off nothingness, depends upon their skilled cultivation of their
capacity for responsibility.

The punishing prison conditions tested Havel's capacity for
responsibility. 'I would say that responsibility for oneself is a knife
we use to carve out our own inimitable features in the panorama
of Being,' he remarked eighteen months into his sentence.[1]
The tone of philosophical defiance built into the remark was
double-edged. It testified to his rebelliousness in the face of
nihilism, the stubbornness of his personal efforts to stand out and
stand up to the crushing pressure of a prison world wrapped in
barbed wire. But the remark also revealed his personal desperation
in the face of a system that aimed to harass, manipulate, repress, and
de-individualize his daily life and nightly dreams, even to offer the
prospect of death.

Pushed to the edge of the world, Havel's daily life was reduced
to frustrated basic wants, half-satisfied needs, yearnings, compensa-
tory reflections, weird happenings. Like being shaved bald and
noticing for the first time the contrast between his smooth skull and
wrinkled face. Or coming to terms with the lack of light by day, the
lack of darkness at night. Living in the same space with people who
swiped his cigarette butts. Getting used to a wide assortment of
pollyannas, perverts, miserable and desperate men, some of them
scoundrels. Adjusting to shortages (or the outright banning) of

---

[1] *Letters to Olga*, op. cit., p. 147.

items he craved most: Stuyvesant cigarettes, powdered juice, lemons, plums, apples, perfumed Kleenex, toothpicks, cheese slices, instant cocoa, strawberry jam, tea, cigars. Intense homesickness for the permitted minor pleasures of late-socialism: sleeping in his own bed wearing his own pyjamas; drinking strong coffee in the morning; strolling through Malá Strana; sweating in the sauna; eating crab cocktail, steak, and cake topped with whipped cream in a restaurant; watching good movies; gathering with artist friends in bars, studios, and galleries; lying in the sun on the lawn; barbecuing chicken at Hrádeček; making the tartar sauce to go with it while sipping white wine and listening to Pink Floyd and the Stones.

Feeling with increasing intensity that prison is an institution designed to rob inmates of free time. Grasping a line in Shakespeare's *Richard II*: 'Grief makes one hour ten.' Attempting to study English. Hoping to learn German. Being victimized by his constant compulsion to reconsider things. Witnessing and hearing buggery. Reading a queer variety of (sometimes bad) books, despite the enveloping hubbub: *Aurelien* by Aragon; a crime novel by Ed McBain; *The Pickwick Papers*; Max Brod's biography of Kafka; Hemingway's *To Have and Have Not*; biographies of Muhammad, Toulouse-Lautrec, and Karl Hermann Frank; *The Triumph* (a look from behind the scenes at American foreign policy); a little book on the Watergate scandal by Václav Borovička; *Treasure Island*; *The Financier* by Dreiser; a novel about capital punishment by the Czech author Jaroslav Maria, *The Sword and the Scales*; Ratzinger's *Introduction to Christianity*; Malaparte's *Kaput*; Stendhal's *Lucien Leuwen*; Saul Bellow's *Herzog*; an autobiographical account by Byrd of living alone for six months at the South Pole. Rescued by the cultivated and clever language of Musil. Pondering *The Stranger* by Camus. Battling with Heidegger's *Sein und Zeit*. Strenuous efforts to counteract hopelessness by doing yoga. Poring over *Rudé právo* the whole day, in effect performing textual analyses by distinguishing what is said from what is not said.

Yearning to hear things once more called by their proper names. Worrying about growing into a humourless old man with no sense of irony. Playing chess with a partner too good for him, and not enjoying it. Fraught attempts to imagine new plays and to analyse the most incredible events and characters of his dreams. Experiencing everything more intensely – and paying more intensely for it. Repeated vivid dreams of women like the VONS activist Jarmila Bělíková and the mysterious 'Andulka'[1], 'who appears to me by day and in my dreams'; old theatre friends like Andulka's ex-husband, Pavel Kohout. Other lavish dreams stained with traces of prison power: being visited by Gert Bastian, former General in the Bundeswehr, dismissed for his opposition to Nato deployment of nuclear weapons; and filming in America with the lucky and successful – and free – Miloš Forman. Suddenly becoming full of energy and élan, gripped by the feeling that there is hope because fundamentally one's life is meaningful.

Good health fertilized by the absence of complications, self-confidence, even the feeling of being able to express things coherently, with a touch of wit. Moved after six months' pre-trial detention from Ruzyně to Heřmanice. After nineteen months, from there to Plzeň-Bory for another thirteen unlucky months, followed by another few months elsewhere. Watching others exhilarated after hitting up with whatever they could manage to get their hands on. Convinced that the tragedy of modern man is not that he knows less and less about the meaning of his life, but that he just doesn't give a toss. Darkness and empty boredom. No sounds of children playing outside his window. No shaking hands, indeed, no physical contact with anybody, except when accidentally bumping into someone or when visited, a few times each year, by Olga and Ivan. Inmates' constant natter about women. Struggling with the burden of inventing a different concept of time. Discovering one way of shortening it: by imagining that one has just been sentenced, only to the time that actually remains. The strange feeling of dependency upon the one-dimensional surroundings of prison. Waving goodbye to the complexity of the outside world, giving up the corresponding art of living responsibly by making decisive judgements about matters like appointments and deadlines. Childish delight in small

---

[1]Havel here referred to Anna Kohoutová, with whom he was having an affair until the morning he was dragged from her bed, to begin this spell in prison. Stories of the affair are told by her daughter, Tereza Boučková, in her *Indiánský běh* (Prague, 1992; first published in samizdat) and an interview published in *Magazín Dnes + TV* (Prague), 10 September 1999, pp. 22–24. Boučková recalls that Havel, nicknamed 'Monolog', consummated the fantasy of sitting in a chair to watch Anna and her daughter strip naked; that Anna tried hard, without success, to get pregnant; and, after Havel was flung into Ruzyně, that his lover attempted to communicate with him by frequenting an adjoining children's playground, where she played waltzes at full blast on a cassette player (*Indiánský běh*, op. cit., pp. 43, 122, 127).

achievements like overcoming anger, darning a hole in a sock, or finding a quiet physical space to write. Discovering that writing, like a good night's sleep, is a biological necessity. Gripped constantly by the feeling that letter-writing to immediate relatives – the only writing permitted by the authorities – is an unsatisfying form of soliloquy addressed to a world that is ever receding over the horizon. Enduring the strictest prison rules of correspondence. No more than one four-page letter per week. No copies of the letters to be retained. No letters to anybody but immediate family. No mention of prison conditions, or politics. No underlining. No scratching out or correction. No illegible handwriting. No quotation marks. No foreign words or expressions. No humour.

Feeling ill. Sinking into hibernation, dragged down by the sweet mental lethargy induced by the oppressive routines of prison life. Cold and sad reveries about autumn leaves. Winter darkness and gloom. Craving alcohol and settling for Earl Grey tea. Toasting the end and arrival of yet another year with prisoners' champagne: a powdered fizzy orange drink called (impressively) Celaskon Effervescens. Celebrating the world première of *The Mountain Hotel*, performed at the Akademietheater Wien, with an American cigarette and a cup of hot powdered milk. Looking forward to travelling by bus, at gunpoint, each day, to work in the nearby Vítkovice Ironworks, near Ostrava. Learning to be a welder. Washing and ironing sheets stained with millions of unborn children. Practising the art of self-control. Astonishment at discovering that shouting at a fellow prisoner relieves tension.

Certain that mental stupidity – forgetfulness, shrinking horizons, losing the knack of writing – is setting in. Shattered by exhaustion, aches and pains at the end of the working week. Craving sweet-tasting foods, like chocolate or crown mints. Six-monthly visits to the prison dentist. The satisfaction of having tartar removed from grimy teeth. Aching gums. Lancing pus with a needle sterilized in a flame. Getting new and stronger lenses in old glass frames. Searching for 'anchor points' – an approaching spring, a visit from Olga and Ivan, the sight of a tree, a warm gesture from a tattooed inmate. Undermined by hearing of the death of an old friend, the free-spirited anti-Chartist Jan Werich, an icon of the cultural confidence of the First Republic. Weighing the remark of Alexandre Dumas – 'A kind word in prison is worth more than the most expensive gift in freedom' – against the vile prison reality of permanent conflict, tension, and stress, some of it caused by tough-guy neighbours called 'kings'. Endless waiting for letters, some of which are not handed over because of something written in English, or because the text was deemed to contain hints, codes or cross-references, or because the prison authorities objected to the name 'Václav Havel' written on the envelope. Savouring brother Ivan's reflections on modern physics. Feeling mentally fit, even enlivened by the clutter of interesting experiences and characters. Terrified by the reality of being inside for several more years. Always keeping an eye on personal belongings. Always chasing something, making arrangements, fearing for something. Otherwise feeling despondent, distracted, uneasy, inattentive, derailed. Bombardment with inmates' talk of how people are naturally lying, selfish bastards who are not worth helping. Learning that other people are indeed hell. Smoking in front of a mirror. Trying hard not to be turned into a curmudgeon. Practising the art of not yielding an inch to the unprincipled hatred of others.

Unlimited time for thinking coupled with the realization, amidst the clutter and lack of interaction with the outside world, of the impossibility of coming up with any decent ideas at all. The impossibility of writing about prison in prison. Struggling for trivial concessions like more sunlight. Daydreaming the first moments of release: telling stories to Olga; sweating it all out in a sauna; waltzing to the theme of the film *Doctor Zhivago*; having good dinners and parties with friends, who will laugh with tears in their eyes; listening to favourite tapes and records; drinking good coffee and rum for breakfast; dropping in on brother Ivan and hugging oldest friends like Zdeněk Urbánek; drinking beer at The Two Suns; paying respects to Egon Bondy; walking dogs through the splendid orchard on Petřín Hill; bumping into conformists unsure of which way they should look; strolling through the Wallenstein Garden; admiring a large pool containing goldfish, gurgling water nymphs, a statue of St George wrestling a dragon; going for a swim at Podolí; praying not to sink like a stone to the bottom.

Then two disturbing questions: What then? What next? The gnawing pain of lumbago. Another hernia. Tennis elbows. Longing for injections to kill pain. Disciplinary punishments. Chasing ideas around the head, all the while worrying about the danger of succumbing to prison psychosis. Fantasizing a natty new suit hand-tailored from dark-brown corduroy cloth. Knowing that a rich meal of grilled chicken, home-made tartar sauce, and white wine would now induce vomit. Comforting colleagues struck down by tears after receiving a letter from home. Battling all day, every day, with the burden of reconciling the need to get along with everyone and the impossibility of suppressing angry emotions against another inmate in a hellishly cramped cell measuring 6 metres square. Experimenting (unsuccessfully) with the art of establishing telepathic contact with others on the outside. Vividly sensual, almost hallucinatory memories – of boarding school in Poděbrady, Ajda shaking the water from her fur after dipping in a pond, the feel and smell of musty old theatre costumes impregnated with make-up powder at the Theatre on the Balustrade. Yet more intense daydreams about the first few days after release. Coping bodily with the impossibility of concentration by becoming bone-lazy and passive. Getting no pleasure out of exercising, losing weight, studying, thinking. Tumbling into a state of profound numbness and fatigue induced by nervous strain. Remembering Franz Kafka: 'Man is an eternal rebel.' Realizing that the source of hope is not outside, in objects or events for instance, but inside. Discovering and being repulsed by a certain type of prisoner, who on the outside is big-talking, bossy, selfish, cynical and interested only in getting rich at others' expense, while on the inside becomes a chronically simpering, self-pitying hypochondriac forever pinning the blame for everything indiscriminately on to others within reach.

Cheered by the sound and smell of rain. Yearning for the return of spring buds, flowers and perfume to the prison courtyard. Eating bread with margarine and garlic. Watching television – a good American documentary on Martin Luther King, even – and suddenly realizing that the outside 'normal' world actually exists, that it is not just a dream or a memory. Watching with delight a variety show put on by prisoners for prisoners. Prison muzak, once in a while good enough to attract dancing inmates under loudspeakers. Looking on, overcome with mounting depression at the pointlessness – and Orwellianism – of it all. Coping with an atmosphere that contains nothing pretty, pure, moving. Observing how many prisoners are grumpy hedgehogs who become irritated or fall into a vile temper by any disturbance of their precise and somnolent daily routines. Facing the grim probability that after calmly falling off to sleep, one will be awakened by a razor-sharp pang of resentment, followed by anger that abates only after arising from bed, furiously scribbling several pages of nonsense in the dark, pigging out on sweets, and smoking three cigarettes. Fearing that release will result in another lock-up.

Looking in the mirror, disgusted, to see only a double chin, baggy eyes, a filthy sagging face, crumpled wrinkles. Haemorrhoids. Always haemorrhoids, so bloody and painful that the prison doctor is summoned and, with luck, agrees to consign the sufferer to bed for days, with the added privilege of long warm baths and perhaps the good news that no tumour has been found. Experiencing the worst bad moods all in a row. Melancholy. Alienation. Hopelessness. Wild anger. Fear. Apathy. Self-doubt. Drawing the conclusion: that everything seems pointless, hopeless and sad, that one is good for nothing else but rotting in prison, that perhaps prison has been deserved. Battling colds and influenza. Bothered by not being able to go for a walk. Bothered more by the emotional incapacity to go for a walk. The fear, felt by everyone who senses the danger of metamorphosis, of being transformed into a tiny, helpless insect. Illness again: sore throats, aching joints, crippled arms, needles, headaches, pills, clogged lungs, and, worst of all, the unspecific prison fever. Feeling shivery, slight headache, watery eyes, always tired, groggy and weak, feeling brain-dead, nervous and absent-minded, compounded by nothing going right and nothing giving pleasure. After all these years, a bowel operation. No cigarettes for weeks. Sleeping off depression. Gaining weight. Staring out of the window. Diagnostic tests. Catheters. Fever. Pain. More pain.

Havel's prison ordeal dragged on until the last week of January 1983. One fateful Sunday afternoon, his body suddenly collapsed under the nerve-wracking weight of the past 189 weeks. Convulsed by a wildly beating heart and a raging fever well off the thermometer scale, he caused his bed to shake so loudly that it kept neighbouring prisoners awake all night. Havel became convinced of the arrival of the grim reaper. Worried that the death in custody of a world-famous rebel might produce an international scandal, his jailers panicked. After administering aspirin, then antibiotics, and X-raying his lungs – Havel was sure that he was suffering acute pneumonia – the authorities arranged for his transfer by ambulance, in pyjamas, handcuffed, back to Prague's Pankrác prison. There was talk of complications, even of some kind of bubble in his lungs. Havel went for broke. Although feeling ghastly, he summoned up enough energy to write a detailed account of his plight to Olga, hoping that the laxer censorship at Pankrác combined with his expressed anxiety that he might be dying would together ensure that his letter from the prison hospital cell just might get through. It did.

Olga, accompanied by Zdeněk Urbánek, rushed to the prison. They demanded to see Havel, to learn details of his condition, even to leave some fruit for the patient. The authorities refused each request, adding only that Havel was alive and his condition stable. Olga exploded. She rushed home and rang Pavel Kohout, now an *émigré* in Vienna. He spent several days and nights telephoning the offices of various notables and heads of state throughout Western Europe, urging them to intervene. Messages on his behalf soon began arriving from all over the world, with quick effect. 'One evening, which I shall never forget,' Havel recalled, 'just as I was getting ready to go to sleep, into my cell there suddenly stepped several guards, a doctor, and a woman official of some kind, who informed me that the District Court of Prague 4 was terminating my sentence.'[1] He was so flabbergasted, even overcome with fear of freedom, that he begged to spend one more night in prison. He was told by the official that that was impossible because he was now a civilian, that without delay he should gather his few belongings, since an ambulance was waiting to take him in his pyjamas to Pod Petřínem civilian hospital.

By the time he reached the intensive-care unit, Havel was in a state of euphoric shock. People were calling him 'Mr Havel' (instead of the impolite 'Havel'). He was no longer handcuffed. Gone were the burly policemen armed with pistols and panting, snarling dogs. He was even able to pick up the phone. Within the hour, Olga, Ivan and Ivan's then wife Květa had arrived, wielding flowers, oranges, sweets, cigarettes, newspapers, photographs, clothes. The distinguished playwright Josef Topol

[1] *Letters to Olga*, op. cit., p. 160.

soon joined them, clutching a chrysanthemum, tears in his eyes, shocked upon hugging Havel that his thin body now flinched at human contact.[1] Everybody then cried, including some of the nurses and doctors. News of his release was broadcast by the serendipitous Voice of America – just one day after it had broadcast a Charter 77 appeal for his release. At the flick of a microphone switch, a panicked regime hoping to unburden itself of a sick dissident by parading itself internationally as liberal found itself represented as having buckled under the moral pressure of democratic forces at home and abroad.

Havel's condition quickly improved. It felt like the happiest time of his life. 'Released from the burden of prison, but not yet encumbered by the burden of freedom, I lived like a king,' he recalled.[2] Holding court from his bed, sometimes on the telephone, he welcomed friends all day long, every day, for a month. He seemed not to need sleep. Samizdat texts piled up on his bedside tables. Flowers and salutations and gifts arrived from all over the world. Cameras clicked. Olga brought him a bottle of gin a day, and Havel the brewmaster quickly perfected the art of converting tinned fruit gifts into fruit punches. These he drank by night either chatting up the young female nurses or alone, propped up on pillows reading Ludvík Vaculík's *Czech Dream-book*, the most talked about literary work in the contemporary Prague scene. Havel himself appears as a character within the text – as a brave non-conformist – which seemed a fitting tribute after all that he had been through.

Everything considered, his life seemed normal once again, perhaps even better than normal. The baleful omnipresence of the state had receded. The secret police visiting his bedside spoke with honey tongues. They apologized, politely nodded, and thanked him for continuing to refrain from speaking with foreign journalists, and from making international calls. The hospital staff were kind. No visiting hours applied. Smiling, chatting well-wishers of every description freely came and went. Havel laughed for the first time for years. He had only rights, and no duties. He felt unconditionally free. Even his body again felt

[1]Interview with Josef Topol (Prague), 6 March 1999.
[2]*Disturbing the Peace*, op. cit., p. 161.

refreshed, light, effervescent. Everything somehow represented a triumph over the evil of arbitrary power – except for the profound personal crisis that he was soon to suffer.

LARGO DESOLATO

The day came when he had to return to the world as it was. Released from Pod Petřínem hospital during the first week of March 1983, he was driven to his family apartment house on the embankment on Rašínovo nábřeží, where he hoped and expected – as he had made clear in a reverie from prison – to spend time with Olga, to renew and develop what he called at one point during his sentence their 'two-in-one identity'.[1] During one sweet fantasy about life after prison, Havel imagined going to a sauna, combining it with swimming and sunbathing, then going home for a snooze, then in the evening putting on some nice clothes and going out with Olga to a good restaurant and eating and drinking to their hearts' content. Within another reverie he re-enacted his favourite morning routine of sleeping late, drinking good coffee and rum, listening to tapes and records, then soaking in the bath, with Olga sitting beside him, on a bathroom stool, summarizing the large pile of newspapers that every morning she and he had once loved to devour together.

These sweet fantasies were entirely understandable. Not only had their relationship survived unbroken since the 1950s. During the past three years, the more pertinent fact was that Havel had come to regard Olga as his anchor-hold, or 'point of stability'. Awash in transience, blown here and there by political storms, culminating in prison, Havel regarded her as the main addressee of his communications with the outside world. Whenever something good, or absurd, or heartbreaking happened to him, and whenever he mulled it over in his mind, which he often did, he would issue a report to her, as it were. Olga honoured his wish. She was always the first to open the letters when they arrived. She would either read them alone, or aloud to friends (like Zdeněk Urbánek) who were with her at the time.[2] Then she would pass each letter to Ivan, who for safe-keeping would make two or three copies on the typewriter. Olga was his penfriend. So it seemed only fitting that after release Havel decided to assemble and publish the letters under the title *Dopisy Olze* (*Letters to Olga*). 'It's true that you won't find many heartfelt, personal passages specifically addressed to my wife in my prison letters,' he later said. 'Even

[1] *Letters to Olga*, op. cit., p. 277.
[2] Zdeněk Urbánek, 'Poděkování', *Ztracená země* (Prague, 1992), pp. 472–473.

so, I think that Olga is their main hero, though admittedly hidden. That is why I put her name in the title of the book. Doesn't that endless search for a firm point, for certainty, for an absolute horizon that fills those letters say something, in itself, to confirm that?'[1]

Letters to Olga is a sad but inspiring work, especially for personally troubled or melancholy readers.[2] Its chosen title was calculated by Havel – with an eye on his public image – to bless the letters with a touch of romantic love. There are certainly plenty of passages in the letters that lend credence to that image Havel desired. 'Last night I dreamt about you. We had rented a palazzo in Venice!' he wrote. 'I'm worried about you!' runs another passage. 'Don't walk over bridges alone at night, and don't go anywhere alone, if possible.' There were also many passages of heartfelt concern. 'I'm really sorry you feel depressions coming on. But you can't afford to have depressions now – wait till I come home! Be cheerful, sociable, active, brave and prudent (but mainly prudent).' And there were the lover's passages: 'I appreciated your saying in one of them that you love me. It's been a long time since you've told me that!'

The interesting thing about these passages in *Letters to Olga* is just how exceptional they are.[3] Those who read the letters as confirmation of a relationship of romantic love battered by months and years of separation in effect have blind eyes for the friction manifested in dozens of contrary passages within the text. We do not know what Olga wrote to her husband – the letters were confiscated by the secret police during a house search, and reportedly went missing[4] – but we do know

---

[1]*Disturbing the Peace*, op. cit., p. 157.

[2]Salman Rushdie (in an interview transmitted on National Public Radio [New York, 21 April 1999]) praised *Letters to Olga* as among the small handful of his favourite books (which included James Joyce's *Ulysses*) that he carried everywhere during his years of hiding from possible execution.

[3]The impression is certainly reinforced by considering one letter *not* included in either the English edition or the published Czech edition organized by Havel's friend, Jan Lopatka. It was a reply to Olga's earlier remark that Kamila Bendová, wife of Havel's prisonmate Václav Benda, had said that Havel never seemed to write such beautiful love letters to Olga as she received from her husband. So Havel tried to prove her wrong by writing just such a letter. 'We nicknamed it The Love Letter', said Ivan Havel later (in an interview, in Prague, on 24 September 1997). It turned out to be an essay on how to write love letters. It revealed how he seemed unable to write an open, warm, loving letter.

[4]Interview with Pavel Kosatík (Prague), 30 September 1997; and with Anna Freimanová (Prague), 9 November 1998.

that her letters did not always win his approval. 'You said you were not sending me a kiss and that I knew why,' he wrote six weeks into his detention. 'I don't know why! I do know, however, that you mustn't write such things to me – I felt miserable for several days. These letters are all one has here. You read them a dozen times, turn them over in your mind, every detail is either a delight or a torment and makes you aware of how helpless you are. In other words, you must write me nice letters.' The demand made of his lover-wife seemed reasonable enough, but in the next breath he issued a string of commands and a reprimand that both contradicted his own principle of romantic civility and revealed some hidden anger at his wife. 'And number them, put the date on them and above all, be as exhaustive as you can and write legibly. After all, it's not so difficult to sit down at a typewriter once in a while and write about everything you're up to.'[1]

Aggression poked its way up between his lines like nettles repeatedly during the next three years. On and on and on *and on* he went about how Olga didn't write enough to him. He often claimed she had 'orphaned' him and regularly signed off by saying that he had run out of paper, as if to remind and chide her that her occasional postcard or one side of a single sheet of paper was thoughtless. At one stage, he wrote in exasperation: 'WRITE MORE OFTEN! WRITE MORE DETAILS! WRITE MORE!' He grumbled constantly, even to the point of nicknaming her The Grumbler. He also chastised her often for not observing the ever-changing rules of prison correspondence: 'I was informed last night that another letter from you had arrived,' he wrote eighteen months into his sentence, adding that the authorities had confiscated it 'because there are greetings from various friends in it, and I am allowed to receive messages and greetings only from relatives. I wasn't even given the photos you included. A pity. It's the third time this has happened.'

Even in the trying circumstances, Havel's reaction was anomalous, considering that he knew Olga actually loved to write. Crafting little plays for fun at the kitchen table in Hrádeček, for instance, was among her favourite activities. She wrote quickly, so quickly in fact that Václav was envious. Her infrequent com-

[1] *Letters to Olga*, op. cit., p. 27.

munication clearly had other and deeper roots, though they seemed lost on Havel at the time. He took little account of the interfering tricks played by the prison authorities on their attempts to synchronize letters. Olga understood the point instinctively: 'Sometimes I would get three at once. Sometimes he would not get my replies before he sent another letter. It was a method they used to make people nervous – psychological pressure.'[1] Havel also underestimated Olga's unshakeable commitment to the marriage. He therefore misunderstood her belief that detailed letter-writing was an exercise in pointlessness, especially since the prison-letter rules dictated that she could only pen the same clichés over and over, which is why she sometimes asked Havel's good friend Zdeněk Urbánek to write on her behalf. Havel's grumbles also overlooked the difficult point that letter-writing meant fundamentally different things to each of them. For him, each one of the 144 letters from prison that he wrote was a matter of life-or-death, a tactic of elementary survival against immense pain. The ensemble of letters resembled Janáček's *From the House of the Dead*: lacking any real plot, the four-page letters read like determined monologues from individual members of a prison chorus who step forward to tell their desperate story before melting back into invisibility. Olga's experience was the inverse: each letter or postcard that she attempted to write induced a great quantity of inner pain. 'Those were letters that were awfully hard for me to write,' she later said. 'I broke down even over the address where you had to write "the accused" and eventually "the convicted".'[2]

Havel also tried to get at Olga in other ways. He managed to master the art of completing compliments with put-downs, sarcasm and pickiness over details. 'I think of you with tenderness,' runs one letter's ending, 'and I even accept with tenderness the fact that you don't write, that you don't do what I ask or respond to my letters (do you at least read them carefully?)'. And another: 'I have an idea for an excellent Christmas gift you might give me: you could write me a long letter at last. Perhaps you could spend one of the holidays writing it.' He added, 'I'd appreciate it if you would answer at least some of

[1] Eric Bailey, 'The First Lady of Prague. An Interview with Olga Havel', *Telegraph Weekend Magazine*, September 1990, p. 18.
[2] Marcela Pecháčková, 'Olga', *Magazín Dnes + TV*, 8 February 1996, p. 10.

the countless questions I've flooded you with in the last six months. Would it be asking too much, for instance, for you to tell me what state you left Hrádeček in, what work you did, and did not, manage to get done, how you're living in Prague, what your plans are, etc. etc.?' And yet another: 'I forgot to tell you I loved the way you looked,' he wrote tetchily after a visit. 'You were smartly dressed and very chic. Even your hair looks good that way (it has, as you know, a tendency to look like spikes or straw – but it didn't during the visit).' Havel occasionally patronized her. 'It seems that this time, being a grass widow has been good for you,' he once wrote after she visited him in Ruzyně, adding: 'But of course I am happiest of all to see that you are living and acting – if I may put it this way – "in my spirit" and that you are effectively standing in for me.'

Havel also seemed to have taken some misanthropic delight in hinting at his extra-marital affairs. 'Greetings to all my friends, kisses to my girlfriends (if I still have any)', he once wrote, as if seeking to annoy Olga. In one of her rare letters, Olga replied by telling her husband of a dream in which she found him in bed with a mutual friend. 'I don't quite understand why your dream pushed me into bed with Markéta, of all people,' he replied cockily. 'She is one of the few beings with whom I have not only, in all politeness, avoided such a possibility, but absolutely forbidden it to myself, even for the future.' Yet there were plenty of other punishing mentions of girlfriends, real and imagined. 'I am not at all surprised,' he wrote at one point, 'that in my dreams (and when I am awake too) various girlfriends appear and try, in all sorts of clever ways, to seduce me (a while ago, for instance, it was Běla. Give her my greetings!).'

Havel's sexual fantasies and actual affairs were an open secret both before and after he left prison. Asked later by the *Magazín Lidových novin* about his 'amorous adventures' he replied, playfully: 'I don't consider myself a Casanova, and I'm not aware that my life has been attended by so-called forays. On the other hand, I do not conceal the fact that I'm a normal man who doesn't shun the world of women. I don't think I have anything either to hide or to publish.' The interviewer then asked: 'When was the last time you told a lie?' Havel replied: 'When answering the last question.'[1] A Casanova in prude's disguise? Like his father, who had had mistresses and two wives? A secret emulator of an early Kundera hero, whose endless copulations amount to sex as amnesia? Improbably the latter, but Havel left his readers guessing, even though there is no doubt that his 'zipper problem' posed problems for his philosophy of living responsibly, in the truth.

Havel's 'amorous forays' – even the one with Anna Kohoutová (the blonde ex-wife of his playwright friend-in-exile Pavel Kohout) on the night he was arrested – were well known. Olga had to 'reconcile herself to them'.[2] The manner in which she did so reveals much about both the personal politics of Havel and Olga's perception of him as a man. Olga could certainly not be described as a subservient woman who ignored the lines of power around her and adored her man through thick and thin. Nor was she looking for a man who adored and loved her until divided by death. Olga was the kind of woman, as the Czechs say, you can't get drunk on a bun. Everybody who knew her well admired her hard-nosed, levelling realism in matters of power, in whatever sphere she moved. She was a typical girl from the poor neighbourhood of Žižkov, where life was frank and not easy, and whining a foreign word. She managed to get through life without bourgeois self-confidence.

The good-looking, blue-eyed butcher's daughter with a gruff voice despised pretension. She was often sarcastic, and normally knew what she wanted and knew how to get it. Whereas her husband was sometimes obsessional about technical details, measuring everything millimetre by millimetre, Olga concentrated more on the overall length and direction of things.[3] She was curious and open-minded about life, but she was not a know-all, even though (according to her friend Dana Němcová) she was impatient with 'intellectual puzzles'. She always knew whether she was for or against something, and acted accordingly, and (like her husband) had a tendency to uncompromising pig-headedness.[4] She always meant what she said. Some mistook this as contemptuousness for others. 'I like personalities, people who are individuals, but I can't stand people who have no spine, try to suck up to the powerful,

[1] Anastázie Kudrnová, 'Šedesátiny Ferdinanda Vaňka', Magazín Lidových novin, volume 1, number 1 (4–10 October 1996), p. 20.
[2] Interview with her good friend and colleague Olga Stankovičová, Prague, 10 November 1998.
[3] Hana Primusová and Milena Pekárková, Olga (Prague, 1997), p. 49.
[4] Ibid., pp. 20, 58.

and are arrogant towards people who have no standing,' she once remarked.[1]

Courage in the face of despair and defeat was one of her most striking qualities. The Havels' friend Zdeněk Urbánek spoke of her as 'the bravest woman among those who took part in defying totalitarianism',[2] and with good reason. 'You shouldn't tell them anything, not even the name of our dogs,' she once said angrily to her husband, after he soft-heartedly invited in for coffee two StB agents standing outside their flat on duty in sub-zero conditions. 'I wouldn't even throw them food for their dogs,' she added.[3] Olga often warned him against being too kind to those who didn't deserve it. She was on the lookout especially for sycophants and self-servers. 'I just can't stand the kind of people we in Žižkov used to call "grubbers"', she once said. 'The sort who think only about themselves and don't care about anything around them. They calculate how much they're making, how they spend it, what to buy, where to go next.'[4]

In contrast to her husband, Olga did not depend upon sexual adventures. If at times strangely embarrassed about her slimness (she didn't like to swim for this reason) and although in public she concealed her left hand (due to the loss of four fingertips in an industrial accident at a state-run Baťa factory when she was sixteen), Olga was certainly sensuous. She simply disliked burdening others with such private details, and was at ease with her body, even in matters of pregnancy and childbirth. In response to prying questions about why she and Václav had never had children, her response was typically frank. He would say: 'I wanted to have children, but God didn't want me to. I have now come to terms with that. Anyway, God probably knows what he's doing. My children wouldn't have had an easy life.' She would say: 'We never tried not to have children, but unfortunately it happens that some people have children and others don't.'[5]

Her matter-of-factness attracted men's eyes. Some (the playwright Josef Topol, for example) thought that she looked and acted like an aristocrat.[6] She was tall, dignified, easily commanded

[1] *Olga*, op. cit., p. 65.
[2] Zdeněk Urbánek, 'Opora', ibid., p. 13.
[3] *Olga*, op. cit., pp. 36, 60.
[4] Cited in Marcela Pecháčková, 'Olga', *Magazín Dnes + TV*, 8 February 1996, p. 8.
[5] Ibid., p. 10. See also *Olga*, op. cit., p. 29.
[6] Josef Topol, cited in *Olga*, op. cit., pp. 20–21.

respect from others, and moved gracefully. She had a ready but unillusioned smile, lots of natural charm, and some men thought of her as sexy. But she had no time for those who talked of orgiastic prowess and she disliked intensely the use of sex as a bargaining chip. She couldn't stand sexual narcissism and (as her secret wedding to Václav revealed) she had the feeling that sacred-sounding promises of love, fidelity and sacrifice were actually selfish displays of raw possession, cleverly disguised but nonetheless fraudulent, deceiving of oneself and others. Despite constant and vigorous denials that she wasn't a feminist, she always said that she considered most men unreliable. She also said that she considered women equal to men, and that in any relationship the two sexes should add to and complement each other's efforts.[1] She certainly considered Václav her equal, and she was convinced that he found her egalitarian independence among her most attractive qualities.

His imprisonment undoubtedly strengthened her sense of independence. She had plenty to do, and lived life to the full, despite huge personal difficulties. She worked long hours preparing manuscripts with Ivan Havel for the samizdat publishing project, Edice Expedice. She tried to keep in touch with people who were going through hard times. Olga also distributed letters, played ping-pong and bridge, walked the dogs Ajda and Golda every day, and trained up a newly acquired German Shepherd guard dog. She liked to go to parties, where she loved to smoke and drink and chat, and (friends noted) would often choose to dance alone. She hatched plans to set up a samizdat project that would later be called *The Original Videojournal*, which tried to capture on film, and distribute video cassettes of, the realities of life in socialist Czechoslovakia. If there was any remaining spare time, she occupied herself with little things that meant a lot in the prevailing circumstances, like shopping, gardening at Hrádeček, mushroom and raspberry picking in nearby forests, collecting books, imagining recipes, browsing antique shops for things art nouveau (her favourite style) that she could use to decorate the embankment apartment or Hrádeček, or (among her favourite activities) rummaging through the rubbish tips at Barrandov film studios, which were richly stocked with bits 'n pieces tossed away

[1]Ibid., p. 25.

by people she denounced as 'unimaginative'.

Olga also started up a reading group, mainly for women. She described it as a 'society of prison widows' and named it 'The Tomb' (*hrobka*), partly because it held its weekly meetings in a dank, dark room in Prague's Old Town, and partly because of the group's passion for reading and discussing trashy erotic and Gothic novels by banned authors (Olga's favourites included *Monsters of Dr Gagra* and *Strange Mandarin* by Sláva Jelínek).[1] The Tomb group tried to live fearlessly. It organized fancy-dress balls, parties and weekends at Hrádeček, and published its own typewritten magazine. The group lived on the edge, with constant secret-police harassment. Many of its core members suffered police threats and violence, and quite a few were forced subsequently into exile.

Olga had her share of dealing directly, and alone, with the secret police. Her movements were constantly monitored, and there were plenty of ugly incidents to handle coolly. When Havel was moved to Plzeň-Bory at the end of July 1981, the StB offered her (and Havel) a passport to enable her to emigrate 'without any problems' to the Federal Republic of Germany. She flatly refused. On another occasion, she was taken into custody for four days (with Ivan) and interrogated about their publishing and book-smuggling activities linked to the Edice Expedice series. She refused to say a word, and was accused of subversion of the state. Then there were the repeated house searches, some of which smacked of sexual harassment, as when two dumpling-headed StB agents, after searching through her belongings, ordered her to go for dinner with them. Typically, cunningly, Olga extracted her revenge by embarrassing them by ordering one clove brandy after another, loudly pointing out to everybody within the restaurant that the public security agents were breaching their own code of conduct. After cutting short the dinner and paying the bill, the red-faced, red-epauletted officers left.[2]

Olga's steely independence reinforced the mild contempt she expressed for her husband's dalliances. They were a source of tension and noisy arguments with him, even though she knew that Václav always confessed that life without her would be

---

[1] Interview with Pavel Kosatík, Prague, 30 September 1997; and '*Člověk má dělat to, nač má sílu*'. *Život Olgy Havlové*, op. cit., pp. 189–223.
[2] Ibid., pp. 40, 41, 39.

unthinkable. Ever since they had been married, she had sensed his capacity for infidelity. Her radars were certainly trained on rambunctiously sexist men – Pavel Landovský, for instance – whom she dismissed as womanizers capable of leading Havel down the path of good times and easy women.[1] In one way or another, she always found out (or was told) about her husband's affairs, and she consistently made it clear to him that she didn't like them. She also disliked the tendency among Charter 77 men to treat Havel's affairs as the butt of back-slapping jokes ('I hear you're at it again!'), sometimes within earshot of Olga.[2] She didn't even approve of his habit of babbling into the ears of women about himself after a few drinks – the habit, as he put it, of being a '"merry drinking companion", a carouser, a bit of a high-stepper, even, some suspect, with inclinations to Don Juanism'.[3] Olga was consistently tough on her version of the proverbial heartless and impious seducer who delights in succumbing to the women he meets. But she didn't take revenge or punish him, in part because she regarded his escapades as harmless juvenile behaviour and partly, some of her close girlfriends thought, because she regarded them with the same ambivalence as a mother does towards her son's sexual experimentations.[4] But although Olga tolerated these affairs, she used her razor-sharp senses to draw the line at sexual encounters that she knew would prove dangerous to their own relationship.

The one she most worried about was Havel's ongoing relationship with Jitka Vodňanská. A trained social psychologist with a young son named Tomáš, Jitka first met Havel just before his long spell in prison. Their affair began immediately after his release, when Havel's skirt-chasing was at its most intense. Although it seemed as if he was simply wanting a fling to punish Olga for 'orphaning' him – or as if all the libidinal energy of the past four years simply had to be discharged in the quickest time possible –

[1] Marcela Pecháčková, 'Olga', *Magazín Dnes + TV*, 8 February 1996, pp. 11–12, where Landovský recalls: 'Olinka didn't like me much, and the worst thing that could happen to Vašek was to be caught with me. She was right in guessing that there were good times and girls around me and she wanted to have him only for herself. I think that Olinka was happiest when he was in prison and no one else was allowed to write to him. She could restrain Vašek best when he was under lock and key.'
[2] Interview with Pavel Kosatík, Prague, 30 September 1997.
[3] *Letters to Olga*, op. cit., p. 184.
[4] Interview with Jiřina Šiklová, Prague, 19 September 1996.

Havel soon found himself in a lustful relationship that lasted six years, after which it turned into a good friendship, with occasional sex on the side. After the misery of prison, he felt uplifted by Jitka's sparkling eyes and wicked sense of humour. Her words were certainly balm to his soul. He wrote to her nearly every day, usually on the back of postcards marked with an artistic or philosophical bent. He loved to let her talk about his character, and he told her often that her astute observations had helped him crawl out from under a big, heavy stone. 'Dear Jitka,' runs one of his early lover's postcards, 'Thank you for your letter and for the very germane analysis of my personality. Except for two details, it's precise. One of them, concerning women, is not exactly a stereotype. I've always been attracted to otherness and unrepeatability. After the good advice, I'm looking forward to seeing you here. You'll be with me in a fortnight. Yours, Václav.'[1]

Jitka's broad view — it was shared by Olga and several of her friends — was that Havel was attracted to strong women to whom he could not or would not make a long-lasting commitment. It was as if he craved hyperprotective women — 'Habsburg' women, Jitka called them — who exercised considerable power over him in order to justify his own need to resist their towering strength. Such resistance came in various forms of active rebelliousness, as when Havel first began to irritate his mother by staying out until all hours of the morning. According to Jitka, his decision to marry Olga carried on this old habit. It was a protest against the dynamic and attractive mother whom he loved, but whom he found both overbearing and distant, especially during those periods when she delegated her son to governesses who made him feel that too much of his childhood was spent doing such things as 'learning how to button up shirts'.[2]

Much the same 'hurtful' emotional protest was now being waged against Olga, Jitka told him. The advice highlighted the abstract point — crucial for understanding childhood — that when power is exercised over us, for instance by our mother, we do not simply 'internalize' or accept its terms and conditions, on our knees. We may do that, of course. Power is indeed sometimes that unequal relationship that presses down on us from the outside,

[1]Václav Havel to Jitka Vodňanská, 17 November 1983.
[2]Interview with Jitka Vodňanská, Prague, 9 November 1998.

only to relegate us as inferiors to a lower order. But in childhood, power in this sense often only functions as such because it *forms* us. We accept its terms of reference. We treat them as the very precondition of our existence, as part of ourselves, and in this way the relationship of power that subordinates us also *empowers* us to act in and upon the world. It turns out that power – in this case, that of Havel's mother over her first-born son – assumes a psychic form. It does not simply press-gang us into submission. Power rather forms our own identity. It renders us into a subject capable of certain forms of action. We then carry that power relationship around with us in later life. If we have lucky childhoods, we are permanently strengthened by its effects, like the strong belief in ourselves or confidence in our own ability to make bold judgements in the company of others. But power also often marks us with its more troubling effects, like regrets, unsatisfiable longings, unrealistic hopes, unfounded fears – and, as as Jitka said of her man Havel, deeply ambivalent, sweet-and-sour feelings for strong women.

In context, of course, Jitka's advice to Havel had different, more carnal meanings. Perhaps the advice was offered simply as a lover's gift. Perhaps it served as an elaborate justification of her own desire for him. Perhaps it simply took aim at knocking down his remaining defences. Whatever the case, the twosome were permanently excited in each other's presence. Freshly out of prison, Havel found she brought him joy through orgasm laced with words and wine. The two made love indiscriminately and often. Jitka quickly became pregnant. Suddenly everything changed. Olga generously proposed a *ménage-à-trois*. Jitka pointed out that Olga's maths were wrong – how young Tomáš would fit in was altogether unclear – and that from a child psychologist's standpoint life would be hell for the child. So Havel began to talk of divorcing Olga. Then he changed his mind. Jitka kept calm – she liked to remind the combatants that her father was named Václav and her mother was called Olga – but she had inner doubts about Havel's resilience under pressure. She guessed secretly that he hadn't much desire for a child. She noted his clumsiness towards children and his ambivalence towards Tomáš. There were memorable moments, for instance when Havel secretly made a medal and presented it to the eight year old in honour of his efforts to gobble up all the dumplings on his plate. But Jitka also noted that Havel often seemed ill-at-ease with Tomáš. He sometimes treated him like a pupil in need of lectures on phenomenology. There were even touches of jealousy, for instance when Havel complained about Jitka taking up precious time to read fairy-tales to her 'spoiled' son.

Faced with such ambivalence, and not yet familiar with the lover with whom she had been sleeping for only a few months, Jitka wrote to Havel to tell him that she had decided to terminate her pregnancy. It was a decision that she subsequently regretted for the rest of her life – a choice she so bewailed that her body shook uncontrollably whenever she was reminded of what she had done. Her thwarting of the power of beginning had the short-term effect of shoring up the affair, even propelling it forwards into passionate love. Havel felt utterly free in her presence. 'Vašek Havel, writer and fat-arse,' began one of his regular postcards, 'sends greetings to his lover of many years and a lifetime – I hope – sweet girlfriend.'[1] The photographs that have survived – Olga burned a pile in a rage – reveal traces of his exquisite happiness during this post-prison period. One image shows him cancan-ing the night away, wearing a big smile and a borrowed diamond brooch; another reveals his suntanned legs, dressed in shorts, as he hiked in the high Tatra mountains; yet another sees him celebrating his fiftieth birthday, Moravian wine in hand, nestled alongside beautiful Jitka.

It is said that nothing is happy in every way, and so it was with Havel, who was heading for a hiding. Olga's ongoing hostility to the affair began to worry him, and he responded by urging Jitka and Olga to meet, to try to resolve the growing tensions. The exercise in male diplomacy ended in a hopeless hangover. Olga was thoroughly fed up. So, over coffee one morning, choosing her moment, she said to Havel, with her usual candidness: 'It's good you have friends.' She paused, then added: 'I've got one, too.' The news of Olga's first-ever affair whistled like a bullet into Havel's spine. He fell speechless, then plummeted into prolonged silence, knowing that his point of anchorage in the world was now potentially smashed into small pieces. It transpired that during the latter part of his time behind bars Olga had become friendly and fallen in love with a young actor named Jan Kašpar. Born in 1953 – his curly-haired youthfulness bothered Havel – Kašpar

---

[1]Václav Havel to Jitka Vodňanská, 12 January 1988.

was talented, good-looking, unmarried, and sometimes kind. He affectionately called Olga 'Šefka' (Boss); for parity's sake, he called Havel 'Boss' (Šefka) as well. Kašpar officially described himself as one of Olga's closest friends and as the 'friendly caretaker' at Hrádeček,[1] but his good friends in Charter 77 knew that that was a euphemism for an affair of the most serious kind. It is unclear where the relationship would have led, but Olga chose to end it, and to move back in with Havel and to rescue their marriage, despite the fact that his affair with Jitka showed no sign of abating. In any event, fate was cruelly to decide things. After Kašpar's separation from Olga, he got married and spent several weeks' honeymoon with his new wife at her country cottage. While pruning a cherry tree, Kašpar slipped and fell to the ground, landing on a pick, severely damaging his spine. Paralysed from the waist down, he was for ever confined to a wheelchair.

It was bad luck that amounted to a personal tragedy, which for reasons of sympathy and guilt circled like an albatross over Havel's head for a long time. Struck down by the fact that Olga had nearly left him, aware that their relationship might now be terminally ill, Havel tumbled into a deep pit of post-prison blues. He had never experienced anything like it in his life, and although he'd half-anticipated their onset while still in prison, the daily reality of trying to cope with serious depression began slowly to destroy him. He drank heavily, slept badly, had no energy for sex, dragged himself everywhere, and slowly withdrew from the world. He began vaguely to resemble Dr Eduard Huml, the 'hero' of his play *The Increased Difficulty of Concentration*, which premièred at the Theatre on the Balustrade in April 1969. Huml, a depressed, exhausted, scholarly writer, whose *magnum opus* is a treatise on human happiness, is preoccupied with striking some balance between the demands of his wife, Vlasta, a manageress of a toy shop, and his girlfriend Renata, who keeps coming for lunch at Huml's flat and romping about in Vlasta's dressing gown. Each woman contrives to monopolize Huml: Renata wants him to get a divorce and marry her, while Vlasta insists that he should stop seeing Renata. Huml flounders. Unable to decide, he lives tediously, tenuously, pressured from all sides, unable to get off the treadmill of daily existence.

[1] *Olga*, op. cit., p. 49.

The depths to which Havel had plunged in this period are best revealed in *Largo desolato*.[1] Perched alone day and night in his study overlooking the Vltava River, guzzling brandy, listening to taped music, he found writing a crutch, a weapon of last resistance against an army poised to overrun his defences. He confessed to one or two friends that *Largo desolato* would examine 'what happens when the personification of resistance finds himself at the end of his tether'.[2] The final version was sometimes interpreted as the most autobiographical of his plays, but that is not strictly accurate. The key motifs and overall theme of the play were certainly inspired by his own experiences, more directly than in any other of his plays. 'When someone comes to write Havel's biography,' said Jan Grossman, 'they should pause when they come to this play, because it is very personal, self-critical, and in a certain sense a caricature of the dissident.'[3] Seen in this way, *Largo desolato* can be understood as a self-caricature of Havel's post-prison depression, but the very fact that he managed to write the play – and to write it as a satire on his own condition – indicates that it is not simply an 'autobiographical' work. *Largo desolato* is better understood as a comic parable about the condition of powerlessness, about what life is like when the individual finally crumbles under the weight of all-consuming power – a chilling, tragi-comic picture of what happens when the power of the individual to think, speak and act in the world is utterly routed by personal and political failure.

At the centre of the narrative is Doctor Leopold Kopřiva, a philosopher who has fallen foul of the state authorities for writing books with titles like *Phenomenology of Responsibility*, *Love and Nothingness*, and *Ontology of the Human Self*. Kopřiva is in an utter mess. His nerves are wracked by the random visits of the secret police. He fears that they will successfully tempt him into declaring that he is no longer himself, and that he will stoop to accepting their offers of freedom in return for signing a confession that he has acted as an 'intellectual hooligan', in breach of Paragraph

---

[1]First published in samizdat in the Edice Petlice series as Václav Havel, *Largo desolato: hra o sedmi obrazech* (Prague, 1984). I have also consulted the German edition translated by Joachim Bruss and edited by Siegfried Lenz, *Largo Desolato: Schauspiel in sieben Bildern* (Reinbek bei Hamburg, 1985), and the English translation and adaptation by Tom Stoppard, *Largo Desolato: A Play in Seven Scenes* (London and Boston, 1987). Dutch, French, and Italian translations also appeared during this period.
[2]*Disturbing the Peace*, op. cit., p. 66.
[3]Cited in the documentary film by Karel Prokop, 'Z Dramatika prezidentem', Česká televize 2 (Prague, 1995).

511 of the criminal code. Kopřiva is also paralysed by pressure
from fairweather friends and supporters, who want him to speak
out, to issue a declaration, to take a stand against despotic power.
But Kopřiva has already buckled. He is tired, desiccated, broken.
Frequently pacing the floors of his apartment like a prisoner pacing
his cell, listening helplessly to the passing of time, he swills rum
from morning to night, shakes, complains of the cold, eats a diet
of onions and almonds only to stay alive, all the while sinking
deeper and deeper into a void.

Kopřiva certainly talks repetitiously about human identity: how
it resembles a pre-verbal existential space in which the individual
can grasp the world through experiencing the presence of others;
how the meaning of life has to be chosen by individuals themselves,
in other words, that it is not something that can be summarized
and handed over to another like an information sheet; and how
he would rather die than abandon his own identity. But Kopřiva
does nothing and no one can help him – not even two workers
who arrive bearing gifts of writing paper stolen from their own
factory, and not even an attractive young woman philosophy
student, who after reluctantly agreeing to drink her fill of the
philosopher's rum tells Kopřiva she loves him. The cruel fact is
that Kopřiva is beyond writing and loving. He suffers more than
writer's block. He has run out of good excuses for putting off
writing. Surrounded by bookcases and walls of bookshelves, his
thoughts go round in a loop and he is capable only of stumbling
over banalities – pen or pencil? Which paper? First tidy the desk?
Suicide by alcohol seems appealing. As for love, Kopřiva has no
strength, no courage, no self-confidence, no joy, no appetite for
life. His failed heart cannot be brought back to life. The curtain
falls with Kopřiva collapsing on the floor, banging his fists, dragging
himself to a sofa, where he sits half-drunk, staring at the front door,
morose, waiting for the police to return.

TEMPTATION

Lead us not into temptation, but deliver us from evil: these ancient words still rumble like thunder through our hills and valleys, not least because the gluttonous act of giving in to enticements, initially against our will, is made to feel morally questionable by the survival deep in our hearts of the belief that we are mere mortal sons and daughters of a fallen apple-eater. Our imagery of temptation is originally religious. That is why the lingering association of temptation with evil has ensured it an important place in the world of power, despite various attempts to reduce the art of governing others to a merely technical or cynical art. Temptation is a thoroughly political matter. Everyone who mixes with power and its resources – property, fame, sex, advantage – knows temptation, whose eventual poisonous fruits are confusion, self-pity, corruption, ruined reputations. Less obviously, temptation is an important resource in the arsenal of those who exercise power over others. It has often been observed that those who rule over others do so by means of guns, money, charisma, sex or law. Missing from such lists is the quietest and often most effective ally of power: temptation.

Before the long spell in prison Havel had known his share of temptations, from cigarettes and booze to sexual infidelities. But more than anything else it was his two spells in prison – the brief one in 1977 and then the extended sentence from 1979 – that dragged him before the devil, threatening to transform him into a toad before power. The dynamics were complicated but they conformed exactly to the rules of temptation. Temptation is a game of seduction whose stakes are high. From the point of view of those who are exercising power, tempting others with advantage – a lighter than expected sentence or material privileges, for instance – must perforce be based on careful calculation. Tight reins must be kept on the advantage offered to the victim, for otherwise they might think that they have scored a victory. The whole point of tempting a victim is to victimize them or seduce them into conformity; in either case, they must be moved to do what they would otherwise not have done. The act of taking the king's shilling normally heaps anguish upon the tempted. They feel in two minds, stretched in several directions, sometimes to breaking point. Guilt and shame are their accomplices. If they succumb, they feel for ever haunted by their own duplicity. If they refuse temptation, then they are left with gnawing doubt about their own capacity for judgement under duress. They are gripped by the feeling that they have unwisely martyred themselves into disadvantage. Either way, the outcome feels unsatisfactory. Giving in to temptation involves cavorting with the devil. Yet the price of integrity is further suffering – and possibly even revenge by the powerful.

From the time of the launch of Charter 77, Havel found himself constantly haunted by this dilemma. His first spell in prison, which followed the launch of the Charter, was hard to bear. 'I didn't know what was happening outside, all I could see was the hysterical witch-hunt against Charter 77. I was deceived by my interrogators, and even by my own counsel. I fell victim to curious, almost psychotic moods.' He was wracked especially by the feeling that his defiance of the authorities made him directly responsible for the misery that now befell his fellow Chartists. 'It seemed to me that, as one of the initiators of the Charter, I had brought terrible misfortune on a large number of people. I of course was trying to shoulder an excessive responsibility, as if the others had not known what they were letting themselves in for, as if it was all just my fault.' Despondency nourished by guilt was fed by his growing awareness that the authorities were preparing a trap for him. During one of his appeals against detention he had made a casual remark about how he felt guilty for the harm he had brought to others – so implying that he regretted his role in Charter 77. The police instantly twisted and hurled it like a dagger back into his heart. Knowing their skill at ruining reputations, Havel panicked. He saw no way out of the trap that his own naivety had helped to set. He caught a glimpse of what it was like to be tempted. He even began to wrestle with the accusation, put about by the authorities, that he had actually succumbed to temptation. 'I had strange dreams and strange ideas. I felt I was being – quite physically – tempted by the devil, that I was in his clutches. I realised that I had somehow got tangled up with him. The fact that something I had written, something I had really thought and that was true, could be misused in this way brought it home to me yet again that the truth is not only that which one thinks, but also under what circumstances, to whom, why and how one says it.'[1]

[1]Václav Havel, 'My temptation', *Index on Censorship*, volume 15, number 10 (November/December 1986), p. 21.

As if to pay penance for his brush with temptation – to spite the authorities' rumour that the world-famous playwright and dissident Václav Havel had accepted that his attempts to defy power were imprudent and ultimately futile – he wrote a new play called *Temptation* (*Pokoušení* [1985]). The drafting process went slowly. Numerous fragments went into the bin. Whole sketches of the individual scenes – Havel's preferred way of writing plays – were also jettisoned. Suddenly, during October 1985, inspiration rushed through his fingers. The play took him only ten days to write, as if it was an act of self-preservation. Driven by the desire to shake off despair and to withdraw from the Faustian pact the authorities had prepared, he wrote 'in a state of increasing feverishness and impatience, you might almost say in a trance'.[1] In prison, he had been sent a copy of Goethe's *Faust* and Thomas Mann's novel on the same subject, *Dr Faustus*, but the script he scribbled out feverishly was unique – and arguably one of Havel's very best.

The play, Havel later observed, is about 'structures' and the fate of people within them. It draws upon the old medieval legend of a man who sold his soul to the devil, and who became identified with a sixteenth-century necromancer named Dr Faustus, in order to tell the story of Dr Henry Foustka, a respected scientist working within a research institute. Life within the organization is all dull-grey ritual. Its white-coated staff are in the habit of hardly noticing one another. Their hearts seem blind. Their bodies are numbed by routine. Their brains are geared to the central task of producing and deploying and protecting the Truth, which contrasts oddly with the staff's immersion in an endless farrago of pointless chit-chat and joking, punctuated by requests for coffee and 'Did you sleep well?', the Director's preferred question of his staff. Bureaucratic thinking reigns, or so it seems. Until it is announced, to a flutter of controlled excitement, that there will be a staff social evening. But that event, and the preparations for it, serve as an absurd canvas on which Havel paints a profound crisis lurking within the organization itself.

The Director makes an official announcement, whose surprising content comes wrapped in language resembling anaesthetic before the knife. 'As you probably know,' he begins, 'there have lately

---

[1] 'My temptation', op. cit., p. 19.

cropped up complaints that our institute isn't fulfilling its tasks in keeping with the present situation.' He continues: 'We're being urged, with increasing insistence, that we go over to the offensive, that is, that we should at last somehow try to implement a programme of extensive educational, popular-scientific and individually therapeutic activity.' The arse-licking Deputy Director, always eager to impress, adds wisdom. He says that the programme should be firmly in the spirit of the scientific *Weltanschauung*. But he is cut short by his pompous superior, who continues to explain to his workers that these are modern times. He appeals to them 'to counter the isolated but nevertheless alarming expressions of various irrational viewpoints which can be discerned in particular in certain members of our younger generation and which owe their origin to the incorrect . . . interpretation of the complexity of natural processes and the historical dynamism of human civilization, some of whose aspects are taken out of context, only to be interpreted, either in the light of pseudo-scientific theories . . . or in the light of a whole range of mystic prejudices, superstitions, obscure teachings and practices spread by certain charlatans, psychopaths and members of the intelligentsia.'

The soliloquy is interrupted several times – by the late arrival to work of a breathless scientific worker carrying a bag of oranges, the Deputy's revelation that typewritten copies of the works of C. J. Jung are circulating among youth, plus a discussion of the daily soap ration. But the interruptions prepare the way for a scene in the dingy, book-lined apartment of Foustka, who is discovered kneeling in the middle of a dimly lit room, in his dressing gown, surrounded by burning candles, another in his left hand, while in his right is a piece of chalk with which he draws a circle round himself and the candles.

There is suddenly a knock at the door. It is Foustka's landlady, informing him that a stranger has come to see him. Foustka is instantly suspicious – his life outside the institute is evidently a risky business – but curiosity gets the upper hand. Enter Fistula, looking like a figure straight from a Beckett play, but actually a stool-pigeon, the secret agent of power who has come to tempt his victim. Fistula is a small, slender man with a limp caused by chronic athlete's foot, he clutches a paper bag containing a pair of slippers, and grins vacuously. Foustka, the secret opponent of the institute, its power over others and all that it symbolizes, stares at his surprise guest with a mixture of curiosity, suspicion and revulsion. So begins the sordid business of temptation.

Foustka reacts initially by scrambling to hide his private life from his unexpected guest: lights are switched on hurriedly, candles are removed, an attempt is made to rub out the chalk circle. Ritual *politesse* is followed by a warning by the tempter Fistula, who is in the habit of grinning a lot, that the encounter should be kept a secret. Foustka is puzzled, then realizes quickly that his unsolicited visitor knows much about him, which makes him angry. 'Out!' he shouts. 'Leave my flat at once and never show your face here again.' Fistula rubs his hands together contentedly, sensing that Foustka's resistance is perhaps a prelude to co-operation. The cunning hunter tries to calm his victim by acknowledging that his host has every reason for suspecting that Fistula is an *agent provocateur*. Fistula, always on the move, then boldly confronts Foustka with three choices: 'You can continue to consider me an *agent provocateur* and insist that I leave. Secondly: not to think of me in those terms but instead to trust me. Thirdly: not to make your mind up in this matter just yet and to adopt a waiting posture, which means not to throw me out but on the other hand to say nothing which, if I were an *agent provocateur*, I might be able to use against you. If I may,' concluded the slippery Fistula, 'I'd recommend the third alternative . . .'

Foustka from here on makes a string of fatal mistakes common to all those who succumb to temptation: pacing up and down the room, he hesitates, then agrees reluctantly to the third possibility. He chooses to be 'flexible' – unwittingly he prepares to welcome the devil – and is greeted with the flattery of a fox. Fistula praises his caution, sharp intelligence, and ready wit, all of which, he goes on to explain, suggest that the two men can work well together. The suggestion upsets Foustka, who moves once again to shake off his tempter by denying he has anything to hide. 'I am a scientist and hold a scientific world view, working in a very responsible position in one of our foremost scientific institutes. If anyone comes to me with ideas that can be defined as an attempt to spread superstition, I shall be forced to act according to my scientific conscience.'

The tempted hangs on to respectability. Everything is at stake, but the unfolding hypocrisy subverts his claim to purity. Fistula, always looking for points of weakness to exploit, responds with riotous laughter, quickly apologizes so as not to repel his victim, then prepares the final trap by offering himself up to Foustka for scientific experiments designed to combat the spread of mysticism. Foustka agrees, then wriggles. The tempter in effect exposes the double standard of the tempted: at a certain stage in the process of temptation, the tempted is required to make the painful acknowledgement that he or she is a hypocrite. That Foustka does silently, at which point he becomes clay in the hands of his master. 'So what's to become of our agreement,' he asks Fistula sheepishly. 'That is entirely up to you,' replies the grinning Fistula.

Back in the company of his colleagues at the scientific institute, Foustka tries to recover his dignity by leading a normal life. He talks philosophy, charms a woman, acts politely in the company of the Director, whom he otherwise assiduously avoids. At one point, daringly, he even lectures the guests at the institute's social evening about the dangers of nihilism: 'When man drives God out of his heart, he makes way for the devil,' says Foustka. 'What else is this contemporary world of ours, with its blind, power-crazed rulers and its blind, powerless subjects, what else is the catastrophe that is being prepared under the banner of science – with us as its grotesque flag-bearers – what else is it other than the work of the devil? It is well known that the devil is a master of disguise. Can one imagine a more ingenious disguise than that offered him by our modern lack of faith? Doubtless he finds he can work best where people have stopped believing in him.' Foustka's talk of the devil is a moment of honesty. It is shortly afterwards followed by a private confession: 'Something is going on inside me – I feel I'd be capable of doing things that were always alien to me. As if something that had lain hidden deep inside me was suddenly floating to the surface.' He knows that those who sup with the devil must use a long spoon, and that his is too short. He grows angry with what he himself has done, brutally striking to the floor, and then kicking, a female colleague.

Honesty, confession, anger provide no hope for the tempted. The deed has been done, and only the public exposure of his temptation remains to be carried out. Like mice fondled by a hungry cat, the tempted are usually tormented by their tempter. So Foustka begins to feel fingers of power around his throat. The Director, reminding his colleagues that the institute is a lighthouse of true knowledge ('What we think today, others will live tomorrow!' he remarks), turns a finger in Foustka's direction, accusing him of indulging pre-scientific deviations, but promises that, since these are modern times, there will be no staged witch-hunts. 'Let the manner in which Dr Foustka's case is handled become a model of a truly scientific approach to facts, which will provide inspiration for us all. Truth must prevail,' he concludes, threateningly, 'whoever suffers in the process.'

The naive Foustka feels relieved. He tries to lie his way out of danger, claiming that he was only acting as a lone soldier doing battle against mysticism. Nobody believes him. He now knows that his days are numbered, and so he grows angry at his tempter, Fistula. 'You're a devil,' he shouts, 'and I don't want to have anything more to do with you.' Fistula replies that he has been no more than a catalyst, and that the honest truth is that in the final analysis Foustka himself *chose* to be tempted. Foustka becomes morose. He confesses his 'unforgivable irresponsibility, for my having succumbed to temptation', but Fistula resorts to sarcasm, diagnosing his victim as suffering from the Smíchovský Compensation Syndrome: a 'hangover' of masochistic self-accusation and self-chastisement caused by the liquors of temptation.

None of this matters. Foustka is done for. He confesses to his indulgence of hermetic rituals; recognizes that he has been too clever by half, and that he has come a cropper by believing that he could play both ends of power against the middle and get away with it. He sees that, in the eyes of those who wield power within the organization, his ultimate crime can be summarized in the devilish maxim: To lie to a liar is fine; to lie to those who speak the truth is permissible; but to lie to the powers who ensure that we can lie with impunity – this is unacceptable and cannot go unpunished. The play does not reveal whether Foustka is promptly fired, made an example of, publicly disgraced, completely destroyed by his act of giving into temptation. He does sing a swan song of opposition to his opponents, railing against 'the destructive pride of intolerant, all-powerful and self-regarding power, which uses science as a handy bow with which to shoot down everything that might put it in jeopardy'. His speech is applauded sarcastically by the head of the organization, after which Foustka's clothes are set on fire, sending him running to and fro in panic across a stage quickly enveloped in smoke. The only player to take a bow is a fireman, fresh on the scene, fully uniformed, looking anxious, a fire extinguisher in hand.

CLIFF-HANGING

The assignment: to conduct a long, carefully prepared interview with the most famous 'dissident' in central Europe for London's *Times Literary Supplement*. Elaborate preparations have been made. My *nom-de-plume* – Erica Blair – is to be used. Through the exile news agency Palach Press, permission is sought and received. 'Tell Miss Blair that I am happy to do it and I am awaiting her visit to Praha.' Exactly how we will meet – or whether Havel himself will be in prison – is unclear. A few days before the departure, my guide and translator, A. G. Brain – now Gerald Turner – telephones to say he has broken his right leg after slipping on black ice. That is exactly what we fear will happen to us once again after arriving in Prague, crutches in hand, pretending to be tourists. For two days, we split up and try to look inconspicuous, mainly by hiding out in the pubs and shops and safe apartments of the city. Then comes the prearranged moment of our first meeting with the man. Crammed around a dark corner table of a dingy pub on the Vltava embankment, Havel is gracious, offers us beer, cigarette in hand. We make final preparations for the following day. My host looks ill and exhausted from his long spell in prison, but he still manages to show his sense of humour. 'Umm, I am sorry,' he says in broken English, 'I had no opportunity to prepare my remarks because I was not today two hours in a prison.'

Next day's meeting made me tremble. Havel's fourth-floor embankment apartment in the heart of art nouveau Prague is a building site, its walls stripped bare in search of concealed microphones. Cigarette smoke blues the air. Havel fidgets constantly with his whisky glass, usually looking at the floor as he speaks. In the era of *glasnost*, the tapped telephone rings often. Two StB policemen now stand guard across the street. Havel's dog, whose predecessor had been shot dead by the secret police on the doorstep, paces nervously at the front door, growling at every creak and thud in the building. The ugly atmosphere gets on my nerves, but my fidgety friend – as in our previous meetings – seems willing to speak with measured passion about his concerns, his tired face occasionally breaking into a warm smile. Short and slight with thinning sandy hair and a pouty moustache, he is described in police files as a 'subversive' and an 'anti-socialist element'; in situations like this, struggling to understand my English and random Czech, he seems shy, soft-spoken, sometimes with a slight lisp, the result of a prison beating, courageous, occasionally sanctimonious, and always stubborn under pressure – a rebel, one of the truly dangerous types, a subversive guided by civilized manners and a taste for freedom.

Time is precious. Olga brings Turkish coffee. Havel opens the bottle of Isle of Skye whisky I have brought him as a gift. There is no small talk. I kick off by asking him how, despite everything, he manages to keep his head above water. He quotes Franz Kafka: 'Why are you watching? Someone must watch, it is said. Someone must be there.' The watchman explains that totalitarian regimes such as Husák's Czechoslovakia and Honecker's GDR, although now on their last legs, are unique in human history. Using more civilized and sophisticated methods of control than the hack dictatorships of the Third World, they are all-embracing and spirit-destroying. 'These regimes get under society's skin,' Havel said. 'From morning to night, everything ordinary citizens do is in some way interfered with by the system. The regime leaves its mark on everything, from the way housing estates are built to the patterns of television programming.' The state is employer, policeman, social worker, judge and jailer rolled into one. It therefore pressures individuals to adapt and to capitulate, to reinforce the foundations of the very regime they spend time bellyaching about in the hidden corners of factories, kitchens, pubs and offices. Havel goes on to say that totalitarianism thereby heaps invisible violence upon everybody. It slowly destroys the individuality and basic human dignity of virtually every member of society, rulers and ruled alike.

Havel's words against the totalitarian regimes of the East are matched – surprisingly – by a deep suspicion of the West. He explains that he is not, and never has been, a professional anti-Communist. Both systems, he tells me, contain huge, faceless organisations which treat people as mere objects. 'The world is losing its human dimension,' he insists, Franz Kafka at his side. 'Self-propelling mega-machines, large-scale enterprises, faceless governments and other juggernauts of impersonal power represent the greatest threat to our present-day world. In the final analysis, totalitarianism is no more than an extreme expression of this threat.'

Havel reaches for another cigarette. Our conversation turns philosophical. We are slowly losing our grip on the world, he

explains, precisely because we strive to be the supreme masters of ourselves and our universe. He points out that one of
his favourite plays, *The Memorandum*, satirizes this trend. Office
workers are instructed by officials to learn a new 'strictly scientific'
language, Ptydepe. It is supposed to eliminate misunderstandings
by maximising the difference between words, so that no word
can be mistaken for another, the length of the word being
inversely proportional to its frequency of use (wombat has 319
letters, he reminds me). Ptydepe paralyses the office and baffles
everybody who tries to learn it. So the bureaucracy introduces a
new language that contains words so simple that they have virtually
infinite meanings – and suitably disastrous consequences for the
organisation. Havel admits that *The Memorandum* is intended
to be riotously funny – that it plays language games before
audiences who are perforce confronted with players caught up
in a power struggle for survival and self-recognition. 'In *The
Memorandum* I saw myself as a free-wheeling pop–art painter
trying to take concrete segments of reality and then rearranging
them in fantastic form,' he says. But he also insists that *The
Memorandum* well illustrates one of his most serious themes: our
modernist attempt to know and to control everything – whether
in scientific research, the development of technology, or politics
– is slowly but surely paralysing our capacity as individuals to lead
meaningful, independent human lives. Several times during our
conversation, he mentions that the world is slipping through
our fingers, and that this slippage cannot be prevented by grand
leaps of faith into the future. He goes on to denounce Utopian
visions, 'radiant tomorrows' he calls them. Life is ever-changing
and lacking an essence. To try to master it fully, to clamp it
down on to a drawing board and to blueprint its reconstruction,
therefore always ends up strait-jacketing and destroying life. So
Havel highlights a direct link between beautiful Utopias and the
concentration camp. 'What is a concentration camp,' he asks, 'but
an attempt by Utopians to dispose of those elements which don't
fit into their Utopia?'

Havel's razor-sharp question reminds me why the West's
enthusiasm for Gorbachev during the era of *perestroika* was often
considered naive, even disheartening, by many people in central
and eastern Europe. The disgust produced by failed Utopias is
something they feel acutely. Havel agrees that his plays aim to

accentuate the aversion to radiant tomorrows. He says that they are inspired by the thought that theatre should question Utopias and encourage people to think and act less dogmatically. They deny that art is a refuge for moral Truth. Havel tells me that he rejects the common complaint of theatre reviewers – repeated at the time in England during Tom Stoppard's elegant adaptation of *Largo Desolato* for the Bristol New Vic – that his own plays are tantalizing because they fail to grasp the moral nettles they themselves plant. Theatre, he insists, is an incomplete dialogue, the playwright essentially a witness to the times. Theatre shouldn't try to thrill or charm playgoers or make things easier for them by providing positive heroes. He admits that his plays provide warnings. But in the same breath he stresses that they don't arrogantly pretend to portray things as they 'really are'. They leave such sermonizing to Brecht and instead try to confront people with themselves – to make them think by prising open their awareness of the unresolved questions and problems facing them. Modern times are gripped by a permanent 'crisis of certainty', he says. Theatre should not pretend to know what is to be done. 'I try to fling my audiences into the heart of a problem that they can't avoid,' he says, pausing to light another cigarette. 'I try to push people's noses into our common wretchedness. Theatre should remind people that the time is getting on, that our situation is bad, and that there's no time to lose.'

Havel agrees to talk about how this idiosyncratic view of theatre as the adversary of totalitarian illusions has earned him considerable international acclaim. He describes how he began working in the theatre as a stage-hand, and how his 'bourgeois' origins excluded him from film school and university. He recalls how he soon became literary adviser at Prague's famous Theatre on the Balustrade, and how his first play there, *The Garden Party*, brought him overnight fame in the early sixties with the tale of a regime racked and ruined by the struggle between the perfectionist Office of Liquidation and the modernising Office for Inauguration. Havel tells me that he mistrusts rigid categories, and that he does not like being pigeonholed as a master playwright of the Theatre of the Absurd. He says that his preferred authors are Hašek and Čapek, Beckett and Ionesco (whose influence is strong, he confesses, in one of his first plays, *An Evening with the Family*), and he acknowledges Kafka's decisive influence on his work. 'When I first read Kafka, I constantly had the feeling that I was writing it myself,' he tells me. 'It was as if I'd had a similar basic experience of the world.' We talk through some of his best-known plays, including *The Increased Difficulty of Concentration*, an adaptation of *The Beggar's Opera* and *Temptation*, soon to be performed by the Royal Shakespeare Company at the Barbican in London. Havel quickly emphasizes that these accomplishments – he modestly declines to discuss his many literary awards, including the American Obie Prize for the best off-Broadway play and the 1986 Erasmus Prize – had had their painful side. His plays have not been performed in his own country for nearly twenty years, and during that time he has also been banned by the Czechoslovak authorities from producing or directing anything. He reminds me that his work did once slip through the net: an amateur production in 1975 of *The Beggar's Opera* in a village near Prague. It led to a police raid, he says quietly, still looking down. All those who took part were interrogated and harassed. Such clampdowns visibly anguish Havel. Theatre needs a home, he says with a wince. A play which remains a mere script is only ever half-finished.

The point helps to explain why Havel, the playwright with an aversion to power-grabbing politicians, has been dragged into politics, apparently against his will, subsequently forcing him to make the best of fate by acting as if he were both playwright and performer in a political opera. He has paid the price: several prison sentences, and more to come. Yet Havel's taste of total power – remarkably – has not seemed to produce hunger for power over others. He appears to harbour no illusions about party politics and professional politicians. He tells me, reaching for another whisky, that he sees himself as an ordinary citizen, endowed with inalienable rights of self-determination. 'I favour a politics growing from the heart, not from a thesis,' he continues, insisting that politics 'from below' is indispensable if individual people are to seek and to protect a meaningful existence in a world threatened by impersonal organizations. Havel acknowledges that small-scale, local activity directed at such organizations is often ridiculed by Western politicians, who consider it as fanciful as the Lilliputians' attempts to tie down Gulliver from below by thousands of small threads. But he strongly disputes this view. 'It's becoming obvious,' he says with Lech Wałesa and Solidarność in mind, 'that politics doesn't have to remain the affair of professionals and that one simple electrician, with his heart in the right place, can influence the history of an entire nation.'

During our five-hour discussion, Havel tries to emphasize several times that he is a reluctant political figure: he says that he wants above all to get back to writing plays and to have them performed in his own country. 'But whether you like it or not,' I reply, 'you are now a star performer in a theatre of opposition.' I add that political figures normally hate irony, which corrodes their own certainties by revealing the ways in which the world is full of ambiguity, and I remind him that in his play *Temptation* a character says: 'I don't give any specific advice, and I don't fix anything for anyone. The most I do is to stimulate now and again.' Havel agrees that that line is his credo as a playwright – and he expresses the hope that it will serve as a future maxim of his own philosophy as a political writer and public figure.

We discuss how Havel's own civic activities have multiplied rapidly during recent years. He had been a founding spokesman for Charter 77 ('a community of people acting independently and trying to voice the truth') and a key figure in VONS, a citizens' group working for the protection of the unjustly prosecuted. At the end of the 1970s, he had been a key participant in the bacchanalian border meetings between the Czechoslovak and Polish democratic oppositions. In the early 1980s, he had conducted an important dialogue with the Western peace movement, urging its activists to swallow the bitter fact that 'peace', a pampered term in the prolespeak of the Communist Party, generated little enthusiasm in central and eastern Europe. This argument, expressed in a number of essays, produced another of the many ironies that had so far defined his life: the prestigious Olof Palme Peace Prize. At the time of our meeting, Havel was also busy with samizdat publishing and the emerging key figure in beleaguered 'dissident' circles.

Havel confesses as well that he has come to sympathize with green politics: 'The green movements have brought to the surface issues – such as whether there is any sense in threatening future generations by the constant drive for increased production – which the traditional political parties have neglected.' The greens' 'non-ideological stance and advocacy of non-violence are close to my own head and heart'. Havel reveals how profoundly he had been influenced as an early teenager by Josef Šafařík's *Seven Letters to Melin*, in which an engineer defects to philosophy, blames modern science and technology for the contemporary crisis of humanity, and concludes that conclusions can only ever be tentative, and that each individual is ultimately responsible for co-determining with others how each shall live. We discuss the prominence of ecological images in his writings. He explains that among his strongest is a powerful boyhood memory of walking down a country lane from Havlov to school in the shadow of a huge munitions factory. 'The chimney spewed dense smoke and scattered it across the sky. Each time I saw it,' he says, 'I had an intense feeling that something was profoundly wrong, that human beings were fouling the heavens.'

Such powerful memories evidently feed Havel's philosophical conviction that the human will to master the world produces poisonous outcomes and that therefore the human species, to avoid disaster, should abandon our arrogant presumption that 'Man is capable of knowing everything, describing everything and doing everything'. We should instead let things be, he urges, all the while trying to nurture a sense of wonder and respect for the world. Havel insists that his call for human modesty is not a plea for apathy. At the end of our meeting, he acknowledges the pitfalls of nihilistic despair; he also stresses the inexhaustible strength that flows from sticking to principles and prodding and poking at the world around us. 'Only by "looking outward" and throwing ourselves repeatedly into the tumult of the world, with the intention of making our voices count – only in this way', he says, 'do we really become human beings.'

The words escaping his gritted teeth were poignant, especially considering that for nearly two decades Havel had been living under constant police watch, ever in danger of arbitrary arrest and imprisonment. His had been a hard and often discouraging life, as his letters from prison bear witness. He tells me that he has tried hard to master the difficult art of waiting patiently, and that nowadays nothing really surprises him. I reply by reminding him that the power of the unexpected can sometimes exceed that of the most powerful governments and politicians. What neither of us realizes is that in a matter of a few months after our meeting his stubborn, civilized patience was to be vindicated, then tested by the temptations of power. Massive crowds were soon to gather in the frozen rectangle called Wenceslas Square to exercise 'candle power' (as he later called it) or, emulating the storming of the

Bastille, to jangle keys together — the keys of the Czechoslovak prison — while chanting 'Give the jesters their cap and bells'. The Party lies of 'normalization' would soon begin to collapse into a twisted heap of confusion. The riot police and water cannon would begin to flinch. Chants of 'Long Live Havel!' would echo through Prague's cobbled streets and narrow passageways. A big surprise indeed was just around the corner. Yet Havel's last words to me remained circumspect on the brink of political success. 'I'm full of hopes, doubts, determination, uncertainties, plans, fears,' he says with a wrinkled smile, gripping my hand to say goodbye. 'For the time being, I'm sure of only one thing: for me it will always be a cliff-hanger.'

VELVET REVOLUTION

(1989)

REVOLUTION

N ever mind cliff-hanging. It was now time for Havel to move to the streets of Prague. It is Friday, 17 November 1989: the first day of the Velvet Revolution. Nobody thought of it that way, of course. A hallmark of revolutionary alterations of power is that they are always unanticipated and unplanned. Revolutions are surprises on a grand scale. Initially, no one is in charge. They never obey the rules of the putsch. *Coups d'état*, the Prague variety of 1948 for instance, are a type of carefully planned seizure of power. They entail elaborate preparations, usually in secret, and they are executed swiftly, often in the wee hours of the morning, when most of the population is in bed, asleep. Their effect is felt instantly: troops surround the central radio and television stations; the international airport is closed; bank accounts are frozen; new or reshuffled faces appear in the ruling group; government orders, instructions, and policies immediately reveal that things have changed, or not changed at all. Revolutions are not like this. They are not calculated in advance; and they may even be described as a long chain of unintended consequences. Revolutions consequently have no easily definable point of origin. And although they are not about trifles (as Aristotle observed) they often spring from what appear at the time to be trifles.[1]

No one had anticipated that sometime during that dark and dreary mid-November day late-socialism in Czechoslovakia would begin to collapse. A crowd of some 15,000 students had gathered peacefully that afternoon outside the Pathology Institute to commemorate the death of Jan Opletal, a student victim of the Nazi occupation fifty years earlier. The commemoration had the Party's approval, and the list of speakers, both official and unofficial, had been organized by the university council of the Communist Youth Union. The students' request to walk on to Opletal Street near Wenceslas Square, after the rally, had been refused by the authorities, so an alternative was authorized. The students were to march to the cemetery in Vyšehrad, where they would gather at the graveside of the nineteenth-century poet, K. H. Mácha. And it was agreed with the authorities that the customary candles would be lit, wreaths and flowers would be laid, the national anthem would be sung, after which the procession was to disperse quietly.

[1] Aristotle, *Politica*, Book 5, chapter 2, section 8.

Everything but the last clause in the contract was satisfied. Instead of dispersing tamely into the evening darkness, thousands of students, feeling their spines straightening, spontaneously began to march towards Wenceslas Square. Tension rose suddenly when the students were temporarily halted by the police at the Botanical Gardens. In the distance police orders were barked. The demonstrators began to sing the national anthem. A flying wedge of helmeted police wielding truncheons cut into their ranks. Scuffles broke out. Shouting and chanting erupted. The awful sound of clumping boots was temporarily drowned by cries of 'We are unarmed!' (*Máme prázdné ruce*) and 'No Violence!' (*Nechceme násilí*). The police with truncheons now pointing at the best brains in the country seemed hellbent on breaking up the demonstration. They began by swooping on a young bearded anarchist named John Bok. They had been looking for a pretext to arrest him for some time, and Bok, a man with unusually sharp senses, knew they were cutting through the crowd specifically to arrest him. 'Tell Vašek! . . . Get a message to him at Hrádeček! . . . Tell him what's happening! Quickly!' he shouted to his friends, gasping for air, as a clutch of mean-looking policemen headlocked him into arrest and dragged him, kicking back while being kicked, through the crowd and dumped him into a nearby van waiting to take him directly to prison.

Bok refused that afternoon to talk to his interrogators at Ruzyně prison. After being charged with assault of a public functionary, he was allowed one brief phone call to his wife, to whom he repeated the message that he had earlier gasped to his friends. 'Please make sure that Vašek, who is at his cottage, gets the message to return urgently to Prague. Something has changed. He needs to be back here. Fast.' Following those words, Bok was beaten, deprived of sleep, and tortured by pushing his body backwards over a chair, so that he couldn't properly breathe. The uncivil police methods presaged the fate of the remaining demonstrators. After losing Bok from their ranks, they marched on defiantly towards Wenceslas Square, edging along the banks of the Vltava River. Scores of curious bystanders, like monks coming to prayer, silently joined in. So did actors and theatre staff. Friday night patrons of the Café Slavia, located riverside just near the Havels' flat, downed their drinks and joined the throng. Outside the famous Klášterní vinárna (the Monastery Wine Bar), waiters and customers came outside on to the streets and called out to the young demonstrators, who by now had lost their fear. They were in a relaxed and cheerful mood, and repeatedly chanted out in defiant tones, 'Join us! Join us!' and 'The nation's helping itself! [*Národ sobě*]'.

Havel, who had gone into retreat at Hrádeček with Jitka Vodňanská, happy to be off 'the Prague merry-go-round'[1], received Bok's message. He hurried back by car to Prague, where he arrived home around midnight. He heard from his brother Ivan, and from Olga, breathtaking news. At a performance of Ivan Kurz's *The Madman's News* at Smetana Hall in Prague, the audience had cheered and applauded Václav Neumann, the director, and the members of the symphony orchestra, who had signed a petition protesting against Havel's most recent imprisonment. Olga reported the irony that during the performance of *The Madman's News* the state television and radio stations had coldly issued a ČTK communiqué which stated that the day of remembrance had been 'hijacked by anti-social elements, well known to the police, and authors of various recent outrages'. The communiqué had denounced those who had chanted slogans hostile to the socialist state. It described them as uninterested in 'dialogue, reform, or democratization'. They were forces of instability, violence, and social destruction. 'Because of this,' it concluded, 'the forces of order were obliged to take necessary measures to restore peace and order.'[2]

A different, but equally exaggerated, version of the events, Havel learned, had just been broadcast by West German television. It informed viewers that reports were being received that an insurrection was taking place in Prague, that its streets were full of young people, that the police were out in force, and that Prague Castle was surrounded by tanks. Something rather different had happened, in fact. After the arrest of John Bok, the originally smallish student demonstration had safely reached the National Theatre, where its numbers had mushroomed to over 50,000 people. At that point, everybody who had been present confirmed that all public places adjoining the demonstration were packed, as if, after all the years of isolation, people could not get enough of each other's company. The protest seemed to take on

---

[1]Václav Havel to Vilém Prečan, 5 November 1989 (Archives of the Czechoslovak Documentation Centre, Scheinfeld, number 1523/89).
[2]Cited in *Svobodné slovo*, 18 November 1989.

a life of its own, as if it had sprouted wings, which is perhaps why at around eight o'clock, as it snaked into Národní třída, it was suddenly greeted with walls of riot police.

Determined not to allow the marchers to reach Wenceslas Square, the commanders of the police operation ordered the leading demonstrators to disperse and simultaneously cut off their long tail of supporters with another thick wall of riot police. Suddenly the crowd realized that it had lost its escape route, and that it was surrounded. All hell broke loose. Many of the trapped and panicky demonstrators began to chant, 'No violence! No violence!' and 'We are unarmed!' Thinking that this might just be another temporary halt enforced by the police, some parts of the crowd called, 'We'll go home from Wenceslas Square! We'll go home from there! [*Z Václaváku domů*]' Other demonstrators, sensing correctly that they were now at the mercy of the white-helmeted riot police, taunted them with shouts of 'Freedom! Freedom! [*Svoboda*]'. Still others bravely made fun of the President by calling him by his first name, and by mimicking his strange ungrammatical way of speaking, deliberately mispronouncing his name in a working-class drawl. 'Jakeš, Jakeš . . .' they called. 'We don't want Myloš! [*Nechceme Myloše*]'.

Once again came the megaphoned order to disperse. The crowd now knew that this was a sick joke, since there was nowhere to go. Many trembled, sat down, then began to sing the national anthem, followed by 'We shall overcome'. Keys were jangled, and a handful of young women were seen giving flowers to the unsmiling police, fixing them on to their helmets and transparent shields. Hundreds of candles were lit. 'No violence! No violence!' the seated crowd again chanted, yellow light flickering on their faces. Some again called out, 'Freedom! Freedom!' The response was swift. Riot police charged from both sides into the trapped crowd. It began rising to its feet, only to be thrown violently against itself, then flung about, jumbled into confusion, and stampeded into the arcades next to the Reduta jazz club.

The crush was so great that individuals began to gasp for air. Many shrieked for help. Cameramen and photographers began to be manhandled out of the way. Then out of nowhere armoured personnel carriers, diesel engines revving, arrived on the scene. Out poured scores of grim-faced Red Berets, the feared Special Anti-Terrorist Forces, who instantly charged at the demonstrators, herding them back to the street, wielding long truncheons on men, women, and children, pushing and shoving each of them in the direction of a carefully prepared narrow path flanked on either side by riot police. The street was filled with sounds of ripping clothing. Glasses scrunched underfoot. Thudding truncheons. Heavy breathing. Screams. Confused shouts. Then shrieks of demonstrators being pushed in ones and twos through the police funnel. Each was punched, kicked or cracked over the head or shoulders. All came through the tunnel looking dazed. Some cursed. Most stumbled. Others crashed to the ground, stunned, bleeding. The lucky ones were dragged into side streets to safety by friends and helpers. The luckless lay there, kicked and struck into unconsciousness.

VELVET POWER

The Velvet Revolution that magically began that afternoon was to produce a fundamental change of governmental power, without sparking civil war. Like all revolutions, it triggered bitter public controversies about who gets what, when, and how. It tore apart the old political ruling class and invented new rules for new political actors. The revolution bestowed the power to govern on new decision-makers. It forged new policies for tackling local and national problems and for reacting with and against international swings and trends. But the revolution did something more basic than this. It also flung everybody temporarily into an everyday world marked by flux, ambiguity, contingency. No doubt, the revolution drew together clumps of previously divided citizens who shared new memories, values, aspirations. The revolution legitimated not only governments and policies – practical outcomes – but also new shared sets of symbolic meanings and emotional commitments. The revolution produced a collective feeling of solidarity of the previously powerless. But in granting citizens a new freedom to speak and act differently the revolution also forced everybody into a state of unease. It catapulted them into a subjunctive mood. All of a sudden, some things were no longer sacred or forbidden. Everything seemed to be in perpetual motion. Reality seemed to lose its reality. Unreality abounded. There was difference, openness, and constant competition among various power groups to produce and to control the definition of reality.

When millions of oppressed people are flung together into a subjunctive mood they naturally feel sensations of joy. Hope and history are words that seem to rhyme. 'Bliss was it in that dawn to be alive,' wrote Wordsworth, and so it usually is in all upheavals of a revolutionary kind. Revolution is a transformative experience. 'It was like a step into an unknown space,' said Havel, as if everybody was staging 'a play that was unfinished'.[1] Revolution is an adventure of the heart and soul. Citizens initially feel personally strengthened by it. Their inner feelings of barrenness, emptiness, isolation momentarily disappear. They lose their fear. They feel lighter, joyful, more enthusiastic, even passionate about their family, friends, neighbours, acquaintances,

[1] Cited in Todd Brewster, 'The People Rise', *Life* (New York), February 1990, p. 32.

and fellow citizens. They feel they have a future. Astonished, they discover boundless energies within themselves. They experience joy in their determination to act and to change the world. Their participation in the turbulent thrill of the revolution becomes a giddy exploration of the unknown. The Germans call this giddiness *Freude*. The French call it *jouissance*. The Spanish call it *alegria*. The Czechs call this state of intoxication *euforie*.

All this is familiar. But it is equally clear that revolutions are also fickle events. Revolutions are times of condensed uncertainty. The joyful solidarity they produce is always countered by a shared sense of menace, danger, foreboding – of the sensed possibility that things will get worse, that evil will be the offspring of good. Revolutions disorientate people. They breed anxiety. Not only do many rediscover the obvious rule that the familiar normally serves as a comfortable home. They also learn at first hand that not everybody gains during revolutions, that indeed many lose out, and that everybody, through the course of revolutionary upheaval, fears to a greater or lesser extent that they will be pushed on to the side of the losers. The history of modern revolutions from the late eighteenth century onwards suggests that revolutions are never 'the irruption of the masses in their own destiny' (Trotsky), for the simple reason that they always – the Velvet Revolution was no exception – unleash the lust for power among jostling minorities of organized manipulators, who seek the ultimate prize: immense power over the lives of millions of others. During revolutions, that is to say, power struggles among political factions always break out. Within the old ruling groups, the knives are usually drawn. Groups of professional counter-revolutionaries are born. Within the ranks of the opposition, groups of professional revolutionaries possessed of great initiative, organizing talent and elaborate doctrines also make their appearance. At first, they appear to listen to their fellow citizens who are rebelling on the streets. Later, these revolutionary grouplets claim to represent them. Eventually, they supplant them, sometimes through violence. The professional revolutionists press home the need to avert counter-revolution and to revolutionize the revolution. The revolution is seen to be an irresistible necessity. This enables the revolutionaries to justify their actions, to sacrifice their victims to the great event, and to absolve in advance any guilt or crime that may be committed in the name of the revolution. Strangely, this idea of the necessity of the revolution is mixed up with the contrary presumption, among both the revolutionaries and their opponents, that human beings have absolute power over their destinies. And so revolutions are usually dangerous affairs. Revolutions are like hurricanes. Drawn into their forcefields, human beings find that it is possible to commit actions that posterity, out of sheer amazement and horror, finds it difficult to comprehend, let alone to justify.

The first day of the Velvet Revolution confirmed these maxims. Whatever observers may now think of the scale and causes of the events, the mayhem that followed undeniably scared many people, revolutionaries like Havel included. He noted that the authorities did their world-historical best to restore calm and to rebuild order and normality. On the morning after the events, on day two of the revolution, Communist Party newspapers reprinted the ČTK communiqué, adding only that by ten o'clock in the evening the centre of Prague was peaceful again. The official press also reported some heavily doctored casualty figures: 7 policemen and 17 demonstrators had been injured; 143 people had been arrested and a further 9 detained for further questioning; 70 others had been caught *flagrante delicto* disturbing the peace; 21 others had been fined and released.

Quite the opposite message had meanwhile spread like fire through Prague. The word 'massacre' began to be heard every-where. Whoever invented it either committed an unintended exaggeration or deliberately produced a white lie. But its effect was to arouse public indignation against the whole Communist system. As each hour passed, talk of massacre ensured that the radical resistance that had sprung up in the university faculties and theatres quickly spread into the streets. Televisions set up in shop windows ran videotapes of the police brutality. At scores of unofficial meetings and in theatres, cafés and pubs all over the city people began to talk of the need to stand up to the Communists, even to defeat them, for instance through strike action and public hearings about police brutality. Inebriated by their own power, crowds began to deface statues, rename underground stations, tear down Communist Red stars. Some people began to hold all-day vigils, lighting hundreds of votive candles at bloodstained sites, and then standing back in silence, as if in prayer.

Whatever fear and vacillation remained on the second day of the revolution suddenly evaporated with the extraordinary news, based on Western media reports that evening, that Martin Šmíd, a young student at the faculty of mathematics and physics, had died from injuries received the previous night. It later transpired that the report was untrue. The standard story is that Havel's Trotskyite friend Petr Uhl had been approached by two StB agents who provided him with details of the death. Uhl was the director of a dissident press agency and in that capacity supplied Western agencies with the world-shattering news. Whether or not Uhl was handling the truth carelessly, or what the motives of the agents were, or why the dithering authorities subsequently spent a whole day searching for the supposed fatality, remains unclear to this day. It was subsequently alleged that an STB secret-police agent had infiltrated the demonstration, provoked it to change course, and then fell down, feigning death, to be carted away by an StB ambulance. The ploy was evidently backed by pro-Gorbachev Party bosses whose aim was to fire up the population, to discredit the hardliners, thus improving the chances of 'the moderates' retaining power. Whatever the case, the truth of the matter did not matter at the time. In thousands and thousands of minds, the death of a young student at the hands of the Communists during a demonstration to commemorate the death of a young student at the hands of the Nazis fifty years earlier proved that the two systems stood on the same continuum of intolerance, totalitarianism, violence.

With danger in the air, Havel was forced to grow concerned about his own personal safety. His friend John Bok especially criticized his habit of walking everywhere and of making his own way home at night after political meetings. He quickly convinced him of the need for protection.[1] Several days into the revolution, long-haired, energetic Bok had organized a private police force to protect the body of the man who would prove to be its principal actor. The Force − 'the boys', Bok preferred to call them − operated from the outset according to the rules of military-police discipline. The thirty or so young men were not especially political. But they had grown tired of the Communist system and were alert to the high risks and dangers of this present moment in history, which their native intelligence told them was of historical significance. The Force was well briefed: their job was

[1] Interview with John Bok (Prague), 1 October 1997.

to protect the lilliputian figure, a man of the people, by operating in secret a rival force to that of the official StB, without it spotting and catching them. The Force looked and dressed like Czech athletes in training, which several of them were in fact. Full of energy, tall and physically agile, they wore track suits and trainers and were strictly forbidden to drink alcohol while on the job. They had excellent road sense and knew Prague like the backs of their big hands. Several were equipped with short-range walkie-talkies, which were used sparingly lest they were detected or monitored by the StB. All were skilled in the arts of seeing and shielding, without being seen.

The tasks of the Force were initially easy to execute: chauffeuring and ferrying Havel here and there all over Prague. Concealing his whereabouts. Keeping watch for the feared official police. Anticipating or foiling any plot they might be hatching to snatch and detain their man. Ushering Havel politely through small crowds of well-wishers. Making sure he shook and kissed hands in moderation, so that he could be on time for the next string of meetings. The problem of scheduling soon mushroomed in size and complexity. For the first time in his life, Havel found himself ever more trapped within a thickening forest of appointments. Individuals and groups, enjoying the new freedom to act with and against each other in opposition to the regime, wanted time with him, and he with them.

Gone for ever was the halcyon tranquillity of trilobite-hunting at Barrandov, peaceful walks through the woods at Hrádeček, long early-morning baths, sipping coffee laced with rum. Some mornings now began before first light. The days usually stretched unbroken beyond nightfall, and often well past midnight. The pace had to be quickened, kept up, quickened again. Amidst mounting chaos, appointments needed to be made and kept. Havel had to be reminded of them; alterations needed to be made; others had to be contacted as and when events demanded; routes and vehicles had to be co-ordinated; and, given the dangers of further police and army crackdowns, everything had to be executed quietly and invisibly.

The job of crowd control was not especially difficult at first. But the technique of gesturing Havel along his route with outstretched hands soon had to be replaced with flying wedges. As each day passed, and especially after the appearance of the first trolley cars adorned with banners reading *Havel na Hrad* (Havel for President), the Force found itself up against thickening walls of people, whose good nature was overpowered by its heaving numbers and, hence, the growing probability that Havel would be mobbed, trapped, knocked down, trampled, injured, wilfully hurt, assassinated even. No one, and certainly not Havel himself, knew the authorities' intentions or tactics, especially after his daring act on the third evening of the revolution: to convene a meeting of citizens at the Činoherní klub theatre to discuss and to decide what now was to be done.

The wise political animal Havel did not know that the gathered group of revolutionaries was destined, in quick time, to lead the struggle against the old order, let alone that it would form itself into a shadow government. But he had the good sense to invite a broad and motley array of individuals and group representatives whose opinions captured something of the various hopes, fears, and angers sparked by the so-called massacre. The packed meeting included Charter 77 veterans, the Pen Club committee, members of groups like the Society for the Protection of the Unjustly Prosecuted (VONS), Art Forum, the Independent Students' Union, the Czechoslovak Helsinki Committee, the Circle of Independent Intellectuals, Renaissance (*Obroda*), the Czechoslovak Democratic Initiative, and independent members of the churches, banned Christian and socialist parties, and other associations. That evening, on Sunday, 19 November 1989, at 11 p.m., after brief but spirited discussion, the meeting voted unanimously to form itself into a new citizens' umbrella group called Civic Forum [*Občanské fórum*]. In the early hours of the next morning, it issued a proclamation. Signed by Havel and seventeen other representatives, the toughly worded document aimed to bring to justice those responsible for the massacre. It sought to remind the population of the tragedy that befell them after capitulating silently in 1968. It aimed as well somehow to split the ruling Communist Party by identifying some of its hardliners. The proclamation called for the resignation of the current Federal Minister of the Interior, František Kincl, and Miroslav Štěpán, as well as those Communist leaders (like Gustáv Husák and Miloš Jakeš) who had actively supported the Warsaw Pact invasion in 1968. It went on to propose the setting up of an independent Civic Forum commission chartered to investigate the massacre and to punish those responsible. And, as if to remind everybody of the need to lift their political sights, it called for the release of all political prisoners, including those (like Petr Uhl) who had been arrested that day.[1]

It would have been easy for the authorities to pick off Havel and his Civic Forum colleagues. They instead kept their fingers off the trigger, probably because for the past two days, ever since the outbreak of the revolution, everything had gone badly for the Communist Party. The silent reprieve gave Havel courage that more could be done. He moved fast to seize the initiative, protected by the Force through all the confused twists and turns of the revolutionary maelstrom. From the moment Civic Forum was formed, Havel manifestly set his sights on becoming Leader of the Opposition. He busied himself initially in securing his immediate power base, for instance by helping to set up and monitor Civic Forum committees concerned with operations, technical advice, information, and planning of strategy. He paid special attention to keeping his fingers on the rapid pulse of events. His days were long and filled with scores of conversations, more or less confidential, laced with endless cigarettes, brandy and beer, snacks and cups of coffee. He quickly looked wrecked, as if to play the part of the rakish revolutionary leader burdened not by the weight of the past, but by the massive uncertainty about the fate of the present.

There are always moments in a revolution (as Jules Michelet pointed out) when actors feel as though normal mechanical time has vanished. This was certainly that moment. Sometimes Havel had the feeling that the revolution – he was now convinced that this was the right word to use – was moving too slowly, and at other times too fast. It never felt just right. Things often moved too slowly because people's actions, including his own, quickly became ensnared within thickening webs of relations, obligations, problems, misunderstandings, all of which gave him and those around him in Civic Forum the feeling that their efforts were being diverted, dissipated, or bogged down in details. Yet events also sometimes seemed to move too quickly. Things happened and disappeared so fast that everybody had to hurry in order just to experience them. The revolution seemed to hurtle forwards at breakneck speed, with such force in fact that the proliferation

[1]The text appeared as *Provolání* (Prague, 19 November 1989). It is reproduced in John F. N. Bradley, *Czechoslovakia's Velvet Revolution. A Political Analysis* (New York, 1992), annex 8.

of surprises and unforeseen events induced flutters and fears in everybody's hearts. In either case, it felt to Havel as if the unfolding revolutionary events could not easily be brought to an end – neither that they could be halted nor that they pointed to a happy ending.

On board the revolution rollercoaster Havel worked hard through Civic Forum both to ensure its survival and to guarantee its role as the beating heart of the emerging opposition body. With his support, Civic Forum dispatched delegates all over the country with the aim of establishing brother and sister chapters. Attempts were also made to embarrass and paralyse the regime by sending delegations of Civic Forum representatives to visit all the strategically important state bodies, such as the Parliament, the Federal Government, the Czech Government, the Presidency, the Czech National Council, and the Ministry of the Interior. The delegations were typically met with sweet words or brick walls, but that did not matter because on each occasion the Civic Forum activists were chaperoned by cheering crowds, which gave the opposition the moral high ground and had the added effect of making the political authorities look as though they were paralysed by crisis. Havel, fearing that they would use violence, like cornered animals, lent his hand to the Forum's efforts to calm public nerves and to appeal for absolute physical restraint within the ranks of the demonstrators, despite police provocations and rumours.

Among the many paradoxes of the Velvet Revolution – its name was drawn from the 1960s New York experimental rock band, the Velvet Underground – is that it began violently and continued throughout to threaten to rain down violence on a torrential scale. Havel told friends that he found the whole saga nerve-wracking, for he knew that any attempt by the authorities to impose martial law would throw everything into the pot of jeopardy. He also knew that the persistent and ineradicable threats of violence – symbolized by the omnipresent walls of grim-faced police dressed in riot gear – might at any moment puff up the street crowds into violent explosions. Everything rested on a knife-edge, especially after hundreds of police moved in on the fifth day of the revolution (Tuesday, 21 November) to surround and protect the building of the Central Committee. The sinister symbolism of that move was compounded by next day's rumour, which ran hot through the street crowds, that all Prague schools and university faculties were being visited by security-police agents; that in nearby Pilsen militia leaders had urged Jakeš to 'stand firm and reject reforms' and to recognize that 'force should be met by force'; and that 40,000 troops were closing in on the city to prepare a Beijing-style crushing of the Czech democracy movement.

Havel hoped against hope that everything would turn out well. Measured calculations dictated the conclusion that the regime would not crack down violently on its opponents. Moscow might not approve. The western enclaves of the Soviet empire were anyway in an advanced state of collapse (Communism had already peacefully collapsed in Hungary and Poland, and neighbouring East Germany was in turmoil). Violence would hardly bring much-needed economic reform or solve any other structural problems of the regime. Violence might well make the country ungovernable. A military crackdown would surely breed resistance from the emerging civil society. There would also certainly be a huge international outcry against a repetition of the Prague Spring solution. And yet within a revolutionary crisis of this kind, Havel sensed, reasoned calculations could count for nothing in comparison with the authorities' fear-driven impulses. So he helped do some fire-fighting, as when he and Professor Jelínek from the Civic Forum leadership made several desperate telephone calls to the Pilsen militia leaders, who were indeed getting ready to issue live ammunition. The tactic of responsibly calling the militia's bluff and sending off a thousand demonstrators to their buildings worked.

The success convinced Havel that the chances of a non-violent or 'velvet' outcome would partly depend on his winning leadership of the opposition. Nothing was certain. But a week into the revolution he had begun to look and act like the moral and political leader of the resistance to late-socialism. The revolution itself was proving to be a great spectacle. It enchanted both observers and participants alike, and so Havel, a master dramatist and compulsive planner of his and others' moves, climbed eagerly on to a stage already clotted with countless actors. Edmund Burke's remark to Lord Charlemont during the French Revolution, 'What a play, what actors!', applied just as well 200 years later to the Velvet Revolution, and particularly to Havel himself. His public quest to confirm his leadership – a show *par excellence* – began at the Prague theatre Laterna Magika. Havel chose that as the site to base the headquarters of Civic Forum, whose inner circles quickly began to function as a government in waiting.

There, in the smoky caverns of the Laterna Magika, he co-ordinated the huge task of drawing up blueprints for the future of the country, helped by a team of experts, including several frustrated *prognostiks* (academic economists), to whom the Jakeš government had refused to listen when the time had come for *perestroika* reforms: Dr Komárek, Dr Dlouhý, and his future enemy number one, Dr Klaus. Reporters from all over the world began to crowd into the theatre, hoping to get a glance or word from the becoming-famous playwright-leader. Havel tried to put some order into the chaos by organizing press conferences, among the first of which was held at 8.30 p.m. on 22 November. At an informal briefing beforehand, his furrowed face radiated confidence as he spoke of the past twenty years of post-totalitarian repression, the misuse of the word socialism, the organized lying about everything, including the Prague Spring and the recent massacre. He said that Civic Forum wanted to replace the powermongering, lies and corruption of the old order with a pluralist democracy. It wanted guarantees for independent economic activity, which was not the same as the restoration of capitalism.

Towards the end of the briefing, Havel said in jest to one reporter, Dana Emingerová, that if details of the briefing were published in the Czechoslovak press then he would pass on to her the prestigious Olof Palme Prize, which he had that day been awarded. In retrospect, the remark was highly revealing of the reigning ignorance within the opposition about the state of morale and fortitude within the upper ranks of the nomenklatura, who were now beginning to panic so wildly that they resembled the swine of Gadarene. Havel's last remark at the briefing reinforced this impression. A messenger had just informed him that a highly secret extraordinary session of the Central Committee had just voted out the compromised leaders in favour of a reformist faction led by Štrougal. 'This probable fall of the compromised calls for champagne,' said Havel with a grin, without knowing that the Party session was not so extraordinary – simply because the *whole* of the Communist Party was in an advanced state of implosion.

Although it took several weeks for Havel and the rest of the inner circle of Civic Forum to realize that they had overestimated the power of the ruling party, he cunningly managed to manoeuvre it into its greatest public test of the revolution. The plan was to put the Party on trial before the emerging public opinion by inviting a senior Communist to address a public rally. The experience of addressing a public without rigging the setting, theme or outcome had almost been forgotten in Czechoslovakia since the military crushing of the Prague Spring. Havel reasoned that the Party leadership, well accustomed to deciding things in committees and behind closed doors, would probably be wrongfooted when exposed to the test of public-opinion-making. He personally had found unforgettable his public debut at Dobřís and more recently – eleven months ago, on 10 December 1988 – he had for the first time addressed a demonstration in Prague's Škroup Square (so named after the composer of the national anthem). Czechoslovak television and amateur video images of that rally show the wispy-haired Havel up on the podium, dressed in a black leather jacket and a brightly coloured scarf, speaking into two loudhailers, attended by a young student, poking fun at the authorities, singing praises to citizens, evidently enjoying the stage performance immensely.[1]

Havel had the chance to repeat this kind of performance on a freezing but sunny Tuesday, 21 November 1989, this time before an immense crowd of over 200,000 demonstrators squeezed into Wenceslas Square. It was the first time Civic Forum figures like Václav Malý, Radim Palouš, Milan Hruška, Karel Sedláček and Havel himself had appeared before such a large crowd. Although earlier that day the air had been rife with rumours about martial law and Chinese-style massacres, the crowd defiantly took refuge in its size, cheering the speakers standing up on the balcony of the Melantrich building, the headquarters of the Socialist Party, whose general secretary, Jan Škoda – a schoolmate from Poděbrady – was a founding member of Civic Forum. The wildest cheers of all were reserved for the nervous Havel. He made a tremendous impression as well on the police, many of whom were spotted sporting the national colours on their lapels and cheering Havel. His political career as Leader of the Opposition was now much clearer, and it

---

[1]See the second of the two-part documentary on *Charta* 77, 'Changes', Česká televize (Prague, 1996), op. cit. 'It seems that we are living in thrilling, extraordinary, even dramatic times,' runs one soundbite. 'State power is on the one hand heightening its repression against citizens, arresting them, squirting them [*stříkat ze stříkaček* – much laughter in the crowd]. On the other hand, society is beginning to lose its fear, and more and more people are unafraid of publicly expressing their true opinions.'

was confirmed within hours by a secret approach to him from a leading Communist, Evžen Erban, sent by Premier Adamec to propose that secret negotiations about the future of the country begin immediately.

Little is known about that first contact with the Party, but Havel's determination to look and act like the next leader of the country was revealed in the letters he immediately drafted on behalf of Civic Forum to Presidents Bush and Gorbachev. The letters aimed to inform them of the deep crisis in Czechoslovakia just before their planned talks in Malta. The quick unofficial replies he received made it crystal-clear not only that Bush favoured a breakthrough to political democracy, but also that Gorbachev, by refusing to back his Czechoslovak comrades with force, was *de facto* of the same opinion. Havel and the rest of Civic Forum drew courage. Their foray into foreign policy, which is what it amounted to, combined with the approach from Premier Adamec, served as the immediate backdrop for Havel's direct backing for the Civic Forum plan to work towards a general strike by hosting a countrywide string of giant demonstrations designed to force the government on to its knees.

There were now large daily demonstrations in Prague, and a taste of things to come was provided by the next one after Havel's Melantrich appearance. An estimated half a million people crushed into Wenceslas Square, amidst extraordinary reports and rumours. News was received of growing confusion within the upper echelons of the Party and of support for Civic Forum from a wide variety of groups and organizations, including the Slavia football club, the Prague Lawyers' Association, the giant ČKD electronics plant, and Barrandov film studios, formerly the property of the Havel family. Demonstrators also knew of the demand for editorial freedom hurled by the employees of State Television at their Communist managers. And snippets of information were circulating fast about the unprecedented spreading of unrest to many towns outside Prague. In Bratislava, where the trial continued of Dr Čarnogurský, who was charged with defaming the socialist system by calling it totalitarian, up to 100,000 demonstrators, many of them workers from Slovnaft Petrol Complex, reportedly had turned out. In České Budějovice, 25,000 protestors braved pouring rain, while policemen searched student hostels for planted bombs. In Brno, perhaps 120,000 people came out in support of the local demand to widen the dialogue 'to involve civil society'. In some cities, like the north Bohemian industrial town of Most, the authorities had tried to prohibit demonstrations, which took place regardless. The significant news also reached Wenceslas Square of the 'disappearance' of seventeen coachloads of Moravian militia-men, newly arrived in Prague to relieve colleagues now exhausted by five days on duty guarding state buildings. Havel told reporters that the militiamen had not been told where they should report for duty – such was the chaos in the capital's police administration – and that consequently they had got lost in the huge crowd gathering for the 4 p.m. demonstration. The militiamen later tried to find accommodation, were refused everywhere they went, and presumably then found their own way back to Moravia, their ears ringing with the chief slogans chanted by the peaceful throng: 'The Soviet Union: Our Model at Last! [*Sovětský svaz, konečně náš vzor*]'; 'St Stephen's Day without Štěpán! [*Na Štěpána bez Štěpána*]'; 'Miloš Jakeš, it's all over! [*Miloši končíme*]'; and a chant that must have thrilled Civic Forum's leader, 'Play Havel's Plays! [*Hrajte Havla*]'.

And so came the weekend of the biggest peaceful demon-strations of all. Moved for reasons of space at the last moment to Letná Plain, high above the Old Town Square, the planned demonstrations on Saturday and Sunday, 25 and 26 November attracted great excitement. The Civic Forum leadership smelled victory. Popular fears of violent counter-revolution were at their lowest ebb. And the Communist leaders, plugging wax in their ears and shading their eyes, pretended to be busy with their official duties. On the day before the Letná demonstrations, the ageing Jakeš had appeared so calm that some of his senior comrades became convinced that he was actually insane. At seven o'clock that evening, Jakeš replied by suddenly announcing that he and his secretariat and politburo were resigning. The news was instantly relayed, in the style of the ancient Greeks, by a journalist who sprinted to Wenceslas Square, where the crowds that were still gathered there greeted the revelations with a roar.

The resignation resembled collective suicide. It was an act of grave political stupidity, and it convinced Havel and his supporters, who immediately afterwards drank a champagne toast to 'A Free Czechoslovakia', that the Party was dissolving into chaos. That was certainly the feeling on Letná Plain, where on the Saturday 750,000 people assembled, some of them having come straight from attending a special mass marking the canonization of Agnes of Bohemia in the Prague Cathedral, celebrated by the ninety-year-old Cardinal Tomášek and shown live for the first time by state television. The Letná demonstrators did not know that Štěpán had just been forced to resign and that President Husák had just agreed to halt criminal proceedings against eight people, including Miroslav Kusý and Ján Čarnogurský. The crowd was nevertheless thrilled to hear speeches from Havel and various other celebrities, and it was agreed by an enormous forest of hands that another demonstration at Letná would take place the following day, at 2 p.m.

With the scent of political victory in the freezing air, nearly a million demonstrators returned on the Sunday to cheer, shout slogans, jangle their keys and listen to the speeches. The gigantic crowd was told through loudspeakers of the Communist counter-demonstration at Litoměřice, where some 1,800 faithful Communists had gathered with shouts of 'Long Live Socialism!', 'Long Live the Party!', 'Long Live the Army!', 'Long Live the Police!', 'We Shall Never Give Up!', and 'Who Is Havel?'. There were jeers and hoots of laughter, then respectful silence followed by some cheering and clapping as Alexander Dubček, the representative of both Slovak voices and of the aspirations of the Prague Spring, mounted the makeshift podium to speak of socialism with a human face and of the past twenty years as a period of national humiliation. There followed live music and a string of speakers, including police lieutenant Pinc. He received a mixed reception after apologizing personally to the crowd for police brutalities and trying to explain that the police themselves did not agree with the ruthless handling of the 17 November demonstration, and that they were only obeying orders. Student representatives replied by reading out a statement by the procurator-general, who acknowledged publicly that the police used excessive violence on the first day of the revolution. A large section of the crowd sounded amused, especially after a Charter 77 spokesman pointed out that not all political prisoners had yet been released. The chuckling turned into rapturous applause when it was announced that Petr Uhl – the first link in the chain of publicity of the massacre – had just arrived at the demonstration, straight from prison.

It was then Havel's turn to stand up before the vast tidal sea of expectant faces. Dressed in black, wearing reading glasses, rocking nervously, to and fro, on his left leg, the man of the people began.

'The Civic Forum wants to be a bridge between totalitarianism and a real, pluralistic democracy, which will subsequently be legitimized by a free election,' he shouted into the microphone. 'We want truth, humanity, freedom as well,' he added, enveloped instantly in a cloud of thunderous applause. After thirty seconds he continued: 'From here on we are all directing this country of ours and all of us bear responsibility for its fate.'[1] Havel went on to announce that the Prime Minister of Czechoslovakia had been invited to speak to the crowd. Havel did not explain why, but those in the crowd who thought about it would have realized that the Civic Forum leadership had put their trust in Adamec as the only senior Communist leader whom they could trust. 'Adamec! Adamec!' some parts of the crowd began to chant, perhaps with the intention of exacting their pound of flesh.

Adamec initially lived up to Civic Forum's and Havel's expectations by telling the crowd politely that the government accepted all of their key demands. The crowd whistled. It roared with joy. But no sooner had Adamec performed well when he made the mistake of qualifying his opening statement. He revealed that he still knelt before the principle of the leading role of the Party by resorting to the ifs and buts for which he had always been famous. He was instantly repaid by the hostility of the demonstrators. Their sea of faces swelled up into a tsunami. It drowned out Adamec. They hissed and booed and heckled and taunted each sentence. Tension rose to the point where the Civic Forum marshals knew that either he was to be pulled from the podium or he would be swallowed up – suffocated, assaulted, even lynched – by the crowd. Adamec's hunch that he could solve the political crisis and save the Czechoslovak Communist Party by appearing at Letná had gone hopelessly wrong. His attempt to outwit Civic Forum had backfired. So too had Civic Forum's attempt to use the Party as a safe bridgehead into the post-Communist future. The revolution was now succeeding. 'Our jaws cannot drop any lower,' exclaimed Radio Free Europe.[2] Communism's time

---

[1] Cited in *Czechoslovakia's Velvet Revolution*, op. cit., p. 102. Other day-by-day accounts include Timothy Garton Ash, *The Magic Lantern: The Revolution of '89 Witnessed in Warsaw, Budapest, Berlin, and Prague* (New York, 1990); and Bernard Wheaton and Zdeněk Kavan, *The Velvet Revolution: Czechoslovakia, 1988–1991* (Boulder, Colorado, 1992).
[2] Cited in Bernard Gwertzman and Michael T. Kaufman (eds.), *The Collapse of Communism by the Correspondents of 'The New York Times'* (New York, 1990), p. vii.

was up. The events boastfully predicted in the Prague scene a few days earlier – a prediction made by British writer Timothy Garton Ash that many thought a wild exaggeration – had come to pass. The political job of getting rid of Communism had taken ten hard years in Poland. In Hungary it had taken ten months. In neighbouring East Germany the revolution had taken ten weeks. In Czechoslovakia it had indeed taken just ten days.

MACHIAVELLI

The end of Adamec led many Civic Forum supporters to conclude that Havel's candidacy for high office was now firmly secured. The inference was premature, but it quickly managed to harden into one of the biggest myths of the revolution. According to the conventional story, Havel was the 'natural candidate' for the country's presidency. This followed from the fact that for a long time – ever since Charter 77, some say – he had been admired and universally popular within the circles that later counted. His reputation seemed to grow unhindered even when he tom-fooled around – as on New Year's Eve, 1988, when, less than a year before the outbreak of revolution, a photograph shows him at a 'Monarchy for All' party, happily sitting on a throne, crowned and drunk, swigging straight from a bottle of wine.

Havel's popularity became especially potent upon his arrest and imprisonment on the evening of 16 January 1989, after laying flowers in Wenceslas Square in memory of Jan Palach. His imprisonment sparked protests and led to a sudden mushrooming of his popularity outwards from narrow dissident circles. Even the Bundestag, in Bonn, passed a resolution, on 16 March 1989, condemning his sentence.[1] A further round of international recognition also came his way, for instance in Toronto, where his friend Josef Škvorecký helped secure his nomination for the Robert F. Kennedy Human Rights Award. Meanwhile, the statesman Henry Kissinger described him as an 'inspirational personality who has shown that all great achievements have to be somebody's dream before they become a reality'.[2] The single sentence uttered by Olga at his trial a month later seemed to capture the inexorable trend towards fame. 'If Václav Havel is sentenced,' she said to the stone-faced judge, 'then all who stand by him in our country, and abroad, including those who have nominated him for the Nobel Prize, will be sentenced along with him.'[3]

His early release from prison, for the last time, on 17 May 1989, consolidated his fame. The welcome-home party held in his honour was attended by everyone who counted in the opposition,

[1] See the various documents assembled in Jan Vladislav and Vilém Prečan (eds.), *Czechoslovakia: Heat in January 1989* (Scheinfeld–Schwarzenberg, 1989).
[2] Josef Škvorecký, 'Ten buržoazní spratek', in *Milý Václave . . . Tvůj*, op. cit., p. 54; the remark by Henry Kissinger is found in the documentary film, *Why Havel?*, directed by Vojtěch Jasný, narrated by Miloš Forman (Los Angeles, 1990).
[3] Cited in Kosatík, p. 251.

including Alexander Dubček. Those who believe the conventional story say that the warm welcome proved that he was now the unrivalled symbol of oppositional integrity, the personification of a principled life lived in the open, the good-looking man who had lost his fear, who always played clean and – despite shy protestations to the contrary – was good at politics. The unprecedented success of 'A Few Sentences' (*Několik vět*), a new petition that he drafted and helped circulate during the early summer of 1989, confirmed these qualities. So did the enormous success, on the Brno stage that same summer, of the last of his plays performed (anonymously) before the revolution, *Tomorrow the Balloon Goes Up* (*Zítra to spustíme* [1989]).[1] And so did his Paulskirche speech, 'A Word on Words', read out in Frankfurt, live on German television, by the actor-director Maximilian Schell to an audience that included André Glucksmann, President von Weizsäcker, and Chancellor Kohl.[2] Or so the conventional tale runs. Then serendipity intervened, it is said. The Party fell into confusion. The regime began to collapse. That left only one alternative to the filth and crumbling authority of the *ancien régime*: the clean-living, smiling and waving Havel, the man who was a master of moral *mise-en-scène*, the honest man of the streets, the political figure with an unblemished past who could, if offered the chance and so long as he accepted, lead the country back into the promised land of freedom.

The view that Havel was naturally destined to be King is fanciful. Its political naivety was obvious to him. Havel knew well that there are tides in political affairs, that good fortune results from catching them when they are rising to their highest. What he could not have known in advance is that before setting to sea he would be required, during the last five months of 1989, to fight his way through a Machiavellian obstacle course of death, intrigue, rivalry and trickery. A portent of things to come was offered by his astrologer friend Daniela Fischerová, whom he visited in early August, just before the twenty-first anniversary of the Prague Spring. It wasn't the first time he had seen her. When the going was rough, he, the embodiment of 'reason', found that he liked the momentary escape from the stress of everyday life

---

[1]Interview with Petr Oslzlý (Brno), 7 November 1998.
[2]'Ein Wort über das Wort,' *Frankfurter Allgemeine Zeitung* (Frankfurt), 16 October 1989, p. 13.

into an occultish world with different prospects. Fischerová told
him that his signs were most unfavourable. She said that he should
take special care of himself. Perhaps this is one reason why he
urged the ragged opposition grouplets in Prague not to provoke
the authorities by holding demonstrations in memory of the Soviet
invasion of the country, and why, during that week of August
1989, he retreated to Hrádeček to avoid being picked up yet again
by the secret police. Perhaps as well it was unfavourable stars that
convinced him, when at Hrádeček, to have the property privately
filmed. Trailed by a crew of video film-makers, he moved slowly
from room to room, describing the events that had happened
there, prefacing his remarks by saying that he did not know what
would now happen, and that in any event the film would serve
as a record for posterity.

Havel soon grew less cautious. Death beckoned. During the
first few days of September, he let his guard down completely
when attending a gathering organized by the Jaroslav Hašek circle
of literary friends at a picturesque countryside retreat in north
Bohemia in Okrouhlice.[1] It quickly degenerated into a bohemian
razzle, and on the night of 3 September, dead drunk, following
a performance by the rock 'n' roll band Sure Thing (*Jasná páka*),
he tried to stagger from an open-air fire to the house where he
was sleeping, arm in arm with an equally pie-eyed accomplice.
Eyewitnesses were uncertain who was the drunker, and who
was really assisting whom. One thing only was certain. As they
snaked past a water mill, the future political leader of the country
tripped and then slipped into the ice-cold waters of the steep-sided
millpond. Desperately trying to claw its stone sides, coughing and
spluttering and grunting for help, he went under repeatedly for
several minutes. A great panic ensued. Less inebriated friends
hobbled to the pond. Several dived in but nobody could help
Havel. Then someone managed to fish his almost lifeless body
out with a ladder. Someone else ran for a car. At high speed,
the waterlogged, vomiting Havel was taken to the local clinic,
where he was plied with oxygen and had his chest massaged.
Miraculously, he woke up next morning covered in scratches
and bruises and suffering severe chest pains. Somehow, he was

---

[1] The following details are drawn from the research note prepared by Blanka Císařovská
(Institute for Contemporary History, Prague, 30 September 1997).

alive. Shortly afterwards, suffering from pneumonia, he rang his historian friend Vilém Prečan in Germany, to say that there was another fact for the archives. 'I was convinced that there was no hope,' said Havel, in the tone of a man born posthumously. 'I had given in.'

It is incredible to think that the leader of the political opposition nearly died only weeks before he became world-famous, but so it was. The stupidity, or near-tragedy, resembled a dreadful parody of an exchange in *Twelfth Night*. 'What's a drunken man like, fool?' it is asked. The answer: 'Like a drown'd man, a fool, and a madman: one draught above heat makes him a fool; the second mads him; and a third drowns him.'[1] The episode had an immediate sobering effect on his judgements, as was evident in the various interviews he gave during the following weeks. Tail between legs, he told the samizdat cultural magazine *Sport* that he had never had political ambitions and certainly didn't want to become a professional politician. 'I would quite enjoy being the kingmaker,' he said, using the English word, 'but I wouldn't enjoy being King.'[2] The point was repeated shortly afterwards in the pages of *Lidové noviny*. He said that although he felt squeezed in the narrowing gap between his roles as 'a bankrupt' (*zkrachovanec*) and 'a politician', he was most certainly not being dragged into politics against his will. He warned against false euphoria, cautioned the opposition against relying upon the tactic of pressuring the state authorities through street demonstrations, and (giving a twist to a famous expression used by Masaryk) urged others to give plenty of emphasis to 'small-scale political work' (*drobné práce politické*).[3] The advice placed him in some tension with Jan Ruml, Rudolf Battěk and others who favoured big pushes from the streets, but very soon neither his caution nor his resistance to official politics counted for much. The outbreak of the revolution and the birth of Civic Forum forced him, not entirely against his will, into playing the leading political role within the opposition.

But now for the moment of intrigue. Among the principal weak points of his efforts during the second half of November to

---

[1] William Shakespeare, *Twelfth Night; Or, What You Will*, Act 1, Scene 5.
[2] From the interview with Ivan Lamper, 'Terén, na který nikdy nevstoupím', *Sport* (Prague), 1, 3 (September 1989), pp. 6–11.
[3] Václav Havel, 'An hour between a bankrupt and a politician', *Lidové noviny*, 10 (October 1989), pp. 1–2.

manoeuvre himself into the dominant role within the opposition was his lack of reputation. He was already something of a hero within Civic Forum, of course, and the massive crowds who heard him speak – not very forcefully or plainly – at least now knew how to recognize him up on balconies at vast distances. But the plain truths were that the revolution was a media event, that very few people in the country had ever heard him speak, and that most did not even know who he was. This was acknowledged on the afternoon and evening of 5 December, during a fateful meeting in Prague of the so-called Crisis Headquarters of the Co-ordination Centre of Civic Forum (*Krizový štáb*).[1] The meeting had been called specifically to examine who would be nominated as Civic Forum's candidate for President. Havel's longtime friend Ladislav Lis began the discussion without beating around the bush. 'The whole nation is calling Havel! Havel!' he said, only to be contradicted by a variety of speakers who thought otherwise. Havel mostly sat in silence as various positions were outlined. Quite a number appealed for 'realism' after Petr Pithart, testing the waters, suggested that perhaps a Slovak like the intellectual Miroslav Kusý should be nominated. Heated cries of 'This is absurd!' and 'This gentleman could never get through!' served as a prelude to discussion of the more serious options. Zdeněk Jičínský spoke powerfully for the view that Alexander Dubček was obviously the only political candidate who was well known to both the Czechoslovak public and the international scene. Someone suggested that Civic Forum should perhaps 'try' the well-known Communist Adamec, who in recent days had confided in him that he wanted to be President. Havel's friend Jiří Dienstbier reported to the meeting that both Olga and the writer Eda Kriseová were backing the Brno left-winger Jaroslav Šabata. At that point, probably sensing that the discussion was slipping through his fingers, Havel felt compelled to intervene, perhaps even with a touch of wounded pride. 'I obviously don't want to be President', he said slowly. 'But if the situation sharpens in such a way that it would be in the interests of the country to have me as president for a short while, then I'm able to be President, since I have always subordinated my personal interest

---

[1] The following account is taken from the gripping transcript of the meeting reproduced in Jiří Suk (ed.), *Občanské fórum* (Prague, 1997), volume 2, pp. 80–90.

to the interests of the country. Otherwise I would not have gone to prison.' Dienstbier, revealing his true colours, jumped in at this point with the claim that it was unrealistic that his friend could be President 'for a short while', and that instead he should realize that millions of people in the squares would indeed support the slogan (he spoke in English at this point) 'Havel for President!'.

The doubts about whether Havel was famous enough to get elected nevertheless lingered. Well after midnight, the only worker representative at the meeting, Petr Miller, pointed out that most middle-aged workers didn't know anything about Havel, except that he was a dissident opposing things. A campaign in the factories would be needed, Miller added. Another passing remark by Zdeněk Jičínský – who pointed out that the Communist-dominated Federal Assembly would more likely support Havel if the proceedings were televised – hit the same sore point. So it was clear to Havel that he was no 'natural' winner of any political prizes, and that the immediate political task was to become popular. That would require opposition to any talk of a directly elected president – which he thought (correctly) that he would lose – and, at the same time, a direct massaging of the will of the parliament and the taking of his campaign for presidency to the country's living rooms and kitchens and pubs by the most powerful available medium of communication: television.

On the 10 December 1989, in the name of Civic Forum, Havel was nominated by his actor friend Jiří Bartoška as a candidate for the presidency. 'I thought it was out of the question that the Parliament we had inherited from the previous regime would elect me,' he recalled.[1] The parliament was indeed hostile to his election. That is why a proposal to hold direct elections of the president immediately surfaced within the radical Democratic Forum grouping of the Communist Party. On 12 December, within the federal parliament, it was argued for forcefully by the Communist deputy Blažej. Havel and other Civic Forum leaders grew worried. Using various means, they spent the next five days trying to kill the proposal. At one point, Havel, watching a live television broadcast of parliament, tried to lobby its members by

[1]'Speech to the Joint Session of the US Congress (Washington, D.C., 21 February 1990)', in *Toward a Civil Society. Selected Speeches and Writings 1990–1994* (Prague 1995), p. 31.

getting a message through by telephone. He didn't know which number to ring, so he and Petr Pithart leafed through the telephone book. Havel eventually got through to the cloakroom. Twenty minutes later, the two men watched someone deliver a letter to the chairman of the parliament. But nothing happened. Havel grew despondent. It is also possible, although still unproven, that during this period Havel put in telephone calls to lobby the student representatives who were at the time (mid-December) sitting on the Parliamentary Commission of Investigation of the Events of 17 November 1989. It was well known that student groups were opposed to the principle of directly electing the President – like Havel, they were convinced that the Party's chosen candidate, probably Adamec, would win a handsome victory, thanks to their choking control over the official media. It was not to be. Although the students sitting on the Parliamentary Commission were prevented from lobbying for Havel, the surprise resignation of Adamec eighteen days before Christmas was an early season's gift to Havel. With the Communist Party leaderless and in a state of collapse, parliament was the only forum in which properly the future President was to be chosen. So Havel now had to raise his profile on television. That meant dealing directly with the Director of Czechoslovak Television, Miroslav Pavel.

A secret meeting between the two men, arranged by Havel, was planned for four o'clock on Sunday afternoon, 16 December at the top-floor studio of artist Joska Skalník, where for the past few days Havel had been in seclusion.[1] Pavel brought with him his newborn baby in a carry cot – his wife was ill – but the 'new man' image was deceptive. He was the former spokesman of Adamec's government, and was a tough and experienced operator. Havel expected trouble, and got it – in the face. Pavel told him that he was a minor political figure, and as such he was completely unprepared to give Civic Forum coverage in the early evening (7.30 p.m.) prime-time news slot. The best he could offer was a late-night slot – when of course most of the nation would be asleep. He smiled, glancing to check his sleeping infant. Havel

[1] The details of the meeting divulged here for the first time are drawn from my interview with Petr Pithart, Scheinfeld, 15 September 1996; my interview with Oldřich Tůma (London, 10 June 1997); the roundtable discussion between Petr Pithart, Jiří Kantůrek and others in *Proměny politického systému v Československu na přelomu let 1989/1990* (Prague, 1995), pp. 78–81; and the brief account provided in Jiří Suk (ed.), *Občanské fórum* (Prague and Brno, 1997), volume 1, pp. 30–31.

instantly welled up with anger. He raised his voice, so sharply that
Pavel's baby woke up and began to scream.

With that anger, at that moment, something changed in Václav
Havel's life. The moment of big-time rivalry had arrived. He
revealed that he was not prepared to back down in the confrontation with one of the two powerful men who now stood
between him and sovereign power. For the next twenty minutes,
the pair exchanged words like boxers exchanging punches. No
progress was made, so Havel resorted to threats. 'You just wait
until I become President,' he scowled, without the faintest note
of irony, testing the rule that he who plunges the dagger never
inherits the crown. 'You'll not last long. I'll make sure we get
rid of you. You'll be nothing!' Havel went on to shout that Jiří
Kantůrek, who was there by his side at that moment, would replace
Pavel if he didn't back down. Pavel raised his voice. So did Havel.
Someone leaned forward to restrain both men. 'All right, have it
your way, arsehole!' snapped Pavel, sensing at that instant that the
tide of history was flowing against him.

With that remark, he grabbed his baby and strode downstairs to
get into his car parked outside. On the way out the door, Havel,
acting the part of the victorious gentleman in a duel, handed his
defeated opponent the tape recording of the meeting. Petr Pithart
ran down five flights of stairs after him – not in honour of some
prior gentlemanly agreement, but because Pithart was worried that
Pavel might try to outfox his opponent with allegations of dirty
tricks and unfair play. 'If he plays it on the radio, we're finished!'
called Pithart to Havel. Just as Pithart got to the street, Pavel was
driving off. Breathless Pithart chased him, banged with his fist on
Pavel's car, and appealed for him to wind down the window,
which he did. 'We agreed not to misuse the tape,' said Pithart.
'We can stick it down the nearest sewer,' he suggested. Pavel
nodded, revving his engine impatiently. But no nearby open sewer
could be found, anywhere. Pithart, the future Prime Minister of
the country, ran back to the car. 'Look, you'd better take it,' he
said. Replied Pavel, just before zooming off: 'No thanks. Stick it
up your arse.'

That evening, the nervous-looking Havel, barely looking up
at the camera, read out a statement during the seven-thirty
evening news, live. Millions watched, but what they thought
went unrecorded. More certain in retrospect was the way in

which the incident leading up to the television appearance suggested a number of disquieting things about the phenomenon of power in human affairs: that the hunger for power over others is polymorphously perverse; that the process of coming to power is usually a costly business; that in the era of mass communications, one of the prizes and privileges of power is the freedom to define reality for others; and that in any conflict-ridden struggle to get the upper hand, good-natured conversational reason is always the loser to raised voices, threats, and outright bullying.

From the point of view of Havel's own stated commitment to living honestly in the truth, none of these things looked very pretty, but at least they had the effect of toughening him up for the coming moment of knavery. In his quest for sovereignty, it was obvious to him and plenty of others around him that by the middle of December there remained only one man potentially standing in his way. By 10 December 1989 – the day he announced that he would be a candidate for President – Havel had effectively won over a big majority of the inner governing circle (*rada*) of Civic Forum.[1] But everywhere there was still talk of another declared candidate named Alexander Dubček. The hurdle had to be jumped, and so the name of his potential opponent must have begun to ring in his ears and to cause him loss of sleep. There were some within Civic Forum, the historian Pavel Seifter for instance, who worried that a power vacuum would result from Havel's departure for the Castle, where in turn he might well fall prey to Dubček, who would wait in the wings for the inexperienced President to make fatal political mistakes.[2] Things were not helped by the fact that Olga was against his candidacy, that Havel's own sister-in-law, Dagmar Havlová, had told him that she supported Dubček, and that the same plausible view had been put eloquently and forcefully within Civic Forum by Zdeněk Jičínský.

Dubček was indeed a threat. After Havel's television performance, Dubček still remained much more a household name than the dissident playwright proto-politician. It was also obvious

---

[1] According to Jaroslav Šabata, reporting the informed estimate provided by a 'worried-looking but resigned' Zdeněk Jičínský on the day before Havel announced his candidacy, 'there were about thirty supporters of the candidacy of Václav Havel, against whom there were about half a dozen supporters of Alexander Dubček.' See Jaroslav Šabata, *Sedmkrát sedm kruhů* (Olomouc, 1997), p. 103.
[2] Interview with His Excellency Pavel Seifter, London, 15 March 1999.

that Dubček was, in the eyes of many, a bridge to the unfinished business of the Prague Spring. Although indecisive, he had learned a few hard lessons in the difficult art of dismantling the Communist system. Moreover, his election would send a powerful message of unity from Prague to Slovakia, and for exactly that reason he commanded enormous support within its population at large. It was also being said that President Dubček – the name sounded more familiar than President Havel – could better secure the loyalty of the nomenklatura amidst the disruptions caused by the revolution, thereby ensuring a smoother transition to free elections sometime during the next six months. And – the critical point – within the Federal Assembly, which was now poised to make the final decision about who was to be the next President, Dubček seemed much more likely to win the hearts of a clear majority of the hard-headed Communist deputies looking for a way to stem the anti-Communist tide.

So Havel had to get above him on the ladder to power, even if that meant trampling on not a few of his fingers. Dubček somehow had to be dealt with – in a civilized, but tough and effective manner, of course. Havel pushed for a solution in two separate, but overlapping, contexts. One of them was the round table, behind-closed-doors talks about the future government that began less than ten days after the outbreak of the revolution.[1] Convened by a group called Most (Bridge) that was put together in the summer of 1989 by the journalist Michal Horáček and prominent rock musician and film-score composer, Michael Kocáb, the regime and Civic Forum and its allies played power games with each other for two weeks. The sometimes tense negotiations culminated in the formation of Marián Čalfa's Government of National Understanding. Havel later dubbed it the Government of National Sacrifice, but it is clear that at every stage his role was central to its formation, and to the negotiated end of Communism's grip on the presidency. The

---

[1]Transcripts of nine rounds of talks that took place between 26 November and 9 December 1989 were printed after the revolution in Vladimír Hanzel, *Zrychlený tep dějin* (Prague, 1991). There were other meetings that went unrecorded, and it is unclear whether, for reasons of confidentiality or reputation, the invisible hand of Havel subsequently touched the manuscript. Further useful comments are to be found in Miloš Calda, 'The Roundtable Talks in Czechoslovakia', in Jon Elster (ed.), *The Roundtable Talks and the Breakdown of Communism* (Chicago and London 1996), pp. 135–177.

Communist negotiators' tactic of appealing for more time, in the hope that that would enable their survival, was countered by Havel's bold initial call for the resignation of President Husák by the end of 1989. Havel also pushed for a resolution that the Federal Prime Minister, Ladislav Adamec, be invited to address a Letná rally, perhaps with the expectation that Adamec could be used as his own personal Trojan Horse. When Adamec, freshly back from Moscow talks, shocked everybody by announcing that he would not head up the new federal government, so implying that he had his eyes on the presidency, he and Havel – on 5 December – met for a private discussion. Havel followed it up immediately with a letter to Adamec (co-signed by the actor Milan Kňažko, of the Public Against Violence) which said that while they saw Adamec as an important guarantor of political stability his proposed candidacy for president would be viewed unfavourably on the streets, and within Civic Forum itself.[1] From there on, Havel used the tactic of putting himself at the centre of things. Like a head of state, he personally assured Vacek, the Minister of Defence, that the opposition trusted him personally and knew that the army would not resort to Tiananmen tactics. Havel also used the tactic of making haste. He repeated many times that any attempt to stall the negotiations about the future government and the next President would produce explosions on the streets. 'The public will overthrow us and nobody knows what will follow,' he said at one point. And Havel tried – but failed – to get agreement that the resignation of Husák now had priority over the formation of a new government. When the opposition's two lawyers (Petr Pithart and Pavel Rychetský) pointed out to him that that tactic would leave no constitutional body to appoint a legitimate government, he backed down. He then put his weight behind powerfully built, sandy-haired, smiling-eyes Marián Čalfa. Havel proposed that he should be the next Prime Minister, on two conditions: that the new cabinet to be formed should 'visibly' meet the opposition's demands, and that the next President should be a Czech who was a member of no political party.

So Adamec was pushed aside and the way cleared for Havel to become President. Dubček now had to be dealt with from within Civic Forum. A clue as to how that was to be done was provided by

[1]Václav Havel and Milan Kňažko to Ladislav Adamec, 5 December 1989.

Havel himself on 5 December, well after midnight, during the long debate within Civic Forum about who would be their presidential candidate. There Havel proposed the principle of turn-taking: he would be willing to accept the candidacy, but on the condition that he would remain President only until free elections were held. This position had strong support both within Civic Forum and its counterpart in Slovakia, Public Against Violence.[1] It was pointed out immediately by Zdeněk Jičínský, in reply, that the proposal was strictly speaking unconstitutional, since the term of office of the President was not tied to that of the parliament, and that presidents were normally elected for five years. But Havel persisted, and in his television appearance on 16 December he reiterated the proposed strategy. 'If it is in the general interest that I should accept the presidential office, then I will accept,' he said. 'But there are two conditions: that I would be temporarily in post as needed only until the one who sits in Masaryk's chair is chosen by a freely elected Federal Assembly. The second condition,' he said, pausing, 'is that by my side, in any post, will be Alexander Dubček.' Havel added: 'I will neither allow any dark powers to erect a barrier between him and me nor between our two nations.'[2]

His audience did not know that on the day before, Havel had met in secret for one hour with the new Prime Minister, Marián Čalfa. In a carefully debugged room, the two men formulated a bold but simple plan. Čalfa promised that he would support Havel's candidacy and would deal with the parliament to ensure it voted that way, before the end of the year. Havel would take care of Dubček in his own way. The two men set to work. Čalfa wined and dined, lobbied and lectured, teased and threatened various groups and individuals 'to stop all unwanted initiatives in parliament'.[3] On 19 December, just as agreed, he appeared before the parliament to appeal to the deputies to elect Havel by the end of the year. Havel had meanwhile arranged, with the help of his cameraman friend and fellow Civic Forum activist, Stanislav Milota, a series of top-secret meetings with Dubček, who was accompanied by his old friend and former Minister of Economic

---

[1] The proposal, which went unrecorded, is minuted in Jiří Suk (ed.), *Občanské fórum* op. cit., volume 2, p. 90.
[2] From the Czechoslovak Television address on 16 December 1989.
[3] *Občanské fórum*, op. cit., volume 1, p. 31.

Planning in the 1968 government, František Vlasák.[1] During the next few days, the foursome thrashed out an agreement, despite some mind-changing. The two opponents shook hands on taking turns to taste presidential power. Dubček initially would not agree to call off his candidacy, but in return for the double guarantee that he would be appointed as leader of the Federal Assembly, and that Havel would say publicly that he indeed supported Dubček's candidacy in the run-up to the forthcoming free elections, Dubček would happily support Havel's candidacy this time around.

The subsequent commitment of both men to keep silent about the deal worked against Dubček. Within the ranks of Civic Forum, Havel carefully planned a nebulously worded declaration of sympathy for the idea that, sometime in the future, a Slovak might become President.[2] He then waited, until the day he enjoyed the advantage of incumbency. 'I feel a special obligation,' he said in a brief passage in his first presidential address to the country, 'to see that all the interests of the Slovak nation are respected and that no state office, including the highest one, will ever be barred to it in future.'[3] Dubček meanwhile kept his part of the bargain to the letter. He spoke warmly of Havel, often standing by his side, all the while clinging publicly to his aim of becoming the next President of Czechoslovakia. That didn't happen – despite the free elections that were held shortly afterwards.

---

[1] The previously unrecorded account of the secret meeting is based on material provided in an interview with Stanislav Milota (Prague), 2 October 1997, and my correspondence (Prague, 24 November 1998) with František Vlasák, who wrote: 'I am very glad to confirm that in mid-December 1989 six brief meetings took place between Mr Havel and Mr Dubček, which I, at the request of both, arranged, and, together with Milota, organized at various places in Prague. The result of these complicated talks was the agreement that Mr Havel would be the candidate for office of President of the ČSSR and Mr Dubček for office of Leader of the National Assembly of the ČSSR. The last meeting took place after 15 December.'
[2] See the transcripts reprinted in *Občanské fórum*, op. cit., volume 2, pp. 263–272.
[3] 'New Year's Address to the Nation', in *Toward a Civil Society*, op. cit., p. 19.

A CROWNED REPUBLIC

The reaction of the uniformed Castle staff who had been assembled in the First Courtyard to welcome the new President surprised everyone. As the tearful entourage passed through the lavish main gates, flanked by monograms of Marie Theresa and Joseph II, statues of battling giants, and symbols of the Bohemian Kingdom (a lion) and the Habsburg monarchy (an eagle), the heat of the revolution seemed to freeze. 'Unsmiling and defiant, they stared at us. Some glared, as if they resented our very presence and wanted us removed,' recalled Petr Pithart, who walked beside Havel on the last leg of what had seemed an endless journey.[1]

The frosty welcome should not have surprised them. Although the Castle symbolized many good things to Czechs – even during the Communist period, from the time of Gottwald, it had often been considered a court of final appeal for commoners or citizens with complaints and requests – the President and his staff were an important source of patronage and, hence, equipped with the power to make and break the destinies of individuals. As Havel and his entourage entered the main western wing of the Castle, they had the feeling – lasting just for a few seconds – of entering a completely enclosed space bathed in sheer darkness. They felt lost. It was as if there was not the slightest chink of light. The air they breathed seemed dead. The dark felt deep, pure dark, darkness so deep that if they had imagined for an instant that they could see something bright before their eyes then it would be nothing but the nimbus of Kafka's castle.

The new President and his entourage were ushered to the second floor and the Emblem Hall, otherwise known as the Hall of the First Citizen of the State. There, around a rectangular table made of teak wood and a marble pedestal inscribed with the words 'Subordinate your personal troubles to those of the community' (*Obci starosti své osobní podrob*), the denim-jeaned and jumpered new tenants gathered to hear Havel deliver a modest speech of thanks to his trusted friends. Champagne was drunk, after which Havel, accompanied by Olga, was first taken briefly to his office – the Office of the President – and then on a guided tour of the

[1]Interview with Petr Pithart, Scheinfeld, 15 September 1996.

bits of the Castle formally closed to the public, escorted by the Castle guards.

Everybody felt bewildered. The building itself posed a problem that urgently needed to be solved: the symbolic shape of the new presidency. The difficulty, to combine the Castle with republican democracy, seemed insoluble. Here, up on the hill overlooking Prague, the pomposity of a massive structure encoded with a thousand years of power over others, a symbol of rulers swelling with ambition, vehement in their greed, sometimes uncontrollable in their lust, drinking their subjects' blood in long draughts. There, down below in the cobbled winding streets of the old city, a bubbling cauldron of dancing bodies and happy faces, renewed hopes, political merry-making, straightened spines, reborn social initiative, excited determination to put an end to hubris, to open up the world, to change it for the better. These were two different universes, as far apart, perhaps, as the humble subject cowering like an insignificant shadow at a remote distance before an emperor's sun. How possibly could the gap between them be bridged? Given the political impossibility of selling off the buildings or somehow bulldozing them down into the River Vltava below, was a new synthesis between the Castle and the democratic republic thinkable and practically possible? And given the constitutional impossibility of Havel refusing to use or acknowledge the Castle, what would the combination of Hradčany and popular power – expressed in the commonplace graffito, 'Havel je kráľ' (Havel is King) – look like?

The strategy for which Havel intuitively opted was *not* to cultivate the institutions of republican democracy, like parliament and a judiciary that upheld the rule of law. Instead, at first cautiously and then later expansively, Havel worked for the creation of a crowned republic. The oxymoron is unfamiliar in contemporary analyses of power. It is also unknown to previous typologies of states, which is odd considering that the first, and still best, schematic outline of a modern crowned republic was provided long ago by a poet and political thinker who was born not far from Prague. Friedrich von Hardenberg, better known by his pen-name Novalis, sketched plans at the end of the eighteenth century for a brand-new type of government that his contemporaries found utterly astonishing, even if many of them thought that such a state would prove in practice to be an impossible contradiction.[1] In a number of writings, and especially in his set of aphorisms entitled *Glauben und Liebe, oder der König und die Königin*, written to celebrate the accession to the throne of the reformist Friedrich Wilhelm III and his wife Luise in mid-November 1797, Novalis defended the French Revolution by denouncing all forms of despotism as corrupt and oppressive. He reckoned the Revolution to be an inevitable 'crisis of puberty' that humanity had to go through so that it could enjoy 'the delightful feeling of freedom, the desire for the new and young, the pride in the brotherhood of man, the joy in personal rights, and the powerful feeling of citizenship'.[2] But against those radicals who assumed that the people *are* by nature free and equal, and that therefore the main political task was to unchain their freedoms, if need be through violent rebellion, Novalis insisted that the people could only *become* so by educating them into the ways of republican citizenship. 'First be human beings,' he urged in an unpublished note, 'and then the rights of human beings will come of their own accord.'[3]

But through which kind of education could people best become citizens? Novalis answered: the ideal form of modern government is a synthesis of republicanism and monarchy. The vital ingredients of a republic – 'electoral assemblies, directorates, and liberty trees' – cannot be nurtured or sustained unless they are harnessed by a king or queen who serves as an inspiration to the people to press for the principles of liberty, equality, and fraternity. Novalis insisted, in an enigmatic passage, that in every

[1]Friedrich von Hardenberg was born on 2 May 1772 at the Castle of Oberwiedenthal in Thuringia, about 200 kilometres from Prague. His father belonged to the Moravians, and he was raised in Pietist circles. After attending school in Brunswick, he studied law at the universities of Jena, Wittenberg, and Leipzig, where he made contact with Romantics like Friedrich Schlegel. He also attended the mining academy at Freiberg and professionally his last years, which were marred by the deep sorrow of bereavement and unconsummated love, were spent in the department of mining of which his father was director. He became known as the region's most important Romantic poet. His principal works include the cycles *Hymnen an die Nacht* and *Geistliche Lieder*, prose tales like 'Die Lehrlinge zu Sais' and 'Heinrich von Ofterdingen', and philosophical and political works such as *Die Christenheit oder Europa* (1799), *Die Enzyklopädie* and *Glauben und Liebe oder der König und die Königin* (1798). His politics were infused with qualified support for the principles of the French Revolution, while his poetry was steeped in the longing for death, of which night is the leading image. Von Hardenberg died of tuberculosis in Weissenfels, Thuringia, on 25 March 1801.
[2]Novalis (Friedrich von Hardenberg), *Schriften* (5 volumes; Stuttgart, 1977–1988), volume 2, p. 522.
[3]Ibid., volume 3, p. 416, no. 762.

genuine republic 'all people are capable of assuming the throne'[1], by which he does not mean that monarchy should be an elected position or form of government. His point is rather that citizens should be uplifted by a virtuous monarch who moves closer to them, as it were, who brings the castle to the people, thereby giving them a sense of mission by appealing to their feelings, desires, and hopes. The monarch should be the instrument of republican *Bildung*. Individuals cannot and will not bind themselves to the state simply because it protects their property or rules in accordance with rational laws to which they have consented. The people will only obligate themselves to the state if they feel 'faith and love' (*Glauben und Liebe*) for the monarch. Faith and love are not naturally occurring substances, however. The people can only learn to love and have faith in themselves as citizens by learning to love and have faith in a ruler whose wisdom and virtue and capacity for making decisions they trust and respect. Republics which nurture active citizenship cannot merely rely upon declarations of rights and the formulation and implementation of good laws; the capacity of their rulers to inspire admiration and respect for the republic is ultimately more important. 'What is the law,' Novalis asks, 'unless it is the expression of a lovable person who is worthy of respect?'

Novalis's proposals for cultivating monarchy within a republic openly acknowledged that the charismatic qualities of the ideal ruler could never stem from divine sources. Novalis detested divine-right theories. Remarkably, he also did not think that charisma flowed automatically from heredity. Although citizens' affection for the sovereign is likely to be enhanced by the fiction of their 'noble birth', Novalis insisted that heredity alone cannot guarantee faith and love, principally because no living person has the unique, infallible, extraordinary qualities that a good queen or king requires to do their job. Republics nurture citizens' capacities for thinking for themselves, asking critical questions, and publicly challenging power relationships that are considered illegitimate. So how then could the monarch develop charismatic qualities in an age of suspicion of power?

How indeed could royal power survive in an age of scepticism? Novalis replied: by surrounding the monarch with artists whose

[1]Ibid., volume 2, p. 489, no. 18.

role is to fuse aesthetics and politics and thereby ensure that the monarch is seen by citizens as a lovable person of extraordinary intelligence, dignity, courage, and standing. The demanding task of the court artists – poets, painters, musicians – is to *invent* a charismatic sovereign who is capable of lending 'the commonplace a higher meaning, the ordinary a mysterious appearance, and the finite the air of the infinite'.[1] The power of the throne must be bathed in pomp. The figure of the ruler is to be draped in such grandeur that the people will watch with warm hearts and open mouths. The job of the artists is to produce plays, operas, symphonies and other alluring works that transform the republic into a 'poetic state', a state that resembles a vast stage performance watched by the public and directed by the playwright monarch and a cast of citizen-actors.

[1] *Schriften*, op. cit., volume 2, p. 545, no. 105. See also ibid., p. 537, no. 55 and p. 534, no. 37.

TE DEUM LAUDAMUS

Novalis's scheme suffered from the disadvantage that the monarch might be uninterested in art or that the King or Queen and the poets might not get along, thus bringing troubles to the poetic state, heaping disrepute upon the Crown and fomenting the suspicions of its citizens. Novalis's plans were stillborn, despite the fact that *Glauben und Liebe* reportedly generated 'a sensation' in Berlin and elsewhere. King Friedrich Wilhelm III, who went so far as to declare himself to be a republican and friend of the revolution, but who confessed that he was not much interested in art, actually read the work. He nevertheless remained unimpressed. Besieged by the job of implementing wide-ranging reforms in Prussia, he was even ultimately angered by its recommendations. 'More is demanded of a king than he can possibly perform,' he reportedly said. 'It is forgotten that he is only a human being. One has only to bring a man who lectures the king about his duties away from his desk and to the throne; then he will see the difficulties that it is not possible to remove.'[1]

The King's reaction revealed the difficulties in modern times of making power sparkle, but the weakness to which he pointed – the gap between the desk and the throne – most definitely did not apply to the poet–politician Havel. Those who talked at the time of Havel as a 'reluctant President', as a man who would rather be writing plays but who had been forced by events against his will into politics, missed the point: Havel had always been a political animal who knew well the art of directing others. And although Milan Šimečka and others were right to plead with Havel not to seek the presidency lest he lose his freedom to write and direct his own plays,[2] they also underestimated the 'transferability' of his playwright's skills into the field of official politics. The point is that Havel had the advantage over most of his rivals of being an experienced political animal and a playwright who knew well the dramaturgical arts of directing others.

So it was not surprising that from the first day of assuming the presidency he began experimenting with his new role as King of the Castle. With mixed success, and always subject to the push and pull of revolutionary politics, the new sovereign

[1]Cited in Richard Samuel, 'Einleitung', in *Schriften*, op. cit., volume 2, p. 479.
[2]Milan Šimečka to Václav Havel, 11 December 1989.

tried to transform the Castle into a giant stage. From there, he tried to direct a new performance – the biggest so far in his life. The play served as the supreme expression of the revolution. It displayed the new-found sense of collective awareness and solidarity. There was a cast of thousands of people, some famous and others previously unknown, whose performances would for a time win the hearts of the country's citizenry and – this Novalis had not anticipated – attract the attention of the whole world.

The performance of Dvořák's *Te Deum* in St Vitus's Cathedral on New Year's Eve was a sign of things to come. Olga was opposed to holding the ceremony – she thought that it would be too pompous and, hence, out of step with the levelling spirit of the revolution. The Havels' playwright friend Josef Topol eventually convinced her to attend the crowning of the new republic. So behind the scenes she set to work, beginning with a shopping expedition to buy her husband a second-hand suit. She came back with various bits and pieces. Contrary to the famous advice of Ibsen that best clothes should never be worn when fighting for freedom and truth, others pitched in. Prince Karel Schwarzenberg improved the wardrobe by bringing along to the embankment flat two suitcases of his own elegant clothing, prompting Havel to say, with a smile: 'I can't wear any of these! I'd look like a gigolo!'[1] He eventually settled for a dark suit with trousers so obviously at half-mast that it was said by wits among the millions who watched the ceremony on television that the Communists had already set to work trimming the powers of the presidency.

Standing in the spot where Gottwald, and before him Beneš and Masaryk, had stood, Havel may not have realized just how much *pre-modern* history was buried within the ceremony. This was admittedly not a repeat of Caesare Borgia's entry into Rome (1500) or the entry of Philip the Good into Bruges (1440) or Richard II's triumphal arrival in London (1392). And those who witnessed it, live or on television, would not have spotted that the vast theatrical ritual called the royal entry, which originated in Europe in the late fourteenth century, drew its ultimate inspiration from the Roman *adventus*, and the medieval church's complex Advent liturgy, its dramatic celebration of the monarchs'

---

[1]Interview with Stanislav Milota, Prague, 2 October 1997.

inauguration into their reign by likening them to Christ's Palm Sunday entry into Jerusalem.[1] Still there were some deeply rooted continuities. There was a feel of conversion about it all. Just as the coming of a king to a city was *like* the Advent of Christ, so the reception by the supporters of the Velvet Revolution of their new political lord was *like* the reception of their Saviour. Here too was the ritualized communal pageantry and drama of it all. The *Te Deum* was like the public celebration of a new sovereign, himself treated as a Christ-like figure, who vowed before his people that together they should aspire towards a certain kind of polity. But it was more than that, for there was the sheer magic of it all. There was no consecration with balm, no wearing of crowns, no bearing of the orb and sceptre, certainly. But there were plenty of citizens who acted like Zacchaeus, who climbed a tree to witness the coming of Jesus to Jericho – tens of thousands of citizens euphoric at the formal entrance of the new Playwright-President of the free Czechoslovak Republic.

The *Te Deum* was the first staged performance by the new President. The appointment of Petr Oslzlý as his cultural affairs adviser further confirmed Havel's wish for a theatrical state,[2] for a refashioned Castle that ensured that citizens and sovereign performed their roles in a drama that aimed to express the truth of the world, to nudge existing conditions of life towards its high standards. During the 1980s, the wild-looking but gentle Oslzlý had worked as one of the most talented and popular actors at Brno's Theatre on a String. He enjoyed a reputation for integrity – he had worked as a 'dissident' organizer of the city's most successful underground university seminar and had acted within a theatre aptly named because it tottered constantly on the edge of nomenklatura- and secret-police harassment. Havel admired his work, and the two had become good friends by the time of *Largo Desolato*. During the summer before the revolution, Oslzlý had even staged anonymously a play by Havel called *Tomorrow the*

[1]On the late classical roots of the royal entry, see Ernst H. Kantorowicz, 'The "King's Advent" and the Enigmatic Panels in the Doors of Santa Sabina', *Art Bulletin*, 26 (1944), pp. 207–231; Gordon Kipling, *Enter the King. Theatre, Liturgy, and Ritual in the Medieval Civic Triumph* (Oxford, 1998); and Roy Strong, *Art and Power: Renaissance Festivals 1450–1650* (Berkeley and Los Angeles, 1984).
[2]Compare the different usages of a similar term by Roy Strong, *Splendor at Court: Renaissance Spectacle and the Theatre of Power* (Boston, 1973) and Clifford Geertz, *Negara: The Theatre State in Nineteenth-Century Bali* (Princeton, 1980).

Balloon Goes Up. Oslzlý was active in Civic Forum from the beginning, but he was utterly surprised when Havel, who was at that very moment trying on the ill-fitting trousers that he would wear the following day for his inauguration, asked him to 'come and help me be President'.[1] Oslzlý accepted, and the two set to work immediately to begin transforming the Castle into a work of art.

They agreed that the building needed a visual overhaul. It felt like an empty, dark and morbid dungeon, symbolized by the state of the original office that had been used by Masaryk, which was now blocked off, dusty and empty. Also symbolic was the state of Husák's office, which was long and sparsely furnished with oversized furniture. It had no clocks, and it was dominated by a long dark table cluttered with about twenty telephones, including a red-coloured one that was reportedly used either to call prostitutes and/or to serve as the hotline to Moscow. Lány Castle, the presidential weekend residence, was in no better shape. 'The fact that you are still living in your old apartment – is that a symbolic decision, or are you simply too lazy to move?' he was asked shortly after becoming President. 'I couldn't possibly live in that repulsive interior so absurdly decorated by Husák,' he replied drily, puffing a cigarette. 'It would be like throwing myself in prison. The presidency is a lot like a prison sentence – I'd rather not emphasize it.'[2] Havel and Oslzlý initially concentrated on going around the Castle with the keeper of plans. On one voyage through the dark unknown, they discovered in the area of Husák's office a mismatch between the plans and what turned out to be a false wall concealing a beautiful door. Havel ordered that it be restored, to make the area feel friendlier. He did the same with the Castle gardens. He asked that a steel fence be torn down, and the graphic design artist Joska Skalník busied himself painting sky and clouds in select places around the courtyard fountain.

The dramaturgs also pushed ahead with smartening up the Castle staff by redesigning both their uniforms and the centre-piece ritual of the Changing of the Guard. 'Give the men new clothes,' Havel told Oslzlý. 'We cannot change history

[1]Interview with Petr Oslzlý, Brno, 7 November 1998.
[2]From *Why Havel?*, op. cit.

in a socialist uniform with a red star on its head.' Under Husák, the Changing of the Guard had been a routine military ritual performed by grim-faced soldiers dressed in baggy khakis. Under Havel, the Changing of the Guard was transformed into a fifteen-minute midday theatrical event costumed by Theodor Pištěk, who designed Miloš Forman's *Amadeus*. Each day, at the stroke of noon, a platoon of guards dressed in red, white and blue (the Czechoslovak colours) marched from their barracks in nearby Martinic Palace on Loretánská Street into the Castle's Courtyard of Honour, where they relieved their colleagues (from here on nobody used the word 'comrade') fatigued from twenty-four hours on duty. The arriving guards were greeted by six horn-players and a drummer, framed in upstairs windows and dressed like toy soldiers, playing resounding fanfares before camera-clicking crowds larger than those assembled under the Old Town Hall clock down the hill and across the river from the Castle.

Meanwhile Havel acquired a fleet of red, white and blue BMWs for use as the President's cavalcade. He was given a personal pedal scooter to speed up his movements, in style, along the impossibly long passageways of the building. Restoration and redecoration work on inner parts of the Castle got underway. Masaryk's library, which had gone to rack and ruin under Husák – it was filled with over 12,000 Party brochures and booklets, and had a tasteless mirrored ceiling to help his astigmatism – was cleared out and restored to its original wood-panelled, carpeted beauty.[1] Under the supervision of Havel's friend Bořek Šípek, the President's office was freshened and brightened and made to feel opulent, but friendly. Aleš Lamr painted splashes of rainbow colour in the corners and on the walls. Havel's favourite paintings – by artists like David Němec and Jiří Sopko – were displayed. A joky fresco containing images of spies, clowns and his dog Ďula was done by Vendula Císařovská. Olbram Zoubek's sculpture of an Egyptian woman with long golden hair was placed opposite an impressively large, elliptical black desk. Oriental rugs were thrown in all directions. And so that the new President could keep an eye on the nearby American Embassy, Petřín vineyards

[1] Interview with Andrej Stankovič, Masaryk Library, Prague Castle, 9 November 1998.

and other parts of Prague, a large mounted telescope was installed at the windows.

These were mostly just trimmings, of course. But Oslzlý and Havel were convinced that they were important first steps in transforming the Castle into the symbol and substance of free cultural expression. Each day, from all over the country, scores of letters arrived from groups and individuals full of ideas about what should be done in the field of culture. Convinced that the building should be made to symbolize the new-found freedom that needed badly to be nurtured, the two hatched a plan to turn the Castle into a giant stage for a day. In the summer of 1990, shortly after the first free parliamentary elections, Havel said to Oslzlý that something had to be done to celebrate 'the victory of the people'. He went on: 'You have a good feeling for how it should be done. The main aim should be to bring the Castle alive.'[1] So a day-long Festival for Democracy was held on the Castle grounds. Under hot and sunny skies, thousands of people dropped in off the streets to witness performances by jugglers, musicians, mime artists. Trade unions and enterprises donated trucks, tables and chairs, and other equipment. Pilsener flowed freely from the taps of barrels donated by breweries. Bands thumped out rock 'n' roll numbers. Strangers chatted. Crowds danced. Lovers kissed. And the brand new President, dressed in blue jeans and a T-shirt, wandered through the throng, hugged by well-wishers, cameras clicking.

Such exercises in re-enchanting political power attracted international attention. During the next two years, offers of artistic help poured in from everywhere, and even foreign governments reciprocated. Novalis doubted that the struggle to transform the state into a work of art might take on an international dimension, but Havel proved him wrong. The earlier appointment of Shirley Temple Black as American Ambassador to Prague was a signal in this direction. So was the agreement of scores of big names to visit the Castle. Philip Roth came for dinner and complained about being stuck in London, and waxed eloquent about just how much rich 'material' was at the disposal of the Castle actors, including Havel. The English playwright Harold Pinter was invited by Havel in early 1990 for the opening of Pinter's

[1] Interview with Andrej Stankovič, op. cit.

The Caretaker. After the performance, the two playwrights had a drink and later went strolling across the Charles Bridge, only to be spotted by a group of young guitarists, who spontaneously played Beethoven's Ninth Symphony for their pleasure. Such was the unprompted affection for the new President, but also a mark of recognition of his early efforts to change the appearance of sovereign power. It seemed everybody who was somebody was there. Jane Fonda's arrival in the spring of 1990 made the Castle seem like a prospective film set. In the summer of 1991, Frank Zappa also agreed to come to the Castle, and to help publicly celebrate the withdrawal of Soviet troops from Czechoslovak territory by jamming at a concert – together with Havel's friend and aide Michael Kocáb, an unusual rock musician who had tirelessly involved himself in efforts to rid the country of the Soviets. On one visit, Zappa caused a big scene by arriving at Prague airport when the new US Ambassador, Shirley Temple Black, was also there. Much to her embarrassment, she hadn't heard of him, as all of Czechoslovakia saw hours later on television. Meanwhile, leather-jacketed, mean-looking Lou Reed flew in, perhaps to talk about Sweet Jane.[1] Then came the Rolling Stones, who returned several times after striking up a good friendship with their groovy president mate from '68.

Amidst the efforts to give the Castle style, Havel didn't forget his own personal image. He arranged through his advisers for the State Education Publishing House to put out a charming sample volume of the thousands of children's letters and sketches sent to him during the first eighteen months of his presidency; each child who wrote to him received an informal letter of thanks, together with a xeroxed photograph of Mr President.[2] He also urged his close friend and inner circle adviser, the author Eda

---

[1] See Paul Berman, *A Tale of Two Utopias: The Political Journey of the Generation of 1968* (New York, 1996), p. 197: 'Head turned away from camera. Face buried itself in hands. Televised mortification! ... The ambassador from the United States volunteered that she did know something about Mr Zappa's daughter, Moon Unit. Czechoslovakia was aghast. People had no way to account for the United States ambassador's boorish airport behavior, except to mark her down as a cultural ignoramus who lacked the aplomb to boast to all of Central Europe about one of America's finest sons, the brilliant Zappa, a world figure in the field of popular music.' See also the transcript of the conversation between Havel and Reed in Hanif Kureishi and Jon Savage, *The Faber Book of Pop* (London and Boston, 1995), pp. 696–709.
[2] The book of letters and sketches, with an introduction by Havel's personal assistant, Vladimír Hanzel, was published as *Mylí pane prezidente* (Prague, 1992).

Kriseová, to write his 'authorized' biography. She understandably hesitated. The form was unfamiliar to her and the timescale of the task – Havel wanted it to appear urgently – was daunting. She told him so. 'Stefan Zweig wrote biographies,' replied Havel, or words to that effect. 'But he's long dead,' the biographer retorted. 'Never mind,' said Havel. 'You should do it – to make me better known. The book should be personal. It should be *your* picture of me.' Kriseová sketched his portrait in less than four months flat. Havel read through a draft, made some amendments before approving it, then – for some as yet unexplained reason – grew uneasy about the book when it was at press.

The biography appeared anyway, to be greeted by strong sales and cool reviews.[1] Kriseová had intended to write a labour of love that provided ammunition for Havel's supporters. Dedicated to 'Vašek', it aimed to turn him into a positive hero, principally because Kriseová reasoned that, immediately after the revolution, with all of its muddling and uncertainty about the future, 'the people' needed a good 'fairy-tale' to help them through the necessary *catharsis* – their cleansing in the flooding waters of filth thrown up by the *ancien régime*, that is, to keep them going along the revolutionary path. Many readers and some reviewers objected to the political misuse of literature. The main fact-minded, empiricist attack came from the typewriter of Vilém Prečan, the country's best contemporary historian, who criticized the book for its 'interpretive chaos' and many factual errors and gaps. He concluded that it was one of those books that would have been better left unwritten. Then there were those who disliked the book's sycophancy. A *New York Times* reviewer spotted that biography had been reduced to hagiography. Meandering 'like the kitchen reminiscences of a loving buddy through Mr Havel's remarkable life', wrote the reviewer Michael T. Kaufman, the book was best summarized as 'an official and genuinely adoring work that helped to introduce the heroic shepherd to his ecstatic flock'.[2]

[1] Eda Kriseová, *Václav Havel. Životopis* (Prague, 1991).
[2] Michael T. Kaufman, 'Once Upon a Time in Prague', *The New York Times Book Review*, 24 October 1993, p. 33.

FUN AND GAMES

The symbolic redesign of the Castle compounded the daily tasks spawned by the revolutionary victory over Communism. Uneasy lies the head that wears the crown, observed King Henry IV, and so it was. Havel instantly had on his newly acquired black desk a mushrooming pile of tasks – new appointments, foreign-policy initiatives, receiving and replying to petitions from individual citizens and their organizations, dismantling the old nomenklatura system, handling the media. The problems seemed all-encompassing. Havel's tempo of life quickened. Gone were the days of sleeping late, drinking coffee and rum, writing a bit, going to the sauna, making love at odd times of the day. Scores, then hundreds and then thousands of letters began to pour each day into the Castle from congratulators and complainants, a growing number of them (Prince Karel Schwarzenberg later recalled) written in the form of petitions to the monarch.[1] The reception was spectacular, sometimes wild. Gifts of all kinds flooded the Castle offices. There were even envelopes stuffed with money – a few with fat wads of greenbacks, which prompted the joke, among the Castle aides, that such gifts proved that the revolution was really a CIA plot after all.

New security structures had to be created. New Castle guards had to be trained to close the gates of the crowned republic at 11 p.m., to escort the security staff from the President's office, to check that all windows and doors were locked and that staff working late knew the night's password, then to patrol inside the grounds, Scorpion machine guns, infrared goggles and radio transmitters in hand. New office equipment had to be purchased from scarce funds to supplement the dusty old Czech and Russian typewriters that had been left behind. Scarce and unusable stationery made life more difficult. 'Someone should retype this,' Havel said to a colleague after spotting that a letter appointing an ambassador was written on a Communist job form. 'It's not your job,' added Havel apologetically, 'but you're the only secretary I can call . . . It's ridiculous. Could you please type it on Federal Republic stationery?'[2]

Personnel had to be recruited – fast. An orgy of patronage went some way towards solving the problem. There were several

[1]Interview with Prince Karel Schwarzenberg, Prague, 19 September 1997.
[2]From *Why Havel?*, op. cit.

typical methods used. Havel picked his own inner circle, whom he treated during the first year as a collective presidency. Other key people – Stanislav Milota, Prince Karel Schwarzenberg – were recommended and contacted by Havel personally. It was a time-consuming business and didn't always work (Havel and Milota went to see the writer Ludvík Vaculík, who decided firmly against coming to the Castle). Others who had been Havel's acquaintances before the revolution were contacted, and they in turn contacted others whom Havel did not know: it was state-building by nods and winks and word of mouth. A case in point was the appointment to the Castle of V. Valeš, who had been Minister of Foreign Trade in 1968, and who had done time in prison with Havel. Valeš called Komárek; Komárek called Václav Klaus; and Klaus spoke to Dlouhý.[1] The tactic of nepotism sometimes produced bizarre combinations – wildly bearded cameraman Stanislav Milota rubbing shoulders with clean-cut bespectacled economist Václav Klaus, for instance – and matters were complicated by the fact that the procedures through which the co-ordination of the newly appointed staff was supposed to take place were initially undefined.

The architecture didn't help. Many newly appointed aides seemed to take ages to memorize the location of the in-house toilets, while most new staff seemed mesmerized by the labyrinthine structures of the Castle. But the most difficult adjustment that Havel and his inner circle of advisers had to make was getting used to the experience of exercising governmental power. Like John F. Kennedy, Havel had an unusually strong urge to govern, which made the adjustment easier. The heartfelt camaraderie, which sprang up around him instantly, also made everything worthwhile. Havel and his team had the feeling that they were at sea on the same tiny boat, and that they should do everything to avoid sinking it. The unconditional trust and loyalty resulted not only from the euphoria of being on the winning side in a revolution. Solidarity not only came from living in each other's pockets for eighteen hours each day, seven days each week. Fear also bred solidarity. The first few weeks and months in the Castle understandably felt dangerous. For the first six months, the Castle was partly policed by Ministry of the Interior guards, some of whom were literally

---

[1]Interview with Stanislav Milota, Prague, 2 October 1997.

hidden away in the woodwork.[1] One day Havel demanded that Richard Sacher, the newly appointed Minister of the Interior, come to open up a keyless room situated near the President's proposed new office. Everybody was shocked when the concealed door was opened. There stood a fearsome-looking soldier on guard, armed with a Scorpion machine gun, listening to the sounds generated by various intercom devices planted in the surrounding rooms. Someone later asked Havel: 'Do you think that soldier knew who you were?' Said Havel cheekily: 'Probably so, because otherwise he would have shot me dead on the spot.'

Experiences like this were commonplace. Sometimes Havel responded by horsing around with his bodyguards – forcing them to work into the wee hours of the morning as he danced and drank at friends' parties – or by pushing the security system to its limits, just for the hell of it, without disrespect for its personnel. He seemed determined to prove the famous maxim of the eighteenth-century *philosophe* Helvétius that men sometimes strive after power so that they can enjoy themselves. During a visit to a Czech village pub, Havel suddenly said to Joska Skalník: 'You wanna see something? Follow me!' Pretending to go to the toilet, the two escapees climbed out of an open back window and began strolling, hands in pockets, down a country road, belatedly followed by scrambling, nervous security men in their macs and on their walkie-talkies.[2] Havel was also skilled at the night-time art of giving his bodyguards the slip – for instance, by pretending to go to bed, waiting for them to fall asleep, then tiptoeing out to a pub for a few drinks. Generally, security was no laughing matter. Guarded only by unarmed karate experts, the group members initially chose to work from one cramped room.[3] They

---

[1] *The New York Times* (31 May 1990) reported that only at the end of May 1990 was the Castle cleared of listening devices ('bugs') planted by unknown persons. See also '"Free" Czechoslovakia? Shadows over the Transition', www.security–policy.org/papers/1990/90–55.html.

[2] Jan Novak, *Commies, Crooks, Gypsies, Spooks and Poets* (South Royalton, 1995), p. 113.

[3] There were initially ten core aides clustered around Havel: the music adviser and organizer of public meetings and events, Ladislav Kantor; Eda Kriseová, who headed the newly established Office of Amnesties and Complaints; Jiří Křižan, a screen writer who shadowed the Ministry of Interior; Miroslav Kvašňák, who was in charge of Havel's bodyguards; Miroslav Masák, the Castle architect; the head of protocol, Stanislav Milota; Petr Oslzlý, who was in charge of promoting freedom of cultural expression; the visual artist Joska Skalník; the foreign-affairs adviser (and subsequently Ambassador to the United States) Alexandr Vondra; and Michael Žantovský, Havel's personal spokesman.

felt like conquerors in enemy territory. Even the straightforward experience of going to the toilet – down the long, red-carpeted corridors lined with Ministry of the Interior soldiers clutching sub-machine guns – was hemmed in with so much anxiety that the word relief assumed a new meaning. Fear made coping with the extraordinary work pressures that much more difficult. So did the lack of free time. It is commonly pointed out – using the obvious example of the imposition of clock time in early modern industrial factories – that those who exercise power over others always seek to determine their daily rhythms, their shared definition of the flows and constraints of time. But it is equally true that power over others extracts a price: the powerful have little or no free time as well.

From the first day, the Castle resembled a time-consuming machine. Havel and his team ran constantly, at high speed, feeling all the while that it was impossible to keep abreast of events. Consequently, everybody in the inner circle lost their private lives, and their sleep. Havel's average of three or four hours per night was typical. Nobody had any time for themselves, or for others outside their immediate circle. Tempers sometimes flared within the presidential group: sometimes those who exploded were simply allowed to exercise their right to explode so as to calm down naturally, or they were grabbed and physically shaken until they regained their senses, or they were ordered to go home to bed to rest. Everybody seemed to develop extra and thicker skins, to become more brusque, less patient, more prone to cause others to cry. Outside friendships became strained. Those with families at home found themselves so consumed and exhausted by their posts that they had little or no time to attend to their children or their partners. Children complained loudly and sometimes turned aggressive. Relationships suffered, partners found it hard to put up with their parvenu politicians, and at least one marriage became a casualty of prolonged absence.

So time-starved power bred mental and bodily stress, which was worsened by the sheer volume of situations and problems to be defined, judged and resolved. Lawyers sometimes sobbed uncontrollably. Secretarial staff couldn't cope. A good administrator was defined as someone who didn't break down sobbing until two in the afternoon. Everybody quickly recognized that some matters were insoluble. Life within the newly established

Office of Amnesties and Complaints, for instance, threw up some extreme, but not atypical cases. A small example: embarrassed confusion descends on the Office of the President when an angry letter arrives, addressed to Havel and written by a man whose daughter had just been murdered by an individual personally amnestied several weeks earlier by the President. A bigger example: twenty-five former nomenklatura staff working within the Castle are fired, upon evidence that they have worked to obstruct justice and tarnish Havel's public image. And an example that is full of political danger: with 7,000 letters per month flooding into the Office of Amnesties and Complaints, it is decided to try to deal collectively with certain complaints by hosting open public meetings in the regions. In Bratislava, more than a thousand citizens crush into an auditorium to meet the President's aides. The venue is carefully chosen to provide an easy back-exit escape route leading to the railway-station shunting yards, where if necessary the presidential aides will sleep that night in empty wagons. The atmosphere is riotous. Many complainants are irate. Each of them expects that after more than four decades of publicly suppressed injustice grievances can and must be righted immediately. As soon as proceedings are opened, many citizens become hysterical, demanding that the omnipotent President pick up his magic telephone to solve problems personally. The wrathful citizens suddenly become calm at the moment one of the aides shouts: 'Listen! You are right! There is no justice in this world.'

Stories of moments like these were swapped among Havel and his advisers, often eliciting the wild laughter of relief. There was a shared sense, confirmed by the gloomy atmosphere in the Castle when they arrived, that totalitarian power was nervous, unsmiling, insecure, uptight. Humour seemed to be confidence-building, rebellious, democratic. Each joke was a tiny revolution. The memorable lighter moments came thick and fast, as when a camera found Havel at his Castle desk, under the gaze of two naked women striding across a wall-mounted canvas by Jiří Sopko. 'What did I sign?' he asks, frowning. 'Wait a minute . . . I was naming an ambassador, but I'm recalling him!' Havel laughed, adding: 'It's all so absurd.'[1] Then there was the big cock-up over a precious letter that had been addressed to Havel at the Castle.

[1] From *Why Havel?*, op. cit.

Havel got wind of a man who so objected to his casual placatory remarks about the need for reconciliation with Germany that he began a hunger strike. Havel – aware that he might be said to be culpable for a death that would get widespread publicity – summoned the protester to his office to discuss the matter. The protester, Havel and his aides sat around in a circle to do business. The man explained that he had fought against the Nazis in Dukla Pass, that he therefore found repulsive Havel's remarks about the 'morally unacceptable' Czech expulsion of ethnic Germans at the end of World War II, and that he was now convinced that Havel was preparing to sell the country to the Germans.

After lengthy discussion, the man accepted Havel's appeal to abandon his hunger strike. He confirmed his decision a few minutes later to a Czechoslovak television crew in the President's office. After receiving a letter personally signed by Havel, the man left the Castle. Everybody felt relieved. But the following morning, Havel's aides received a telephone call from the same man, who was waiting downstairs with the security guards, at the stairway entrance to Havel's office. An aide went down to see what was the matter. The man was shaking and pale. He explained to the aide that he hadn't slept a wink because of the letter he had been given. 'But what is wrong with yesterday's letter?' asked the aide. 'It is a letter from Gorbachev to President Havel,' came the reply. Realizing that the petitioner had been given the wrong letter, the aide invited the man upstairs to pick up the correct letter. Havel spotted the two men. 'What's wrong?' he asked. 'Our friend was given the Gorbachev letter by mistake,' said the aide, who did not notice that at that moment the grey-suited Soviet Ambassador was sitting all ears on a nearby sofa.

Then there was the first state visit by Havel and his aides to Poland. It felt a bit like a re-run of the Charter 77 and Solidarność meetings a decade earlier, but with a difference or two. As Havel and his long-haired advisers descended the aircraft steps that led on to soft, red carpet, with a brass band playing the old Czechoslovak anthem, the Polish guards glared at the revolutionaries. 'They'd have made us into Siberian sausages if they'd had a chance,' recalled an aide. Sweet revenge came that evening, at a state dinner attended by everybody's old enemy, the Polish President General Jaruzelski, whose nickname was 'the crow'. Every effort was made to get him drunk. The revolutionaries succeeded. 'All things considered, you're not a bad guy,' slurred the famous writer and public intellectual, Adam Michnik, towards the end of the evening, Havel and the others chortling loudly. 'But you should give up and step down,' continued Michnik. At which moment President Jaruzelski lurched towards the floor, rescued from a nasty bump by several pairs of dissident hands.

THE MANIPULATOR

Almost everybody who had contact with him – or had no contact at all – during the first period of his presidency noted his aloofness. Some pointed out that he'd always been coldly calculating when it came to keeping company. Others confessed their nostalgia for the old 'dissident' times when Havel seemed always to be available – and always willing to talk, drink and be merry. Stories began to circulate about how he had changed, and about how he seemed even to be embarrassed by the great Chinese walls of power that had come between him and his former friends and working colleagues.

A typical version ran something like this: During the first weeks of his presidency, Vašek is invited to a flat for drinks and political discussion. He arrives, dressed in blue jeans, looking crumpled and withdrawn, and is instantly greeted with hugs and kisses – and a barrage of laments about how nobody ever sees him any more, except on television. He seems to hang his head in embarrassment, reaches for a drink, wedges his tired body on to the arm of a chair or on to a bare patch on the crowded living-room floor, rolls a cigarette, and sits quietly as others speak, others looking on. Later the guests begin to mingle, laugh and dance. He receives another barrage of laments about how distant he has become. He again hangs his head and rolls another cigarette. And then another – as if rolling tobacco into paper is an involuntary defence reaction against guilt. Almost everybody then gets drunk with the President – partly because that's what always used to happen, partly because a revolution is taking place, and partly because everybody is thrilled to have a loved political actor back in their midst.

Then there were those who complained that his aloofness – the aloofness of the monarch of the crowned republic – hampered their job of trying to establish links between the emerging structures of government on the hill and the world beyond the Castle walls. This was a more serious objection, for it touched on the whole question of his accountability before the public, as well as his personal responsibility for the hundreds of decisions of consequence that he was now making on a daily basis. A strong version of this political type of objection came quickly, and almost spontaneously, from within the ranks of Civic Forum. The Forum had been his power base up until his election as President. It began to work hard to prepare and fertilize the soil out of which free parliamentary elections were to grow by the summer of 1990. Civic Forum thought of itself not as a party – the word was anathema to its many activists – but as a potentially country-wide para-political structure, run directly by citizens, whose aim was to institutionalize, as quickly as possible, the procedures and institutions of an electoral system that had been destroyed long ago by the *coup de Prague*. Civic Forum was a catalyst network geared to driving the revolution towards parliamentary democracy. Its activists were interested in the Polish and Hungarian examples of 'government by round table', but as an improvised citizens' initiative it was based on no political theory or thinker. It deliberately worked against the Machiavellian rules that state power should be sought after, that official politics was everything, that it was imperative, if only for the sake of survival, to fill power vacuums with strength wherever they existed. Civic Forum instead worked to change the rules of state politics from the outside. Wherever possible, subject to finding sources of funding, it tried to set up 'election centres' as well as teams of advisers supplied to local groups trying to form themselves into pressure groups or 'democratic' political parties. It was of course a tactic designed to benefit Civic Forum, but at this stage it was to be neither a social movement nor a political party – nor even a future government. 'Parties are for party members!' ran one of its posters for the forthcoming elections. 'Civic Forum is for all!'

Given Havel's stated commitment to free elections, it was indeed odd, his critics said, that from the outset he broke off virtually all contacts with Civic Forum. 'From the beginning there was a constant problem,' said Jan Urban, who later became chief spokesperson and convenor of Civic Forum. 'Havel and the rest of the Castle became totally separate, and very secretive. Their links with the outside world were uncoordinated. They contacted others only on their own terms.'[1] Many within Civic Forum sensed that Havel's aloofness was politically undesirable – there were even occasions when the Castle seemed deliberately to be giving out contradictory information and advice, for the

---

[1]Interview with Jan Urban, Prague, 3 November 1998. See also his important article, 'Bezmocnost mocných', *Listy*, volume 23, 5 (1993), pp. 3–10.

purpose of playing off the federal and two national governments, perhaps (so some within Civic Forum suspected) with the ultimate – unconstitutional – aim of creating a 'fourth government', a crowned republic rotating around President Havel.

The key players within Civic Forum were initially reluctant to blow the whistle publicly on Havel. The basic rule of 'dissident morality' – that individuals and groups refrained from screaming at each other publicly after sitting in prison with them – was observed, especially since everybody within Civic Forum remained scared of secret-police provocation and infiltration, and continued as well to treat the shadowy Communist Party as enemy number one. So there were efforts, from the last week of January 1990 onwards, to create a private 'pipeline' between Civic Forum and Havel. An informal, private meeting held regularly on Sunday evenings at Jan Urban's house was set up to exchange views and information – to act as a damage-limitation exercise. Havel's spokesman, Michael Žantovský, regularly attended and later so did others, like Ivan Gabal, Jan Ruml and Vladimír Mlynář. The pipeline meetings continued after the summer parliamentary elections, indeed they survived until the end of 1991, when a row with the Castle about its proposed constitutional amendments ended in acrimony.

The conviction that Havel had withdrawn into the Castle to become a power unto himself was quite at odds with his former self-image as a man who lived openly before others, in the truth. Although it shocked a good many former friends and political acquaintances, those who knew him well were less than surprised. Something like Havel's Law of Oligarchy was at work from the beginning. This was no 'iron law' of the kind outlined earlier this century by Robert Michels, for whom oligarchy springs up wherever there is organization.[1] That so-called law rested upon faulty premises – including its supposition that 'the masses' are naturally docile and gullible, and its claim to be a universally applicable law. Havel's Law of Oligarchy was quite different. It grew out of a specific revolutionary con-

---

[1] The first edition of the book by Robert Michels was published in Germany, with the title *Zur Soziologie des Parteiwesens in der modernen Demokratie* (Leipzig, 1911). A new edition, somewhat revised, with an added chapter on the war, was published in Italy in late 1914. The English edition, published in 1915, was based on the Italian version.

text and nourished itself on the efforts to build a crowned republic.

To begin with, communication with anybody and everybody was generally difficult. There were few phones, no photocopiers, no fax machines. Even paper was in short supply. The presidential office also inherited from the *ancien régime* an immensely large workload that simply had to be dealt with. *Raison d'état* had to be followed, or so it was said. A new foreign policy had to be negotiated. Laws had to be reviewed and signed. New ministries had to be constructed. More staff had to be recruited, brought to the Castle and trained. New ambassadors had to present their credentials, and foreign delegations of government, business and civic organizations had to be received officially. The decision to switch over to the forms of protocol that operated during the Masaryk presidency of the First Republic was time-consuming, and also off-putting to would-be visitors to the Castle. Then there was the profoundly intimidating security system operating at the Castle. Not even Havel himself initially knew how it worked – at least not until the day that an alternative surveillance system provided by the American Embassy, and dubbed 'the refrigerator', was set up. Even that did not make it any easier for individuals and groups to make appointments, or (as some had hoped) to drop by for a quick chat and a coffee or brandy with the new President.

The absurd time pressures on Havel worked to prevent that in any case. Not only locals, but contacts from the four corners of the earth often had the experience – and do so still – of being squeezed out by a bureaucratic schedule which was strict and inflexible. After five or fifteen or thirty minutes, if the callers have been lucky, time is up. There is a firm knock at the door. 'Mr President', says the faintly smiling but businesslike assistant with a craning head, 'would you be so kind as to prepare for your next appointment, who is now waiting.' The distancing effects of such treatment were reinforced, from the outset, by the privileges affixed to the presidency. 'I find myself in the world of privileges, exceptions, perks, in the world of VIPs who gradually lose track of how much a streetcar ticket or butter costs, how to make a cup of coffee, how to drive a car and how to place a telephone call', he soon observed, adding: 'I find myself on the threshold of the very world of the Communist fat cats whom I have criticized all my life.'[1] Havel's urge to have guaranteed access to the mass media inflated the privileges he enjoyed. The elbowing ratpack of newspaper and radio and television journalists began to take up valuable appointments. They in turn required minding, lest they said the wrong things, which in turn necessitated spokespersons, watchdogs who guarded the sovereign power carefully, at all times. Soon, it seemed as though hardly anybody, or that even nobody, could 'get' to the President.

No contemporary head of state can live without media coverage, it is true, but from early January 1990 it was obvious that a special dynamic, one traceable to his preferred role as a political *Ichspieler*, provided crucial nourishment for Havel's Law of Oligarchy. Those from outside the Castle who tried to deal with him during this period found that he strongly preferred to operate outside institutional forms and procedures and to handle things personally. He no doubt found a certain freedom in presidential power. There were times when he found it a stimulant. 'I worry about him,' said his good friend, playwright Josef Topol, to Olga over coffee one morning, a year into his presidency. 'You shouldn't,' snapped Olga, rolling her eyes. 'He adores it! He'll never give it up!'[2]

The role of *Ichspieler* meant making decisions by personal wheeling and dealing, the art of which he had mastered from the time of the group of Thirty-Sixers. Especially before the revolution, in apartment meetings for instance, Havel had been admired for the way he would listen to many opposing or contradictory opinions, then take the floor for a few minutes to formulate a statement or a position that was acceptable to everybody present. Combined with his courageous struggle against imprisonment for two decades, it made him into a moral authority within the opposition. After the revolution, he continued to practise this art, but mainly within his immediate circle of trusted advisers. So when it came to dealing with outsiders, in encounters with members of the public for instance, Havel resorted to *ad hoc* personal negotiations.

In Vojtěch Jasný and Miloš Forman's film *Why Havel?*, he confessed that among the most enjoyable things about the presidency

---

[1] From a speech in acceptance of the Sonning Prize, Copenhagen, 28 May 1991, in *Toward a Civil Society*, op. cit., p. 137.
[2] Interview with Josef Topol, Prague, 6 March 1999.

'are these surprise visits, where I unexpectedly arrive at factories, offices, pubs, discos. All of a sudden, the President's there. It's unheard of. A woman sits in her office pretending to work while she munches on a roll. Someone knocks – 'Come in' – and in I walk. She's in shock. The roll feels like a rock in her throat. She starts babbling and the truth spurts out. Two minutes after I've left, she realizes she should have lied.'[1] Exactly the same habit of acting as if he were the *deus ex machina*, as a figure who personalized everything in order to resolve everything, was obvious to those who dealt with him daily through Civic Forum. 'Havel never understood the value of institutions, negotiations, and the need for compromise,' concluded Jan Urban, who found that negotiations were often fraught and frustrating, because for Havel Castle policy-making was 'always about making direct deals, personal compromises and, above all, manipulation. These tactics work perfectly well in small groups within a small opposition. But it would never have worked within a large opposition like that of Solidarność in Poland. And it most certainly never worked during the first months of his presidency, when power was seen simply as manipulation.'[2]

Havel's propensity to manipulate others was nourished by his skill at playing the role of *Ichspieler* before adoring audiences bubbling and throbbing with praise. During the first year of office, he joined the ranks of 'the world's great leaders'.[3] Celebrity was a great aphrodisiac. He was blessed with a special kind of power – the power of charisma – whose mechanics were daily lubricated by his air of divinity before enthusiastic crowds devoted to his every move, his every word and gesture. Those individuals who want to believe should kneel, said Pascal, and kneel down they did. Projecting themselves outwards towards the Leader, individuals introjected him into their souls. He began to seem like a mortal endowed with immortality. Many were smitten by his theanthropic qualities. Public expectations of the extraordinary followed him everywhere. The humdrum routines of everyday life vanished in his presence. Like a prophet endowed with premonitions of a better world, he seemed to have the knack of inventing new ideas, of getting things done, of being in the

[1] From *Why Havel?*, op. cit.
[2] Interview with Jan Urban, Prague, 3 November 1998.
[3] Clive James, *Fame in the 20th Century* (London, 1993), p. 243.

right place at the right time. There were moments even when individuals felt *driven* to be near him, to talk to him, even to touch his body. In the industrial town of Opava – the following story was typical – a young teacher dashed from her classroom at the end of the school day to try to catch a glimpse of him as he attended an official function at the municipal hall. Gripping a bunch of bright flowers, she nudged her way through an excited crowd. A policeman caught sight of her and kindly cleared a path for her to present the flowers to His Royal Highness – at exactly the moment that he was descending the steps of the municipal hall. The schoolteacher was ecstatic. There he stood, smiling at the teacher, who curtseyed before showering him with flowers. Her heart fluttered, head dizzied, and mind went completely blank. She later recalled that he was shorter than her – she had not expected to look down on him – that his nose was yellowed by pollen from a previous bunch of flowers – he looked like a happy clown – and that he smiled warmly and said in a hoarse statesman's voice, 'Thank you very much.'[1]

'Charisma' is originally a theological term (from the Greek *kharis*, favour or grace) meaning the gift of grace. It now refers to the apparently superhuman powers of a single individual to magnetize others like iron filings. The charismatic personality is as magical as it is unstable. For a time, charisma is blessed with the capacity to dignify the mundane, to glorify the obvious. Yet charismatic power usually doesn't last long. It fades with time and sometimes (as Shakespeare's character Antony discovers while lying in his tent, abandoned by the god Hercules) it can disappear overnight. Immediately following the Velvet Revolution, Havel seemed to be an exception to the rule of fading charisma. His habit of playing the role of charismatic *Ichspieler* caused sensations, which made life hard for his critics. Whenever confronted with objections, concerning matters of style or policy, he would if necessary cut off the personal negotiations and go silent on his opponents. Several times he told his aides: 'Don't bring me messengers bearing bad news.' He could well have been uttering the words of a messenger in the company of the Queen of Egypt: 'Though it be honest, it is never good / To bring bad news / Give to a gracious message / An host of tongues; but let ill tidings tell

[1] Interview with Gabriela Müllerová, London, September 1997.

/ Themselves when they be felt.'[1] So during the first months of his presidency – the habit continued throughout his political career – Havel worked hard to cultivate people who bore him good tidings. His appointment of Saša Brabcová as his personal translator was a case in point. Everybody working on the fringes of the Castle, and even some within, found her a puzzling woman in the Prague sense. Nobody really knew who she was and where she had come from – except that before the revolution she had been the personal aide of Miroslav Štěpán, the last First Secretary of the Communist Party of Czechoslovakia. Now working with Havel in the innermost circles of Castle power, she was party to the most confidential discussions and decisions. Some people within Civic Forum and within the Castle objected. Havel initially reacted with deaf ears. When pushed, his reaction was curt. 'She brings positive vibes to the Castle,' he said. And that was that.

[1]William Shakespeare, *Antony and Cleopatra*, Act 2, Scene 5.

DECLINE

(1990–1999)

DEFECTIONS

T he republican monarch soon had his first taste of the maxim that elected political men who get mixed up in state politics are strongly pressured into playing by its rules, which means that they quickly learn the arts of manipulation, keeping matters secret, pulling strings, turning others' weaknesses into sources of strength, even turning themselves into devilish creatures who stop at nothing to get their ways – and, in so doing, creating adversaries ready to cause 'trouble'. Within the Castle, in accordance with this maxim, there was an immediate tendency for people around the elected Havel to act as if they themselves had been chosen by divine force. Not surprisingly, 'trouble' began immediately to come Havel's way.

There were aides, Stanislav Milota for example, who openly criticized the working practices of the Castle.[1] The rugged, good-looking Milota was a former cameraman with a sharp eye for people. He was a good organizer and an articulate and down-to-earth working-class man from Žižkov, the rough district of Prague in which Olga had also been born. He had been a close friend of Havel's before and during the revolution and on 2 January 1990 he received a telephone call from the new President, inviting him to become Head of the Secretariat. 'Do you want an easy retirement with a big pension, or do you rather want to help me?' began Havel. According to Milota, the self-answering, either/or structure of the question was rather typical of how Havel manoeuvred people into making the decision he wanted. But Milota willingly agreed. Havel was pleased, and added, with a touch of irony. 'Good. I need someone to be my opponent in the Castle.'

Critical opposition he certainly got from his friend. Milota's instincts were proletarian, and he tried often to remind Havel that his own class background should not blind him to how most of the country lived. He was personally critical of Havel's attempts to crown the republic with works of contemporary pop art. 'I know you can't force this nation to like Beethoven and Shakespeare. But then can you do the same with Michael Jackson and the Rolling Stones?' Milota pointedly asked him one day. 'I have a different view from you of the wood from which this country has been

[1]The following material is drawn from an interview with Stanislav Milota, Prague, 2 October 1997.

hewn,' he continued. 'From your bourgeois background, you learned not to eat with your knife, and not to kiss the arses of comrade women. But I learned other things. Just as Olga did.'

These were rough and tough words. Milota was no friendlier towards what he dubbed the 'amoral behaviour' of senior officials during the first few months of the new regime. Havel's helpers were inclined to behave in ways familiar under the Communist *ancien régime*. The backscratching, toe-sucking and breast-fondling efforts that used to go into obtaining a visa to France, say, were now potentially in evidence around a new President actively committed to 'living in the truth'. It was not that Havel himself was becoming corrupted. It was rather that the Castle seemed to attract mindless profligates, said Milota. He was appalled by the heavy drinking on the first presidential flight to Moscow. 'Have you seen yourselves through the eyes of the flight attendants? Do you know how you're behaving?' he asked a group of them on board the plane. The earthy Milota was frank with Havel about the need for a more spartan approach to protocol. 'This is a nation that's demoralized. You should set an example. Don't take taxis and chauffeur-driven limos. Catch a tram up to the Castle. Have bread and a jug of water for lunch. You too need the occasional kick in the arse.'

Havel was normally a very precise person and would usually have kept excesses and amoral behaviour at bay, Milota later said. But during these early weeks, Havel was tired. He found it hard to keep control of the high-pressured dynamics of Castle life. Besides, he himself had an appetite for power and bohemian excess. He eventually told Milota to stop disrupting business with objections. 'I don't want to hear any more about all this,' he said. Relations between the two men worsened, especially during the preparations for the first presidential visit to the United States. According to Milota, Washington's fascination with Havel – 'the cleancut bourgeois guy who looked different from his rough-tongued Polish electrician counterpart' – served to overinflate the Castle's sense of its own power in the world. The planned delegation, the second biggest ever (after De Gaulle's) in the history of the United States, was too fat to fit into one aircraft. Milota told Havel that he was making the mistake of acting as if he were the President of a country like the People's Republic of China. 'Why do we need thirty bodyguards on this trip?' Milota asked. 'We're a country of only 15 million people. What is all this going to cost?' The reaction among Havel's advisers ranged from puzzlement to frosty suspicion that Milota was trying to get rid of them. He decided to get out first, to leave behind what he considered to be an orgy of powermongering. One afternoon in mid-May 1990, after sixteen weeks as Head of the Secretariat, he quietly plucked his jacket from the office coat rack, said to his secretaries that he was just stepping out for a moment for some fresh air, and never came back again to the Castle. Later that day, he sent a message to Havel, explaining (as the Communists used to do) that for health reasons he was 'taking early retirement'.

The message from Milota (he later heard) was received with stony silence. The notable exception was Olga, who not only liked and respected Milota, her fellow Žižkov radical, but also shared his feverish complaints, and said so loudly. She never found the Castle an especially hospitable place, and liked to dismiss it as 'the submarine'. Here were scores of people trapped eighteen hours a day inside an airless, dimly lit space, cut off from the real world, way out of their depths in treacherous waters, deeply uncertain of either their mission or their machine. Her husband's aides were mostly unqualified for the job, she told some of them to their face. Others were womanizers and drunkards. Still others were insecure narcissists who spent their time gazing at their own media images. Olga disliked fame. She was impatient with journalists who flattered her, or asked her such questions as what flowers or food she liked. She was not averse to telling them off, or interrupting them to say she had to empty her washing machine. She also disliked being trapped in the cage of Castle security. She often said to her bodyguards that she'd rather be playing bridge or walking in the countryside, and naturally got enormous pleasure from giving them the slip – as on the first American state visit, when unannounced she entered a lingerie shop, leaving her young male bodyguards standing pink-faced among bras and knickers and laced bodygloves.

Olga had high but simple moral standards. She disliked snobbishness and despised prejudice, for instance against Romanies or the elderly. She insisted on frankness, simplicity, honesty, and no bullshit – and it is unsurprising that she clashed with some of the key Castle personnel. Mutual friends confirmed that she had a much better eye for people's character than did Havel. She could spot daggers in castlemen's smiles, and if she had her way, she told a friend during the first few weeks of the Castle under Havel's leadership, she would rid the place of some of them by 'hanging them with their own bloody neckties'.[1] Some bit back at her for sentiments of that kind. Ladislav Kantor was among the targets of her criticism. She considered him a 'red-haired cretin', and several times tried to rap him over the knuckles – for instance when he queried, on security grounds, the proposed appointment of the great exiled Czech conductor Kubelík to the National Theatre. She said openly that Kantor was a flatterer of her husband, and that he was in danger of falling for it. Kantor responded by trying to draw Havel into such disputes, even on one occasion offering to get rid of the cuckoo in the nest. 'I can get you a divorce,' Kantor said.[2]

Olga, as dignified and tough as polished old boots, was unmoved. At an early stage after the revolution, she made up her mind to turn her back on the Castle and instead of playing the hollow role of First Lady she devoted her energies to the fledgling civil society. She considered it a more meaningful option with credible precedents. As a young teenager, just before the *coup de Prague*, she had been involved in running a Žižkov club-residence called Milíčův dům. Set up by a Christian pacifist, Přemysl Pitter, it functioned as an alternative community for young people whose family life had been shattered by poverty, war, bigotry. The club-cum-residence had sheltered Jewish children during the Reichsprotektorat, while during the years Olga was there many children came as refugees from the Sudetenland pogroms and concentration camps. The refuge offered tastes of other worlds. The children were encouraged to live as equals within a community; they were taught how to resolve their conflicts non-violently; and they were offered access to a big library, courses in art-appreciation and theatre, and generally to join in group activities like singing, gardening, sewing, knitting and ping-pong.

The director of the community centre fell out with the Communists, and in 1951 narrowly escaped to Switzerland after refusing to be drafted to the uranium mines at Jáchymov. Olga never forgot him or his bold initiative. Immediately after Havel went to the Castle, she began to wonder whether a similar kind of experiment

[1]Interview with Jiřina Šiklová, Prague, 19 September 1996.
[2]The dispute with Kantor is confirmed in interviews with Olga Stankovičová, Prague, 10 November 1998; and with Stanislav Milota, Prague, 2 October 1997.

could be made in defence of the fledgling civil society. She had had some thoughts of setting up an organization to protect animals or the environment, but her dream began to come true after making a state visit to Canada in February 1990. There she was approached by a rich Czech *émigré*, a Montréal manufacturer of nuclear-reactor equipment named Karel Velan. He wanted to donate money to a Czech hospital, especially for the purpose of showing Czech doctors how things were done in the West. Olga soon spotted the advantages to be won from appealing to others to pool funds to help the disabled victims of Communism live in dignity. And so upon her return from Canada she set to work founding an organization called the Good Will Committee.

It was the first of its kind in post-Communist Czechoslovakia. Olga wanted it to be small, and to serve mainly as a clearing house for sponsors' and donors' money. Things turned out differently, in part because as each day passed the new organization attracted dozens then hundreds of letters seeking support. There were also hundreds of offers of financial support from post-'48 and post-'68 emigrants, Czech and Slovak businesses, and older citizens, especially poor women who sent 100-crown notes through the post. In its first phase, it was decided that the primary goal of the Committee was to re-equip and humanize the prison-like institutions of incarceration inherited from the *ancien régime* – large institutions like borstals for children and centres of confinement for the disabled. Later, after a change of law covering the work of charities, the Good Will Committee – despite Olga's original desire to keep the initiative small – grew much larger and was renamed the Olga Havlová Foundation. She left the day-to-day management to her staff, instead concentrating on lobbying members of parliament and the social-welfare ministries, fund-raising, and – above all – visiting groups and individuals with the aim of deconstructing the old institutions and setting up new, smaller, civil-society institutions with a human face.

Václav Havel reacted supportively. Although at first he was 'a bit amused that his wife had found a hobby'[1], he quickly grew proud of its intrinsic merits – so much so that he set up his own foundation, The Václav Havel Foundation, which until 1995 served to fund projects like the refurbishment of

[1]Interview with Olga Stankovičová, Prague, 10 November 1998.

the Castle library and guided tours through the Castle for the blind. The desire for emulation was understandable, but the effects were different. The Good Will Committee proved that it was possible to pose a different – hopefully complementary, but potentially contradictory – understanding of politics, power and empowerment than that of the Castle. The President's big house on the hill: the seat of state power, wrapped in its imagery of flags, ornaments, guards, arms, courtiers. Its role: to draw upon tax revenues to issue orders, sanction laws, issue prepared statements, grant amnesties, provide symbolic and moral leadership, to bind the country to the outside world by means of diplomatic missions, meetings with heads of state, trade agreements, troop deployments, or (in the last instance) force of arms. By contrast, a charitable organization: a small and independently funded organ not of the state, but of civil society. Its role: to address the self-defined needs of its clients, to provide some stability and justice in their lives, to shield and protect them from the inconveniences resulting from state neglect, market forces, or social bigotry and discrimination – overall, to help the disempowered to feel stronger in the world by encouraging them to see and feel the importance of what the ancient Greeks called the *metaxu*. Through the charitable organization, in other words, the disempowered can come to sense the importance of nests in which they are warmed and nourished and gain self-confidence. They are encouraged to rely less on 'distant' and 'inflexible' governmental institutions. The powerless come to learn that power is not synonymous with large-scale organizations like states and corporations. They learn, on the contrary, that lines of power run through every nook and cranny of our lives, that large-scale organizations rest on these foundations of 'micro-power', with the implication that amendments and reversals of these same local relations of power – the empowering of the powerless – can be a counterweight to 'macro-power', and can have wider effects upon the overall structures of the state and civil society.

PARLIAMENT

The active defence of civil society against the castled state, combined with criticism of the *Ichspieler*, effectively called into question the practical vision of the crowned republic. So too did the active defence of parliamentary government during the first week of 1990. At the time, one of Havel's closest collaborators during the long years of Soviet-secured normalization recalled meeting him alone at the Castle for an hour on the day before his first major parliamentary speech. 'He was relaxed after lunch. He made himself comfortable, stretched out on a *chaise-longue*, undid his tie, and talked quietly and frankly,' said the colleague. 'He told me that he had decided to be President for a year, after which he would make a public speech, perhaps before parliament, in which he would announce that he was standing down and that he had decided on a successor. He added,' continued the colleague, 'that there would not be a dry eye in the public during the speech.' The surprised colleague asked him whom he would nominate as the heir apparent. 'Havel refused to say, pointing out that the room in which they were sitting, the President's Office, was probably still bugged.' So the colleague wrote a well-known name on a piece of paper and passed it to him. Havel laughed, shook his head, then exclaimed: '*He's a political intriguer!*' Later the colleague learned that Havel instead had in mind Magdaléna Vášáryová, a well-known beautiful star of Czechoslovak stage and screen.

The exchange between the new President and one of his most trusted friends was of no political consequence, except that it revealed something of Havel's rather cavalier attitude towards the parliament at the time. It also helps explain the political trouble that came his way next day. The hitherto unrevealed events went something like this. In the first few weeks after the revolution, public whisperings began about the future name of the Czechoslovak federation. Mistrust and bad feelings quickly developed. Various Czech politicians openly made fun of the Slovaks; some were even heard to say that a hyphen should be used between Czech and Slovak in Bratislava, but not abroad. Some Slovaks replied that their state should be mentioned first, as in Slovakoczechia, but this was treated in Prague as a good joke, then a bad joke.

Havel decided to act. On 23 January, driven by an instinct that it was time to move, he came to the Federal Assembly building, with the stated aim of addressing its members. Like

Lycurgus or Solon – or Charles de Gaulle coming to the French National Assembly in 1958 – Havel would for a time occupy the four-storey, steel-beamed, ugly green glass structure, which was situated (Prague people often quipped) near Wenceslas Square, between a museum and a theatre. Havel would act as a popular sovereign battling against those trying to interpose themselves between the people and himself. Equipped with the full powers of a herald, he would urge the parliament to change the name of the country, alter its coat of arms, and rename its armed forces, and to do so by a disciplined parliamentary debate followed by a show of hands.

Before entering the Federal Assembly, Havel had coffee and a chat with the standing committee called the Presidium. Most of its members seemed afraid to speak against him.[1] He was, after all, the ruler of the crowned republic, the unchallenged symbol and driving force of the revolutionary changes that had begun. And his reasoning was as precise as ever. He explained that he would say to the assembly that he was led by 'a responsibility to negotiate in accordance with the awakened will of the public'. Havel went on to reveal that he would present 'proposals for mutually implemented changes' that were 'expected by most people'. The proposals were inspired and called for by 'the public, to whom I feel my primary responsibility', he added. He then divulged that he would put a clear and concrete proposal for altering the name and key symbols of the country, dropping the word 'socialist'. The new name of the country was to be virtually the same as that used during the First Republic: The Czechoslovak Republic.

Not every member of the Presidium agreed with his tactics and intentions, as was explained on the spot by the country's leading constitutional lawyer, Zdeněk Jičínský. The slim and short, grey-haired, goatee-chin-tufted, fox-faced, calm-mannered and highly intelligent Jičínskí was a seasoned politician, and he had no difficulty telling some bad news to the charismatic Havel, whom he had come to know during the early days of Civic Forum. 'It is simply impossible that you read out your proposals and then expect the members of the Assembly to raise their hands in acclamation,' Jičínský told Havel to his face. 'These are proposals of a special

[1]Interview with Zdeněk Jičínský, Prague, 25 September 1996; see also his *Československý parlament v polistopadovém vývoji* (Prague 1993), pp. 106–111.

kind. Under the existing constitutional rules, they most certainly cannot be altered in this immediate way. In our federal system, state symbols cannot be changed by the Federal Assembly without the prior consultation and agreement of the republican parliaments: the Czech National Council and Slovak National Council.'

Havel, as headstrong as ever, went ahead with his plan. He even had the cheek to insist before the parliament that his proposals had to be treated as a package, that is, that in the interests of smooth passage they were not divisible. But Jičínský had correctly anticipated the mood of the assembled parliament. Havel's attempt to transform the parliament into a stage and to perform solo in front of its members – to cast himself in the role of *Ichspieler* – failed. The deputies sent Havel packing; according to one eyewitness, his eyes were as glazed as a Greek statue. The Assembly refused to approve his package of proposals, and instead acted as catalyst of a wider public controversy about the themes that Havel had raised.

Naturally, the problem of the relative 'invisibility' of Slovakia instantly surfaced, and some Slovak deputies began to insist that the new name and symbols of the country should express the fact that Slovakia was also a republic. Their preferred solution was to insert a hyphen in the country's name – just as the country had first had after the Munich fiasco. Within the Czech lands plenty of angry voices began to make themselves heard – enabling a bizarre compromise to emerge. The Federal Assembly eventually passed legislation that enabled the country to have *two* names: to be spelled without a hyphen in the Czech lands ('Czechoslovak Republic') and with a hyphen in Slovakia ('Czecho-Slovak Republic'). The new law was greeted with howls of protest at a big public rally in Bratislava on 30 March 1990. In the end, the law had to be amended to fulfil the requirements of 'making Slovakia visible'. As postage stamps from this period reveal, the country was from here on to be called the Czech and Slovak Federated Republic. The first battle in what would later be called 'the hyphen war' had been concluded.

Future historians will dispute whether or not Havel was culpable for his part in prematurely triggering off a bitter conflict that eventually soured Czech and Slovak relations for years to come. Beyond dispute is the little-known fact that prior to this conflict there was another: the issue of whether or not the new President really wanted to allow the development of a parliamentary democratic system of government. It sounds overdrawn to put it this way, but at the time, during the first weeks and months of the revolution, there were plenty of people inside and outside the Federal Assembly who worried that Václav Havel, the symbolic leader of the struggle to live in the truth under conditions of open government, was potentially a threat to the realization of exactly that goal. The feeling crystallized that there was a fundamental contradiction between Havel's desire for a strong and stable executive and the need in any democracy to control demagogy. The same feeling was strengthened by Havel's tendency to describe himself, in self-important terms, as the voice of Being, as 'an instrument of the time' who was being compelled 'to do what had to be done'. Some observers grew particularly nervous after his full-blooded attack on the status quo on the afternoon of the twenty-first anniversary of the military crushing of the Prague Spring. Standing on the balcony of the pollution-stained Civic Forum building, overlooking Wenceslas Square, flanked by aides and photographers and camera crews, Havel called for a 'second revolution' to get rid of the rubbish left over from the *ancien régime*.[1]

Such words served to confirm the suspicions of key players like Jičínský, who dug in their heels and so handed the President his first political defeat. Havel was a mite indignant. 'Experience has taught me that it is best to do the opposite of what Professor Jičínský advises,' he later said. 'Whenever I heeded his advice, whose common denominator was always the recommendation that I ought to postpone something, it had disastrous consequences.'[2] Jičínský later confirmed that he neither regarded Havel as a personal enemy nor really worried that he would turn out to be a Jacobin figure like Robespierre. 'Václav Havel was at the time a figure of absolute power. But, unlike Robespierre, he had no intention of acting in an absolutist way. Not only that, but Havel wanted disputes to be resolved peacefully. He didn't want people to settle scores in the streets. He was opposed to revolutionary violence.' But the allergic reaction of the Federal Assembly towards Havel – expressed most eloquently in the constitutionalist opinions of

[1] Václav Havel, *Summer Meditations on Politics, Morality and Civility in a Time of Transition.* (London and Boston, 1992), pp. xvi–xvii; Václav Havel, *Vážení občané* (Prague, 1992), pp. 16–18
[2] *Mladá fronta Dnes*, 16 June 1992, p. 1.

Jičínský – reveals the grains of truth of the old maxim that all revolutions tend to breed professional revolutionists possessed of great initiative, organizational talent and elaborate doctrines. That old maxim implied that professional revolutionists initially appear to listen to their fellow citizens who are rebelling; later, they claim to be representatives of their supporters, who eventually become the objects of manipulation of the self-appointed revolutionaries, usually by violence.[1]

Havel, who constantly appealed for non-violence and 'velvet' solutions, certainly did not fall victim to, let alone flirt with the second half of this maxim. Jičínský pointed out as well that Havel's anti-parliamentarian instincts were understandable. After all, it was a parliament dominated by unelected Communists whose next moves in the revolutionary power struggle were unknown. The parliament, Jičínský noted, had indeed elected Havel as President – it was among the sweetest ironies of the Velvet Revolution – but it might not have done so had voting been by secret ballot instead of by a show of cowed hands. Yet the trouble with Havel's position, Jičínský reasoned, was that he and his closest advisers knew little about constitutions and had little feel in particular for the actual and potential relationship between the presidency, the federal parliament and the constitution.

Havel and his aides set to work on the hunch that the constitution was a Communist device, and therefore rotten, and that the parliament ultimately consisted of a bunch of Communists who needed to be kept in check before being thrown out by a general election. Their presumption, argued Jičínský, ignored the basic point that the existing constitution, introduced in 1960 and amended in 1968, contained many clauses found elsewhere in parliamentary democratic constitutions. The first steps toward the 'democratization' of that constitution had been taken in the dying moments of the Husák presidency: the principles of the leading role of the Communist Party and the people's militia had been removed; the parliamentary procedure through which Havel was subsequently elected was introduced in the form of

---

[1]One version of this old maxim about the unintended dynamic consequences of revolutionary politics was presented during the French Revolution by the greatest German liberal of the time, Georg Forster. See his *Kleine Schriften und Briefe*, ed. Claus Träger (Leipzig, 1961), p. 344: 'The Revolution is a hurricane; who can harness it? Galvanized by its spirit, human beings find it possible to commit actions that posterity, out of sheer horror, will be unable to comprehend.'

an amendment; and the wording of the oath of allegiance to be sworn by incoming presidents was changed so as to get rid of all references to 'socialism'. These various amendments Jičínský welcomed. Their content was an improvement on what had existed before. They also helped to preserve and cultivate a spirit of constitutionalism and the commitment to the principle – vital in abnormal conditions like the Velvet Revolution – of what he called 'legal continuity'.

Jičínský was especially critical of Havel's habit of playing the role of *Ichspieler*. 'Havel's personality was that of an artist, a dramatist,' said Jičínský later. 'He had no grasp of political science, no legal background, and only limited familiarity with the constitutional relationships in which he was acting.' Matters were exacerbated by his natural impatience. The insistence by a playwright that an instruction be carried out right away may be appropriate on the stage. But it was actually counterproductive in these early weeks of the revolution, when time was needed to get the new balance right among various branches of the constitution. 'Havel did not behave arrogantly,' he concluded. 'That was not his style. But when he realized he couldn't get his way immediately, his mood plummeted. He found strange the political terrain of parliament and constitutional change, and he did not know how to move about within their forms. Although he had absolute powers, he nevertheless should have had some respect for the institution of parliament.'

In the context, Jičínský's criticisms may have been judged as pedantic, as fun-spoiling, as curmudgeonly. But they were politically revealing, and although he didn't quite put it this way, they highlighted the precious role of parliaments as power-sharing and flexible power-taming devices, especially during the establishment and consolidation of democracy.[1] During the first weeks of the revolution, Havel took the view that the current federal parliament was not only full of crooks and Commies, but that within the crowned republic that was being born, parliament functioned as an obstacle to living freely 'in the truth'. His hoary prejudice against parliament was worrying, especially in view of its rich history and – above all – its indispensability in

[1]See Juan J. Linz, 'The Perils of Presidentialism', *Journal of Democracy*, volume 1, number 1 (Winter 1990), pp. 51–69.

democratic regimes. Parliaments are assemblies of decision-makers who consider themselves formally equal to one another in status, and whose authority as members of parliament rests on their claim to represent a wider political community. Parliaments in this sense superseded the traditional medieval assemblies (such as the German *Hoftage* or English *witanegemots*), which had functioned – note the parallels here with Havel's attitude – mainly as loosely organized, *ad hoc* consultative bodies summoned by the monarch for the purposes of seeking their counsel or opinion, or publicizing among the monarch's subjects special events, such as dynastic marriages, international treaties and new judicial and legislative measures.

In contrast to this medieval arrangement, parliaments in the modern sense first developed in the field of high tension between the public power of feudal monarchs and the cluster of private interests represented by the estates of nobility, clergy, peasantry and burghers.[1] Bodies like the Spanish *cortes* and the French *parlament* (or *parlamentum*) met more frequently and regularly, and also functioned as both consultative and deliberative bodies. Especially when the cohesion and influence of estates increased, and when at the same time government typically assumed the form of the *Ständestaat* – a monarchy ruling over a society dominated by orders – parliaments became a vital intermediary between monarchic rulers and the (elected or appointed) representatives of the most privileged estates, who sought to define and defend matters of concern to the whole 'realm'.

These early European parliaments were by no means weak or intermittent. Not only the English parliament – often assumed to be the unique example of a powerful representative assembly – but nearly all Continental parliaments began to exercise considerable powers of granting taxes, participating in legislation and determining the justice of matters as diverse as succession and foreign policy. Here were the seeds of the more recent understanding of the necessity of parliaments to democracy. Although it is true that parliaments can play a variety of roles, two sometimes tensely interrelated functions of parliament are of special importance to

[1] The dualism between monarchs and estates – which developed nowhere else in the world, and was the forerunner of the polarity between state and civil society of the early modern era – is basic to understanding the origins of European parliamentary assemblies, as is pointed out in the classic essay by Otto Hintze, 'Weltgeschichtliche Bedingungen der Repräsentativverfassung [1931]', in *Staat und Verfassung* (Göttingen, 1970), pp. 140–185.

democracy. First, parliaments are vital means of aggregating, co-ordinating and representing diverse social interests. This integrative capacity of parliament has often been misunderstood – by the Marxist tradition especially – as a mechanism of bourgeois class rule. Parliament *may* become the political means of class domination – as Lenin put it, 'simply a machine for the suppression of one class by another'. But a cursory familiarity with the long history of European parliamentary assemblies suggests that there is no *essential* relationship between parliament and bourgeois power. The effects of parliamentary forms are not necessarily produced by the forms themselves.

To express this first point differently: only when there is a supreme and *accountable* political body – like a federal assembly – can *final* decisions be taken which fairly and openly balance and transcend the particular, conflicting group relations of civil society. There is never a 'natural' harmony among social groups, and there is never a 'natural' equilibrium between society and the state. There is indeed a constant danger in a democratic system that party competition, freedom of association, the rule of law and other democratic procedures will be used to defeat democracy. Hence, parliament is an indispensable mechanism for anticipating and alleviating the constant pressure exerted by social groups upon each other, and upon the state itself. And, when faced with recalcitrant or power-hungry organizations or charismatic figures in crisis situations, parliament becomes vital for checking and ordering the suppression of those groups committed explicitly to destroying pluralism.

Parliaments have a second function: they are vital means of checking the secretive or unaccountable operations of state power, and hence, of dampening the desires of would-be dictators. Parliaments make it difficult or impossible for rulers to govern without open debate and organized opposition to state policies. The oppositional role of parliaments is based on the (originally medieval) premise that there is no necessary incompatibility between effective government and effective opposition. It is also based on the premise that opposition to state power can be effective only when the special privileges traditionally monopolized by those who rule – immunity from prosecution, rights freely to criticize and guaranteed pay and political status – are shared with their opponents. And the oppositional role of parliament rests on the perennial insight – ignored by Havel in the heat of the revolution, but outlined more than two centuries ago by a wise defender of power-sharing – that 'constant experience shows us that every person invested with power is apt to abuse it, and to carry that power as far as it will go'.[1]

[1]Charles Louis de Secondat, Baron de Montesquieu, *De l'esprit des lois* (Paris 1979), volume 1, Book X1, chapter 4, p. 293.

LUSTRATION

Freedom of speech is said to be the elixir of democratic life, a basic entitlement of citizens endowed with powers to act freely upon the world. Listen to Milan Kundera at the stormy Fourth Czechoslovak Writers' Congress in Prague in 1967, quoting Voltaire. 'In his letter to Helvétius, Voltaire wrote that beautiful phrase: "I disapprove of what you say, but I will defend to the death your right to say it." This formulates a fundamental ethical principle of modern culture,' said Kundera, to warm applause. He continued, more earnestly. 'Any suppression of views,' he said, 'even when the views that are being forcibly suppressed are erroneous, must lead, in the final analysis, away from the truth, for truth can be attained only through the interaction of views that are equal and free. Any interference with freedom of thought and words, no matter how discreet the technique or name given to such censorship, is a scandal in the twentieth century and a shackle on our emerging literature.'[1]

Now consider the competing view that the vital principle of freedom of speech must have at least some limits, since freedom of expression, under certain conditions, can otherwise cripple freedom of expression.[2] This view points out that standard free-speech arguments, like Kundera's, have all the earmarks of an ideology, essentially because they presume that counter-arguments are dangerous and must therefore be rejected by all right-thinking people. Free speech about free speech is frowned upon. The toleration of free speech is *intolerant* of those who doubt that freedom of expression is an absolute principle. The critics of free expression add another objection. There are times, they insist, when saying certain things publicly is insulting or defaming of others, which means that their capacity for action is damaged. Even the simple naming of another person – as in the court trial of someone who has been victimized, or is accused of victimizing another – can be damaging. Freedom of expression can be a refuge of scoundrels. And so, it is argued, defences of freedom of speech must be countered with legal restrictions upon what is said to others. The right to speak and the duty to be silent are like twins – the closest of relatives who dislike

---

[1] Reprinted in *The Prague Spring 1968*, op. cit., p. 8.
[2] Stanley Fish, *There's No Such Thing as Free Speech and It's a Good Thing, Too* (New York and Oxford 1994); John Keane, *The Media and Democracy* (Oxford and New York, 1991).

living apart, but who find it hard to live together without quarrelling.

The vexed relationship between speech and silence is a key dilemma of the modern condition. Within the first few months after Havel's election as President, it resurfaced with a vengeance – and sorely tested the principle, defended by Kundera, that words should be unmuzzled. The central political problem was this: What should be done about the 'crimes' committed by the Communists and their collaborators against citizens' rights? Should publicity about repression in the past be unlimited? Should the old nomenklatura be punished, initially by exposing their crimes before the public? Or should such publicity, which was bound to cause fear and ill-feeling, be restrained so that everybody could forgive and forget, and work together towards a more open and tolerant society?

Havel was aware during the revolution that such fraught questions were bound to stir up political trouble. The news reached him in early December 1989 that the shredding and burning of important StB files on a massive scale was underway. The first press reports appeared on 8 December, and within days the burnings were the butt of newspaper cartoons and street-level jokes. So during the roundtable talks with the Communists, a day before the announcement of the new Government of National Understanding, Havel moved to solve the problem by proposing Richard Sacher – a lawyer and senior functionary in the Czechoslovak People's Party – as the next Minister of the Interior. Sacher was a good man, he said. He was flexible, dynamic, and peace-loving. Others were less convinced, and Havel had to eat humble pie. The negotiators agreed in the end to entrust the whole police apparatus, including the StB and its files, to a triumvarate of Marián Čalfa and his two first deputies, Valtr Komárek and Ján Čarnogurský. The decision made no impact on the mass destruction of files – 15,000 were reportedly weeded and shredded – so that one day after his election as President, on 30 December, Havel finally got his way by appointing Sacher as the new federal Minister of the Interior.

The appointment bred trouble. It produced a bitter political row that some Czechs soon came to call 'Sachergate'. The episode that broke out just before Easter in 1990 was arguably more of a political thriller than its American counterpart, and the only reason it did not bring down the President of the country was because, at the time, Havel's potential critics around the Castle held fast to the view that 'solidarity' with the Castle was vital if the *ancien régime* was to be defeated. According to these critics, there was plenty of evidence that Sacher, immediately following his appointment, had set to work organizing his own personal collection of old security files, into the so-called 'Z-files'. His move was understandable – it was better to safeguard sensitive files in the inner vaults of the Ministry of the Interior than to trust others with them. But his critics were adamant that Sacher's tactic was both illegal and charged with blackmail potential. He was said to be refusing to co-operate with the newly established Office for the Protection of the Constitution and Democracy, directed by Zdeněk Formánek, who was now laying claim to the files, without success. Sacher had also secretly screened members of the cabinet and parliament. He was as well turning a blind eye to the ongoing removal of files by his StB agents.

This wasn't all. Some opponents of Sacher even suggested that Havel, who clearly knew about the whole business, and who was aware that there were scores of former dissidents with fat StB files, was being fed some of these (and perhaps other) files from Sacher's collection, and so was drawn into a cat's cradle of suspicion of others. Sacher's critics found puzzling his motives, which might have included his old loyalties to the Czechoslovak People's Party, which bore grudges against both the dissidents and the Communist Party. Sacher's links with Havel were also puzzling. It could not be ruled out that he was co-operating with Sacher, and learning to use the files, for the purpose of protecting his fledgling presidency against scandalous exposés. Whatever the case, Sacher's critics were convinced that there was mounting evidence that he was deliberately slowing down the reform of the Ministry of the Interior, that he was surrounding himself with Communist men and women from the 'old structures', and that he had just botched an attempt to sack some 800 StB officials. After signing their redundancy notices, which contained a right of appeal, Sacher was forced to reinstate them, and to pay them compensation, which cost Czechoslovak taxpayers millions of crowns.

Jan Urban, representing Civic Forum, dashed to the presidential country estate at Lány to confront Havel with the need to act decisively.[1] At an opportune moment, when Havel was alone, Urban appealed to him. 'Václav,' he began quietly, looking him straight in the eye, 'I am playing a role in public life, but I don't presume that I should know everything about the inner workings of state. I understand that there may be matters of national security of which I should know nothing.' He hesitated, trying to get the emphasis right. 'But tell me, as President, is this Sacher affair of this type?' Urban added: 'I'll take you at your word. If you say "yes", then I'll not delve into it further. I promise I'll back off.' Not wanting to lie, Havel winced, but gave no straight answer. 'Václav, we are in total opposition,' snapped Urban, who after some brief pleasantries scampered back to Prague to propose independent mediation of the dispute. Havel, knowing that he was cornered, consented. The respected moral philosopher Ladislav Hejdánek agreed to be the mediator and a stormy but closed six-hour meeting to consider his findings took place a week later at Civic Forum headquarters. Outside, pro-Havel demonstrators noisily protested that Civic Forum was preparing a *coup d'état*. Inside, Hejdánek vindicated the position of Civic Forum. Havel was thus forced to accept a deal that included the appointment of the seasoned Charter 77 activist Jan Ruml to the post of first Deputy Interior Minister, with special responsibility for the StB. A few days later, with rumours circulating that the security forces were mutinous, Ruml proved that political power sometimes needs gun barrels to get its way. He handed out a new set of legally watertight redundancy notices to the StB, flanked by mean-faced paratroopers armed with Scorpion sub-machine guns.

These were crazy times for Havel, who now went everywhere flanked by two female bodyguards. One was blonde, the other was brunette, so distinguishing him – he told friends – from Colonel Gaddafi, the only other head of state who used women to fend off assassins. The cool image was of little help in protecting him against the much more serious trouble, again to do with the StB, lurking around the corner. The taming of Sacher left unresolved the basic problem of what to do with the security files. For a while, Havel treated the matter as people's private business, as he did,

---

[1]Interview with Jan Urban (Prague), 3 November 1998. The Sacher affair first surfaced in the Czechoslovak press during mid-April 1990, for instance in *Lidové noviny* (Prague), in the week beginning 18 April, and in *Respekt* (Prague), 25 April – 1 May 1990.

with a look of amusement, when finding out the size of his own StB file.[1] He soon became wiser, especially after February 1991, when the Federal Parliament appointed a commission to review the police files and to expose publicly parliamentarians who were listed therein as agents or collaborators. The commission ruled that elected politicians enjoyed immunity, and could therefore not be dismissed. It proposed instead that members of parliament listed in the StB files had two options: they could either resign quietly or be exposed publicly. A few weeks later, on 22 March 1991, a special televised session of parliament pointed fingers at ten elected MPs who were alleged to be StB collaborators, but who had refused to resign.

A Commie-hunt had begun. It soon led to the enactment of the most ethically dubious and politically controversial purging legislation in all of central and eastern Europe: the so-called lustration act, agreed by the Czech and Slovak National Assembly on 4 October 1991.[2] The term 'lustration', derived originally from Latin (*lustrare*, to purify through sacrifice), had older connotations in Czech and other European languages of moral purification through washing in holy water, and of going around, viewing or surveying or making a census of land or troops. The old meanings conveyed exactly what the new lustrators had in mind. Their chief aim was to bring into the public domain basic information about the extent of Communist misdoings, even to bring to justice those people who were up to their ears in the old system. Armed with truth, the lustrators insisted that freedom of expression was an unconditional right. Lustration involved not only exercising the basic right to expose state secrets. It also meant exercising the basic right of citizens to inform the wider public of the truth. The lustrators deplored the slow pace of revolutionary reforms. They insisted that unfulfilled expectations were rising, and that a new political census was urgently required. Some of the lustrators came close to saying that the Velvet Revolution had been too soft, and that the body politic now needed quick purification.

[1]Interview with Petruška Šustrová (Scheinfeld), 14 September 1996.
[2]The following draws upon Herman Schwartz, 'Lustration in Eastern Europe', *Parker School Journal of East European Law*, volume 1, number 2 (1994), pp. 141–171; Jiřina Šiklová, 'Lustration or the Czech Way of Screening', *East European Constitutional Review*, volume 5, number 1 (Winter 1996), pp. 57–62; the interview with Petruška Šustrová, op. cit.; and detailed correspondence from Václav Žák (Prague), 14 March 1999.

Hence, weeding out collaborators – eliminating fear of the truth by widening the circle of fear and mutual recrimination against Communists – was a necessary price to pay for nurturing citizens' freedom of communication.

The lustrators acted with moral urgency, especially after the attempted *coup d'état* in the Soviet Union during the summer of 1991. The lustrators loudly applauded the provisions of the new law, which passed by a very slim majority. It targeted at least a million people. These included former Communists who had held positions of power from the district level up, former secret-police agents, their collaborators (a term vaguely defined in the legislation), and anybody who received police training in Moscow. The law also applied to anybody who had belonged to Party-run groups, like the People's Militia, as well as to bodies such as the National Front Action that were used by the Party after 1948 to weed out undesirables from workplaces, sports clubs, schools and universities. The lustration law specified that all former members of these listed groups should for five years be banned from holding top-level administrative jobs in all branches of the state, including government ministries, the military, universities, the courts, broadcasting, and enterprises such as banks, railways and foreign-trade companies. The law also required that everybody in post, or seeking a post, in these sectors must from hereon present to their employer a document, issued by the federal Ministry of the Interior, to prove that they had been postively 'lustrated'.

The law triggered off country-wide howls of protest. Many grew nervous – understandably so, since Communism after 1948 and (especially) late-socialism after 1968 had been systems of power in which everybody, in one way or another, had been implicated. The critics of lustration pointed out that many of those seeking vengeance against the Communists – like Václav Klaus, the upwardly mobile Finance Minister – had political motives. The critics also pointed to the miserable irony that the architects of the law – 'right-wing Bolsheviks' Havel's friend Jiří Dienstbier dubbed them, sarcastically – had invested their trust and loyalty in the secret police. Their handwritten and computer records, containing at least 140,000 names, were presumed to be accurate, despite the well-known facts that the secret police used trickery, threats, bribes and lies to lure individuals into their nets of suspicion. The critics of lustration thus accused its defenders of ignoring the facts behind the facts. They charged the lustrators with allowing the secret police to rule – unquestioned – from their graves.

The lustration-law opponents also criticized its loopholes. Thousands of files of well-placed Communists had already been weeded, and probably destroyed. Top Communists who now worked in private business or those who had already retired with handsome pensions – like Miroslav Štěpán, the former Prague Party boss who now ponced around the country signing copies of his memoirs after serving only six months of a longer prison sentence for giving orders to use violence against demonstrators on the first day of the revolution – were also not covered by the law. Presumably, they were to get off, scot-free. Worst of all, said its critics, the lustration law, in the name of freedom of information, encouraged a climate of repressive incivility. Pelting each other with truth was destroying trust and loyalty to the public good. So, for instance, employers, anticipating trouble, were quickly getting on with the nasty business of 'lustrating' their staff, whether or not there was any reasonable suspicion of their culpability. Children of former Communists were suffering discrimination. Former Charter 77 supporters were discovering the names of informers in their ranks. Brothers and sisters were finding out that they had spied on each other. Many decent individuals who accepted the anonymous telephone caller's invitation to meet for coffee the following day now were being turned into guilted scapegoats. Truth was breeding hatred. Daily life was beginning to resemble an unpleasant scene from Hitchcock's *Rear Window*. Everybody was potentially the object of suspicion. Nobody was beyond victimization. The whole society could end up criminalizing itself.

Havel was caught in a squeeze. He reacted to the lustration controversy using the tactics of balanced diplomacy. When travelling outside the country, or speaking to foreign guests and hosts, he pointedly criticized the hysteria, name-calling and atmosphere of bitterness and suspicion produced by the lustration. In an interview with his friend Adam Michnik, he confessed his mounting anxiety about the 'lawless revenge and witch-hunts'. He told Jeri Laber of Helsinki Watch that the legislation was a recipe for injustice. 'We have not yet found a dignified and civilized way to reckon with our past,' he said. 'The lustration act affects the small fish. The big ones are laughing at us. They have become capitalists; the act does not affect them.'[1] And he told an audience in New York that the legislation was anti-democratic. 'The problem is that the legislation is based on the principle of collective responsibility,' he said. 'It prohibits certain persons solely because they belonged to groups defined by their external characteristics. It does not allow their cases to be heard individually. This runs counter to the basic principles of democratic law.'[2]

At home, in the local political scene, Havel was more circumspect. Chastened by Sachergate, he tried various ways of walking the tightrope stretched beween honest public appraisals of the Communist past and the current and future need to drain off the poisons of fear and revenge. He sided with those who feared the worst by confessing that his own blood had curdled after being handed a big, official-looking envelope, sealed and stamped, containing details of his candidacy for the Writers' Union in the mid-1960s.[3] But he also sided with those who were unprepared to forgive and forget. He agreed that those who had committed clearly defined crimes should be brought to justice – and that (as the Czechs say) the only way to wash a staircase is from the top. He agreed as well that there needed to be public acknowledgement of the sufferings of the victims of Communism, especially of people killed or tortured. 'Parliament's desire to purge the public service is entirely legitimate,' he said. Lustration was 'a necessary law, an extraordinary law, a rigorous law'. So, he continued, he had no alternative but to sign the lustration bill into law. Otherwise the whole body politic would have suffered a convulsion following a head-on collision between the presidency and the parliament.

After confirming the lustration act, Havel submitted a letter to the parliament announcing that he would seek to amend the legislation, to ensure that every citizen should have the individual right to subpoena witnesses and cross-examine their accusers in an independent court. The letter pointed to the need to institutionalize free speech, but it was deliberately not worded in legalese. No parliamentary debate was required. The strategy of

---

[1] Both quotations are from Jeri Laber, 'Witch Hunt in Prague', *The New York Review of Books* (23 April 1992), p. 8.
[2] From a speech in acceptance of an honorary doctorate awarded by New York University, 27 October 1991, reprinted in *Toward a Civil Society*, op. cit., p. 158.
[3] In an interview with Dana Emingerová and Luboš Beniak, 'Nejistota posiluje', *Mladý svět* (Prague), 13 May 1991, p. 16.

soft compromise with lustration was typical. Mostly, Havel stuck to generalized disapprovals of the whole business. He notably refused to discuss particular cases. Symptomatic was his calculated public silence about the extraordinary case of Jan Kavan, who had been accused – illegally, it turned out – of being an StB agent who had cleverly disguised himself at Palach Press, an opposition press agency in London.[1] In December 1991, Havel met Jan Kavan and several of his old friends – Petr Uhl and Anna Šabatová – for drinks in a restaurant in central Prague to discuss Kavan's lustration. Havel made it clear to them that he had no doubt that the allegations about Kavan were false. Kavan was encouraged. But Havel went on to say that the whole case had become so politicized that it was impossible for him as President to take sides publicly. He was unable to pour water on a hot case that the ignorant said proved that where there is smoke there must be fire. Havel explained that it would put him on a confrontation course with the current government, especially because the matter was *sub judice*, and would remain so until the courts handed down a decision. Kavan left the meeting with a good feeling of having been vindicated privately, although Havel – playing the role of prudent politician – had his agreement that the detailed contents of their discussion would not be divulged publicly to journalists.[2]

Havel's tactic revealed a subtle but important change that had now descended upon his presidency. He had evidently bidden farewell to his old noble habit of drawing black–and–white distinctions between 'truth' and 'lies'. Before entering official politics, he had always insisted that the truth is always the truth. When asked what living in the truth actually meant, he always answered along the lines of Polonius: 'To thine own self be true / And it must follow, as the night the day / Thou canst not then be false to any man.' Truth is within ourselves, he told Antoine Spire shortly after his long spell in prison, it is a matter for our consciences, and its public expression is always justified, even in the face of threats and throttling.[3] Once upon a time, even further back in his career, he liked to draw the corresponding distinction – famously

---

[1] An account of Kavan's case appears in Lawrence Weschler, *Calamities of Exile* (Chicago, 1998), pp. 63–135.
[2] Interview with Senator Jan Kavan, Prague, 23 September 1997.
[3] William Shakespeare, *Hamlet, Prince of Denmark*, Act 1, Scene 3; compare the almost identical formulation in the typewritten and hand-corrected samizdat interview, originally conducted by Antoine Spire in Prague, and finally dated 3 April 1983.

outlined during the Prague Spring to Antonín Liehm – between truth-loving intellectuals and politicians who perforce are slaves to power. 'The reason intellectuals make such poor politicians,' he told Liehm, 'is that they are used to serving the interests of truth rather than using truth as a means of serving the needs of power.'[1] Using truth cautiously, as a means of repairing and oiling the machinery of state power, and his seat within it, was now a much closer description of his actions. It turned out that the biblical injunction to seek the truth because truth sets us free is not always true. Lustration taught Havel that in official politics there is indeed no such thing as pure freedom of speech. He came to see that truths are sometimes out of season, that truth, like fruits, should only be plucked when ripe. Havel learned to watch his words. He learned the value of 'tact, the proper instincts, and good taste'.[2] He understood that politics loves politesse – that presidential power is a friend of *measured* truth.

[1] *The Politics of Culture*, op. cit., p. 374.
[2] Václav Havel, *Summer Meditations on Politics, Morality and Civility in a Time of Transition* (London and Boston, 1992), p. 11.

MARKET POWER

Baroness Thatcher – bright-red lipstick, bouffant blue-rinsed hair, blue suit, matching bag – calls for Scotch on the rocks for two, in honour of her friend's swanky performance. Drinks promptly arrive in cut-crystal glasses, on a silver platter, courtesy of an unsmiling waiter wearing white gloves. The two friends engage in polite conversation, flanked by several hundred admirers attending a public lecture sponsored by London's Institute of Economic Affairs. At an opportune moment of silence, the unknown author of a forthcoming biography of Václav Havel butts in politely to ask the Iron Lady's friend, Dr Václav Klaus, what he thinks of his country's President. 'He is a half-socialist,' says Klaus, in a frank mood, pursing his lips. 'He has always been in favour of collective solutions. His speeches about so-called civil society are just the latest version of the same dogma. He is in love with state power.'[1]

So few words, so much confidence. The public lecture that he had just delivered – in honour of the well-known Austrian economist Friedrich von Hayek, the darling of contemporary neo-liberalism – was equally strident. In a chandeliered ballroom setting – it was a full house of 300 invited guests – Dr Klaus had tried to convince his audience that he and his colleagues had begun to transform the Czech Republic into a free-market paradise. What was once among the most Stalinist states of the Warsaw Pact empire was now the most vibrant, bustling, and open society in the region, potentially an economy that could in future outpace the economic performance of its long-established Western democratic neighbours. It had taken great determination and fortitude to shift a whole nation of people from totalitarian servitude to a market system of liberty, but he and his government colleagues had managed it. The catastrophe of socialism was that it had turned an aquarium into fish soup. It had posed a massive challenge: to turn fish soup back into an aquarium. And it had been done, thanks to one of the most remarkable privatization plans in modern history.

Klaus went on to explain that elsewhere in the post-Communist bloc, in Poland and Hungary for instance, privatization had been carried out without clear legal rules. That had led many investors

[1]From my conversation with Václav Klaus after he delivered the Hayek Memorial Lecture, London, 17 June 1997.

– both domestic and foreign – to discover with regret that they did not have clear legal title to their investments. So rather than lurch haphazardly into quasi-market reforms and 'spontaneous privatization', Klaus and his government had insisted upon the systematic re-creation of the foundations of an efficient market and a free society – the rule of law, clearly defined property rights, an efficient system of contract. The so-called voucher scheme was exemplary of this strategy. The starting point of the scheme, Klaus argued, was to take the ideologists of socialism at their word when they insisted that state properties and industries 'belonged to the people'. Vouchers were accordingly offered for sale at a nominal price to all citizens of Czechoslovakia. A system of auctions and bids had been created to enable the transfer of ownership of property into private hands. There it belonged, Klaus said. And the scheme had been enormously successful, he concluded. It had created widespread public support for privatization. It had proved to be an efficient way of transferring ownership rights from an irresponsible state to responsible private parties. And – since power and property are twins, as the seventeenth-century English political thinker James Harrington famously observed – the voucher system of privatization had laid the foundations for a political system capable of maximizing its citizens' freedom.

Throughout the lecture, and in the question period that followed, Klaus presented his case with great polish and dignity – and got roundly applauded for it. Those who know him well and who have worked around him often say that he is a shrewd political actor who in his dealings with others can be ruthlessly calculating. It might even be said, with a touch of exaggeration, that Klaus's political style in fact resembled that of a late twentieth-century Septimius Severus, the Roman emperor much admired by Machiavelli.[1] The Czech Septimius Severus – tortoiseshell glasses, short grey hair, smart suits and ties – naturally had a late-modern look about him. But, like his Roman predecessor, the Czech Septimius had learned to combine the arts of manly charm and decency with the political qualities of a savage lion and a tricky fox. These qualities were first noted by others during Klaus's first dealings, on behalf of Civic Forum, with the Communists during the Velvet Revolution. Then an economist at the Institute of

[1]Niccolò Machiavelli, *Il principe*, chapter 18.

Forecasting of the Czechoslovak Academy of Sciences, he quickly
proved himself to be a good organizer, a tough bargainer, and a
brilliant spokesman for the neo-liberal alternative to late-socialism.
He developed a reputation for resolution, professionalism, and a
big ego – so big that it later spawned the commonplace joke that
the only difference between God and Václav Klaus is that God
doesn't think that He's Václav Klaus.

The Czech Septimius Severus played an active role in the
co-ordinating committee of Civic Forum and, under the so-called
Government of National Understanding led by Prime Minister
Marián Čalfa, he had been rewarded with the post of Minister
of Finance. He was not only a competent economist but also
a talented political animal who had a sharp ear for what people
were saying and thinking. He was unafraid of telling people
about unpleasant realities or of taking risks. He proved that he
was an ambitious fighter by deciding to run for office for Civic
Forum in the June 1990 elections. He was convinced he could
win anywhere, so he chose to stand in a coal-mining district of
northern Moravia, in one of the inhospitable heartlands of the
Communist Party – and won. Klaus soon after (13 October 1990)
surprised many observers by winning 70 per cent of delegates'
votes for the post of Chairman of Civic Forum at its Congress
held in the Prague district of Hostivař. There should have been
no surprise. For several months, he and his supporters had been
very active, especially in the regional structures of Civic Forum.
They had ambitions, as became evident in April 1991, when Civic
Forum split and the breakaway Civic Democratic Party (ODS)
was founded in Olomouc, in opposition to Jiří Dienstbier's Civic
Movement (OH) party, which remained sympathetic to Havel.

Klaus, by now playing the political role of Septimius Severus
with confidence, made publicly known his strong dislike of Civic
Movement's undisciplined, left-wing laziness. Many within Civic
Movement responded with the charge of careerism, which was
true. Klaus worked hard to model his party on Mrs Thatcher's
Conservative Party. The Civic Democratic Party was supposed
to be a party of self-confident and enterprising individuals who
together would accelerate the drive to post-Communism by
legislating for the reintroduction of a market economy. Convinced that socialism was just a short and disastrous interlude
between capitalism and capitalism, he was for the strong state

and the free market. Despite claims to the contrary, Klaus always seemed less than interested in legal and political reforms for the sake of democracy. It was the mark of a man whose theories of free-market economics were formed during the period of late-socialism. Unlike the earlier advocates of democratic 'market socialism', Ota Šik for instance, Klaus worked during the 1970s and 1980s for the introduction of a free-market economy, if possible under the rubric of a powerful (late-socialist) state. With the outbreak of revolution, that Utopian vision of a free market suddenly became practical. Klaus lost no time in pushing the principles of free-market economics – using bossy political tactics and existing state structures wherever possible.

Both the aims and methods of the politics of the 'strong state, free market' contradicted the crowned republic, and put Klaus on a collision course with Havel. Their friendship got off to a bad start during the revolution, when at one point in an early meeting with the state authorities, Havel, effectively the leader of Civic Forum, introduced Klaus to the other side as 'Václav Wolf'. Klaus reportedly winced at the absent-minded – or unconsciously motivated – slip.[1] The mutual respect thereafter dissolved in the emerging acids of party politics, so that by the summer of 1990, when Klaus was already an important force in both Civic Forum and the government (as Minister of Finance) Havel – still dreaming of a crowned republic – tried hard to get rid of him by offering him the post of Governor of the National Bank of Czechoslovakia. Septimius refused to take the poisoned bait. By now he was a seasoned political creature. He correctly sensed that Havel was mainly worried about threats to the presidency. Klaus responded by trying to clip Havel's political wings using every available sharp instrument. He built a new power base by campaigning for the founding of the new Civic Democratic Party, which he soon ruled, unchallenged. After becoming Czech Prime Minister in June 1992, Klaus also put the frighteners on Havel by proposing the idea that the then Prime Minister of the Federal Republic, Jan Stráský, be considered as the next serious candidate for the presidency of the country.

Then there was the ongoing political war of nerves that Klaus waged against Havel. Neutral observers frequently noted Klaus's

---

[1]Interview with Ivan Havel, Prague, 23 April 1996.

pretended omnipotence: his political unwillingness to listen to anybody and his penchant for treating his opponents as children, or as morons. Another observer, sympathetic to Havel, noted the different political characters of the rivalling Václavs. In certain contexts, the President 'might think that he knows what's true and right, and that his opponent is an idiot. But he would never put it that way. Normally, he is reflective, tentative, and gives no simple answers'. Klaus, by contrast, always 'understood something of the psychology of winning power over others by aggression'. He always had 'a perfectly prepared strategy, which typically began with a punch in his opponent's stomach. He detested "wetness", even though, after conquering his opponent, he could pour on the charm.'[1]

Behind the scenes, the different political styles produced considerable friction, as when the two men appeared on a nationwide television talk-show filmed in Brno, in December 1992. Before their appearance, which was hosted by the well-known presenter Antonín Přidal and featured several other guests, everyone gathered in a hotel lounge to have drinks. The mood was friendly – until Septimius arrived, late, hobbling along on crutches, nursing a leg recently injured while playing tennis. The atmosphere stiffened. It did not improve after the group moved to the dinner table. Everybody began to stare at their plates as Septimius rounded on each guest in turn. In a loud voice he told Přidal, who turned as pale as a ghost, that his programme was full of intellectual bullshit. Septimius then attacked another guest for his Europhilia. 'Brussels! A socialist nightmare that we must live without!' he snarled. Septimius then ticked off Havel, who ate his dinner in silence. Septimius went on to sermonize against intellectuals, whom he denounced as useless and sometimes dangerous meddlers in the world of power. After everybody had been told off, the party moved to the state television studios, where Václav Klaus was in fine – dynamic, buoyant – form. Like a bull at a gate baying for blood, Klaus charged at his opponents, including the shaken Havel, who spent the session defending himself with tentative statements and complicated formulae. After the filming was over, the whole group returned to the hotel for a parting drink. Suddenly, Septimius Severus became genial, charming

[1]Interview with Jacques Rupnik, Paris, 29 April 1998.

even. He offered around the drinks, even though nobody felt like drinking with him. After a few minutes, sensing his absence to be imperative, Klaus left, with handshakes and smiles. The rest of the group, including Havel, slowly recovered, as if from a foiled encounter with a charming bully. They stayed on until half-past three in the morning, reminiscing, chatting and joking.

The Brno encounter was not atypical, for Havel often felt unnerved by the political abrasiveness of Klaus. Havel, never a morning person, found especially unpleasant his opponent's early-morning telephone calls, beginning with impossible statements like, 'I can't believe that you said what you did yesterday,' or unfriendly questions like, 'So can you tell me where we now stand?' Nearly every Wednesday morning, when the two met at the Castle for a briefing session, staff noted that the polite Havel would tense up beforehand, unsure of how today he would handle the 'attacking sarcasm'[1] and other rough tactics of his unpredictable opponent. The tension was compounded by an ever-lengthening history of spats over one matter or another. Many of them were traceable ultimately to Klaus's hard-headed, savage-minded economism – and to his intense dislike of Havel's defensive resort to philosophical abstractions like 'the crisis of humanity' and the need for 'human decency'. Klaus had one – only one, but historically big – Idea, and he repeated it constantly to Havel's face. The Big Idea: no post-Communist society can become successful unless it quickly develops a dynamic and fully modern market-based system of commodity production and exchange. Compared with the unproductive stagnation of late-socialism, Klaus argued, economies driven by commodity production and exchange have the great advantage of enhancing their overall power by minimizing collective losses. Market forces ensure that factors of production that fail to perform according to the current (international) standards of efficiency are continuously and swiftly eliminated and forced to find alternative, more productive uses. Factors of production that are 'uncompetitive' go the wall. Klaus's Big Idea, in other words, was that markets mimic Abraham Lincoln's famous maxim that those who need a helping hand should look no further than the end of their right

---

[1]From the essay on Klaus by Petr Nováček in *Týden* (Prague), 8 December 1997, pp. 30–34. The same point was made in my interviews with Pavel Tigrid, Prague, 18 September 1996, and Prince Karel Schwarzenberg, Prague, 19 September 1997.

arm. In this way, markets invite the victims of competition to blame themselves – and to survive and then thrive by adapting to new standards of efficiency.

Ever since his teenage years, Havel had had difficulty with these arguments. He complained to his Thirty-Sixer friend Radim Kopecký about the supposed principle that life is 'an eternal struggle, tough, even cynical and merciless egoism'.[1] The sixteen-year-old Havel tried to stake out the countervailing principle of 'soft humanism'. Sympathy for others was important, for no society could function without it, he insisted. Kopecký replied by accusing him of supposing that he somehow was living in the ancient world, in which the separation of markets from morality, politics and law went unrecognized. Modern times are different, Kopecký argued. Private property, market competition and its corresponding values of individualism tinged with nihilism are today unavoidable, whatever Communists and socialists and other moralists might think or say.[2]

Many years later, thanks to the aggressive political rhetoric and manoeuvring of Klaus, Havel was forced in practice to live with a competitive party system and – a greater humiliation – to acknowledge the domestic and international imperative of developing the *non-state* institution of legally guaranteed market forces. Klaus taught him, against his will, that the ideal of a crowned republic was just that, and that instead there must be *economic* limits placed upon the scope and power of state institutions. Thanks to Klaus, the subjects of the crowned republic endured tremendous structural change: output from the private sector quickly eclipsed state production; the proportion of working people employed in agriculture dropped three times; most of Czechoslovak trade switched to OECD countries; while during 1991 alone, real wages fell by 30 per cent. It might even be said that Klaus's greatest political success against Havel was to force all Czechoslovaks to wake up suddenly to market realities – by giving each of them a taste of what it is like to return to medieval times, when (in matters such as military service, marriage and spiritual salvation) many more activities than now, paradoxically, were considered tradable items with a price tag attached.

[1]Havel to Kopecký (Prague, 17 December 1952).
[2]Kopecký to Havel (Prague, 16 December 1952); Kopecký to Havel (Prague, 28 December 1952).

There was a further irony produced by the tussle between Klaus and Havel. In attempting to counter the rise of Klaus, who threatened his sovereign power, Havel eventually latched on to two effective themes – democracy and civil society – that implied the need to draw stricter limits upon his own power. Not only did Havel come to accept the indispensable role of markets. He also came to call publicly for more democracy and to acknowledge the *non-state* sources of social morality and co-operation that both democratic institutions and markets require to function as markets.

Havel's defence of democracy against his opponent's mean-spirited politics was evident in a widely reported speech before the chandeliered Czech Parliament in the spring of 1996.[1] Arriving to the sounds of Smetana's *Fanfáry*, standing before a forest of microphones, dressed in a smart black suit and a matching black-and-white-striped tie and pocket handerkerchief, sporting glasses, sipping water, a frog permanently in his throat, Václav Klaus looking on over his shoulder, Havel talked earnestly, in long sentences for over an hour, about the importance of democracy in the Czech Republic. He acknowledged the common-sense understanding of democracy as a form of rule that sub-divides the powers of making, implementing and adjudicating laws. Democracy is 'free competition among different political parties, the rule of law, the principle of civic equality', he added. But he went on to emphasize that democracy must not be treated merely as a technical mechanism (*soustava*), or as a political machine (*soustrojí*). Democracy, he proposed, is 'a certain attitude towards the world'.

What kind of attitude? Václav Klaus momentarily looked away and down as Havel began to speak of humility. 'Democracy is a way of being [*způsob bytí*],' he argued. It nurtures and thrives upon 'respect for others, honesty, creative work, good manners and taste, solidarity and respect for the cultures of different social groups and nations'. Democracy is the rule of humility. *Hubris* is anathema to it, since democracy thrives on the humble willingness 'to behave as one expects others to behave'. Democracy demands humility towards the underdog. Respect for a minority by a majority is required in a democracy. So is 'humility towards the order and

[1]Česká televize 2 (Prague), 12 March 1996.

beauty of nature, as well as humility towards the beauty of things created by previous generations'. Democracy is a political system in which the exercise of power over people and power over matter, being inseparable, must be publicly controlled. Democracy cultivates a shared sense of the fallibility of human beings living in the natural world, which means, he concluded, that the quest for democracy must be 'a never-ending obligation' humbled by the awareness of its own fragility.

In the same speech on humility – it earned him long applause – Havel emphasized the need to cultivate a tolerant and open civil society. There were many sources of Havel's deep interest in the subject.[1] Struggling to find a public language in which to do battle with the fox- and lion-like Klaus, Havel was forced to call into question his own earlier presumption that a crowned republic led by a charismatic *Ichspieler* could serve effectively to replace the Communist order. In this and other speeches and writings, Havel began to develop a brilliant modern idea: that economic actors always and everywhere go about their business and do their work, and can only ever do so, insofar as they tap into, and cultivate, sources of 'social capital'. A market economy, he insisted, can only function as such if its members are 'embedded' in a wider civil society that harbours social interaction based on such norms as trust, reliability, punctuality, honesty, friendship, resolution, the capacity for group commitment, humility, and non-violent mutual recognition.

The point against Klaus was put with special force from the time of his 1992 New Year's Address to the Nation. 'Dear friends, I wish you success in your work in the New Year', he said. He added the kind of words that always irritated Klaus: 'I wish you health, peace, steady nerves, much patience, hope, and strength, and that you will all understand and help one another.' He went on: 'We must face difficulties and people of ill-will with a wise and united perseverance. In an atmosphere of decency, creativity, tolerance and a quiet resolution, we shall bear far more easily the trials we have yet to experience, and resolve all the large problems

---

[1]See the contributions by Havel and others to John Keane (ed.), *Civil Society and the State. New European Perspectives* (London, 1988; reissued 1998). Compare his interesting comment, written in 1988, on the dustjacket of *Democracy and Civil Society*, op. cit.: 'The various political shifts and upheavals within the communist world all have one thing in common: the undying urge to create a genuine civil society.'

we must yet face.'[1] The sentiments were arguably more than a principled reminder that markets require morality. Havel was taking political aim at what elsewhere he called the 'Wild West mentality' unleashed by post–Communist conditions. 'Spreading corruption, gold-fever, and the view that life is a jungle and so man must be a brute to man', he said, 'all these are simply the most familiar manifestations of that strange condition of a society in which the values of a totalitarian state have collapsed and the values of civil society have not yet come to fruition.'[2] Havel here pointed, by implication, to the widespread looting of state assets in the name of privatization, for instance the practice of 'tunnelling' out of assets by majority shareholders taking advantage of inadequate protection by securities laws for minority shareholder rights. Havel was also in effect criticizing the Klausite uncivil effects of the obsession with state-backed privatization, especially for its blindness towards the way markets tend to 'fail', in the process weakening or destroying the structures of civil society upon which they otherwise depend for their survival and growth. Havel mentioned no examples, many of which however spring readily to mind. For instance: market forces tend to spread into all the nooks and crannies of social life, so violating the plurality of *non-market* voices and identities – friendship, household life, religiosity, community life – that are otherwise crucial to the functioning of market forces. Market forces also suffer from a certain blindness towards losers: in market competition, certain groups and individuals, and sometimes whole regions and countries, necessarily lose, and yet such losses cannot be dealt with by markets, exactly because losses ('externalities', Klaus calls them) are easily translatable into 'price signals' and market criteria. Such 'market failures', Havel implied, demonstrate that market interaction cannot create the vital ingredients of social order upon which it otherwise depends. Klaus was blind to a basic 'law' of modern market economies: where there is no flourishing civil society, there can be no flourishing markets.

[1]'New Year's Address to the Nation' (Prague, 1 January 1992), in Václav Havel, *Toward a Civil Society. Selected Speeches and Writings 1990–1994* (Prague, 1995), p. 174. Compare the tougher words against Klaus in 'A Crying Need for Intellectuals: an interview', *The New Presence* (April 1999), p. 16: 'He sees things solely in terms of responsible individuals, the blind laws of the market and a centralized state: everything else he regards as nonsense. It is a very short-sighted, political attitude – if not actually suicidal.'
[2]*1992 & 1993*, op. cit., pp. 90, 53–54.

VELVET DIVORCE

On the thundery summer's afternoon of 17 July 1992, members of the Slovak National Council – the Slovakian parliament – gathered at two o'clock in the old parliament building nestled under the Bratislava Castle on the banks of the Danube. A beautiful setting indeed for ugly business. Before the Council lay the job of deciding the future of the people, property and international standing of the Slovak lands. Members hushed as the Convenor began to read out the motion for the last time. The question was apparently straightforward: Did those members of the Council present in the chamber support or not the proposed Declaration of Sovereignty of the Slovak Nation?

Since the matter had been debated repeatedly during the past weeks, no discussion was allowed. Some dissenting members tried to disrupt the proceedings with shouted quips and questions. But the gag was vigorously applied, and the vote taken. By acclamation, out of 147 deputies, 113 voted for the motion, 10 abstained, and 24 deputies, most of them from Hungarian minority parties, bravely voted against. An hour later, upon hearing news of the vote relayed instantly by telephone to the Castle in Prague, a wrinkle-faced Havel announced to an agitated press pack his resignation as President of the Czech and Slovak Federated Republic. The country that had lasted seventy-five years had begun to end. Suddenly, and unexpectedly, the provincial city on the Danube was to become the capital city of a new state. The hope that post-1989 Czechoslovakia would prove to be a model multinational post-Communist democratic state, and that accordingly it would play a major stabilizing role in central Europe, was smashed to pieces. The leader of the crowned republic had already lost much ground to personal defections, parliamentary obstruction, a newborn party system, and the privatization of property. Now, with the loss of half his realm, the *Ichspieler* had suffered a decisive blow. An important phase of Havel's political career – like many political careers – had ended in ruinous failure.

The evening headlines on television and radio, and in the next morning's press, were divided. In Prague, few welcomed his resignation and most were stunned into speechlessness, as if they had just received an unexpected electric shock from an unknown source. But there were also some who spoke of his departure from the Castle as an inevitable consequence of the deep-rooted enmity between the country's two predominant nations. According to this view, common among the hard-headed nationalist minds of the political elite of the republic, the ideal of a common Czechoslovak state had been doomed from the country's birth. The moment of birth of Czechoslovakia, a state populated primarily by Czechs and Slovaks, but also by Hungarians, Germans, Ukrainians and Poles, was also its moment of death. Czechoslovakia, on this view, was always an ill-conceived, artificial construction, which without external support and under external pressure would have disintegrated much earlier. So its moment of reckoning had finally arrived.

This nationalist view supposed that the history of Czechoslovakia resembled a ragged band of carriaged travellers bumping their way along a rocky path that led past the camouflaged hiding place of a man of decision called Procrustes, who at an opportune moment one midsummer's afternoon pounced unexpectedly on the carriage, dragged its occupants into his secluded stone cottage, flung them on a stretching rack, and tightened his ropes to the point where their state simply snapped in two. The view that there was a hidden logic of tragedy within Czechoslovakia, and that it triumphed finally in Bratislava in the Declaration of Sovereignty of the Slovak Nation, was a dangerous, if useful fiction. It was dangerous inasmuch as it fed the nationalist presumption that all nations are caught up in an animal struggle for survival, and that only the fittest survive. It was exactly this presumption that had fuelled the flames of the Yugoslav conflict going on at the same time. At the heart of the ideology of nationalism – and among the most peculiar features of its 'grammar' – is its simultaneous treatment of its opponents as everything and nothing. Nationalists, strictly defined, warn of the menace to their own way of life by those who are alien. The Other is viewed as a (potential) knife in the throat of the Nation, and nationalists are therefore driven by friend–foe calculations. Yet nationalists not only suffer from a judgement disorder that convinces them that Other nations live at their own expense. Nationalism is also arrogant, confidently portraying the Other as a worthless zero, as inferior rubbish. It follows that the Other is unworthy of respect or recognition, that it has few if any entitlements, not even when it constitutes a majority or minority of the surrounding population. Nationalists consequently suffer from a single-minded arrogance that leads them to label the Other as worthless, to taunt and spit at them or, in the extreme case, to press for their expulsion – or murder, even.[1]

This image of the dangerous logic of nationalism is necessarily simplified, but within the Czechoslovak political class that emerged out of the Velvet Revolution there were certainly Czech and Slovak nationalists in this sense. They quickly found out that the rhetoric of nationalism was a politically useful fiction. It nourished the lives of two types of political animals: 'excretory' Czech nationalists, for whom the split-up of Czechoslovakia through the excretion of Slovakia represented a final triumph of 'pure' Czech statehood; and backward-looking Slovak nationalists, for whom the Declaration represented the final emancipation of the Slovaks as a captive nation – a positive contribution to the process of disintegration of old political boundaries triggered by the Versailles system formed after 1918.

The odd thing about these nationalist tensions is just how absent they were immediately after the revolution, that is, not much more than two years before the Slovak declaration of sovereignty. The point is important, since it suggests that the fiction that Czechoslovakia was a tragedy waiting to happen was groundless. It overlooked the most obvious three facts of all: that the difficulties between the Slovak and Czech lands were not somehow in the blood of their peoples; that the tensions that surfaced between the political elites of the two nations were mainly caused by Czech lethargy about Slovak grievances; and that the velvet divorce, as it was later to be called, was never popular with the citizens of either the Czech or Slovak lands of the country.

Havel himself quickly grasped the latter point. It was a paradox, because for many months before the announced carve-up of the country popular opinions about the past, present and future had become ever more agitated. For most people, post-Communism meant disorientation. Standards of living seemed to fall, jobs were insecure, services declined, existing political institutions

---

[1]See my discussion of national identity and nationalism in *Civil Society: Old Images, New Visions*, op. cit., pp. 79–113.

and political leaders felt ever less competent, as Havel anxiously noted in an interview with Stanislava Dufková at Hrádeček in early November 1991. 'We are living in a time of peculiar – I would say – social and pyschological chaos,' he said in the conversation that was transmitted a day later on Czechoslovak Radio. 'People are unsettled by the fact that they cannot see firm order, structure of values, or orderly community life anywhere. Everything has been thrown into uncertainty. The whole legal system and the constitutional set-up are uncertain. Political parties are quarrelling among themselves. They attack each other. Everybody says something different. Everybody proposes something different. It is not known what the reform will bring or what social shocks it will cause.'[1]

Given this climate of profound uncertainty bordering on chaos, it might have been expected that Czechoslovaks would have grasped for certainties. Appeals to the Nation might have been expected to work like a magic healing potion capable of restoring a sense of balance in their personal lives. But virtually the opposite happened. With daily life in a state of extreme flux, large numbers of people took shelter in the safe harbours of the given state. Czechoslovakia took on a new meaning as a bedrock of their existence. So in the autumn of 1991 Havel moved to harness this popular conservatism by calling for a state-wide referendum to decide the future of the country. The tactic – appealing over the heads of institutions to *il popolo*, to preserve the state – was discussed at length with his close friend and adviser, Pavel Tigrid, who agreed to organize a petition for signatures in support of the status quo. It was to be called *Za společný stát* (For a Common State),

The call for a referendum correctly read the aggregate public mood. By the summer of 1992, opinion polls showed more than eight out of ten respondents agreed that the future shape of the state should be determined not by politicians, but by citizens themselves.[2] The petition collected nearly 2 million signatures, mostly in Bohemia and Moravia. Yet Havel's whole tactic of campaigning

[1] Stanislava Dufková, 'Hovory z Lán', an interview with President Václav Havel recorded at Hrádeček on 2 November 1991, broadcast on Československy Rozhlas Radio Network at 13.15 GMT on 3 November 1991.
[2] Sharon Wolchik, 'The Politics of Ethnicity in Post-Communist Czechoslovakia', *East European Politics and Societies*, 8, 1 (1994), p. 178.

for a referendum failed for a variety of reasons. It pandered to the presumption, traceable to the eighteenth century, that every nation is entitled to its own chosen form of government, and in so doing, unwittingly, it highlighted the 'fictionality' of nations living together within a multinational state like Czechoslovakia. A properly conducted referendum might well have produced a clear majority of voters in favour of preserving the country – let us call them Czechoslovaks – but precisely that result would have highlighted the fact that at least a *minority* did not think of itself as 'Czechoslovak', that 'the Czechoslovak nation' was not therefore a univocal entity, and indeed that it was a controversial and contradictory phenomenon, if only because it contained people who thought of themselves primarily as *Czechs* or *Slovaks* – which was precisely the opposite (divisive) effect that Havel had intended.

Exactly this irony surfaced during the early stages of the referendum campaign, which in Slovakia tended to be understood by growing numbers of people as a further example of arrogant Czech efforts to rule Slovakia from Prague.[1] The irony was accentuated by Havel's implicit impatience with the tasks of bargaining and making compromises within a framework of existing constitutional rules and procedures in need of alteration. Immediately after the revolution, Havel (unlike Adolfo Suárez in Spain) made no effort to modify the constitution. In fact, nine months into his presidency he began actively to campaign for its retention. In a major speech to the Federal Assembly in September 1990, he declared himself in favour of the federation and the overwhelming number of 'federal people' who saw it as legitimate. The federation admittedly required some minor tinkering, he recommended; if that were done, the shining example of American federalism should be kept in mind.[2] The speech backfired on him in Slovakia. Jozef Prokeš, the new leader of the Slovak National Party, struck back immediately, in a published open letter. 'Your reference to the American Constitution,' he wrote, 'has left the strong impression that you wish to continue with the ideology of Czechoslovakism,

---

[1]Zdeněk Jičínský, 'Ke ztroskotání československého federalismu', in Rüdiger Kipke and Karel Vodička (eds.), *Rozloučení s Československem* (Prague, 1993), p. 77.
[2]Václav Havel, 'Základ identity splečného státu', *Narodna obroda* (Bratislava), 18 September 1990.

that is to say one nation in this state which, it seems, your statement about a federal people confirms. Until now this has not brought anything good in the relations between Czechs and Slovaks.'[1]

Havel pounced on such criticism. On the first anniversary of the outbreak of the Velvet Revolution, he appeared on television before an audience of several million viewers.[2] He dramatically called on the people to support him against their elected representatives. The *Ichspieler*'s performance was dramatic, but revealing of the degree to which his strategy suffered from political nausea – from an active disregard for the flawed power of the given institutional procedures of the Czechoslovak state inherited from the Communists. Havel seemed to underestimate the severe irritation to the body politic caused by the Soviet-style federal constitution inherited from the '89 revolution. Although this constitution was not wholly a child of Soviet 'normalization', it nonetheless was stamped with the marks of that period. It resembled (as Havel's friend and Prime Minister from 1990 to 1992, Petr Pithart, noted) a two-member union of governments that made federation in the strict sense impossible, since there was in effect no way of voting to resolve differences between the two parties.[3] The system was pseudo-federal. The system presupposed the existence of two separate constitutions which in truth did not exist, if only because *de facto* power was exercised absolutely through the Party-state organs (the KSC or Czech Communist Party and, nominally, the KSS, or Slovak Communist Party). Each nation was excessively protected from the laws of its neighbour, for instance by strong rights of veto and, ultimately, by the right to secession that the law on the Czechoslovak federation of 1968 guaranteed to both republics.

Havel's impatience with negotiations and his resort to the referendum principle not only underestimated the burdens of the old constitution – and the urgent need to alter it. His antipolitical impatience also failed to foresee the ways in which that constitution

[1]Jozef Prokeš, 'Otvorené list prezidentovi SFR', *Slovenská národ* (Bratislava), 24 October 1990.
[2]Karl-Peter Schwarz, *Tschechen und Slowaken: Der lange Weg zur friedlichen Trennung* (Vienna, 1993), p. 222.
[3]Interview with Petr Pithart (Scheinfeld), 15 September 1996. See also his 'The Break-Up of Czechoslovakia', *Scottish Affairs*, 8 (Summer 1994), pp. 20–24.

produced bitter divisions about its future – so bitter in fact that the status quo, which Havel implicitly supported, became simply untenable. It is true that the Czech–Slovak struggle was conducted without threats of violence. The outbreak of war in the former Yugoslavia and the bloody birthpangs of the Russian Federation served as a warning to the political elites of every persuasion that *violent* nationalism was to be avoided at all costs. Hence the *velvet* nature of the dispute – the constant emphasis on the need to end the federation 'in an orderly manner', 'without hysteria', 'intelligently', and always with due respect for procedural rules. But still, from the outset, negotiations were marked by great bitterness, which raises the pertinent question of whether, or to what degree, Havel's own behaviour was salt to the festering wound.

There were some observers and participants who insisted that the Slovak withdrawal from the federation was in no small measure traceable to Havel's personal behaviour as President. An old Slovak adage that a nightingale must be judged by what it sings arguably applied well to Havel, whose popularity within Slovakia gradually diminished from the time of the revolution. Up to and during the revolution, many had loved him as a Czechoslovak patriot. He seemed to have no strong feelings of nationality and he certainly despised Czech and Slovak folklore, which the Communists had used as a cultural weapon to combat modernist and cosmopolitan cultural trends. His younger brother was married to a Slovak, and many Slovaks knew, by word of mouth, that he had received a rapturous reception in Bratislava during a public concert featuring Joan Baez. And immediately after assuming the presidency, Havel's immense popularity as the shining symbol of the country's hopes for the future had undoubtedly been fixed by his public appearances with Alexander Dubček, himself a Slovak who spoke Slovak, unlike others who went to Prague and spoke only Czech, a man who symbolized both the dramatic failure of the Prague Spring and a man with a sense of humour and a sense of justice who had suffered much under 'normalization'.

But Havel's reputation among the Slovaks was shakier than it seemed. Trouble brewed well before the revolution, indeed right back to the period of the launch of Charter 77, which eventually attracted a thousand Czech signatories, whereas only fifty Slovaks

signed. There was at the time some feeling in Bratislava, where
there were no embassies and, hence, none of the links to the
outside world which the embassies provided the regime's opponents, that everything important involved going though Prague.
And it seemed that people in Prague complemented this picture
of themselves by talking of Slovakia as a poor and primitively
beautiful place for walking through spring fields, swimming in
summery lakes, crossing swelling autumn rivers, or skiing in
wintery mountain snows. Immediately after the revolution, this
Slovak suspicion of Czech indifference began to be trained on
Havel himself.

During and immediately after the revolution, some recalled,
leaders from Bratislava came to talk to Havel about the Civic
Forum apparatus in Slovakia, only to be sent packing by him,
with the advice that they should set up their own organization,
later to be called the Public Against Violence. People noted as
well how Havel's ears blocked out talk that the capital of the
federation should be in Brno, which is halfway between Prague
and Bratislava. It was noted too that no Slovak politician was
close to Havel; that he never read Slovak newspapers, which
were anyway unavailable in Prague; that he was unaware that
there was a festering Slovak problem, even hints that he seemed
to treat Slovaks as nice Catholic peasants who lived in the
mountains, but whose education out of the old (fascist) ways
would take time. Havel remained unmoved by the whispered
criticisms, but his reputation suffered its first serious setback
in Bratislava circles when he decided, under pressure from his
advisers, to travel to Munich and Berlin to meet Chancellor
Kohl in the first week of January 1990. It was his first foreign
visit as the new head of state and, indeed, his first visit outside
of Prague. The symbolism was obvious – the newly integrating,
still powerful neighbour Germany was an obvious priority – but
in Bratislava the visit was received as a slap in the face with a wet
Czech carp.

Relations worsened during the preparations, in February 1990,
for Havel's visit to Washington and other North American capital
cities. Juraj Mihálik, a sculptor turned international relations
'specialist' on the twelve-member Co-ordinating Committee of
the Revolution, reported that the delegation consisted of over
200 people. The new government rang from Prague, presumably

with Havel's consent, to announce that the number of Slovaks in the delegation had to be reduced from eight to four. There were howls of protest from Bratislava, and the number was put back to eight.[1] Slovaks in governing circles were even more astonished by the subsequent trip to Israel at the end of March 1990. The delegation included not a single Slovak politician; although there were two representatives of the Slovak Jewish community, the planned absence of Slovak politicians made it difficult to organize an official apology from the new Slovakia for the terrible crimes heaped upon Jews by the old Slovakia. It was as if Havel's men and women were bent on shoring up an old stereotype: Czechs were progressive, intelligent, liberal, whereas Slovaks were unreliable, anti-Semitic, unrepresentative of the newly freed Czechoslovakia. In the end, Milan Kňažko, a popular film, television and theatre actor, one of the leaders of the revolution in Bratislava and at the time Havel's single Slovak adviser at the Castle, went to Israel to make a speech of apology on behalf of the Slovakian population. Kňažko's political career never subsequently flourished.[2] Although he accepted the post at the Castle on the understanding that he would later become a vice-president – a move that would have been warmly welcomed in Slovakia – the job never materialized. Kňažko instead found himself transformed into an ardent defender of Slovak interests. Open disagreement with Havel and his team ensued. After only several weeks in the Castle, Kňažko lost direct access to the President, who sometimes made his key adviser wait several days before agreeing to meet. Kňažko soon resigned.

The Slovak tensions with Havel thereafter publicly worsened, beginning with the outbreak of the so-called hyphen-war in the spring of 1990. Havel quickly developed a reputation for acting without consultation with the Slovaks – thanks to his (rebuffed) decision to instruct parliament to pass legislation about the country's name. Then there was Havel's announcement that Czechoslovakia was no longer going to produce arms for the world's armies, guerrillas, and gangs. He said publicly that he had given careful consideration to the ethics of the

---

[1] Juraj Mihalík, from the manuscript *Vzpomínky na zlyhania*, cited in Colm Tóibín, *The Sign of the Cross. Travels in Catholic Europe* (London, 1994), p. 234.
[2] *The Sign of the Cross*, op. cit., p. 235.

gargantuan arms trade, and had decided firmly against feeding it further. But somehow he seemed not to see either the
importance of pre-negotiating the matter with a wide variety
of the country's opinion-makers, including those resident in
Slovakia, or that ethical principles can and often do collide,
and that in this case the policy of disarmament, of a sudden
shut-down of arms factories, would have a devastating effect on
the economic and social life of Slovakia, where the arms industry
was primarily based. The principle of opposing the production
of guns in Slovakia overrode the principle of putting butter on
its tables.

And so on, down the slippery slope of enmity. It wasn't long
before Havel became the object of multiplying insults from
Slovak secessionists. The President's clarion call for Czechoslovak
unity 'faded into the voice of a Greek chorus'.[1] In Bratislava,
on 14 March 1991, during celebrations of the establishment of the
Slovak state just prior to the outbreak of World War II, Havel
was attacked by a small but noisy demonstration of between 2,000
and 3,000 people. Communists, fascists, anti-Semites, nationalists
– all of them jeered, cursed and swore whenever Havel's name
was mentioned. Events got out of hand when Havel, without
informing the Slovak Minister of the Interior, began an impromptu
walkabout in the heart of Bratislava while the demonstration
was still taking place. The surprised demonstrators saw it as a
provocation. Local observers added that there was an unusually
large pack of foreign print and radio journalists and camera
crews, and that that implied that the Castle had leaked news
of the President's lightning visit to Bratislava. Whether Havel
intended to attract a counter-demonstration or be martyred is
unclear, but if local opinion in Bratislava is to be believed,
then the President's office must have been delighted with the
pictures and stories of the best-loved politician in the world
being attacked by the primitive peasants of Slovakia. Havel was
spat on, kicked, scratched, and told to fuck off home. It all
seemed to confirm that the Slovaks were the troublemakers. A
few months later, on 28 October 1991, during a rowdy celebration of the founding of Czechoslovakia, he was again attacked

[1] Eric Stein, *Czecho/Slovakia. Ethnic Conflict, Constitutional Fissure, Negotiated Breakup*
(Ann Arbor, 1997), p. 2.

publicly, this time viciously. Havel's reputation in Slovakia was being ruined.

Symptomatic of these changes was the slow downturn in Havel's opinion-poll fortunes in Slovakia. Not much more than a year after the revolution, the person who had symbolically embodied the country's hopes for the future was suffering from popular mistrust. The proportion of Slovaks (60 per cent) willing to believe in him in January 1991 fell considerably below the corresponding levels of trust in the Slovak government (85 per cent). By August of that same year, less than half of Slovaks were willing to trust Havel compared to 84 per cent of Czechs. Although support for him rose somewhat in Slovakia towards the end of the year, and during early 1992, the corresponding level of popular trust remained far lower than in the Czech lands.[1] Throughout this period, Mečiar and Dubček consistently remained the two most popular and trusted politicians in Slovakia, whereas Havel's rating at one point in the autumn of 1991 plummeted to a mere 9 per cent.[2]

Havel's loss of popularity in Slovakia may be seen as the story of the public exposure of his unresolved ambivalence about his own national identity. Prior to the revolution he had always acted, written and spoken as a Czech, as a Czechoslovak, as a European, and as a cosmopolitan. From within this rather syncretic perspective, he took for granted the importance of the principle of national self-determination. On a doorway leading towards the study in his Prague flat there was a prominent red, white and blue sticker that read 'Free Czechoslovakia!'. But what is interesting about his Masaryk-like commitment to Czechoslovakia, especially when one looks carefully at his texts, is just how easily Havel wobbled between feisty declarations of support for the idea of Czechoslovakia and potentially contradictory, mawkish expressions of his underlying Czechness. 'My home is my Czechness, my nationality', he wrote before the break-up, 'and I see no reason whatsoever for not acknowledging this layer of my home; after all, it is as essentially self-evident for me as, for example, that layer of my home which I would call my male

---

[1]Sharon L. Wolchik, 'The Politics of Transition and the Break-Up of Czechoslovakia', in Jiří Musil (ed.), *The End of Czechoslovakia*, op. cit., p. 229.
[2]See 'Komu věří Slováci' ('Whom the Slovaks trust'), *Lidové noviny*, 25 October 1991, p. 2.

sex.'[1] In moments such as these, Havel saw no necessary conflict between the principle of a multinational state and the principle of defending different people's national identity within that state. But when tempers began to flare in the Slovak lands after the revolution, Havel, like many other Czech politicians, was forced to choose between these two principles. They chose to act as the wronged partners of the crumbling federation.

Havel found himself an exponent of what might be called the subtle ideology of Czech clean hands. This ideology, like all ideologies that serve to rationalize particular interests through talk of generalities, ultimately blamed the Slovaks, with their hot-headed nationalism, for destroying the federation. Rather like the politely arrogant man who feels insulted and vindicated by a woman who grows furious at his uncomprehending arrogance and who, if he doesn't change his ways, is then left with no option but to leave or divorce him, many Czechs, Havel included, felt the Slovaks ultimately to be the failed partner of the federation. They were accused of backward-looking emotionalism, and from that accusation it was only a millimetre's jump to condescending talk of how the Czechs had never wanted to stifle the Slovaks' desire for freedom, that Czechs were now sad about the breakdown of the federation, even if in the end Czechs had been made to look like fools for having been so tolerant of their emotionally 'volatile' partners.

In practice, although Havel had flirted with this ideology of Czech clean hands he had neither anticipated nor supported its perverse results. Although mostly unintended, the ideology of clean hands oiled Czech resentment and insult directed at the Slovaks which meant, paradoxically, that previous supporters of the federation could quickly be converted to the view that the Slovaks were a rotten tooth in the Czech body politic and had to be pulled to stop the toothache and to prevent further decay. Czech innocence quickly turned into talk of ridding the Czechs of the Slovak infection. Slovaks' worst fears about Czech prejudices materialized. Slovakia was said to have a weaker democratic tradition, to be politically less advanced, above all to be an 'economic burden' – despite the fact that at the time prospects for economic growth were generally much brighter

[1]Václav Havel, Letní přemítaní (Prague, 1991), pp. 18–19.

in the Czech lands – and certainly an impediment in any future attempt successfully to convert the ramshackle Communist mode of production into a healthy, functioning capitalist economy. Too bad about respect for constitutional niceties or the democrats in Slovakia who would suffer isolation following the dissolution of the state. The choice was stark, as Václav Klaus and other spokesmen of the Civic Democratic Party (ODS) made perfectly clear after Havel's resignation: either radical economic reform or the regression into socialism in a common state.

It followed from this uncompromising attitude on the Czech side that all Slovak offers of a looser federal belt had to be rejected. The federation should be strangled. Like two armlocked wrestlers whose faces begin to look alike under strain, Czech separatists strengthened the hand of Slovak separatists. Pincered between them, Havel's position soon became unsustainable. The final humiliating blow against his reputation in Slovakia was hammered in by the least popular Slovak politician in the Czech-speaking regions of Bohemia and Moravia, Premier Mečiar. Just a fortnight before the Slovak declaration of sovereignty, on 3 July 1992, Mečiar, backed by the largest party in Slovakia, the HZDS (Movement for a Democratic Slovakia), successfully moved in the Federal Assembly to block the re-election of Havel as President, whose term was due to expire in October. Havel had at last been forced to pay the political price of his ambiguous role in the drama of the velvet divorce.

Nothing now stood in the way of the carve-up of the state without a referendum. The tempo of events quickened.[1] In August, leaders of the two main parties (the HZDS and the ODS) from Slovakia and the Czech lands wrote the script for the smooth break-up of the state by agreeing to pass laws to end the federation, to divide up property in a ratio of 2:1 (according to population), to guarantee the powers of the successor republics and their recognition in international law, and to form a customs and monetary union. On 1 September 1992, the new Slovak constitution was ratified. The transfer of powers from the federation to the republics and the outright liquidation of federal institutions gathered momentum. In the last week of November, the Federal

---

[1]An excellent account of the events is provided by Václav Žák, 'The Velvet Divorce – Institutional Foundations', in Jiří Musil (ed.), *The End of Czechoslovakia* (Budapest, London and New York, 1995), pp. 244–268.

Assembly committed suicide by approving the break-up of the federation. Within a few weeks, the break-up of the state would become a reality.

The peaceful coexistence of two close nations living in one state ended with the sound of popping corks and clinking champagne glasses on New Year's Eve, 1992. Against Havel's wishes, and partly because of them, Czech negligence and Slovak grievance parted company. The country agreed to divorce itself. Friends reported that that evening Havel was melancholy. Communism was repressive; post-Communism now felt depressive. Whether he felt a touch of repentance for what he had – and had not done – is unknown, but whatever feelings he harboured were transformed into sadness upon hearing the news next day that his old rival and friend Alexander Dubček had been fatally injured in a car crash on his way to the Federal Assembly. The revelry and mourning that followed on New Year's Day, 1993 in Slovakia pretty much summed up the fate that had befallen the country. Some were jubilant, most were hesitant or nervous, but everybody now understood the new reality: Czechoslovakia was now the name of a country from the distant past.

OH EUROPE!

The story may be apocryphal. But those attending the David-like President during his inaugural state visit to Germany in January 1990 were reportedly left as breathless as Goliath-like Chancellor Helmut Kohl during the early seconds of their first-ever encounter. 'How would you react to this idea?' asked the crumpled Havel, less than diplomatically, mug of beer and cigarette in hand. 'Why don't we work together to dissolve all political parties? Why don't we set up just one big party: the Party of Europe?' Chancellor Kohl evidently glanced sideways and fell silent for a few seconds before recovering his footing. He reclaimed protocol by issuing the customary warm diplomatic congratulations to the new President of Czechoslovakia. He then asked his distinguished revolutionary guest whether he would care for something more to drink before formal talks got underway, as they promptly did, on matters other than the Party of Europe.

Something of the exuberance of political youth no doubt animated Havel's upstart question, but the theme of Europe – regardless of whether or not the story was true – quickly matured into one of the favourite and most effective weapons within his arsenal of political speeches and foreign-policy initiatives. His familiarity with the subject extended back to his teenage years, when for instance he and Radim Kopecký had made plans to develop a European-wide federation of youth along non-Communist lines. Havel had also done enough browsing in the family library to know by heart the oft-quoted and re-printed remark of Karel Čapek, first published when Havel was two years old: 'If you were to look for Czechoslovakia on the map it would suffice to place your finger precisely in the middle of Europe; it is there,' wrote Čapek. 'Just halfway between North and South, and between West and East, just in the middle between the four Seas whose shores outline the complicated contour of Europe. To be anchored in the very heart of Europe is not merely a geographical location, but it means the very fate of the land and of the nation that inhabits it.'[1]

Following the triumph of totalitarianism in Russia and Germany, and the Munich agreement, this type of pro-European sentiment tended to become unfashionable, even embarrassed

[1] These are the opening words of Karel Čapek's 'Introduction', in Karel Čapek *et al.*, *At the Cross-Roads of Europe. A Historical Outline of the Democratic Idea in Czechoslovakia* (Prague, 1938), p. 3.

by finding itself in a verbal alliance with violent power. Europe tended to become a dirty or suspicious word, soiled by Mussolini's talk of 'European civilization' and Nazi propaganda against 'Asiatic and Jewish Bolshevism'. The subsequent defeat of German and Italian fascism, combined with the military advances of the Soviet Union into central Europe, meant not only the geopolitical subdivision of European territory. It also meant that the attempted symbolic revival of 'Europe' and the political quest for peaceful European integration – beginning with such experiments as the European Coal and Steel Community and the Treaty of Rome – necessarily excluded Czechoslovakia, confirming its consignment to the sphere of 'Eastern Europe' under Soviet domination. Havel himself never accepted the geopolitical arrangement, and tried repeatedly to challenge it publicly. The Charter 77 initiative was in this respect a turning point, because the whole underlying principle of the Charter was its bold attempt to act *as if* European-wide agreement and co-operation on matters of human and civil rights actually existed in legal and political form. The revolutions on the western fringes of the Soviet empire in the autumn of 1989 dramatically confirmed this presumption. Suddenly, like the walls of Jericho, the barbed wire and concrete and guns dividing Europe lost their function. Europe was again free to negotiate its own peaceful reunification.

Havel's cheeky question to Chancellor Kohl pointed in this direction. Kohl may have retreated into his shell – according to the story – and vowed from there on to handle Václav Havel with a loud voice and powerful manner, and to restrict political arguments with him to *in camera* sessions. For Havel, the outcome of his cheeky question was altogether different. Quick off the mark, and well ahead of most of the political spectrum in his own country, he chose to embark on the boldest move of his time in the office of the President. His foresight was to be rewarded with the greatest single achievement of his presidential career: to bring back international respect and recognition, even admiration, for his tiny country by beginning the slow and delicate and fraught process of negotiating the re-entry of the Czechs into the structures of European integration.

His campaigning for the Czechs' formal re-entry into Europe, using the Velvet Revolution as a springboard – 'bringing the Czech Republic into the European Union and into the twenty-first century', as he put it to a close friend,[1] was undoubtedly helped along by the remarkable parallel resurgence of wider interest in European integration, stretching from the second half of the 1980s into the 1990s. During Havel's several presidencies, many observers and whole electorates welcomed various treaties, including the Single Europe (1992) Act, while most political leaders throughout the region willingly co-operated in such forums as the European Parliament and the annual meetings of the European Council. The spirit of European unity also appeared on the military front. Franco-German co-operation seemed nothing short of a miracle; the formation of a European Common Security and Foreign Policy was widely interpreted as a small (if incomplete) victory in Europe's struggle to control its own affairs; while for the first time ever – during the Gulf War – European countries acted in unison to defend their perceived interests outside of Europe. Even some part of the elites within the two countries that had traditionally felt least at home in Europe – Britain and Russia – seemed to be persuaded of its importance.

Picking up the threads of this trend, Havel began to sew using the same sharp principle that Jean Monnet, the most famous political architect of Europe, himself applied to the subject of European integration: if you want to change the world, find the most powerful point of leverage against the status quo instead of short-sightedly mucking around with present-day details. Havel did so in various different ways, each pursued simultaneously.

Intense efforts to repair and consolidate diplomatic relations with the various member states of the European Community (as it was still called in January 1990) was the most obvious step to be taken. During the first flying year of his presidency of Czechoslovakia, Havel made state visits to Berlin, Munich London, Paris, Rome, Lisbon, Strasbourg, Madrid and Barcelona, among other European cities. Meanwhile, he foresaw that his country's re-entry into the European mosaic of states required

---

[1]Interview with Paul Wilson, Toronto, 17 November 1996.

some co-ordination with the other newly independent central-
eastern European states that had just emerged from under the
Communist rubble. 'Good relations with our neighbours are
in the fundamental interest of each of our countries as well
as in the fundamental interest of Europe as a whole,' he said
to a NATO summit in Brussels, called in early January 1994
to foster ties between itself and the four member states (the
Czech Republic, Poland, Slovakia, Hungary) of the so-called
Višegrád group.[1] The speech was well received. It convinced
enough domestic opinion that going into NATO – the American-
dominated military alliance whose formation was spawned in
part by the *coup de Prague* a half-century earlier – would help
to stabilize Czech democracy and make the Czech economy
more attractive to foreign investors. The speech also evidently
helped to consolidate agreement favouring the redefinition and
acceptance of the Partnership for Peace, a scheme conceived in
the previous October by NATO defence ministers as a way of
fostering ties between central-eastern Europe and the alliance.
'Our countries have very similar views on the Partnership for
Peace', said Havel following a handshake from President Bill
Clinton after the Brussels meeting. 'I would be happy if today
the city of Prague could emerge as a symbol of Europe standing
in alliance.' Shortly afterwards, Czech entry into the military
alliance that acts as policeman of the European region seemed
a foregone conclusion – as it proved to be in March 1999 –
with the NATO announcement of plans for joint training and
the holding of military exercises on the soil of the Višegrád
states. A few weeks later, as NATO bombs rained down on
Serbia, Havel told delegates to the fiftieth-anniversary summit of
NATO that the Czech Republic now formally belonged to 'the
Western sphere of civilization. The same is true,' he added, 'of
Slovakia, Slovenia, Romania, Lithuania, Latvia, Estonia, Bulgaria
and other Balkan States.'

Then there was the need to tackle some difficult questions
concerning relations with Germany. Just before the Velvet Revolution, Havel drafted and sent a private letter to President Richard
von Weizsäcker.[2] Anticipating controversial remarks made during

---

[1] *The Prague Post*, volume 4, 3 (19–25 January 1994), p. 1.
[2] Václav Havel to President Richard von Weizsäcker, Prague, 5 November 1989.

a Czechoslovak Television interview a few weeks later, Havel apologized on behalf of the citizens of his country for the 'profoundly immoral' treatment of the ethnic German populations of the country immediately after the military defeat of Nazism. Havel confessed that no peaceful and good-willed *rapprochement* between the new Germany and his own country – and no new relationship with the wider Europe – would be possible unless public recognition was given to the scale and brutality of the Czechs' treatment of their own ethnic German citizens. He noted that during the years 1945–1946 – Havel was speaking from experience as the owner of property at Hrádeček once owned by a victim – at least 2.5 million ethnic Germans were violently hunted out of the country, leaving behind perhaps only a scared minority of 200,000 survivors of the exodus. Such treatment was unacceptable, argued Havel. No good reasons could justify it. All Czechs and Slovaks should feel ashamed of what they or their distant relatives had done. The memory of it should for ever be preserved, and any future repetition of it could only be avoided, he implied, if a new treaty of understanding between the two countries was drafted, and signed. He concluded: 'Czechoslovak democrats owe German democrats something.'

Howls of protest greeted the proposal. But Havel was unflinching. There were many who pointed out that the exodus of ethnic Germans was just punishment for their support for Hitler's totalitarianism. While they claimed their right to a homeland, they had in fact renounced their home country of Czechoslovakia. They deserved everything they subsequently got. There were other critics who spotted that the apology to Germany was a prelude to negotiating entry into the European Community of states, in which Germany already exercised important powers. The reaction was something like: 'We've only barely begun to free ourselves as a country after more than fifty years, and now we're being asked to subordinate ourselves again, this time to the Germans and their Brussels agents.'

Havel aimed two barrels at such rhetoric. He singled out 'Czechocentrism' and 'provincial mistrust' towards the wider world as the rotten foundations on which anti-German xenophobia rested. Time and again – on television and especially during his weekly radio broadcast from the presidential estate at

Lány[1] – he attacked narrow-mindedness, ignorance of the wider world, and intolerance of others. He maintained that such attitudes were pointless, except to justify Czechs and Slovaks taking a political path that led nowhere except into a blind alley of isolation. Such attitudes also served secretly to reinforce the widespread unspoken assumption, to which Neville Chamberlain notoriously gave voice, that central Europe is another world, well off the main highways of world affairs, and really not worth a detour. Finally, he said, such attitudes had had murderous effects in the past, and they might well do so in the future, unless checked.

Havel tried to buttress his attack on anti-German xenophobia by standing on ramparts made from several different – not entirely compatible – arguments. He continued to remind his audiences that a cosmopolitan sense of responsibility for others is a citizen's duty – just as he had emphasized in the play *Redevelopment, or Slum Clearance* (*Asanace* [1988]), when the character Zdeněk Bergman reacts to news of the death of the wise idealist Plekhanov: 'Confronted with his death, we realize that we must bear our portion of guilt for it, for we, too, are responsible for the sad state of this world.'[2] Havel tried to add substance to his call for cosmopolitanism by repeating Čapek's theme of the Czech lands as the geopolitical crossroads of Europe. He tried as well to recast the same theme as a defence of *Mitteleuropa*. 'It was often in Vienna or Prague before anywhere else that potential threats to humanity appeared,' he told an Austrian audience. The long and often unhappy history of cultural and political contacts among the peoples of *Mitteleuropa* – Havel's definition was fuzzy – now placed the region in 'the front line of the fight for democracy and stability in the whole of Europe'. Czechs and Slovaks should not gaze at their navels. They had the duty to think of themselves as members of a wider proto-political community that could serve as the hub of 'the West's ongoing efforts to live in peace and security'.[3]

[1]Examples include the President's attack on 'provincial mistrust' and 'Czechocentrism' in the address from Lány on 14 January 1994.
[2]*Asanace: hra o pěti jednáních* (Münich, 1988 [first published the previous year in samizdat in Prague]), p. 95. Compare the almost identical remarks in the interview, 'The struggle to be free needs support', *The Nation* (Bangkok) 18 February 1994.
[3]*1992 & 1993*, op. cit., p. 83; see also his treatments of the *Mitteleuropa* theme, ibid., pp. 124, 148, and his introduction, dated August 1996, to a small brochure about the Barrandov studios.

Havel's vague definition of *Mitteleuropa* was perhaps deliberate, considering that in his hands it functioned as something resembling a future Utopia designed to stimulate the hopes and dreams of present-day citizens and governments. The idea of *Mitteleuropa* evidently excluded 'Eastern' countries still haunted by the ghosts of Russian power and 'Western' countries like Britain, for whom the post-Communist lands were still regarded as far-away countries about which we know nothing (a prejudice voiced by Neville Chamberlain when Havel was still in nappies). But whether Havel intended to include in *Mitteleuropa* countries as diverse as Sweden and Slovenia, Poland and Hungary and (parts of) Italy, was unclear. Presumably, his defence of the region included Germany, which is perhaps one reason why in his various efforts to demonstrate the need for cultural and political solidarity between Czechoslovaks and Germans he was strangely hare-lipped about the Holocaust. It was as if Havel made a political calculation not to stir up trouble with his country's neighbours. When the subject of the Holocaust did arise, Havel's vague argument – surely one of the most problematic in all of his political and artistic career – was as soothing to guilted Germans and quisling Czechs as it was objectionable to concerned Jewish ears in both countries. In the Holocaust, he said in a 1993 address at The George Washington University, 'the Chosen People were chosen by history to bear the brunt [of responsibility] for us all. The meaning of their sacrifice is to warn us against indifference to things we foolishly believe do not concern us.'[1] Terms like 'history' and 'Fate' seemed designed to highlight the undeniable fact that the Holocaust is now part of our received historical tradition, so that any present and future efforts to look forward to a future freed from totalitarian power are *compelled* to look backwards, to force us, again and again, to face up to what some human beings did to others for the first time ever. Yet the trouble with Havel's talk of 'Fate' and 'history' is that it so easily caused insult. Personal and group responsibility for the

---

[1]From the speech after receiving the President's Medal at The George Washington University, Washington, DC, 22 April 1993, reprinted in *Toward a Civil Society*, op. cit., p. 228. The same argument that 'Fate' chose the Jews to make 'modern humanity face up to its responsibility' appears in Václav Havel, *Vážení občané* (Prague, 1992), p. 108. Note the foul version of the understanding of the Holocaust as Destiny: Hitler's certainty, from 1936, that his actions were ordained by Providence. 'I go with the certainty of a sleepwalker along the path laid out for me by Providence', he told a jubilant crowd in Munich on 14 March 1936 (quoted in Ian Kershaw, *Hitler, 1889–1936: Hubris* (Harmondsworth 1998), p. 527.

Holocaust was fudged, or dissolved into talk of abstract non-actors going under the name of forces with a will of their own.

No such depersonalized talk of 'history' infected his discussions of nationalist politics. With one eye on the Balkans war unleashed by the Milošević regime in the early 1990s, Havel roundly condemned nationalism, 'the hatred for anyone who seems to be playing the traitor to his roots or who claims different roots'. He pointed out that Communism and nationalism have a common mind-set. 'Both simplify the world,' he said, 'divide it into friends and enemies, the chosen and those condemned to contempt, into "us" as the better people and "them" as the worse. They do not examine individual merit or guilt, but prejudge, pigeonhole and, thus, divide society into the meritorious and the culprits.' And he went on to warn that the germs of nationalism are highly contagious. 'Czechocentrism' could ruinously conspire with Balkan nationalisms to succour little nationalists elsewhere in Europe. 'The fate of the so-called West', he concluded, 'is today being decided in the so-called East.'[1]

These various arguments against 'Czechocentrism' were greeted with yet more howls of protest, at which Havel took aim with a second barrel. It was imperative, he argued, to move as quickly as possible towards a new treaty that resolved once and for all the bad feelings produced on both sides of the border by the cruel expulsion of ethnic Germans and the brutality of Nazism. A breakthrough along these lines came at the end of February 1992, when Havel met with Chancellor Kohl to sign a friendship treaty that included assurances of German support for Czechoslovakia's full membership in the European Community. In spite of a week of small but lively street protests – in Prague demonstrations of up to 5,000 people voiced concerns about the dangers of German territorial and economic domination – the atmosphere of the endorsement ceremony in the Castle's opulent Spanish Hall was festive. Havel, Kohl and their advisers raised champagne glasses in honour of the new 'spirit of commonality'. Havel was forthright. 'We are laying the foundations for good, friendly relations between our nations,' he said. 'We are shaping the future, setting the grounds for a fast way for Czechoslovakia into the family of European nations.' Kohl reciprocated the generosity. 'We have

[1] *1992 & 1993*, op. cit., pp. 91, 80, 174.

stood over too many graves in this century,' he said. 'We have
shed too many tears. The time has come for us to learn from
history. It is in this way that I understand our decision to help
your country.'[1]

After the break-up of Czechoslovakia, the friendship treaty in
effect had to be renegotiated all over again. It was nonetheless
a watershed agreement, and not only because it served as the
written precedent for a pattern of inter-governmental negotiation
that would lead ultimately to full membership within the European
Union. The treaty – acting like a lance to a boil – also served to
publicize the lingering grievances against such agreement. Few
denied the material advantages offered by the treaty, which in
addition to German support for Czechoslovak membership in
the European Community also included provision for security
measures, scientific collaboration, environmental protection and
basic cultural, economic and governmental co-operation. The
critics were vociferous about other matters, especially the reference
in the treaty to the 'expulsion' of 2½ million ethnic Germans
four decades earlier. A spokesman for Landsmannschaft, a pressure
group representing them, told the business daily *Hospodářské noviny*
that the pressing question of restitution had been left unresolved by
the treaty. The Czech Septimius, who had by now worked his way
up the political ladder to become federal Deputy Prime Minister,
agreed. 'We are now signing a treaty that leaves unresolved the
most dangerous issues,' Klaus said bitterly. He too objected – on
free-market grounds, as ever – to the word 'expulsion', which
'could be a friendly gesture offering [Germany] certain moral
satisfaction for the severity of this process carried out after the
war'. But, he continued, 'the context in which this word is used in
the treaty could germinate certain legal claims [by ethnic Germans]
in the future'.

Czechoslovakia's privatization laws specifically precluded restitution claims by owners who lost their property before 1948
and, in any case, the negotiators of the treaty supposed, as Kohl
himself openly admitted, that the European Community would
serve as the future framework within which 'solutions for the
settlement of foreign claims' would be found. Havel was more

[1]All quotations concerning the signing of the treaty are from *The Prague Post* (Prague),
3–9 March 1992, p. 1.

strident. He implied — it was not put quite so cynically — that the problem would wither away with the decline in the numbers of 'first generation' ethnic Germans. 'This issue, which seems to be controversial and dramatic at the moment, will gradually lose its controversial and dramatic nature,' he predicted. To which he added remarks about the basic principles of European integration. Those who continued to think in narrowly retributionist terms understated the co-operative spirit that Brussels was now trying to foster. The key point, Havel said, was that the European Community vision of a Europe without borders would make it 'possible for any European, including a Sudeten German, if he or she wants, to work, live, and invest in our country'.

The remark typified another move made by Havel in support of the Czechs' return to Europe: his efforts to provide a sophisticated moral-philosophical justification of the long-term process of European integration. Compared with other statesmen and stateswomen in the European region, Havel proved that he could himself write unaided the best — and the most thoughtful — speeches on the subject. His inaugural address to the European Parliament in Strasbourg in early March 1994 was typical.[1] Havel acknowledged all that had been so far achieved through negotiation. Given how much 'unrest, chaos, and violence' Europe had suffered in the twentieth century, it was a near-miracle that so much common agreement and successful institution-building had been achieved in so little time, he said. He criticized those — he surely had in mind personalities like Margaret Thatcher and Václav Klaus — who misrepresented the European Union as a new Moloch with an insatiable appetite for otherwise freedom-loving individuals, groups, regions, nations, and states. He instead spoke of the Union as 'a space that allows the autonomous components of Europe to develop freely and in their own way in an environment of lasting security and mutually beneficial co-operation based on principles of democracy, respect for human rights, civil society, and an open market economy'.

Havel pointed to the nightmare alternative — genocidal war in the former Yugoslavia — before reiterating that the post-Communist countries of Europe had seen enough of such blood-

---

[1]Speech delivered to the European Parliament, Strasbourg, 8 March 1994, in *Toward a Civil Society*, op. cit., pp. 291–303.

shed this century. He stated bluntly what many of his fellow
Czechs would not dare even to whisper. 'Yes,' he said, Czechs
were ready to join the European Union 'because we know
it will repay us many times over, as it will all Europeans'.
He then praised the Maastricht Treaty of Union as a 'great
administrative work', as 'a remarkable labour of the human spirit
and its rational capacities' – in order to criticize its lack of 'a
spiritual or moral or emotional dimension'. European integration could only succeed, he concluded, if it were given 'charisma'. Something like a new charter of European Union was
required. It would give to 'millions of European souls an idea,
a historical mission and a momentum'. The European charter
would 'clearly articulate the values upon which it is founded
and which it intends to defend and cultivate'. It would also
'take care to create emblems and symbols, visible bearers of its
significance'.

Subsequent speeches tried to clarify and detail exactly what
he meant by the European 'idea'. The efforts were unusually
philosophical, the turn away from practical politics definite. It
was as if the *Ichspieler* had once again found his footing, a last
remaining stage on which to perform to an audience – this
time, significantly, one that stretched from Madeira to the Urals,
from the frozen Arctic to sunny Cyprus, and even beyond,
to interested audiences living in Tokyo, Beijing, Washington,
Santiago, Canberra, New Delhi, Cairo, or Johannesburg. The
stunning width of his audience matched the breathtaking height
of his thoughts. The acrobatics involved talk of Schiller's 'Ode
to Joy' and its insistence that freedom requires giving allegiance
and commitment to 'the judge above the stars'. There were
frequent mentions of the need for Europe to abandon its traditional quest 'to spread – violently or non-violently – its own
religion, its own civilization, its own inventions, or its own
power'. Havel even insisted that Europe should stop preaching
'the rule of law, democracy, human rights, or justice to the
rest of the world'. Europe's key task, he said repeatedly, is
'to discover its conscience and its responsibility, in the deepest sense'.[1]

---

[1] An example of this (typical) kind of reasoned argument is 'The Hope for Europe',
a public address delivered in Aachen, 15 May 1996, reprinted in *The New York
Review of Books*, 20 June 1996, pp. 38–41.

The acrobatics were brilliantly executed and good to watch. And they certainly helped to consolidate his global reputation, and to win him prizes, gold medals, honorary doctorates, several shortlistings for the Nobel Prize, even the honour of being labelled 'the moral leader of Europe'.[1] Yet the odd thing is that nobody spotted the tragic irony lurking within his efforts to become the moral leader of Europe with a global reputation. His campaigning for the Czech Republic's full entry into the European Union, if successful, would for ever prevent a repetition of the kind of unchallenged charismatic presidential power that he had once enjoyed, during the first months of the glorious Velvet Revolution. During his ten-year string of presidencies, on the domestic front, that charismatic power was subsequently tamed and permanently humbled, check by balance, push by pull, confrontation by confrontation. But on the international scene, in principle, Havel's power remained unchallenged. According to the Constitution of the Czech Republic (ratified on 16 December 1992), the President of the Republic 'shall be the head of the state' and 'shall not be answerable for the exercise of his function' (Article 54). Subject to the countersignature of the Prime Minister, or by a member of the government authorized by that minister, the President is sovereign in respect of such matters as representing the state in external affairs, negotiating and ratifying international treaties, acting as the supreme commander of the armed forces, appointing and promoting generals, appointing judges, and accrediting and receiving the heads of foreign diplomatic missions (Article 63).

Havel's statesman-like battle for Czech accession to the European Union effectively spelled the end of these sovereign powers, in substance if not in name. His daring rescue of a small, humiliated and insignificant country from the Soviet empire, his reinsertion of that country on the map of the world by pushing it towards the European region, had a political price. Full membership in the European Union actually required the creation of a *post-sovereign presidency*, a sovereign leader who was no longer sovereign. European Union membership required a leader who ceased to be *primus inter pares* within the upper echelons of the state, who instead is just one leader among three or four

[1] Timothy Garton Ash, 'The moral leader of Europe', *Independent* (London), 21 October 1998, p. 5.

handfuls of leaders, who are themselves subject to the constraints and opportunities afforded by obedience to the so-called *acquis communautaire*, the body of treaties, laws, and directives already agreed by the earlier political architects of European integration.

Future presidents of the Czech Republic may wish to thank – and some will want to curse – Havel for this spectacular change. But, whatever transpires and whatever is thought of the change, the Czech presidents who follow in his footsteps will feel the difference. They will of course sit beside the heads of large European member states; from time to time they will amend or veto their wills. But future Czech presidents will know that among the terms of their election is their acceptance of the fact that they can no longer engage in power politics in the early modern sense. Like the oxygen they breathe each few seconds, they shall have to operate within the kind of institutional framework anticipated in the Maastricht Treaty of Union. Thanks to that treaty, and Havel's efforts to extend it eastwards, all future heads of Czech state will not be heads of state. They will instead make politics within a three-pillared structure, comprising the original European Communities – the ESCE, EAEC and EC – plus the newly founded Common Foreign and Security Policy (CFSP) and co-operation in Home and Judicial Affairs (HJA). They will accept that the stated goal of 'creating an ever-closer union among the peoples of Europe' (Article A) requires not merely acceptance of the *acquis communautaire*, but also a relative shift away from policy-making by consensus towards qualified majority voting, plus a quickening pace of Euro-legislation in all policy fields. All future heads of state will recognize that the Treaty of Union 'constitutionalizes' the principle of the 'Union Citizen'. They will understand that the combined effect of such changes, including the monetary union of existing and future member states, is to weaken and dissolve the principle of the sovereign territorial state. In other words – let us call this the European law of power-sharing – all heads of state will accept that they are subject to countervailing *supranational* powers, even in such fundamental matters as representing the state in external affairs, negotiating and ratifying international treaties, acting as the supreme commander of the armed forces, and accrediting and receiving the heads of foreign diplomatic missions.

METAMORPHOSIS

'Dear Mr President.' The calm physician paused. 'I think it best that you have some tests, which we could begin this afternoon in nearby Innsbruck. They should not take long, and I emphasize that they are just routine. There is absolutely nothing to be worried about. I give you my word.' Minutes later, the Austrian staff in the local hamlet clinic in Reutt telephoned for an air ambulance, which promptly whisked the President of the Czech Republic to hospital for emergency surgery to remove 30 centimetres of heavily perforated intestine. So began his fourth hospitalization in a year. Despite fears, there were no signs of cancer and Havel, enmeshed in tubes and confined to hospital for several more weeks, was soon off the critical list, reportedly in a good mood, and even capable of a few post-operative jokes befitting a lucky head of state.

He was indeed lucky that bowels recognize no borders, and that he had had the good fortune to be out of his own country in mid-April 1998, on holiday in a small Austrian village in the Tyrolian Alps. 'The hospital is better than anything we have in Prague,' the President's brother Ivan remarked. 'And luckily Czech surgeons were not involved. It is not that they are less competent. It is that most of them might have hesitated or refused to do what had to be done, out of fear of failing and perhaps ruining their careers as a result.'[1] The comment contained more than just a hint of concern about the imperfect state of the Czech health-care system, which can be so unresponsive (as the local joke has it) that the waiting list for pregnancy tests has been stretched to ten months. The comment pointed to some hard political facts: that despite the failures of the crowned republic, Havel's body and persona had in a way become royalized; that his illness was an instant media event; and that nobody around him dared put a foot wrong because a royal tragedy of epic proportions was now unfolding before everyone's eyes.

The sad public performance at the Prague Castle had begun seventeen months earlier. In early December 1996, a public scandal erupted during his first medical crisis, which pushed Havel towards the grave and left him permanently weakened.

[1]Telephone conversation with Ivan Havel, Prague and London, 16 April 1998. Compare the remarks of Karel Srp, in *News* (Vienna) 23 April 1998, p. 74: 'Had it happened in Prague, he would have died. The Austrian doctors and his wife Dagmar saved him.'

Some said that official secrecy, political incompetence and medical misjudgement had almost cost him his life. The facts were these. On 16 November 1996, Havel's personal physician, Michal Šerf, X-rayed his lungs. A spot was seen, but Serf considered that Havel's pneumonia first needed to be treated. Havel was so treated, but failed to respond. The symptoms – fever, shivering, double vision – worsened so his new girlfriend, the blonde actress Dagmar Veškrnová, sacked the physician, who had been a trusted friend from before the Velvet Revolution. At Prague's best hospital, Na Homolce, she made contact with other doctors, who administered sedatives and again X-rayed his lungs – anonymously.

Illness never strikes at an opportune moment, and Havel's was no exception. In the middle of crucial negotiations to effect Czech entry into NATO, his good health was both a practical necessity and a symbol of the Czech Republic's ability to see through high-powered negotiations at this level. So the doctors chose to keep the medical crisis a top secret, even from the rest of the medical profession. His lungs were X-rayed incognito, and the plates were circulated to other specialist doctors bearing the name of his chief bodyguard. It was evident that the right lung of the patient was marked by a black spot, so another opinion was sought, this time from one of Prague's leading medical professors, Dr Pavel Pafko. He wasted no time recommending surgery, which was carried out at his teaching hospital, the Third Surgical Clinic, located on Londýnská Street, just near where Havel had been born.

Minutes before the surgery began – as if facing his own execution – Havel and his Minister of Health lit up cigarettes under the glare of television lights, watched by a hundred reporters, jostling to get the last shot before the brave President disappeared into the operating theatre – perhaps into the grave. The procedure lasted four hours, during which Dr Pafko and his team located and promptly removed a malignant tumour more than half an inch long, together with the surrounding tissue. The President with only one-and-a-half lungs was then put into the intensive-care unit, separated by screens from the other patients.

From here on, opinions about what happened are divided, in no small measure because those closest to Havel began at that

moment to disagree about what should be done.[1] Shortly after
the operation, Havel's left lung developed a new pneumonia. His
pulse rate soared, and Dr Pafko, calling in another doctor, six nurses
and a lung ventilator, carried out a tracheotomy – opening a hole
in Havel's throat, so that he could breathe. No sooner had that
been done than Havel developed heart trouble. A genuine crisis
quickly followed. The lung ventilator stopped operating and were
it not for Veškrnová, who walked into the intensive-care unit to
find Havel asphyxiating, he would certainly have died.

That episode in the life-or-death drama rocked everybody's
confidence. Veškrnová summoned a faith healer, who made three
visits to Havel's bedside. His brother Ivan, convinced that the
presidential staff were no longer on top of the situation, called
in an independent doctor, whom he trusted. That prompted
Veškrnová to get on the phone for international help. Eight days
after the operation, as the patient's heart improved but overall
condition worsened, a new infection developed. Although the
laboratory-test results were inconclusive, and Havel was given
a blood transfusion, splits developed within the team of twelve
doctors led by Dr Pafko. Some wanted urgently to move Havel
out of the Third Surgical Clinic. Others considered such a move
unnecessary; still others were certain only that moving Havel was
too dangerous. At exactly that moment Fortune – described by
Machiavelli as 'mistress of one half our actions'[2] – intervened
to bring, on an overnight flight to Prague, a thirteenth doctor,
a distinguished American named Robert J. Ginsberg. Head of
thoracic surgery at the world-famous Memorial Sloan-Kettering
Cancer Center in New York, Ginsberg had an instant stabilizing
effect on the whole situation, despite some background grumbling
about his medical credentials. He took one look at Havel before
ordering the hospital staff to turn down the oxygen content of
the ventilator. He personally cleaned the inside of Havel's airway,
and then announced to the team of quarrelling doctors that the
patient's fever would subside, and that he was on the road to a
normal recovery. He was proved right.

As Ginsberg boarded his flight back to New York two days later,
a rancorous public debate erupted in the Czech Republic. Why did

---

[1] The best-researched account is provided by Paul Berman, 'The Philosopher-King
is Mortal', *The New York Times Magazine*, 11 May 1997, pp. 32–59.
[2] *Il principe*, op. cit., chapter 25.

Havel's X-rays bear the name of his chief bodyguard, some asked, and why was he allowed to smoke until a few seconds before he was wheeled into the operating theatre? Why on earth was a faith healer summoned to his bedside? And why, others asked, were events at Prague's reputedly best hospital allowed so obviously to slip out of control? Why did his surgeons quarrel themselves into doing nothing at the most critical point? The questions were not directly answered, and rumours circulated that Havel, who returned home to convalesce on 27 December, had slumped into deep despondency enforced by compulsory abstinence from cigarettes and alcohol.

Things didn't improve, politically speaking. On the eighth day after returning from hospital, Havel left his friends and the Czech public breathless by marrying Veškrnová in a private ceremony, to which not even his brother Ivan was invited. Some of his closest friends warned him not to go through with it. He told them, in reply, that he had reached the conclusion that Dáša had personally saved his life, and that he was besotted – since well before his operation, when they were already living together. There was apparently plenty of flowing libidinal energy. He initially loved the way she eyeballed him, he said, and she also found his bohemian-playwright side sexy. The day after the wedding – a twenty-minute ceremony held shortly before noon on 4 January 1997 at Prague's Žižkov Town Hall, where thirty-three years earlier he had married his first wife Olga – Havel addressed the country on his regular 'Talks from Lány' programme. 'I believe, or hope', he began, 'that we will be happy. And I believe in something else: that this new stage will help make me in some ways a better man than I have been.' Havel didn't elaborate his past shortcomings, but interestingly he did have much to say about Olga, who had died from cancer less than a year ago. 'Olga was my companion for almost forty-five years. She is and will always be an irreplaceable part of my soul. I married Dáša not to replace Olga, but simply because we love each other and want to live together.' Havel mentioned that a symbol of this continuity was the choice to get married in the same location. He then – inappropriately, thought some – went on to invoke Olga's support for the choice of his new forty-three-year-old wife. 'Before she died,' he said, 'Olga said I should remarry. At the time, I ruled it out categorically, and I was resolved to end my days alone. She was convinced that I can't live alone, and that I shouldn't. She was right, and life itself confirmed that when I was lucky enough to get to know Dáša.'[1]

Press and television photographs from this period show the thin-looking Havel to be radiant. Yet whatever personal happiness he gained from the marriage seemed quickly to backfire upon him politically. 'Even if Dagmar Veškrnová had been an angel,' said one of Havel's trusted advisers later, 'the newlyweds would not likely have landed on their feet.'[2] Public opinion indeed became restless, and even showed strange signs of vindictiveness. Havel began to resemble the kind-hearted king – in the well-known Czech nursery rhyme – who dabbed honey on his nose for his favourite bee to feed on, only to plummet into shock after the ungrateful insect grew restless and stung him. Just a few months into the marriage, his new wife told an invited audience of children and journalists at the Castle that her current favourite story-book character was the Golden Fish (released by fishermen after granting them three wishes) because she wanted to 'fulfil my husband's every wish'[3]. Havel looked on, smiling. The state of sexual politics in the Czech Republic showed itself to be a few strides ahead of the performance, which was widely interpreted to border on bad taste. Some even said it resembled a tawdry scene out of one of Havel's absurdist plays. The observation highlighted the lingering public sympathy for Olga. It also underlined the fact that Havel's second marriage – 'our presidency' he subsequently called it in a Czech Television *faux pas* – quickly became a political liability. Love is always a poor adviser, which is perhaps why during the year 1997 Havel acted like a besotted playwright swooning after a young actress rehearsing the part of Her Serene Highness. 'All her life, she had to play roles, to slip into them,' well-placed Prague observers remarked, or words to that effect. They added something like: 'She has no identity, and she is looking for a new role. It is quite probable that she is playing the role that he expects of her, especially considering that he has been ill and that from here on death is permanently on his mind.'

Havel had not had any practice in experimenting with these expectations. His first wife Olga had refused on principle to

[1] *Hovory z Lán*, Czech Radio (Prague), 5 January 1997.
[2] Interview with Jiří Pehe, Prague, 5 March 1999.
[3] Česká televizé 1 (Prague), 24 December 1997.

play the political role of First Lady; she preferred instead to busy herself with projects that aimed to empower the socially downtrodden. Dáša Veškrnová, by contrast, appeared to fancy a political role. Her discovery that, within the Castle, she had no automatic right to visit her new husband, upset her. So did her discovery, after drafting a reply letter to Madame Chirac, that she had no special rights, and that she was required to wait in a queue for her letter to be typed and forwarded to Paris. Veškrnová's disquiet fed her political aspirations, proof of which came during the last week of August 1997, when she told the Czech daily *Mladá fronta Dnes* that she had been 'thrown into deep water' when she had married President Václav Havel, and that she now wanted a law to govern her functions, including a formal guarantee that she receive assistance from the President's staff. All hell broke loose. Pavel Rychetský, chairman of the Senate's important Commission on Constitutional and Legal Affairs, voiced typical criticism of Dáša's ambitions. 'The wife of the President is not a position,' he reminded her in the pages of *Lidové noviny*, 'and it is definitely not a constitutional position'.[1] He added that it was mistaken to think that the law had to be changed every time that family members of state officials had unsatisfied needs. There were rumbling noises from within the Castle and rumours began to reach the outside world that some staff were rather disgruntled, and even that one of Havel's most trusted aides had left after saying to her face something like: 'As you know, I have already handed in my resignation. You should know as well that, unlike other satrapies, this country is a parliamentary democracy with an elected president. You are only his wife.'

Havlová bit back. In a prepared statement, she told *Mladá fronta Dnes* that she was 'shocked by television and newspaper reports . . . which, without exception, accuse me of wanting to be a constitutional body, wanting to have my own law or even change the constitution'. She repeated that there were presently no legislative guarantees of her important position. How otherwise could she fulfil her duties? 'Almost every one of my decisions or letters,' she added, 'has some political significance

---

[1] *Mladá fronta Dnes* (25 August 1997). The ensuing controversy is documented in *Lidové noviny* (26 August 1997) and *Mladá fronta Dnes* (27 August 1997).

and can, in one way or another, touch upon the interests or prestige of the head of state, and therefore the state itself.' Havel's spin doctor Špaček tried to make peace by reiterating in softer tones Dáša's key points. While the First Lady currently had two assistants, she honestly needed more help. 'She only wants a sentence in the existing law ... that stipulates that the First Lady will receive as much help as is necessary.' This was hardly convincing, since the term necessity – a favourite of state-mongers, we learn from Machiavelli – was itself both the sore point and the unresolved issue.

Havel's political troubles were deepened by backing Dáša's perceived public indiscretions. There were quite a few of them, including a press conference outburst against journalists for failing to recognize her husband's 'right to free weekends, like every other employee'.[1] Quips and vulgar jokes about her – and the corresponding state of her husband's health and political judgement – naturally began to circulate throughout Czech society. Dáša was quickly forced to learn that contemporary politics and high-profile media coverage are a married couple, and that the old distinction between on-stage and back-stage in politics is now obsolete. The more 'private' political stars try to be, the more 'publicity' they get. So tabloid journalists and image consultants rudely criticized her Versace wardrobe as too 'extravagant'. Unkindly, some said Dáša looked like a flight attendant, that she should lose a few kilos, or that she wore too much bright-red lipstick. Still others sneered that her nails were improperly manicured, or that her hair was a mess.[2]

Havel meanwhile (perhaps unfairly) was made to look like the

---

[1] See the insightful remarks of Jindřich Ginter, 'Z herečky se první dáma nestala', *Slovo* (Prague), 8 November 1997.

[2] *Blesk* (Prague), 30 October 1997. Worse was to come. In October 1998, Prague's TV Nova, the most talked-about private television station in central-eastern Europe, reported that the marriage of the presidential couple was in crisis. The claim was based on a then-unpublished book co-authored by Přemysl Svora, *Sedm týdnů, které otřásly Hradem* [*Seven Days that Shook the Castle*] (Prague, 1998). Following the programme, the Havels vigorously denied the allegations and filed a libel suit against TV Nova. Dáša accused its mogul, Vladimír Železný (whose name means 'iron' in Czech) of trying to blackmail the President into pardoning Železný's son David, a convicted rapist. Železný replied that the President's wife made him nauseous. 'I consider the statement by the First Lady, I stress 'lady', of this country, to be a fishwife's argument.' He went on to express surprise that Havel co-initiated the libel suit. 'Well,' the smooth-tongued Železný added, 'husbands don't always have it easy.' A few months later, after an out-of-court settlement for an undisclosed sum was reached, TV Nova apologized to the Havels on its evening news programme.

partner of a pin-up blonde featured in a down-market tabloid newspaper. 'Did you hear that Havel is planning to spend next Christmas with Olga?' ran one of the most cruel, popular jokes. 'But do you know who she is going to marry next?' ran a reply. 'Yeltsin!' Havel reacted defensively to such irreverence – he reportedly instructed his immediate staff at the Castle several times that they should like her[1] – and in so doing began to act as if he were a politician cocooned in his own hubris. Things were not helped by the absence of Olga, who had always made efforts to check his indiscretions and to complain to him about the arselickers and skirtchasers within the ranks of his own staff. Neutral observers complained that the President seemed unusually ill-tempered and prone to mood-swings, possibly due to his prescribed medication.[2]

Matters were worsened by Havel's loss of contact with acquaintances, friends and family – even his brother Ivan began to report to friends that he now regretted seeing him only once a year, whereas during his time in prison he used to see him the permitted four times a year. Machiavelli's comment that princes sometimes do things for the fame that outlives them seemed to rebound on him cruelly: fame brought him no friends, only attention. Havel's own predilection for playing the role of *Ichspieler* consolidated this impression. On his wedding day, typically, he told reporters that he himself would decide how to handle the morality of what he had done, and what he would do in the future. 'Anyone who knows me a little,' he said, 'knows that when its comes to the important things in my life, I've always done what I consider to be right and that I've never taken into consideration how much people like or dislike my decisions.'[3]

Some observers began to re-describe this self-justification for

[1]Interview with Olga Stankovicová, Prague, 10 November 1998.
[2]'Politologům se nelíbi Havlovo příliš emotivní vystupování', *MF Dnes* (Prague), 9 December 1997, p. 3. Later evidence of his continuing depression is found in the leaked memorandum, 'Mým podřízeným' ('To my subordinates'), reprinted in *Lidové noviny* (Prague), 10 October 1998, p. 27. The memorandum outlines a media strategy ('I want to be seen less and heard less'), and begins with a confession: 'This weekend I was in one of the deepest depressions in a long time. It was probably evident at our meeting, or in my introduction. If I put anyone in a bad mood, I apologize for that. On the other hand, I tell myself that it doesn't do any harm if my colleagues occasionally have a peek at the sombre spirit of their boss.'
[3]Cited in *The Prague Post* (Prague), 8–14 January 1997, p. 1.

'living in the truth' as pig-headedness. During 1997, all sorts
of stories, some of them poisonous, began to circulate. Their
veracity was uncertain, but they had the effect of stripping away
the remaining layers of Havel's charisma.[1] There were those who
cited the Russian poet Joseph Brodsky, who had earlier warned
Havel not 'to create illusions' by repeatedly using terms like
'global responsibilities', which 'are not much better at the core
than the retrospective utopias of the latter-day nationalists or
the entrepreneurial fantasies of the *nouveaux riches*'.[2] Brodsky had
implied that Havel was showing signs of clinging dogmatically
to favourite philosophical tenets, perhaps because he had ever
less time to read and to keep up with things, so that, naturally,
he began to nourish himself on old literature and to parrot
old intuitions. On a different note, foreign journalists treated
to chain-smoking lunches in wine cellars at the foot of the
Castle noted that he now talked more like a politician than a
poet, a playwright, or philosophical critic of the modern world.[3]
Such perceptions, whatever their accuracy, fed deeper feelings
that presidential power had cramped Havel's imaginative literary
style, that political power had turned him into a maker of rote
speeches defined by state duties. The possible implication was
spelled out long ago by a wise philosopher: 'The possession of
power unavoidably corrupts the free exercise of reason,' he wrote.
Another philosopher harshened the point: 'Coming to power is a
costly business,' he wrote, 'power *makes stupid* . . . Politics devours
all seriousness for really intellectual things'.[4]

Havel's self-portrayals as a 'post-modern' president were a
case in point. During his first term as President of the Czech
Republic, his preaching 'post-modern' argument – that the modern technological age is ending, fortunately so because it has
been defined above all by human arrogance towards both nature

[1] The Brno newspaper *Moravsko slezský den* (21 November 1997) reported that,
although 65.7 per cent of Czechs still 'trusted' Havel, his popularity had dropped
20 per cent during 1997 alone.
[2] Joseph Brodsky to Václav Havel, printed in the *New York Review of Books*, 41, 4
(1994), p. 30
[3] Christopher Hitchens, 'Havel in the Castle', *The Nation* (Washington, DC), 16
December 1996, p. 8.
[4] Immanuel Kant, *Zum ewigen Frieden. Ein philosophischer Entwurf* (Berlin, 1795), second
supplement, in *Immanuel Kants Werke*, ed. Ernst Cassirer, volume 6 (Berlin, 1914);
Friedrich Nietzsche, *Götzen-Dämmerung, oder Wie man mit dem Hammer philosophirt*
(Leipzig, 1889), p. 59.

and other humans – was refreshing. It served as an important reminder that democracy thrives on humility. There were even moments when his public attacks on modernity exuded bravery. An example was his 4 July speech on the steps of Philadelphia's Independence Hall, when he told his American audience, some of them dressed in smart suits, others ambling by in cut-offs and T-shirts and licking ice-cream, that the 1776 revolution was founded on the mistaken 'anthropocentric' presumption that the doctrine of inalienable human rights, conferred on humanity by the Creator, subsequently encouraged Man to forget about the Creator and to act as 'the pinnacle of creation and lord of the world'.[1]

Later repetition of this theme turned it into a stale cliché, and made it vulnerable to the common-sense objection that the content of Havel's 'post-modern' speeches was contradicted by the recognizably *modern* spectacle of a head of state attempting to stave off political decline by reaching for abstractions and looking to the heavens. That suspicion of his motives was confirmed by other critics, who pointed to the need to rethink Havel's dissident period. The story circulated that those who once knew him well sometimes found him to be arrogant, and that some of his (former) acquaintances remember well a rowdy dispute he had had with Jan Vladislav about *Charta 77*, shortly after its formation. According to the story, Vladislav objected to Havel doing things behind his and others' backs, for which Havel, when caught out, had the sense and good grace to apologize, adding with a strained face: 'You now know me. I am a manipulator.' That secret confession, observers began to say, revealed something of Havel's long-standing, deep-seated lust for being at the centre of things. Old friends began to mock his choice of Smetana's *Fanfáry* as official muzak, and everybody – not merely those who had been politically booted upstairs or downstairs – complained about his aloofness. 'Several days ago,' recalled his loyal classmate from the King George School at Poděbrady, 'I was parking my car at Dejvice, when a presidential cavalcade suddenly came screaming down the main street. Václav was being driven home after returning from a state visit and the display of flashing lights and sirens was unbelievable. We used to laugh at

---

[1] Speech in acceptance of the Philadelphia Liberty Medal, Philadelphia, 4 July 1994.

such pompous displays of power in Communist times,' said his friend.'[1]

Behind such complaints was the feeling, however vaguely expressed, that Václav Havel was now suffering from another illness: the kind that affects politicians who lose the art of knowing where to draw the limits and to bow gracefully out of politics, and who perforce fail to see that their political careers often end in tatters. After the break-up of Czechoslovakia, in the autumn of 1992, he clung to the role of the presidency, telling friends who visited him at Hrádeček that the Czech Republic needed a monarch-like symbol of continuity with the immediate past.[2] Now, it was as if Havel was simply afraid of leaving politics, that his ego was now dependent on retaining office, that the advice of the banished Lord Belarius (in Shakespeare's *Cymbeline*) applied well to him personally: 'The art o' the court / As hard to leave as keep, whose top to climb / Is certain falling, or so slipp'ry that / The fear's as bad as falling.' The impression that he was fearfully clinging to power – the perception that the once-beneficial *pharmakon* of political power was now wearing off and producing pernicious effects – was certainly reinforced when Czech audiences watched with amazement as Havel did public battle over restituted family property with his sister-in-law, Ivan's wife, the mathematician Dagmar, who was the co-owner of the art deco extravaganza, Lucerna Palace, built by the President's grandfather earlier this century. The dispute quickly turned nasty, and the President decided to put the case in the hands of one of his advisers, former Communist Prime Minister Marián Čalfa. He turned out to be a legal consultant to a large firm with rumoured arms-trading connections, the Chemapol Group, which before going into liquidation in February 1999 then proceeded to buy out the President's share. The whole deal had a whiff of crony capitalism about it – and it felt to many that it was quite at odds with Havel's long-standing commitment to the ethical principle of living responsibly in the truth. The Lucerna dispute was compounded by the growing feeling, more or less vaguely

[1]Interview with Alois Strnad, Prague, 28 September 1997.
[2]Interview with Paul Wilson, Toronto, 1 June 1998. According to Wilson, Havel rejected any suggestions that he might in future play the kind of public role carved out by the former Canadian Prime Minister, Pierre Trudeau. 'I can't see that I would have as much, or more, influence as a writer than as a president,' said Havel.

expressed by growing numbers of journalists, politicians, office workers, young people, taxi drivers, that the Havel presidency was no longer (as is said in America) agenda-setting, that it was fast losing its sense of mission, dynamism, openness, its enthusiasm for the people.

More and more citizens began to conclude that it was a lame-duck presidency. The wise noted that Havel's career as a playwright was for ever destroyed. 'Is there no play,' he may have continued to muse, 'To ease the anguish of a torturing hour?'[1] During a visit to Oxford in the mid-autumn of 1998, he said that he'd like to get back to drama, to write 'an absurdist play'. But the sad reality was that Havel, even if he still had the time and inclination, could not return to the world of theatre without being dogged by controversy. Other citizens began to say that his presidency displayed too much will power and too little won't power, that it no longer had much to do with the precept (emphasized in Oxford) that the politician 'should humbly look for the truth of this world without claiming to be its professional owner'.[2] Others lamented the simple lack of courtesy of the presidency. A not untypical example, one that annoyed quite a few people, resulted from the promise by Havel's office that he would personally attend the fiftieth anniversary of the founding of his old school at Poděbrady. Although the organizers of the event arranged everything around Havel, and even though they hosted two visits beforehand by a squad of security agents, he let everybody down. At the very last minute, he sent an apology with a curt alibi that wasn't believed by anybody. Worst of all, growing numbers, in all walks of life, began to say that the presidency was publicly inaccessible – much more so and differently than during the early months after the revolution. Instead of the Castle coming closer to the people, Havel's critics said, it appeared to be drawing away into its own world, leaving the people behind and underneath, as if in a Kafka novel, where the Castle is permanently inaccessible. 'You cannot greatly influence the Castle's intentions any more,' commented one of his former trusted colleagues, choosing his metaphors with care. 'Havel's priorities are set so precisely and firmly that you cannot influence them. He is surrounded by

[1] William Shakespeare, *A Midsummer Night's Dream*, Act 5, Scene 1.
[2] Address in acceptance of an Honorary Degree from Oxford University, Oxford, 22 October 1998, posted at http://www.hrad.cz/president/Havel/speeches/1998/2210_uk.html.

courtiers [*dvořané*]: men and women who serve *auf dem Hof des Monarchs*, courtiers whose job is to serve the King.'

Some of his harshest critics, speaking from experience, extended the point. Havel's courtiers, they said, were busy performing a variety of tasks. 'Good morning, sweet lord! How dost thou, good lord?' said the courtiers. They cooked his food, tailored and ironed his clothes, arranged his schedules, cut and blowdried his hair, put cushions behind his back, fitted slippers on his tired feet, as it were. But these same courtiers found that their utter dependence on the monarch was not negotiable. Naturally there was rivalry among them to get close to him. Eager to have him for themselves, they displayed the bad habit of boasting about how often they saw him. That bad habit had been noted during the first Havel presidency, but in the changed circumstances of this bad period, the habit had perversely image-damaging consequences: the more the courtiers struggled to have his ear, the more they became dependent upon the monarch – and the more he became dependent on lackeys as reality-definers and protectors. The courtiers' job was not to criticize him by flinging fresh ideas and opinions at him, for if they did that they risked confusing or irritating the monarch, for which they would then get the sack. No, Havel's critics said, the paltry job of the Castle courtiers was to confirm his intuitions and judgements. He consequently became cocooned in their words, smiles, nods, soundbites and press releases. The courtiers became mirrors to his reality, even to his vanity and – unfortunately for the monarch – they could not do differently. The mirrors became incapable of reflecting any other reality. Soon the King, who began to resemble a mirror of his mirrors, lived in a house of mirrors.

During this period of bodily illnesses and political decline, there were undoubtedly crowning moments Not all the water in the rough, rude sea of politics could wash the balm from the anointed King. Havel's success at playing the game of offering himself to the people for re-election – the reality was that he wanted the presidency at any price – and his subsequent re-election in late 1997 by the slimmest of parliamentary majorities to another term of office, despite brushes with death, was one example. Another was the skilful outmanoeuvring of his chief political enemy, Václav Klaus. Havel's splendid speech in defence of 'civil society' to the Czech parliament in early December 1997 also counted as an important highlight. And of greatest significance, and undoubtedly a big personal triumph, was the decision of the Czech parliament to back entry into NATO, despite rancorous criticism of his own long-standing support for that policy; and (in March 1999) the standing ovation given him by the French Senate after urging the creation of a federal Europe with a two-chamber parliament modelled along the lines of the American Congress.

Supporters and friends capitalized on these achievements. Acknowledging the political threats to his authority, they found time to regroup, to remind the world of the high stakes of his decline. 'Havel's one of the Czech Republic's best exports – along with Škoda cars, the Charles Bridge and pilsener beer,' said the wags. 'He is our best political asset,' said the more serious-minded lionizers. 'Whatever mistakes he's made, we have to support him. We'll otherwise not make it into the European Union – and end up with someone like Václav Klaus as our next president.' Such remarks, designed to touch up his fading image, made plain, at home, that Havel's authority was no longer naturally charismatic, and that it had to be fought for politically. For the bitter truth was that the events following his first illness, like dripping acid, had conspired to tarnish and corrode his political and moral authority. Havel-hunting had become a sport. It was almost as if Václav Havel were once again becoming a dissident.

The trend was anticipated by his old friend Adam Michnik, the distinguished Polish intellectual and publisher. 'A charismatic leader initially wields almost metaphysical power,' he said, mentioning Havel in the next breath. 'His entitlement to authority springs from the past: it is he who has worked the miracle, it is he who toppled dictatorship and brought about freedom. But this charisma is apt to fade under democratic conditions. No more miracles happen and the leader of an anti-Communist movement turns into a normal man marked by human weaknesses . . . At this stage,' Michnik added, 'the charismatic leader becomes a caricature of himself.'[1] Shortly before Havel became first President of the Czech Republic, Michnik pursued the same point. 'Vašek,' he said, 'it's all very well riding high on applause and acclamation. But what will you do, how will you feel, when the clapping stops and the hissing and heckling begins?' That was a good question, to which Havel seemed no longer to have any good or surprising

[1]Adam Michnik, in a speech to the Friedrich Naumann Foundation (Berlin, 1995).

answers. Perhaps the only person suitably qualified to reply, if only he could, was the figure of death on the enchanting medieval clock in Prague's Old Town Square. Every hour, it shakes its head in disagreement with men's follies, for it knows that, come what may, time and the hour run through the roughest day.

So the Prague tragedy gradually unfolded. For the first time, voices here and there could be heard to whisper that the rule of the monarch-like Havel was perhaps coming to an end, and that the country would soon be on its own. 'Havel was the man who was able to stage this miracle play,' remarked his friend and Deputy Foreign Minister, Martin Palouš. 'The sacrifice was to cast himself in the lead role.'[1] There were moments when Havel seemed to agree, as when he confessed that the Czechs' growing mood of despondency was perhaps inevitable, 'even if the country were ruled jointly by Pericles, Jesus Christ and Buddha'.[2] Other voices suggested for the first time that his departure might be a positive challenge to Czech political thinking, political culture, and the political institutions themselves. A few even said openly that Havel had trapped the country's political class in a vicious circle: the longer he stayed, the more difficult it was for potential 'fresh blood' presidential candidates to surface. The probability seemed high that with the passing of time such whispers would grow into conversations, then into raised voices, even transformed into loud calls for his resignation. A small country in the heart of Europe was slowly learning that modern media coverage does not suffer either fools or heroes gladly . . . and that hubris gets rough treatment in a democracy.

[1] Cited in Jonathan Steele, 'Crushed-velvet revolutionary', *Guardian* (London), 13 March 1999. A similar remark was made in my interview with Palouš, (Prague) 24 September 1997.
[2] 'A Crying Need for Intellectuals', *The New Presence*, op. cit., p. 18.

THE GIFT OF DEATH

D eath and dying: two nasty little words that send shivers down the spines of most people. The word dying means the declining capacity to make a mark on the world; it means growing isolation from others, pain, embarrassment, eventual extinction. The word death means the opposite of birth. It is the endpoint of dying, the moment at which the power of the living individual is finally extinguished – once and for ever. For most people, this endpoint of life is exactly as Thomas Hobbes described it more than three centuries ago – 'a perpetuall and restless desire of Power after Power, that ceaseth only in death.'[1] Death – in the Christian world at least – is a blackened and lonely event filled with sobbing, brave speeches, dirge, mourning, loss. Death is exhaustion, melancholia, sadness, guilt. Death is no laughing matter; it is solemnity, for around the dying and the dead wit and laughter are unseemly, if only because death means nothingness. There are of course many ways of dying. But from this conventional standpoint there is only one end result: you are no more, you are no longer to be found anywhere, you are dead.

The popular understanding of death as the extreme borderline of power is not quite right. It correctly grasps that the lonely process of disappearing from the face of the earth ends in nothingness. But by treating dying and death as a *fact* of life it overlooks their inescapably *political* dimension. All individuals, presidents and other authority figures included, are confronted with the task of coping personally with their own effacement through death. Dead people have no troubles, but dying and death are inescapable problems for the living. Their resolution requires more than simply working through the gentle and painful sadness of disappearance from the company of others. That is the easy part. The task of coping with death – as Havel's friend Jan Patočka consistently taught – is much more and above all a matter of individuals cultivating *responsibility* for their own death.[2] This follows from the fact that everywhere, and at all times, death stalks life. 'Life as a self-respecting human being wouldn't be what it is unless it was constantly accompanied [*provázet*] by death,' Havel told a television interviewer curious about his recent introduction to the Czech edition of *The Tibetan Book of the Dead* (*Bardo Thötröl*). 'We know about death. We

[1] *Leviathan*, op. cit., Part 1, chapter 11.
[2] Jan Patočka, *Heretical Essays in the Philosophy of History*, translated by Erazim Kohák (Chicago and La Salle, Illinois, 1996), p. 105.

know that we all die, and that this [knowledge] distinguishes us from other beings,' he continued, before drawing his key conclusion: 'The individual must first of all think about if and why s/he either acts only within a given time on earth or tries to behave, as Masaryk said, *sub species aeternitatis*, that is, reckon upon eternity when acting, as if everything is being recorded and evaluated [*zhodnocení*], and as if each one of our actions may or may not be an event that can for ever change the universe.'[1]

Havel's remark was astute. Death is indeed the constant companion of life, and never more so than during the act of dying, when a certain measure of freedom can be exercised by individuals. They may choose not to exercise this freedom, but in every case they are called upon to take it upon themselves (*auf sich nehmen* as the philosopher Martin Heidegger puts it) to decide how they are to die and what their death means. Their death is always their own death – each is forced to speak in the first-person singular of 'my death' – which means that no one can step into their shoes and act out their role in the drama of dying. When individuals seek to do that – by passing on their powers to a doctor, for instance – they in effect refuse to explain themselves, to answer for their thoughts and actions before others. They act irresponsibly. They suppose or pretend that they cannot look death straight in the face. They stop 'practising for death' (as Socrates put it in Plato's *Phaedo*). They give up wrestling with the basic problem of making judgements about how best to die. They do not receive the rich gift of death – the power to give life to the process of dying, to prove, in the face of impossibility and defeat, that it is possible to exercise vigilance over oneself in the presence of others.

From the time of his sixtieth birthday, when his health began rapidly to worsen, Havel found himself in the company of five of the country's past presidents, each of whom was squeezed between the imperative to act responsibly in the face of bodily death and the choice to carry on as President of the body politic. There were moments, for instance immediately after part of his lung was removed, when death was much on his mind – so much so that he secretly instructed a friend to prepare a tombstone

---

[1]Interview with Antonín Přidal, 'Z očí do očí', Česká televize 2, Prague, 1996.

for him, to be placed when the time came in the family crypt, located in the fourteenth arcade in Vinohradský cemetery.[1] There were other moments when he confided that his body was too worn out for the presidency. His friend Jaroslav Šabata recalled accompanying him on a flight to Berlin to meet President Herzog and German ex-dissidents in November 1996, just before lung cancer struck. 'Havel was lying back one seat in front of us. He had a mild temperature,' Šabata noted. 'He thought it was flu – he didn't yet know what was going on. He was free and relaxed with his thoughts, both personal and political. At one point, like a bolt from the blue, he leaned over to us and whispered, "I've had enough of this presidency." He said it very expressively.'[2]

A similar remark, using different words, slipped out into public eighteen months later, thanks to a tiny microphone hidden by journalists within a forest of large microphones and television cameras. In early June 1998, the ill-looking, ashen-faced Havel was recorded as saying that he was 'fed up with everything' – including his lazy office staff, journalists, and the political situation in general. The *faux pas* caused him some public embarrassment. It even forced him to field questions on Czech television about whether he was giving consideration to his own 'abdication' (*abdikace*). 'I can imagine that I would abdicate if my struggles against death, illnesses and operations went on indefinitely. But . . .' He paused, breathing heavily. 'I don't think I would abdicate because I became fed up . . . A characteristic of democracy is that governments are changed through elections, and that means that the president sometimes finds it easier to work with elected leaders than at other times.' Pressed by his television interviewers, he said that he had abdicated only once in his career – during the break-up of Czechoslovakia, when his role as the elected President sworn to uphold the country's federal constitution prevented him from signing legislation that would split the state. He went on to reiterate that he could not see any 'serious political reason' why

---

[1] Of the eight former presidents of Czechoslovakia, six either stepped down for health reasons (Masaryk [1918–1935]; Beneš [1935–1938; 1941–1946; 1946–1948]; Svoboda [1968–1973; 1973–1975]); or died when in office (Gottwald [1948–1953]; Zápotocký [1953–1957]); or died in prison shortly after being arrested (Hácha [1938–1945]). See Vladimír Kadlec, *Podivné konce našich prezidentů* (first published in samizdat, Prague, 1989 [1991].
[2] Jaroslav Šabata, *Sedmkrát Sedm Kruhů* (Olomouc, 1997), p. 107.

he should now abandon his post. 'The only reason may possibly be my health,' he added. Sitting in a golden chair, dressed in a smart summer suit and tie, speaking often with his hands, the double-chinned President went on to confess that he was greatly bothered by his decline, that he understood that the absence of health is the same as the acute consciousness of having a mortal body: 'During the whole of my life, I've not been interested in my body,' he commented. 'I took it for granted that it was something like a natural carrier of my personality and spirit. It was in prison, when suffering from chronic pneumonia, that I noticed for the first time that I had a body. I was half-dcad, and because of that they released me early. Since 1996, I've again had to realize that I have a body, and that I have to look after it. It's a novelty for me. I admit that it's hard to get used to.'[1]

Public and private confessions of mortality were not especially typical. Something odd about the early winter life of President Havel is that he preferred to sing swan songs into the ears of death. Words like dying and death seemed to get smothered in elaborate denials, or to have no meaning at all. The more laden with illness he became during the course of the year 1998, the more he appeared officially to presume death to be a distant, quite unlikely event. Perhaps conceit always works strongest in the weakest bodies. Perhaps he was simply unused to not getting his way. Or perhaps his life had become such a habit that he no longer knew or cared what death was, or even that he had become unsuited for death. One afternoon, he paced nervously in circles around his seated physician, demanding an instant cure for all of his aches and pains, physical and spiritual. 'Would that I could change the weather, Mr President,' replied the physician respectfully, mocking his conceit.[2] Havel's denials in public were equally forceful. When replying to journalists' questions about his deeply uncertain health and political future, the President consistently brushed aside the implication that he may have to 'abdicate'. In hospital, several times at the edge of the abyss, he reacted in exactly the same way. 'Václav Havel seems always to be above his illness,' remarked his Austrian

---

[1] All quotations are from the pre-recorded interview with Havel conducted by Bohumil Klepetko and Jolana Voldánová and transmitted on ČTV 2, 13 June 1998.
[2] Interview with Michal Šerf, Prague, 2 November 1998.

surgeon, Professor Ernst Bodner. 'Václav Havel is probably the only patient who cannot wait to have his next operation,' he added.[1] Less restrained before journalists than Czech doctors, the grey-haired, golf-loving Professor Bodner was unusually frank in describing Havel's hospital behaviour. 'Václav Havel has a very strong will, and that sometimes complicated life for us,' he said. The impatient Havel always got upset when something didn't happen at the right moment, but otherwise he acted like a man of iron fully prepared from within for everything. He insisted that stitches from his neck be removed without anaesthetic. Immediately after operations, after coming out from the narcosis, he always insisted on drinking wine, despite firm resistance and quiet protestations from the professor. Havel also clamoured several times against his confinement within the intensive-care unit. 'I feel as if I am in prison,' he grumbled. Professor Bodner balked. He explained that it was imperative that he stay in the unit. Bodner pleaded with Havel to help the team of doctors promote his full recovery. 'How long do I have to stay here?' snapped Havel. Bodner hesitated, then stated quietly, holding his breath, that it would probably be two days. 'Promise!' snapped Havel again. The professor didn't have a chance, and two days later, when he came to examine Havel, he was greeted instantly with the words: 'We're moving today.'

Havel was discharged from Prague's Central Military hospital on 28 August 1998, more than a month after undergoing yet more abdominal surgery, this time with numerous post-operational complications. After undergoing an operation on 26 July to remove a colostomy attached five months earlier to his lower intestine, he developed respiratory problems a week later while recuperating. Doctors performed a tracheotomy – the fourth in two years – that is, they inserted a tube into a hole made in the chain-smoking President's trachea to enable him to breathe. The next day, Havel's heart began to beat fast and irregularly. It took about two hours – using electrical shocks administered to his heart – to return his heartbeat and blood pressure to around normal. By then the beginnings of bronchial pneumonia had been spotted, and Havel was heavily sedated and forced

---

[1]The following quotations are drawn from the interview with Professor Bodner conducted by Marek Wollner, *Týden*, 31 (27 July 1998), pp. 18, 20.

to rest. Eventually, three weeks later, after slow but gradual improvement, the tube stuck in Havel's throat was removed, and the incision (reported Havel's personal doctor, Ilja Kotík) spontaneously closed. Everybody remained upbeat. Boris Štastný, one of the President's medical team, told the news agency ČTK that the surgery to remove a cancerous tumour from Havel's right lung in December 1996 had been completely successful, and that his lungs were now in 'perfect shape'. The odd reassurance resembled a scurvied ship's surgeon congratulating himself on sparing the whole crew from food poisoning. It was backed up with Professor Bodner's verdict that the ups and downs of surgery had drawn himself, the President and his wife together like a family. Then came the slicker words of the President's senior political adviser, Jiří Pehe. 'He's on top of things,' said Pehe, adding that in preparation for his planned trip to the United States on 15 September, the bed-ridden President Havel had carefully monitored Czech and world events – and had even commented publicly on the thirtieth anniversary of the Soviet invasion of Czechoslovakia.[1]

Meanwhile, on the streets and around pub and kitchen tables, the spreading talk of Havel's bodily demise proved that many Czechs were wiser and more open than their President about the subject of death. Many familiarized themselves quickly with new words like bronchopneumonia and arrhythmia and kept track of the latest medical reports and complex details of procedures like tracheotomies and the removal of colostomies. Most of the big medical questions: 'Do his doctors know what they're doing?' and 'Is he dying?', and several large political questions: 'Should such a sick man carry on as President?' and 'Is anyone talking about a successor?' were repeatedly raised and dissected, answered and disputed before finding themselves relegated to a limbo of cautious indecision. Other citizens laced words with black humour that revealed the simple fact that nothing more than death was at stake. 'Do you know why Havel ran for President again last year?' went one of the most popular jokes. 'Because if he weren't at the Castle, he'd already be in Olšany cemetery!'

Dark humour often unnerves. It forcibly reminds individuals

---

[1] *The Prague Post* (2–8 September 1998), p. 2.

that they alone of all living beings *know* that one day they shall
not exist as individuals. Dark humour plays on their sense of
the uncanny. It exposes the familiar way in which individuals
process their strong childhood anxieties about dying by imagining
themselves to be immortal. Dark humour reveals that death and
dying are not subjects that the living like to contemplate, even
in the healthiest moods. This golden rule applies especially to
politicians and heads of state. They happen to be busy beings who
can rarely, if ever, spare a moment's thought to the 'meaning'
of anything that is basic, let alone to the process of dying.
Always on the run, they often consider talk of their dying,
or their need for urgent medical treatment, to be exaggerated,
as Havel himself did when rejecting the advice of doctors to
undergo further treatment.[1] Politicians, and especially heads of
state, are also prone to dismiss the subject of their own death
because the considerable power they exercise over others seduces
them into believing that they have full power over themselves.
Like everybody else, they aspire to further life, to additional
sums of being; but the thought that everything that individual
human beings do and achieve ultimately turns against them seems
far from their minds. Their lives are full of public attention
and admiring glances. They swagger around their worlds; act
self-confidently in the face of adversity; and often behave in
defiant and domineering ways. Political success tricks them into
presuming that the moment will never come when they will be
unable to take a step in any direction, when literally nothing more
will be possible.

That presumption is nourished by the certainty that simply
by achieving the highest office they have achieved fame and
therefore a certain form of immortality. They are treated as
special beings endowed with god-like tendencies. Heads turn
and bodies bow whichever way they walk. They reciprocate by
playing the peacock to perfection. They bathe constantly in the
halogen of televisual publicity. They appear on websites and –
like Havel – have large and elaborate ones of their own. Print
journalists write endlessly about them. Even the art of biography

---

[1]*Rytmus života*, 31 (29 July 1998), p. 5; cf. *Lidové noviny*, 27 July 1998, p. 3. Compare
the remark of Miroslav Čerbák, head of the Doctors' Concilium responsible for
treating Havel during this period: 'He is the type of person who, when he feels
a task and duty, comes alive' (*MF Dnes* [Prague], 4 December 1997).

– one of whose many possible effects is to turn them into smouldering volcanoes, to lift them out of time and confer upon them a form of immortality by preserving their lives in words and pictures – helps them to forget that they live close to their skeletons. From time to time, famous political figures may wonder whether their fame resembles a gift of pearls that triggers self-doubts about their genuine or cultivated qualities. The wiser among them know that fame can be cruel by bringing loneliness, jealousy and dispute their way. But even those politicians whose fame proves short-lived feel their fame to be a glass that magnifies their power and rescues them from the oblivion of 'vulgar death'.[1] So they tend to become incapable of seeing themselves except from the inside. They think of themselves as necessary, even indispensable. They feel themselves to be an absolute reality, as a whole, as the whole . . . as therefore a being who *is* God.

Enter the compulsory fact that each individual must learn to be the loser, and the corresponding question of whether or not the individual chooses to act responsibly in the face of death. The undeniable misfortune of an ageing and unwell head of state like Havel was that despite all appearances and denials to the contrary he was forced to observe at close range the slow but methodical degradation of his organs. Each extra day of his life saw him lose ground. His body gradually gave him the slip. One by one, sometimes obviously and otherwise discreetly, his organs took their revenge upon his power by detaching themselves from his body. It was as if they escaped from him and no longer belonged to him – that against his own orders his heart and lungs and bowels turned traitors, committed acts of indefinable treachery that were impossible to denounce or arrest, since they stopped at nothing and put themselves in no one's service. Such treachery threatened to turn him into a flesh-and-blood ghost and forced him in turn to reconsider his strong yearning to ignore death. Dying confronted Havel with the utterly personal problem of coming to terms with his own demise – with solving the insoluble problem of needing to reconcile the feeling of being everything with the evidence of becoming nothing.

The problem of how to square the power of dying sover-

---

[1]Homer, *Iliad*, Book X1, 1, 394.

eigns with the jagged fact of their own eventual powerlessness
is especially pertinent in contemporary parliamentary democracies, including the unconsolidated Czech kind. Had Havel
lived like a king in early modern times, the subject of death
would have been much less troubling to him and his subjects.
Once upon a time, say during the second half of the fourteenth
century in Europe, sovereign monarchs like Edward VI and
Queen Elizabeth I regarded themselves as immortal.[1] According
to the famous (originally medieval) formula of a *rex qui nunquam
moritur*, a 'king that never dies', every regal head of state is at
the same time a flesh-and-blood mortal and the indestructible
embodiment and head of the political community. Just like
the body of Jesus Christ, the monarch has two bodies. One
of them is visible, individual and mortal; the other is invisible,
immortal and collective. Within the single body of the monarch,
that is to say, two forms of power are melded: the power to
make marks on the earthly world by means of government,
and the power of the body politic, which although it cannot
be seen or touched consists of all the mechanisms of law-making
and government constituted, for the sake of the people and
the public good, to compensate for the imperfections of the
fragile human body and thus to withstand the ebb and flow
of time.

This formula of the indestructible power of the monarch
implied that the body politic always lives on unharmed when
the body of the monarch becomes terminally ill, or suffers death
by accident. Even the hands of an assassin cannot harm the body
politic or the monarch. For that reason, contemporaries preferred
to speak not of the *death* of the monarch, but to use the word
demise to describe the process of transferring and relocating the
body politic in the body of a new flesh-and-blood monarch.
When the natural body of the monarch suffered demise, the
body politic was reincarnated, at once and without controversy,
in the mortal body of the successor monarch. Yet in a certain
sense the deceased lived on too. The incarnation of the body
politic in the body of the monarch did away with the problem
of death; the deceased monarch never really died but – like King

[1]Ernst H. Kantorowicz, *The King's Two Bodies. A Study in Medieval Political Theology*
(Princeton, NJ, 1957), especially pp. 3–23, 314–450.

Henry VIII who survived for many years after the death of Henry Tudor – lived on as an immortal superbody.

Definite traces of this doctrine of the immortality of the monarch and monarchy reappeared in the totalitarian and late-socialist regimes under which Havel lived most of his life; whether called Stalin or Mao or Fidel or Gottwald, the bodily figure of the omniscient, omnipotent great leader – the Egocrat, to use Solzhenitsyn's term – towered over everybody and everything, like an invulnerable masculine body endowed with amazing strengths and talents, a mortal body which defied the laws of biological nature to attain immortality, precisely because it expressed and at the same time merged with, and drew sustenance from, the immortal body politic of the totalitarian system. So, for example, when President Klement Gottwald died in 1953, he was embalmed – like Stalin just before him – and put on display. Unfortunately, the Czechoslovak mortician, inexperienced in the techniques of embalming, bungled the job. The corpse began to rot, had to be replaced by a dummy, and eventually was moved from public view. Gottwald's fate pointed to more democratic times. For under democratic conditions, the immortality of the political body and its leader is not presumed. The body politic is split asunder permanently by the separation between the institutions of government and the myriad organizations of civil society. Within both domains, positions of power are not associated with bodies laying claim to immortality. Nobody sits on thrones. Nobody supposes themselves or others to be angelic. Nobody pretends that positions of power are properly 'merged' with the bodies of particular actors. Nothing is sacred. Everything is publicly questionable. Compared to absolute monarchies, relationships of power are disembodied and lose their sacred quality. There are no thrones. Power is not exercised by angels; often enough (it is presumed) power is wielded instead by potential or actual devils. And those who exercise power over others are considered mere mortals who occupy offices and positions temporarily, subject to good health, election and public controversy – and to removal from office.

As the twentieth century ended, the Czech Republic found itself caught up in the throes of a transition towards a disembodied presidency. Although a majority of its citizens – revealing their not-yet-democratic habits – still found it hard to distinguish

between Václav Havel and the role of the Czech President,[1] the
republic and its citizens began to live in the subjunctive tense. No
one quite knew what was going to happen and details of the events
to come were still unknown. How long he would survive, whether
he might recover, how he would die and who would succeed him
couldn't be grasped. Yet one outcome was certain. The time of
his state funeral was coming. A whole nation would fall silent,
and so too would admirers within many other nations – from
the United States of America and Canada to Russia, Japan and
China. His corpse – its stubble still growing – would be expedited
odourlessly and with technical perfection from his deathbed to the
grave. But his death would be a global media event – on a scale
much bigger than the state funeral of Masaryk.[2]

Prague would double in size. As he lay in state in the old Castle
of the Bohemian kings above the city, a queue some miles long
would spring up. Mourners would wait all day, and all night,
to see his body for the last time. The day of the funeral would
be a public holiday. Hundreds of thousands of people, dressed
in black and clutching flowers, would be seen lining the route
taken by the cortège on the way to his final resting place. Huge
black banners would fly from every office; his photograph, draped
in black, would crowd every shop and news-stand and public
place. Shared feelings of embarrassment would hold words back.
Half-buried or forgotten anxieties about death would collectively
resurface; fantasies of personal immortality would temporarily
weaken. Around the graveside a forest of microphones, tripods,
cameras, pads and pens would suddenly spring up. Obituaries,
many of them written long ago and updated several times already,
would appear in all four corners of the earth. Millions of words
would be uttered. Many hundreds of different and conflicting
points would be made. The words of the dead man (as Auden
said) would be modified in the guts of the living. It would be said
that he was a good man, a great man, a hero of the century. Harry
S. Truman's remark that a statesman is a dead politician would be
confirmed. Loud sounds of grinding axes would also be heard. His

[1]*Lidové noviny*, 21 November 1997, p. 3. In a readers' poll, the same newspaper
reported that there were some Czechs who liked what Havel had done for their
country, but who were emphatic that 'the atmosphere of irreplaceability' enveloping
the Castle (*atmosféra nenahraditelnosti*) was bad for the role of the presidency.
[2]See the first-hand account by H. Gordon Skilling, 'Letters from Prague 1937',
Kosmas, Journal of Czechoslovak and Central European Affairs (London, 1982), p. 71.

enemies would wish him good riddance. The wags would say that in democracies death is for some politicians a good career move. And through all the din of commentary and commentary upon the commentary, some wise voices would insist that one thing should be for ever remembered: that Václav Havel was a man who had the misfortune of being born into the twentieth century, a man whose fate was politics, a man who achieved fame as the political figure who taught the world much more about power, the powerful and the powerless than most of his twentieth-century rivals.

ACKNOWLEDGEMENTS

Acknowledgements – fond memories of the heart cast in words – are especially difficult to summarize in a project that stretches back nearly two decades, to the early 1980s, when I first made scholarly and political contact with the unhappy paradise called the Czechoslovak Socialist Republic. So I shall say only that I am most grateful to the many scores of people who have helped me to prepare and complete this book, especially during the past five years of intensive research and writing. For reasons of space, I cannot mention them all, although it would be wrong to let three groups of people suffer in silence the condescension of posterity.

Many individuals generously contributed their time and energy in interviews that I conducted in various countries around the world. A very few interviewees wished to remain anonymous because they personally feel too close to Václav Havel, and therefore do not wish to offend him, for instance by breaking a compact to remain silent about a certain phase of their lives together. There were others who asked for their anonymity because they felt, just prior to publication, that their political solidarity with him could be jeopardized by the book's uncompromisingly tough praise for Havel's achievements. I have naturally respected the wishes of the former small handful of people; the wishes of the latter group, consisting of only two individuals, I have accepted, with some puzzlement. Then there were those individuals who gave everything, sometimes more than once, always generously. I gratefully acknowledge the stimulating conversations with Václav Havel, to whom I explained at the outset of the project my intention to write an unauthorized biography with a difference, but without malice. His brother, Ivan Havel, understood from the beginning that the book was to be a serious work of scholarship, and accordingly gave his time and advice with great intelligence, wit, prudence, and patience. There were also many other interviewees whose comments and advice I have tried hard to incorporate in the book. They include: Rudolf Battěk; Václav Bělohradský; John Bok; Petr Brod; Karel Brynda; Barry Buzan; Ivan Chvatík; Penelope Connell; Viola Fischerová; Anna Freimanová; the late Ernest Gellner; Marketa Goetz-Stankiewicz; Vladimír Hanzel; Pierre Hassner; Dagmar Havlová; Milena Janišová; Zdeněk Jičínský; Jan Kavan; Václav Klaus; Radim Kopecký; Pavel Kosatík; Hana Ledecká; Tapani Lausti; Naděžda Macurová; Louise Mares; Adam Michnik; Stanislav Milota; František Novák; Martin Palouš; Jiří

Pehe; Harold Pinter; Petr Pithart; Vilém Prečan; Adam Roberts; Richard Rose; Jacques Rupnik; Michal Schonberg; Prince Karel Schwarzenberg; Pavel Seifter; Michal Šerf; Jiřina Šiklová; Joska Skalník; H. Gordon Skilling; Josef Škvorecký; Andrej Stankovič; Olga Stankovičová; Max van der Stoel; Alois Strnad; Jiří Suk; Petruška Šustrová; Pavel Tigrid; Josef Topol; Jacqueline True; Oldřich Tůma; Jan Urban; Zdeněk Urbánek; Ludvík Vaculík; František Vlasák; Jitka Vodňanská; Phillip Whitehead; Paul Wilson; Václav Žak; and Milan Znoj.

Other individuals helped by providing invaluable materials and vital forms of technical assistance during the preparation of the book. My very special thanks are due to Derek Paton, a research assistant at the Centre for the Study of Democracy in London, and the Institute of Contemporary History in Prague. For nearly four years, he was a constant companion who tirelessly gathered documents, provided honest advice, arranged meetings and provided excellent translations, always with professional dedication, unending patience, outstanding intelligence, and lively humour. He should certainly not be implicated in any errors of judgement or public controversies spawned by the book. The British Academy's generous Fellowship is gratefully acknowledged. Gabriela Müllerová helped me improve my basic Czech and to analyse hundreds of stories and reports about Havel during a twelve-month period. Eva Skryová, Wendy Stokes, and Nancy Wood were partners in underground crime. Many staff and students at the Centre for the Study of Democracy provided indispensable help, especially Sara Amos, Patrick Burke, Bridget Cotter, Niels Jacob Harbitz, Simon Joss, Chantal Mouffe, John Owens, Richard Rose, and Richard Whitman. Many other colleagues at the University of Westminster provided invaluable support for my research work, including Professor Margaret Blunden, Professor Geoffrey Holt, Professor Keith Phillips, Professor Michael Trevan, and the Vice-Chancellor and Rector, Dr Geoffrey Copland. Some individuals generously supplied me with photographic illustrations, including Alexander Dobrovodský, Ivan Havel, Bohdan Holomíček, Martin Hykl, Jaroslav Krejčí, Tomki Němec, Magdalena Tichá, Jitka Vodňanská, Vladimír Weiss, Petr Zhoř, and the Czech News Agency. Still others have helped satisfy manifold requests, for instance by providing materials ranging from rare newspaper clippings to valuable primary source documents. They include:

Timothy Garton Ash; Anthony Cantle; April Carter; Mita Castle; Vojtech Čelko; David Daniels; Marzia Ferrari; Klára Hůrková; Jan Kavan; Pavel Kosatík; Jiří Kuběna; Alan Levy; Paul Mier; Jana Nálevková; Petr Oslzlý; Jiřina Šiklová; Roger Scruton; H. Gordon Skilling; Eva Šormová; Alfred Stepan; Marketa Goetz-Stankiewicz; Viktor Stoilov; Jan Šulc; Helena Taylor; Oldřich Tůma; and Gerald Turner. For help during the past five years in translating and interpreting Havel, I should especially like to thank Paul Wilson and A.G. Brain, Derek Paton and Marzia Ferrari. In the world of publishing, I am especially grateful to Sara Fisher, Bill Hamilton, and Jim Gill at A.M. Heath; Petra Tobišková and Alexandra Panthel; and the fabulous group at Bloomsbury Publishers, especially my wise and skilled editors Liz Calder and Mary Tomlinson; and Penny Edwards, Jane Ellis, Nigel Newton; Matt Richell; and Will Webb.

The other members of my household enabled the book to reach press in numberless ways. There is no need to embarrass them by describing in detail their efforts to keep up my spirits and rescue me from gross obsessions. Rebecca Allison and Leo Lawson-O'Neil helped in more ways than they know. Big hugs and many kisses for George Keane and Alice Keane; and ditto for Kathy O'Neil, to whom I dedicate this book, with love.

ILLUSTRATIONS

I gratefully acknowledge the generosity of those who furnished the photographs included in this book, and described below:

Following the contents page: the centre of attention, by Vladimír Weiss

Beginnings: during his first year, from the family archives

Folly: at the family gravesite, Košíře Cemetery, Prague, 1940, from the family archives.

Republicans: the Havel family strolling at Havlov, from the family archives

Devil's Playground: the javelin thrower, at Havlov, from the family archives

Zoology: 'My home, my castle!', at Havlov, from the family archives

Resistance: Miloš Havel, from the family archives

Cold Peace: Václav Havel with younger brother Ivan, on the first day he attended school, September 1944, from the family archives

Red Stars: With a Lenin hat, from the family archives

Coup de Prague: Dressed up as a musketeer, during summer holidays at Havlov, 1949, from the family archives

Flying Splinters: Božena Havlová, in the swimming pool at Havlov, from the family archives

Trials: Dressed as a Roman notable, with brother Ivan (left) and Jan Škoda (right), at Havlov, 1949, from the family archives

Thirty-Sixers: with the poet Jiří Paukert, from the family archives

Ashes on Ice: seated at a desk, with brother Ivan, in the embankment flat, Prague, September 1954, from the family archives

The Public Poet: with a cup of coffee, from the family archives

Stalin's Carcass: dressed like an eccentric family guest, at Havlov, pipe in hand, from the family archives

To Barracks: in uniform, as First Lieutenant Škrovánek, in the staged performance of Pavel Kohout's *September Nights*, 1957–8, from the family archives

Socialist Realism: with Olga Šplíchalová, from the family archives

Garden Party: dressed for a performance at Hrádeček, 1976, by Bohdan Holomíček

The Crisis: at the Divadlo Na zábradlí, from the family archives

The Memorandum: with Arthur Miller, 1963, by Inge Morath

Summer Friendship: tie-dyed in a field of flowers, by Bohdan Holomíček

Mid-summer's Night: in London in 1968, by the *Guardian*

A Politician of Retreat: profile, in shades, from the family archives

Normalization: carrying a ladder in the orchard at Hrádeček, by Bohdan Holomíček

Late-Socialism: reading a book on the art of brewing, by Bohdan Holomíček

Beggars' Opera: the première of *Žebrácká opera*, 1975, by Bohdan Holomíček

Charter 77: with Adam Michnik and Jacek Kuron (to Havel's left), at an illegal meeting with Solidarność, Krkonoše, from the Czechoslovak News Agency

Violence: reading, gramophone behind, from the family archives

Courage: as Caesar, about to die at Brutus's hand, from the family archives

The Powerless: gun-toting gangster, from Jitka Vodňanská and Alexander Dobrovodský

The Victim: clutching a bag of apples, after returning from prison, from my collection

Prison: dressed in black, smoking, from the family archives

Largo Desolato: 'All you need is love': with Olga at Hrádeček, by Tomki Němec

Temptation: 'You're Number One': with Jitka Vodňanská, on his fiftieth birthday, from Jitka Vodňanská

Cliff-Hanging: with whisky bottle, during an interview with Erica Blair, November 1986, by Gerald Turner

Revolution: at a Civic Forum meeting, by Jaroslav Krejčí

Velvet Power: Waving to a giant crowd from the balcony of the Melantrich building, Wenceslas Square, from the Czech News Agency

Machiavelli: facing Alexander Dubček, Ruzyně Airport, 1990, by Tomki Němec

A Crowned Republic: with tailors, Prague Castle, 1990, by Tomki Němec

Te Deum Laudamus: Olga and Václav on their knees in St Vitus's Cathedral, by Petr Zhoř

Fun and Games: with the Rolling Stones, Prague, 18 August 1990, by Tomki Němec

The Manipulator: watching himself on the BBC, Lány, 1990, by Tomki Němec

Defections: reversing his BMW at Lány, by Tomki Němec

Parliament: before a joint session of the US Congress, with Vice-President Dan Quayle and Speaker of the House of Representatives, Congressman Thomas S. Foley, 21 February 1990, by Tomki Němec

Lustration: in shades, guard in background, by Martin Hykl

Market Power: with Václav Klaus and Prince Karel Schwarzenberg, by Tomki Němec

Velvet Divorce: informing the Speaker of the Federal Assembly of his resignation, 17 July 1992, watched by Pavel Tigrid, by Tomki Němec

Oh Europe!: with Umberto Eco and Olga, on Capri, by Tomki Němec

Metamorphosis: with Dáša Havlová, by Tomki Němec

Death: on the beach at Cabo da Roca, in Portugal, 14 December 1990, by Tomki Němec

GUIDE TO CZECH PRONUNCIATION

Czech is a phonetic tongue, and that means that it is pronounced as it is written. The main stress of a word is always on the first syllable. The following brief guide to pronunciation should satisfy most demands of this book:

Vowels:

a	as in p*u*b
á	as in c*a*rp
e	as in g*e*t
é	as in tod*a*y
ě	as in y*e*llow
i or y	as in s*i*t
í or ý	as in p*ea*t
o	as in g*o*t
u	as in l*oo*k
ů	as in c*oo*l

Consonants:

c	like the *ts* in rats
č	like the *ch* in chubby
ch	like the *ch* in loch
g	like the *g* in god
h	like the *h* in had
j	like the *y* in yoke
r	like the *r* in ripe, but rolled
ř	similar to the *rsh* in Pershing, as in Dvořák
š	like the *sh* in shop
ž	like the *s* in pleasure

INDEX